DEVON COUNTY COUNCIL

THE DEVON LANDSCAPE

AN APPRAISAL OF DEVON'S LANDSCAPE AT THE BEGINNING OF THE 21ST CENTURY

DEVON BOOKS

First published in Great Britain in 2002

British Library Cataloguing-in-Publication Data
A CIP record for this title is available from the British Library

ISBN 1 85522 824 6

DEVON BOOKS
OFFICIAL PUBLISHER TO DEVON COUNTY COUNCIL

Halsgrove House
Lower Moor Way
Tiverton, Devon EX16 6SS
Tel: 01884 243242
Fax: 01884 243325
email: sales@halsgrove.com
website: www.halsgrove.com

Devon Books gratefully acknowledges the support of the
Countryside Agency towards the publication of this book.

Printed and bound in Italy by Centro Grafico Ambrosiano.

Whilst every care has been taken to ensure the accuracy of the information contained in this book, the author disclaims responsibility for any mistakes which may have inadvertently been included.

CONTENTS

*Colour coding on contents pages refers to coloured sections throughout book.

ACKNOWLEDGEMENTS

Production of *The Devon Landscape* would not have been possible without reference to other documents. Acknowledgement is made here of the debt to those documents, whose input has been invaluable.

The Character of England: landscape, wildlife and natural features
(Countryside Commission and English Nature, 1996)

Interim Landscape Character Assessment Guidance
(Countryside Agency, 1999)

Tranquil Areas
(Countryside Commission and Council for the Protection of Rural England, 1995)

The Tamar Valley Landscape
(Cobham Resource Consultants for Countryside Commission, 1992)

The Blackdown Hills Landscape
(Cobham Resource Consultants for Countryside Commission, 1989)
The East Devon Landscape
(Derek Lovejoy Partnership for Countryside Commission, 1993)

The South Devon Landscape
(Derek Lovejoy Partnership for Countryside Commission, 1993)

North Devon Landscape Assessment
(North Devon District Council, 1993)

The Torridge Landscape
(Chris Blandford Associates, 1995)

Exmoor Environmentally Sensitive Area Landscape Assessment
(ADAS, 1994)

Dartmoor Environmentally Sensitive Area Landscape Assessment
(ADAS, 1994)
Greenscape Assessment for the City of Plymouth
(Land Use Consultants for Plymouth City Council, 2000)

South Hams Landscape Character Assessment and Guidelines, Consultation Draft
(South Devon Coast and Countryside Service, 2001)

Teignbridge District Landscape Assessment, Consultation Draft
(Teignbridge District Council, 2001)

Archaeology of the Devon Landscape
(Devon County Council, 1980)

Financially supported by the Countryside Agency

5

The spire of Modbury Church punctuates the South Hams skyline.

INTRODUCTION

Devon's landscape is a valued inheritance. Its character and beauty make the County outstandingly attractive as a place in which to live and work, or as a place to visit. As we enter the 21st century, the landscape must rank among Devon's greatest assets.

As such an asset, the Devon landscape has its own intrinsic importance. It is valued for its diversity and character, for the aesthetic qualities that give rise to strong, even passionate, personal feelings, and for its historical and cultural associations.

These positive qualities of the landscape are also translated into wider values. Devon's landscape must be seen in national context, where it is almost a byword for so much of what is most valued in the country's scenery. This perception helps to sustain an important tourism industry, providing millions of pounds annually to the Devon economy and supporting thousands of jobs. It is also a major factor in attracting investment into the County, and increasing the value of a rural economy which is having to adapt to changing circumstances.

The Devon landscape should also be viewed within the wider perspective of the overall quality of the Devon environment. The quality of Devon's environment received international recognition in 2001 when UNESCO designated the Dorset and East Devon Coast as a World Heritage Site in view of its geological significance. This is the first natural World Heritage Site in England and joins such renowned features as the Grand Canyon and the Great Barrier Reef.

The national significance of the Devon landscape has been recognised by the designation within Devon's historic boundaries of the whole of one National Park (Dartmoor) and part of another (Exmoor). In addition there are three Areas of Outstanding Natural Beauty (North Devon, South Devon and East Devon, and parts of two others Blackdown Hills and Tamar Valley). These designations, representing England's finest landscapes, cover a total of one third of Devon's area.

Devon County Council is committed to working with its partners to conserve the County's outstanding landscape and further everyone's enjoyment and understanding of it. This book is the first element of the Council's new Landscape Strategy which will guide our work in the future.

The Devon Landscape is an appraisal of this environmental and economic asset at the opening of the new Millennium. It has two main thrusts. Firstly, it identifies the key themes that go toward the making of the Devon landscape. Secondly, it sets out how differing elements of these themes result in identifiable areas, each with its own distinctive characteristics. These 'Landscape Character Zones' form the basis for the understanding and appreciation of the landscape and for actions to maintain and enhance them.

Devon County Council recognises the fundamental principle that the character and quality of the Devon landscape should be appreciated in its entirety, not just its international and national importance. The typical and commonplace should be cherished as well as the rare and the special. Subtle variations in landscape character should be recognised and strengthened and there should be an understanding of the role of local distinctiveness in giving us all a 'sense of place'. This approach is perhaps the key message of *The Devon Landscape*.

The County Council is very grateful to the Countryside Agency for its financial support for this book, and to all the people and organisations who have helped with its preparation. It has benefited especially from our working in partnership with Dartmoor National Park Authority, Exmoor National Park Authority, Plymouth City Council and Torbay Council. Steve Church, who advises on landscape policy in Devon County Council's Environment Directorate, has undertaken background research and has brought his deep professional knowledge to *The Devon Landscape*.

Councillor David Morrish MSc FRGS
Executive Member for the Environment,
Devon County Council
Exeter April 2002

Human and natural influences interact on the landscape of the Dart Estuary.

CHAPTER 1

BACKGROUND

HISTORY OF THE APPRAISAL

The importance of the landscape to Devon in environmental, cultural and economic terms has been recognised by Devon County Council for some time. There is a long history of the County Council adopting policies relating to the conservation of the landscape in its Development Plans and Structure Plans, dating back to the 1950s. While such policies tended to concentrate on the conservation of designated landscape areas, be they nationally or locally designated, there has been an increasing recognition of the need to conserve, maintain and enhance all landscapes for their own sake.

Corresponding with this increasing awareness of the importance of the entirety of Devon's landscapes has grown an appreciation of the need to recognise the landscape character of an area, as much as its more obvious aesthetic attractions or otherwise. This has been very much in line with national thinking on this issue, especially as contained in landscape advice published by the Government's statutory countryside advisory body, the Countryside Agency, and its predecessor, the Countryside Commission.

Encouraged by such thinking and advice, Devon County Council first undertook the preparation of a Devon Landscape Strategy from 1992 onwards. The draft strategy was completed in 1994 and approved as the basis for consultation with interested Authorities, organisation and individuals.

Consultation was undertaken during 1994-95. Responses were invited from all Devon MPs, all District Councils in Devon, both National Parks within the County, all surrounding local authorities, over 50 local and national organisations and agencies, all County Council departments and appropriate County Council officers and members.

The general response to the document was positive. A large number of comments was received suggesting amendment of detail, but the general approach of the document was widely supported. However, this period coincided with a time of rapid change and progress in the national landscape appraisal framework. This was exemplified by the publication of the Countryside Commission document 'The New Map of England; A Directory of Regional Landscapes', followed by the Commission's joint publication with English Nature of 'The Character of England; landscape, wildlife and natural features'. A study of 'Tranquil Areas' in England, again by the Commission this time jointly with the Council for the Protection of Rural England,

introduced an additional element to the landscape debate. Discussions on landscape issues at the regional level by the South West Regional Planning Conference and the issuing of an 'Interim Landscape Character Assessment Guidance' document by the Countryside Agency further accentuated the rapidly changing background to landscape matters.

This fast-moving setting was not the ideal environment for publication of a landscape strategy for Devon which would have to, out of necessity, be related to a particular point in time and which could, therefore, be very quickly rendered out of date. However, with the arrival of the new century it had become apparent that there may never be an ideal time for such a publication and that consequently there was no advantage to be gained from any further waiting.

It should be noted that *The Devon Landscape* covers the whole of the historic county. The Unitary Authorities (Plymouth, Torbay) and the National Parks (Dartmoor, Exmoor) have, in political and administrative terms, complete or considerable independence from the rest of Devon. In landscape terms, however, it is agreed that the strategic county level represented by treating the historic county as a whole is the appropriate treatment for Devon.

A Landscape Strategy for Devon

The draft document of 1995, although overtaken by some of the events outlined above, remains a good basis for a Devon Landscape Strategy. However, it has been considered that the earlier document tried to include too much in one publication. The scope of that document has therefore been divided into three elements, each with its own subject area and its own projected life-span. The three elements are:

1. An overview of the Devon landscape, to include an investigation of the various themes that go to make up the landscape and a division of the County into discrete zones of distinctive character. It is a document with a relatively long lifetime.

2. An examination of the background context in policy terms, both national and local. It contains some detailed issues and some critical actions to address them. Updating is required as the policy context moves on and thus this is a document with a medium lifespan.

3. The role of Devon County Council in landscape matters and a specific action plan. This contains policies, action and guidelines to ensure the maintenance and enhancement of the landscape features which typify local distinctiveness, and relates to action within the remit of the County Council to undertake or influence. This document requires frequent updating and therefore has a relatively short lifetime.

The Devon Landscape is the first of these three elements. It constitutes an overview of the Devon landscape at a point in time, the beginning of the 21st century. As such, it provides a useful academic landmark on the state of the Devon landscape as well as acting as a reference point to monitor landscape change. It provides the fundamental groundwork, the body of information on which the actions of the overall strategy will impact. It is not, of itself, the Landscape Strategy, which comprises all of the three elements listed above; it is, however, the bedrock at the foundations of the strategy, the element on which all the other elements depend.

POLICY CONTEXT

The approach adopted follows the current advice of the Countryside Agency in the Interim Landscape Character Assessment Guidance (1999). It also complies with the advice contained in the Government's Planning Policy Guidance No. 7 (PPG7, February 1997; The Countryside – Environmental Quality and Economic and Social Development) and in the current Regional Planning Guidance for the South West (RPG10, September 2001).

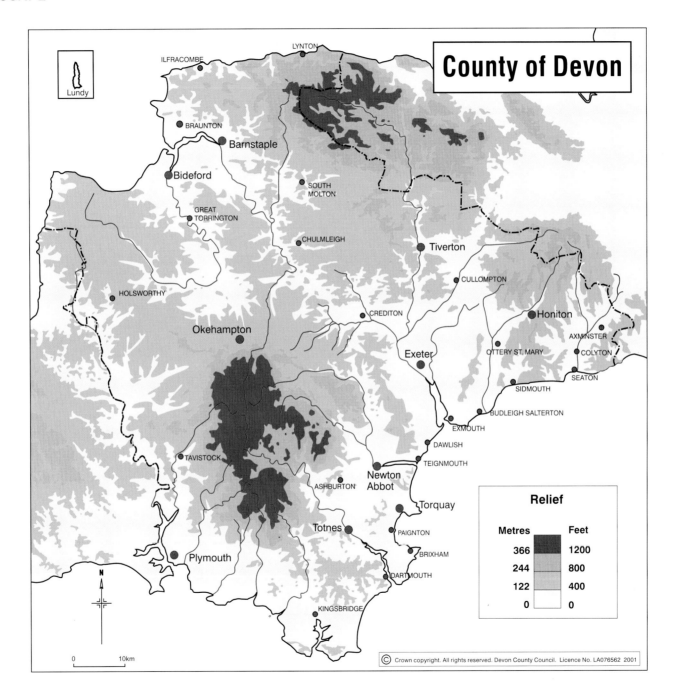

County of Devon

Lundy

ILFRACOMBE
LYNTON
BRAUNTON
Barnstaple
Bideford
GREAT TORRINGTON
SOUTH MOLTON
CHULMLEIGH
Tiverton
CULLOMPTON
HOLSWORTHY
CREDITON
Honiton
Okehampton
AXMINSTER
OTTERY ST. MARY
COLYTON
Exeter
SEATON
SIDMOUTH
BUDLEIGH SALTERTON
EXMOUTH
DAWLISH
TAVISTOCK
TEIGNMOUTH
Newton Abbot
ASHBURTON
Torquay
Totnes
PAIGNTON
Plymouth
BRIXHAM
DARTMOUTH
KINGSBRIDGE

N

0   10km

Relief

Metres	Feet
366	1200
244	800
122	400
0	0

CHAPTER 2

USE OF A LANDSCAPE STRATEGY

As was pointed out earlier, *The Devon Landscape* is not itself a landscape strategy, although it is fundamental to such a strategy. However, even by itself it does have a usefulness.

Its main uses will be:
- to provide an academic landmark on the state of the Devon landscape at the beginning of the twenty-first century;
- to act as a reference point to monitor landscape change;
- to promote an understanding and appreciation of the Devon landscape, and the nature of local landscape character.

These uses are also relevant to the strategy as a whole. In addition, however, the further elements which go with *The Devon Landscape* to form the overall strategy combine to give a wide range of uses, valuable not only to the County Council but to a wide range of other bodies and individuals. In general terms, the strategy will:

- identify forces of landscape change and explore the best mechanisms for controlling, influencing and planning for change at a strategic level;
- foster a collective responsibility among all interested parties to consider how their actions might influence the landscape and how to make such actions a positive contribution;
- help identify agreed priorities to target existing resources and potential grant aid, to support applications for potential financial assistance for relevant programmes and to develop ways of monitoring actions;
- encourage authorities and agencies to work and co-operate with farmers, landowners, amenity bodies and the local community and to support and strengthen existing partnerships.

The landscape is integral to a range of issues, especially perhaps development and nature conservation. A strategic approach to landscape matters can help guide the location, nature, size or, indeed, desirability of development. In addition, principles relating to the visual landscape will in turn have an effect on bio-diversity issues, habitats and landscape being closely inter-related.

In addition to these general aims, a landscape strategy for Devon will also have more specific applications. A lengthy list, almost certainly not exhaustive, is set out below:

- Providing strategic advice to aid the development of government policy especially in relation to national countryside and heritage agencies such as the Forestry Commission, DEFRA, Countryside Agency, and English Heritage; such policy will help refine the agencies' grant programmes and objectives and thus has the potential to address Devon's 'local' landscape issues.
- Guiding Devon County Council spending and internal budget allocation for landscape projects by identifying countywide and local priorities.
- Acting as a basis for developing targeting statements and more rigorous criteria for countryside grant applications and project proposals; helping to demonstrate appropriate resource allocation, and providing a measure of a scheme's benefit to the landscape.
- Providing a landscape reference document for the assessment of major development, e.g. a basis for developing criteria for Environmental Assessments.
- Raising issues and possible new approaches for future County Structure Plan policy and promoting discussion about the future of designated areas.
- Fulfilling the role of county-level assessment within the hierarchy of assessments from the national to the local level.

- Identifying strategic landscape principles for countywide planning policies e.g. minerals and waste-disposal local plans, transport and development policies.
- Identifying landscape principles for the development of district-wide local plans, and acting as a potential source of supplementary planning guidance, particularly relating to local distinctiveness, for developers and development control officers.
- Providing a wider context for more localised landscape appraisals, management plans, river catchment studies, wildlife surveys, and other similar documents.
- Raising awareness and appreciation of Devon's landscape in the widest sense, including the provision of an educational resource.
- Promoting the quality and character of the Devon landscape, thus offering inspiration to the individual and encouraging commitment to become involved in shaping the future landscape.
- Complementing other strategic countryside strategies.
- Identifying means of fostering greater co-operation and involvement in landscape conservation and enhancement.

The Devon Landscape and its companion documents are thus aimed at a wide audience; professionals, including planners, designers, countryside managers and advisors, engineers, national and local agencies and organisations, developers, farmers, interest groups and individuals all of whom have a direct involvement with, or interest in, the landscape and the potential to shape and enhance it. *The Devon Landscape* will also be of interest to groups and individuals who have an interest in the landscape as academics, historians, local residents or visitors and who wish to have a greater understanding and appreciation of the great range of diversity which goes to make up Devon's landscape.

CHAPTER 3

SCOPE OF THE DOCUMENT

The great variety of Devon's landscape relies on an almost infinite number of features which make up the whole – all important in their own right, but needing a context to understand their contribution to the landscape. It is often the association of a number of related components around a particular theme which contributes to the flavour of the whole landscape. For example, a waterside landscape typical of many Devon river valleys will be the composite of a number of components – riverside trees, historic quays and mills, steep valley woodlands, open valley floor.

Consequently, an important element is an examination of a series of key themes which permeate the County, giving a unifying aspect to locally distinctive areas which in turn combine to form the Devon landscape. These themes in total go to make up what is called 'the Essence of Devon' and this topic is fully explored in Chapter 5, which comprises approximately a third of *The Devon Landscape*.

In addition to having an essential landscape character which relies on a complex mix of inter-related components, Devon also contains a rich diversity of distinctive landscape types and local character areas, each themselves the product of a unique mix of components. *The Devon Landscape* identifies a series of distinctive landscape character areas which are relevant at a county level and identifies their key characteristic features. This groundwork forms the basis for highlighting local issues and opportunities for action to help conserve, enhance and restore landscapes, including townscapes and the built environment, and detailed discussion of these issues is included in the companion documents to *The Devon Landscape* which, together, go to make up Devon's landscape strategy.

The examination of what are termed Devon's 'Landscape Character Zones' is set out in Chapter 6 and occupies the greatest part of *The Devon Landscape*.

This two-fold approach to landscape appraisal adopted by *The Devon Landscape*, i.e. identifying universal themes and the Landscape Character Zones, forms the basic framework for the whole strategy, and provides the structure on which all the actions and proposals discussed in the strategy depend. Underpinning the whole strategy, and especially evident in *The Devon Landscape*, is an overall vision of the future where:

- the value of the landscape in its widest sense is acknowledged;
- the character and quality of the landscape is appreciated in its entirety, cherishing the typical and the commonplace as well as the rare and the special;
- the potentially conflicting forces of conservation versus social or economic change have been integrated and harmonised;
- everybody appreciates they have a role to play in shaping the Devon landscape.

CHAPTER 4

THE WIDER CONTEXT

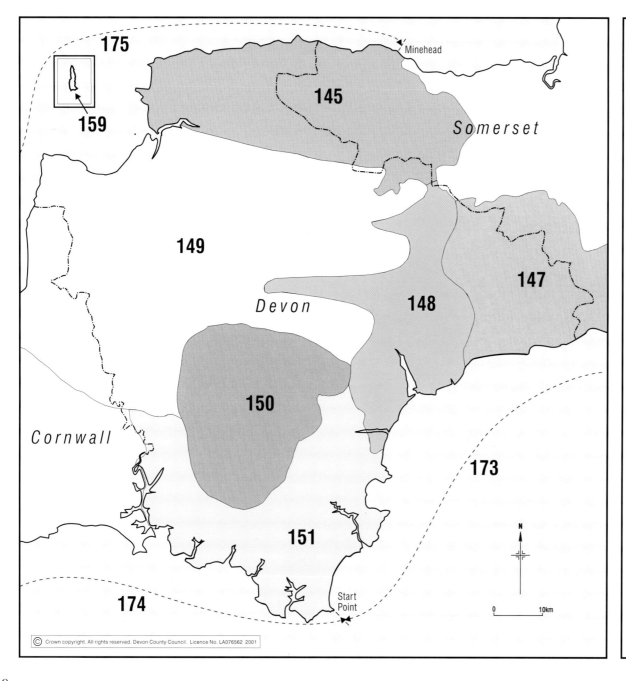

Map 1.
The Character of England

Character Areas :

145 - Exmoor

147 - Blackdowns

148 - Devon Redlands

149 - The Culm

150 - Dartmoor

151 - South Devon

159 - Lundy

Maritime Character Areas :

173 - Lyme Bay

174 - Start Point to Land's End

175 - Land's End to Minehead

---·---·--- County boundary

THE CHARACTER OF ENGLAND

In the same way as *The Devon Landscape* derives a series of Landscape Character Zones, a map of the whole of England has been produced which depicts the natural and cultural dimensions of the landscape at a national level. This map, produced jointly by the Countryside Agency and English Nature, divides England into some 180 Character and Natural Areas. The former are areas with a broadly similar landscape character, exactly analogous to the Landscape Character Zones set out in *The Devon Landscape*. The latter are areas with similar types of wildlife and natural features. To a large extent they also share similar land-scapes, and there is a close correspondence between the Character and Natural Areas.

Devon is included within all or part of seven Character Areas, plus three Maritime Natural Areas, which include the relevant coastal margins. The Areas in question, together with their Character of England reference numbers, are listed below, and shown on **Map 1**.

CHARACTER AREAS

145	Exmoor
147	Blackdowns
148	Devon Redlands
149	The Culm
150	Dartmoor
151	South Devon
159	Lundy

MARITIME NATURAL AREAS

173	Lyme Bay
174	Start Point to Land's End
175	Land's End to Minehead

A list of the main features of the Character Areas, taken from the Character of England document, is as follows:

145 Exmoor

- a range of landscape elements, from open bleak heather and grass moorland to deep, well-wooded and sheltered valleys;
- below the open moorland, a landscape of enclosed land divided into hill farms, surrounded by small irregular fields and deep sunken lanes;
- other, later, straight-sided fields enclosed by earth and stone banks topped with beech hedgerows;
- narrow, steep-sided valleys leading to the coast, often thickly wooded.

147 Blackdowns

- an intimate landscape of lowland farmland;
- plateaux and ridges divided by river valleys;
- ancient semi-natural woodlands linked by hedgerows;
- a coastal fringe dominated by irregular head-lands and unstable cliffs.

148 Devon Redlands

- dominated by arable and pasture fields of mixed farmland;
- small farm woodlands and hedgerows break up the landscape;
- pebble bed heathlands on infertile, acidic soil a distinctive feature in part of the Character Area;
- estuaries, rivers and floodplains a characteristic feature;
- striking red sandstone cliffs on the coastline.

149 The Culm

- small to medium fields of grassland with characteristic tussocks of purple moor grass and rushes;
- often neglected, flower-rich hedgerows on steep banks divide the fields;
- abrupt, high sea cliffs on a spectacular coastline;
- wooded river valleys in a landscape dominated by a series of ridges.

150 Dartmoor

- upland heaths, grass moor and pasture provide an open landscape;
- peat bogs a significant element;
- river-cut valleys mark the edge of the granite area;
- characteristic hedgebanks and granite drystone walls lining narrow lanes and small fields of the moorland edge;
- mines and quarries prominent features.

151 South Devon

- rounded hills of pink and red soils among areas of green pasture;
- a network of narrow country lanes enclosed by high hedgebanks;
- inland valleys often deep and enclosed;
- broad, tidal drowned estuaries or rias with steep, often wooded hillsides that dip abruptly into the water.

159 Lundy

- exposed and open rolling heathland dominat-ing the northern end of the island;
- improved and semi-improved pastures enclosed by wire fences and stone walls in the south, around the small settlements;
- spectacular, near-vertical granite cliffs.

The Maritime Natural Areas are defined largely for their nature conservation rather than their landscape character. However, their nature does impact on the landscape character of the adjacent land-based Character Areas, as indicated below:

173 Lyme Bay

- a coastal geomorphology of numerous classic landforms – spits, constantly crumbling cliffs, landslips;
- estuaries, lakes and lagoons;
- littoral and sub-littoral marine wildlife of importance;
- the open sea as a habitat for marine mammals.

174 Start Point to Land's End

- drowned estuaries or rias;
- open water estuaries;
- coastal cliffs of important maritime grassland and heathland habitats;
- sandy beaches and dunes;
- inter-tidal rocky shores.

175 Land's End to Minehead

- sea cliffs;
- nationally important maritime grassland, heathland and woodland;
- sand dunes and shingle spits;
- large estuary and bay;
- rocky and sandy sea-bed habitats.

A HIERARCHY OF LANDSCAPE CHARACTER

These Character Areas help to provide a basis of national consistency in appraising landscapes and landscape character. At a Devon level, however, while providing a valuable starting point, they are perhaps a little too general to address the more detailed distinctiveness appropriate at this scale. The Landscape Character Zones set out in Chapter 6 obviously have a close relationship to the national Character Areas but they assess the landscape at a more detailed level. To a large extent, they are effectively sub-divisions of the Character Areas, with some minor variations arising from the more detailed approach which are explained in the descriptions.

In the same way that *The Devon Landscape* undertakes an examination at a level appropriate to the County, it is also the case that these Landscape Character Zones can themselves be sub-divided on a yet more detailed level. The next more detailed level appropriate to such an examination is the District Council, Unitary Authority or National Park. Work has already been completed in some cases and is under way in others, and the ideal situation will be for a hierarchy of landscape appraisals, from national (the Character Areas), through County (*The Devon Landscape*) to District or equivalent. The potential may even exist for yet more detailed breakdown in some instances.

The Devon Landscape thus fits as an integral part into this hierarchy of landscape assessments.

For information, **Map 2** shows the areas of the District Councils, Unitary Authorities and National Parks in Devon.

TRANQUIL AREAS

While the physical appearance of an area is obviously very important in appraising landscape character, it is not the only factor. Also very important is the degree of perceived remoteness, quietness or tranquillity.

In 1995 the then Countryside Commission, in conjunction with the Council for the Protection of Rural England, undertook a study of the 'Tranquil Areas' of England, including a comparison of the situation in the 1960s and the 1990s. The study used certain set criteria to define the Tranquil Areas. Under these criteria, a Tranquil Area lies:

- 4km or more from the largest power stations;
- 3km or more from the most highly trafficked roads; from large towns; and from major industrial areas;
- 2km or more from other motorways and major trunk roads and from the edge of smaller towns;
- 1km or more from medium disturbance roads (i.e. difficult to cross in peak hours, 10,000 vehicles per day) and from some main-line railways.

A Tranquil Area also lies beyond military and civil airfield noise lozenges as defined by published data and beyond very extensive opencast mining.

Elements of lower disturbance are noted as falling within generally Tranquil Areas; these include roads of lower disturbance, 400KV and 275KV power lines, some well-trafficked railways, large mining or processing operations, groups of pylons or masts, settlements greater than 2500 in population, some half-abandoned airfields and most windpower developments.

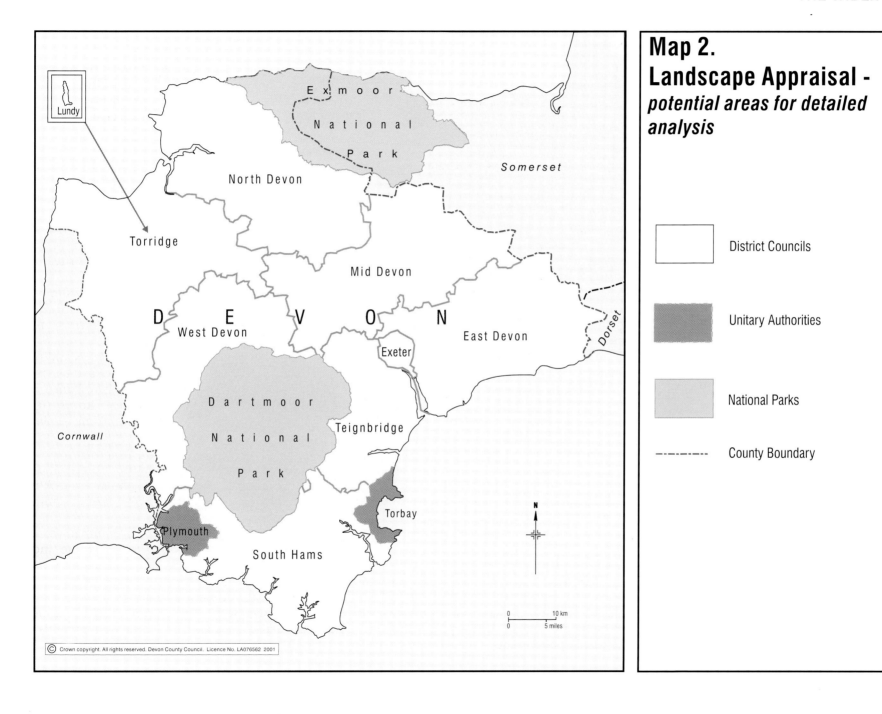

Lundy

Exmoor
National
Park

Somerset

North Devon

Torridge

Mid Devon

D E V O N

West Devon

East Devon

Exeter

Cornwall

Dartmoor
National
Park

Teignbridge

Dorset

N

Torbay

Plymouth

South Hams

0   10 km
0   5 miles

Map 2.
Landscape Appraisal -
potential areas for detailed analysis

☐ District Councils

▨ Unitary Authorities

▨ National Parks

–·–·–·– County Boundary

Map 3.
Tranquil Areas

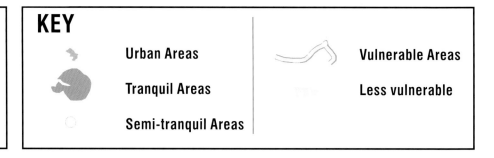

Urban Areas

Tranquil Areas

Semi-tranquil Areas

Vulnerable Areas

Less vulnerable

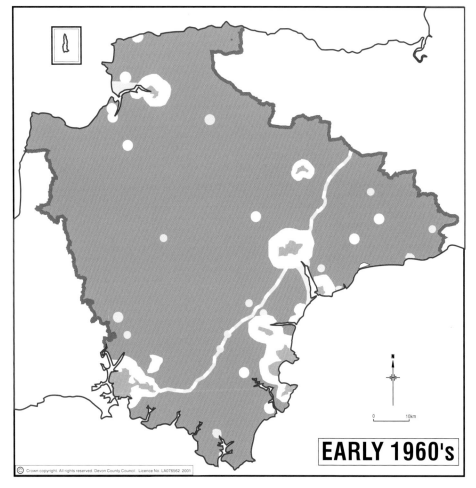

EARLY 1960's

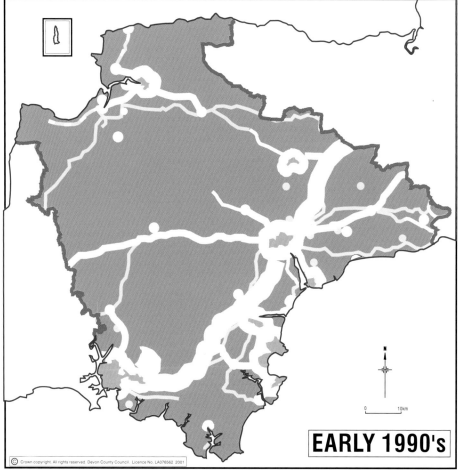

EARLY 1990's

The maps produced as a result of this study are drawn on a level sufficient to ignore local effects, in order to provide an essentially broad-brush picture of areas of the countryside which are free from urban intrusion. Within the Tranquil Areas lower-level semi-tranquil areas are also shown. In addition, disturbance created by some roads is projected to increase and these areas are identified as 'vulnerable'. In certain other cases, such as power lines, disturbance is unlikely to increase significantly and the affected areas are 'less vulnerable'.

The resulting outcome of the study, for both 1960s and 1990s, is shown on **Map 3**.

An examination of the study in relation to Devon gives the following figures:

Tranquil Area

        1960s   5936 sqkm
        1990s   5003 sqkm

        change 933 sqkm, 16% loss

Percentage of Devon in Tranquil Area
        1960s 89%
        1990s 75%

        change 14% loss

Size of average Tranquil Area in Devon
        1960s 660 sqkm
        1990s 111 sqkm

The figures highlight the following:

- the total loss of Tranquil Area, while appreciable, is lower in percentage terms than almost any other rural county;
- the percentage of Devon which remained tranquil in the 1990s was among the highest in England, and the highest in southern England;
- the average size of a Tranquil Area in Devon, while much reduced from the 1960s to the 1990s, was among the highest in England and, again, the highest in southern England.

In national comparison terms it may be seen that Devon remains among the most blessed counties in England for Tranquil Areas. The change from the 1960s to the 1990s is, however, revealing and should be used as a warning.

Nevertheless, the maps should be taken as guidance only. It is true that tranquillity is an important element of landscape character, but the broad-brush effect deliberately adopted by the study obviously causes anomalies. Most people who know Devon will be able to point at individual locations in Tranquil Areas which may be anything but tranquil; in contrast, numerous locations excluded do in fact have a perceived tranquillity, and some of the descriptions in Chapter 6 note this.

As a general guide, however, the Tranquil Areas are an important pointer; the relatively large size of Devon's individual Tranquil Areas, including a good part of the largest one in southern England, is especially important to an appraisal of the landscape character of Devon.

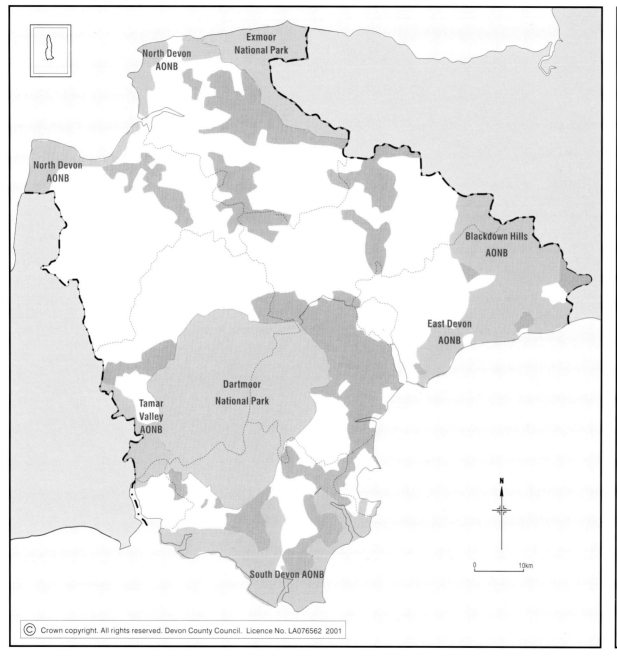

North Devon
AONB

Exmoor
National Park

North Devon
AONB

Blackdown Hills
AONB

East Devon
AONB

Dartmoor
National Park

Tamar
Valley
AONB

South Devon AONB

0   10km

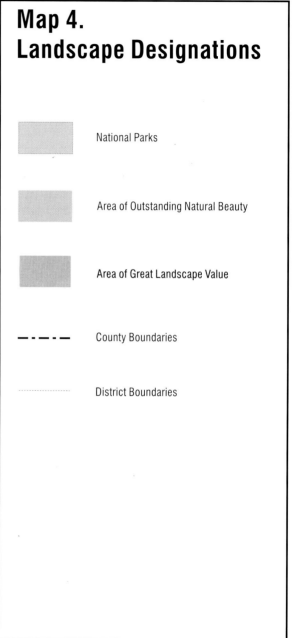

Map 4.
Landscape Designations

National Parks

Area of Outstanding Natural Beauty

Area of Great Landscape Value

— · — · — County Boundaries

··········· District Boundaries

LANDSCAPE DESIGNATIONS

There is a long tradition of Government identifying what are deemed high quality landscapes and specifically designating them for special treatment. Two types of designation are relevant, National Parks and Areas of Outstanding Natural Beauty. Both are designated by the Countryside Agency on behalf of central Government, under the 1949 National Parks and Access to the Countryside Act. While National Parks tend to have the higher public profile, it has always been made clear that, in landscape terms, the two types of designation are of equal status. This has been reiterated yet again in Planning Policy Guidance Note 7 from Government, and the Countryside and Rights of Way Act 2000 gives additional strength to the Area of Outstanding Natural Beauty designation.

The quality of Devon's landscape has been widely acknowledged, both as a whole and in terms of certain identified areas. This has led to large areas of the County being designated for the quality of the landscape. Devon covers the whole of one National Park (Dartmoor) and approximately one third of another (Exmoor). In addition, three designated Areas of Outstanding Natural Beauty fall wholly within Devon (North Devon, East Devon, South Devon) and approximately half of each of two others (Blackdown Hills, Tamar Valley). These areas cover over one-third of Devon's area in total.

In addition, designation of landscapes has also been undertaken at a County level. Areas of landscape regarded as being of considerable, if more localised, importance, areas of significance at a County level, have been designated as Areas of Great Landscape Value. The future of this County designation is currently under debate, and is addressed more appropriately in a companion document to *The Devon Landscape* which deals with the policy discussions. At the time of the appraisal of the landscape for the beginning of the 21st century, 13 Areas of Great Landscape Value were recognised, some of them contiguous, covering almost 15 per cent of the County area.

All the designated landscapes are shown on **Map 4**.

While there are inevitably many correspondences between the designated landscape areas and the Landscape Character Zones, the bases on which these two sets of areas are identified are not the same and there is much criss-crossing of landscape designations and Character Zones. These relationships are noted in the discussions of the appropriate Landscape Character Zones and there should be no presumption of a weakness on the part of either a designation or a Character Zone if the two do not coincide.

Devon County Council also has a designation 'Coastal Preservation Area', whose purpose is to protect the finite resource of undeveloped coastal land. This designation has no implications of landscape quality, but relies purely on visibility from the coast, estuary or sea coupled with being substantially unaffected by development. The vast majority of Devon's coast, and all of it outside the settlements, is covered by this designation which has played an important part in maintaining Devon's coastal landscape integrity.

A further relevant factor is the Heritage Coast. Heritage Coasts are defined by the Countryside Agency on behalf of central Government as areas where management is important to maintain the quality of the coastal landscape. While not strictly a landscape designation, definition of a Heritage Coast does depend on the quality of the coastal scenery of an area.

Inland Devon as probably most often thought of – 'Redlands' near Cheriton Fitzpaine.

CHAPTER 5

THE ESSENCE OF DEVON — LANDSCAPE THEMES

The harsh but dramatic Atlantic coast near Hartland Quay.

Contrasts of deep wooded valley and moorland at East Lyn Cleave, Exmoor.

INTRODUCTION TO LANDSCAPE THEMES

An appraisal of the Devon landscape soon makes it apparent that a large variety of key components makes up its composition. It is the sum total of all these features, in a unique combination, that shapes the Essence of Devon as a landscape entity. It is also the individual mix of these features which creates each locally distinctive individual Landscape Character Zone. This chapter on the Essence of Devon identifies the key features and classifies them into a series of themes, in order to try to give some sort of shape to what is otherwise a confused picture.

It has often been said that the dominant factor in Devon's landscape, indeed, in the landscape of everywhere in England, has been the hand of mankind. The appearance of almost every square metre in the County, from the centre of Exeter or Plymouth to the middle of Dartmoor, can be attributed, directly or indirectly, to human intervention. It may be argued that occasional cliff faces or landslip areas have escaped such influence, but even here, human action on adjacent land probably means that there has been some peripheral impact.

This scenario is fully accepted, but at the same time human influence needs a canvas on which to work. It is therefore the themes which create this canvas, which create a blank screen on which human factors can work, which are considered first. The themes which reflect the work of mankind, and which act upon the shape provided by the natural processes, then follow.

The themes are not unique to Devon. However, as indicated earlier, it is the individual mix of the themes which gives the various parts of Devon their individual characters. Further, the overall Essence of Devon is a product of the impact of all these factors which may be regarded as the basic building blocks of Devon's landscape.

A total of seven themes are identified and considered:

THEME 1: GEOLOGY

More than any other single factor, the underlying geology shapes the distinctive character of Devon. It gives us, for example, the famous red soils, as well as a range of **landforms** from steep rocky valleys to soft undulating farmland. **Inland rock formations** provide distinctive landscapes and building materials, and are often the basis for the existence of **quarries** and other signs of past mineral wealth and activity. Cliff formations and a deeply indented coastline provide a wealth of geomorphological features, landmarks and widely valued **coastal scenery**.

THEME 2: WATER

Water, its sight and sound, permeates every corner of Devon. It is present over the range from black, peaty moorland **streams** to the major wooded valleys of the rivers which dissect the County. Regionally distinctive are the **estuaries** and drowned river valleys, or **rias** which represent major tidal landscapes and inland waterways. In contrast are the smaller, less well-known water landscapes provided by canals, ponds and **other bodies of water**.

THEME 3: FARMED LANDSCAPES AND WOODLAND

Devon's landscape is primarily a farmed landscape. A range of pressures, political, scientific and economic, inevitably give rise to a **changing agricultural landscape** and **agricultural diversification**; such pressures will doubtless continue to have an effect on the landscape. While agriculture is the predominant use, the landform and soils of Devon have led to the existence of **woodland** throughout the landscape, especially but not exclusively on the steepest slopes. The appearance of specific **tree features**, often the result of the actions of individuals, can also have an effect on the character of the landscape.

THEME 4: FIELD BOUNDARIES

Throughout Devon the **land use pattern** and the results of **enclosure** provide a unifying feature. The substantial nature of the field walls and, especially, Devon's hedgebanks, and the variety of construction practices and **hedgerow management** create a variety of landscape features both characteristic and highly valued. This value is not only visual but includes the importance of the boundaries as **natural corridors**. Also relevant is the evidence of early farmers' influence on the landscape – ancient reaves, grazing systems, open fields and the legacy of archaeological features conserved on land which has remained uncultivated, give rise to an important **historic landscape**. Indeed, in Devon the majority of field boundaries may be regarded as 'historic' and the Theme is thus very important in terms of understanding historic developments.

THEME 5: SETTLEMENTS AND BUILDINGS

Devon has a range of **settlements** varying in size from over a quarter of a million people to the smallest hamlet; this also represents a range of origins. In addition, because of the essentially rural nature of the County, individual **buildings** often represent **landscape elements**; traditional Devon farmsteads especially characterise the County, giving rise to such renowned features as cob barns, thatched cottages and Dartmoor longhouses. The location of the settlements is also a factor. **Village form** throughout Devon often displays a distinctive relationship with the surrounding landscape. The internal appearance of the settlements is also a factor and **townscapes** have their own contribution to the landscape of Devon and its character.

THEME 6: DEVELOPMENT, ROADS AND PEOPLE

This theme especially reflects contemporary pressures on various elements of the landscape. The problems, and opportunities, presented by areas of **urban fringe**, less marked perhaps in Devon than some places, are nevertheless relevant; **new development in the countryside** is a contentious and often emotive issue and **road and highway improvements** can provoke similar reactions. Finally, the presence of **people in the landscape** can have an effect; historically, people working on the land, now, primarily people using the land for leisure.

THEME 7: PANORAMAS, SKYLINES AND LANDMARKS

Although drawn out as a theme in its own right, this element crosses the realms of most of the previous themes, and all or any of them will contribute to this way of looking at the landscape. The **panoramas** include inland and coastal vistas, 'wildscapes' and cultivated land; **skylines** can be vast and relatively featureless, marked perhaps by isolated trees or clumps, can relate to intricate and detailed landforms, or can focus on specific features; **landmarks** range from features in the centre of an urban area to isolated buildings or landforms deep in a rural area.

Through all these themes the widest definition of landscape is followed – recognising that it includes nature and wildlife and reflects the historic heritage rather than simply visual aspects. However, it is such a visual appraisal which is the baseline of *The Devon Landscape*; for detailed discussions on the other aspects of landscape the appropriate documents should be consulted ('Devon Biodiversity Action Plan', 'Devon Historic Landscape Characterisation Project').

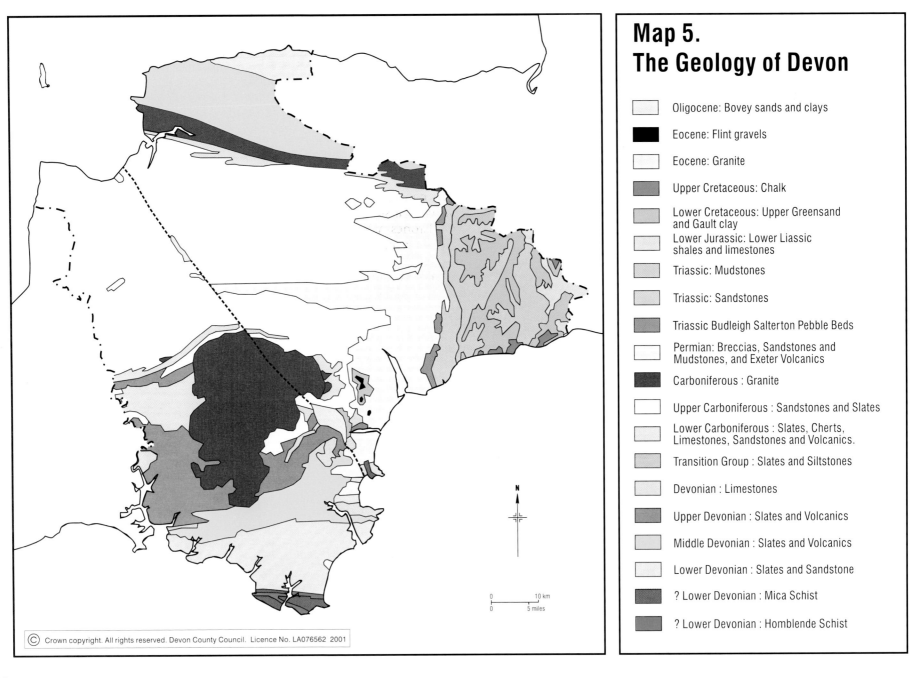

Map 5.
The Geology of Devon

Oligocene: Bovey sands and clays

Eocene: Flint gravels

Eocene: Granite

Upper Cretaceous: Chalk

Lower Cretaceous: Upper Greensand and Gault clay

Lower Jurassic: Lower Liassic shales and limestones

Triassic: Mudstones

Triassic: Sandstones

Triassic Budleigh Salterton Pebble Beds

Permian: Breccias, Sandstones and Mudstones, and Exeter Volcanics

Carboniferous : Granite

Upper Carboniferous : Sandstones and Slates

Lower Carboniferous : Slates, Cherts, Limestones, Sandstones and Volcanics.

Transition Group : Slates and Siltstones

Devonian : Limestones

Upper Devonian : Slates and Volcanics

Middle Devonian : Slates and Volcanics

Lower Devonian : Slates and Sandstone

? Lower Devonian : Mica Schist

? Lower Devonian : Homblende Schist

THEME 1 : GEOLOGY

BACKGROUND

The underlying geology and the resulting landform and soils has probably had the strongest physical influence in shaping the character of the Devon landscape. Directly or indirectly it affects settlement, farming patterns, mining activities and even vernacular building styles through the construction material historically available.

From oldest to youngest, Devon's geology shows the following progression:

Devonian:

Laid down in seas over 395 to 310 million years ago, Devonian rocks in northern Devon are composed mainly of sandstones with thin shale beds. In the south, rocks of the same age are different in character as here, only fine deposits accumulated on the seabed of the time. Shales were laid down and at times marine creatures lived and reefs developed, forming the limestone beds around Torquay and Plymouth.

Carboniferous:

The Devonian sea conditions continued into the carboniferous period, resulting in a succession of sandstones, shales and mudstones which date from 350 to 280 million years ago. In places, sooty deposits resulted from accumulated vegetation; this is known locally as 'Culm', which has become a name synonymous with Carboniferous strata in Devon.

At the end of the Carboniferous era a period of mountain building occurred which gave rise to volcanic activity. This created a lake of molten material which welled up to form the granite body of Dartmoor. It also folded and faulted the older Devonian and Carboniferous rocks, giving rise to the steeply inclined strata visible at many points on the coast and transforming the shales into slates in central Devon and schists in the far south.

Permian and Triassic:

The newly formed higher land emerged into sub-tropical arid conditions which gave rise to a sequence of red sandstones between 280 and 195 million years ago. In the river valleys of the time, sands and gravels were laid down to form the Bunter Pebble Beds in the east of the County.

Dramatically inclined strata exposed on the coast near Hartland Point.

Jurassic:

Another period of marine incursion 195 million years ago flooded small areas in the south-eastern part of the County where a succession of limestones and shales were deposited. Most of the rest of Devon was unaffected.

Cretaceous:

Sea re-entered most of Devon 125 million years ago, although Dartmoor may have remained as an island. Sands and clays settled, forming the Greensand and Gault Clays of East Devon. As the sea got deeper calcium was deposited as the chalk that makes up the cliffs at Beer.

Tertiary:

Another period of mountain building 65 million years ago raised Devon out of the sea again.

Erosion then removed most of the earlier chalk, leaving behind areas of flint gravel in the east of the County and on Haldon. The Sticklepath Fault occurred 30 million years ago, causing local subsidence to create the Bovey and Petrockstow Basins which filled with sand and clay deposits.

Quaternary:

Unlike most of the country, Devon did not experience the full effects of this Ice Age of 10 million years ago; the southward moving ice sheets halted on the northern cliffs after crossing the Bristol Channel. Glacial clays formed in this area. Subsequently, river erosion created much of the present-day shape of Devon. Rises in sea level caused by the melting of the ice sheets caused many of Devon's river valleys to be drowned, creating the rias and estuaries of the Taw-Torridge and the south coast.

The geology of Devon is shown on **Map 5**.

A brief glance at the map will show that the 'newer' rocks in the list are largely confined to the east of the County. This reflects the southern end of what has been recognised as a national division between old and new rocks, the so-called Exe-Tees line. There are, of course, complexities of detail; the new red rocks are found west of the Exe on the shores of Tor Bay, and two tongues stretch west of Tiverton and, even more marked, west of Crediton; on the other hand, older rocks appear here and there east of the Exe. Nevertheless, this is a basic geological and landscape division and goes towards creating the very different character of the eastern and western parts of the County.

Below: *Limestone at Berry Head contrasts with older rocks nearby.*

1(A) LANDFORM

Devon is hilly, characterised by a variety of generally undulating landforms. The detailed forms can vary considerably – the brooding skyline of Dartmoor, punctuated by its granite tors, rising abruptly from the surrounding farmland; the broad sweep of the Culm Measures with its long rounded ridges and wooded valleys; the steep-sided 'fingers' of greensand in East Devon; North Devon's downland plateau, dissected by valleys; and the steeply undulating, scattered hillocks and hidden valleys of Mid Devon. Even in the few flatter parts of the County, as, for example, on Braunton Marsh, the landform is a characteristic feature largely because of its great contrast to the undulating hills.

It is therefore not surprising that geology, and its resulting landform, have emerged as perhaps the key factors determining the extent of local landscape character. This is reflected in the strong echoes of the geology map to be seen in the boundaries of the Countryside Agency's Character Areas and of the Landscape Character Zones of *The Devon Landscape*.

As has been acknowledged earlier, landscape character is at least as much a product of human activity as natural processes. However, throughout Devon's history, geology, through the soil, landform and drainage patterns that it creates, has governed human responses. For example, transport links followed the open ridge lines when the valleys were still wooded or wet. Altitude, steepness of slopes, spring lines, soils and drainage affected forest clearance for cultivation and thereby dictated which woodland was left. The same influences affected the sequence of enclosure and subsequent field patterns. Aspect, shelter and natural places for surveillance or defence often influenced the location of settlements, while the landform frequently dictated their shape.

Today, many of the limitations of landform can be overcome. For instance, the land can be re-shaped, flattened or cut through; settlements have less regard for aspect or shelter; and the lack of flat land in Devon has meant increasing use of steep slopes now that this has become technologically feasible. All these factors have implications for the future of Devon's landscape.

Devon Landforms:

Greensand ridges meet the sea at Sidmouth.

Christow and the Teign Valley.

Undulating countryside near the Raddon Hills, Mid Devon.

1(B) INLAND ROCK FORMATIONS AND QUARRIES

The most obvious aspect of Devon's geology reveals itself in its rock formations. Best known, and probably most spectacular, are the granite tors of Dartmoor, whose outlines have become instantly recognisable as a shorthand form for wild, inland Devon.

More subtle, however, are the relics of mankind's use of less obvious landforms. In past times, many, perhaps most, of Devon's parishes would have their own quarries for use as local building stone. This would reflect on the local architecture (see, for example, North Devon 'slate' use, greensand chert, pebble bed and flint use in East Devon, schist drystone walls in the far south); they also, usually in a small way reflect on the local landscape. Most are now overgrown, almost forgotten, but some have developed and adapted to a modern use.

Modern use of such areas can be varied and include landfill and education as well as extraction. There is now an increasing awareness of the need to protect the wider earth science resource, including such features, as an integral part of the landscape. English Nature has launched the principle of Regionally Important Geological Sites (RIGS) as part of its Earth Science Conservation Strategy. English Nature promotes the establishment of local RIGS groups to conserve rocks, fossils and landforms through voluntary co-operation, beginning with the selection of potential RIGS sites. In Devon, such sites are defined by the Devon RIGS Group and referred to as 'County Geological Sites'.

The importance of Devon's geological resource for education and research also needs to be emphasised. A whole geological period – the Devonian – is named after the County and a large proportion of Devon's Sites of Special Scientific Interest (locations designated under statute by English Nature) are important for geological reasons. In addition, Devon's inland rock formations and landforms are of value as an educational tool for understanding how Devon's landscape has evolved, as well as providing distinctive landscape features. The tors, outcrops, quarry faces, boulder fields and caves are obvious examples, but the locally distinctive construction materials already mentioned also form an educational tool in their own right to the geological heritage of the local area. It can sometimes be a fascinating educational project to trace the source of such local materials to a hidden or forgotten quarry.

Left: *Holmingham Quarry – an important landscape feature in the Exe Valley.*

Opposite page:
Left: *Berry Head.*
Middle: *Thurlestone Rock.*
Right: *Near Hartland Quay.*

1(C) COASTAL SCENERY

Devon relies heavily on its geological resource to provide its dramatic coastal scenery. More than 'just' dramatic, the range of this geological resource has also given rise to a very diverse coastline. The Devon coast includes such varied features as the limestone cliffs of Berry Head; the crumbling slabs of the north 'Culm' coast; awesome granite sea cliffs on Lundy; the schist outcrop at Prawle Point; red sandstone sea stacks at Ladram Bay; striking vertical and convoluted strata at Hartland; white chalk cliffs at Beer; classic landslips of the Axmouth – Lyme Regis undercliffs.

This remarkable coastal landscape is highly valued nationally. An indication of this national importance can be obtained by looking back at **Map 4**. The greater part of Devon's coast is included within three of the nationally designated Areas of Outstanding Natural Beauty or within Exmoor National Park. In addition, most of the Devon coast has been defined nationally by the Countryside Agency as Heritage Coast. While this definition is made for management purposes only, it is only applied to those lengths of coastline deemed to be of the highest quality nationally.

The Devon Heritage Coasts are:

Exmoor	(Somerset – Combe Martin)
North Devon	(Combe Martin – Taw/ Torridge Estuary)
Hartland	(Westward Ho! – Cornwall)
South Devon	(Plymouth – Torbay)
East Devon	(Budleigh Salterton – Dorset)
Lundy	

The geological importance of one length of coast has been internally recognised. At a meeting of UNESCO's World Heritage Convention in Helsinki in December 2001, the Dorset and East Devon Coast was inscribed as a World Heritage Site. There are four criteria for natural World Heritage sites and the Dorset and East Devon Coast was considered under the following:

The site should be an outstanding example, representing major stages of Earth's history, including the record of life, significant ongoing geological processes in the development of landforms, or significant geomorphia or physiographic features.

The site extends for 155 kilometres (25 miles) from Orcombe Point in East Devon to Studland Bay in Dorset. It includes the area from the top of the cliffs to Mean Low Water Mark, and is interrupted only by the presence of coastal development; the settlements have an important role as gateway towns to the Site. The Dorset and East Devon Coast, to be known as the Jurassic Coast, is the first natural World Heritage Site in England and joins such renowned features as the Giant's Causeway and the Grand Canyon.

Devon has been fortunate in that so much of its coastal land has been protected from large-scale development, and this has meant that coastal geological formations are under less threat from the need to construct major sea defences than is the case in many parts of the country. However, man-made sea defences do remain a potential landscape issue around some coastal towns and geologically vulnerable areas, such as shingle spits or friable cliffs.

The main pressures on the cliff tops themselves and on potential access points to the coast probably arise from recreation. Recreational pressures and opportunities are fairly widely spaced, but tend to be concentrated around coastal towns and other 'honey-pot' sites. The existence of the South West Coast Path along the length of the Devon coast is important in that it spreads usage and reduces concentration on certain locations. It also gives the opportunity to manage recreational use of the coast through the implementation of the South West Coast Path Strategy.

The cliff-faces themselves are generally inaccess-ible to human beings, and thus they represent valuable wildlife havens, especially for breeding seabirds. However, a few cliff areas are popular with rock climbers. This activity has more of a potential con-flict with ecology than with the landscape; indeed, some might say that the presence of climbers can be an added interest to the coastal scene. There may be some small-scale landscape concerns, such as the legacy of in situ bolts and spikes, and cliff top erosion associated with belay points. A loss of a character of remoteness may also accompany such activity.

One aspect of coastal geological landscapes often neglected is their appearance from the sea. Devon's distinctive coastline has long provided landmarks and hazards for sailors and the coastal rock formations, the form and appearance of seaside towns, lighthouses, landmarks and daymarks have been documented in pilot books and charts for centuries. They represent an important part of Devon's history, as well as providing attractive landscape features for today's visiting recreational yachtsmen to navigate by.

Devon County Council policy has been to retain coastal areas visible from the sea as undeveloped as possible, and this has had an important and positive effect on the landscape integrity of these coastal geological and historical features.

The remote coast near Hartland Point.

Clovelly – picturesque location and landmark for mariners.

THEME 2: WATER

BACKGROUND

One cannot really escape the presence of water in Devon. Nowhere is more than 25 miles/40km from the sea and the South West Peninsula, dipping its 'toe' into the Atlantic Ocean, gathers more than its fair share of rain. The result is a myriad of small streams and wooded gorges which feed into the major river valley systems, culminating in the creeks, estuaries and rias (drowned estuaries) of South Devon and the wide estuary mouth of the Taw-Torridge on the north coast.

Devon is truly a landscape shaped by water. It is a softer landform than counties further north which also have a high rainfall and whose landscapes have been covered not only by water but by the glacial ice which Devon just managed to avoid.

The mild maritime climate has created lush and often well vegetated streams and rivers, but the topography has not provided opportunities for lakes to form. As a result Devon's inland water landscapes of intimate river valleys and streams are more unobtrusive and secretive treasures than, for example, Cumbria's lakes, but they still represent a key landscape theme contributory to the essence of Devon.

Instead of lakes the South West Peninsula offers large-scale water landscapes of national importance along its indented coastline. The distinctive rias and estuaries are recognised for their landscape, ecological and recreational value nationally.

The boundary of the South Devon Area of Outstanding Natural Beauty has been drawn to include all the rias of that part of the coast, as well as the more inland estuarine and middle-valley landscapes of two of the major rivers, the Dart and the Avon. Further west, the Tamar Valley Area of Outstanding Natural Beauty has been designated specifically around the middle and lower courses of that river. Further, and representing landscape in its wider definition, national and, in places, international recognition has been accorded to the nature conservation importance of all or part of the major estuaries, as well as a variety of inland water bodies.

The rias and estuaries must represent one of the key distinctive features of the regional landscape and their conservation, enhancement and management warrants identification as a major priority.

One of the South Devon rias – the creek at Stoke Gabriel on the Dart.

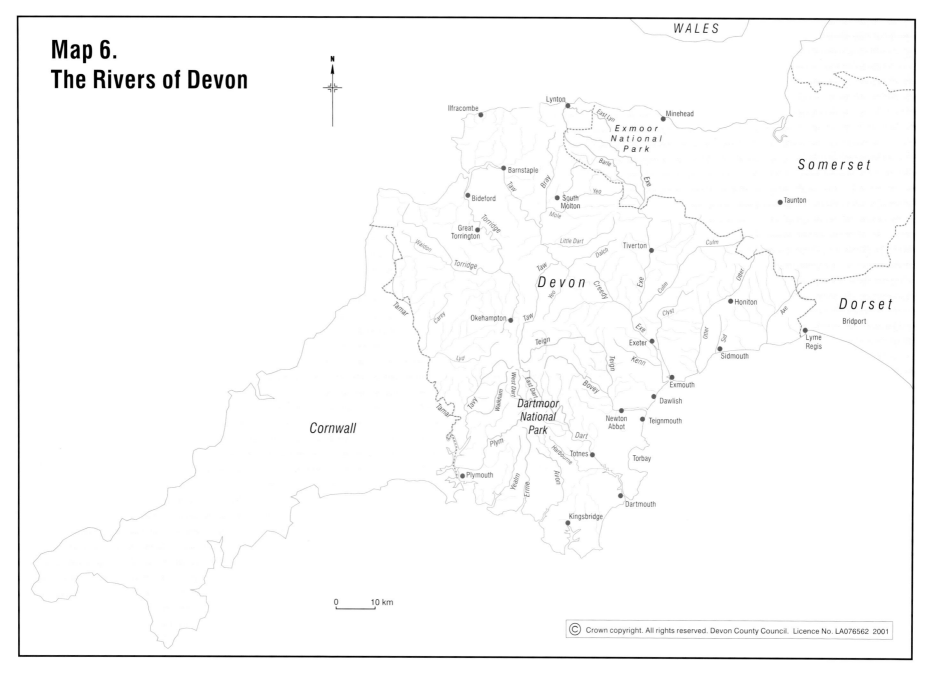

Map 6.
The Rivers of Devon

2(A) STREAMS AND RIVERS

In W.G. Hoskins' much-quoted book 'Devon', he refers to Dartmoor as the 'Great Source', not only for granite, the building stone for buildings both famous and humble, but also for providing a high altitude catchment area to feed Devon's major rivers. **Map 6** shows the location of the rivers, and clearly indicates how so many of them radiate in all directions from Dartmoor. The East Devon rivers are a separate case, but apart from them only the Tamar, Exe and Torridge have their source away from Dartmoor and even these are fed by streams and rivers draining off the high moorland. The link between moor and sea is especially strong in the south where the Plym, Yealm, Erme, Avon, Dart and Teign dissect the complex farming landscape between the high moor and the coastal estuaries.

The nature of Devon's river landscapes changes delightfully from source to sea. Dartmoor streams are strongly acidic and as they drop off the steep edges of the granite they cut deep gorges. These tend to be choked with boulders, which results in the constant sound of rushing water. Shade and shelter create a lush water landscape of mosses, ferns and wet woodland flora. Being alone by one of these streams the landscape seems almost primeval, overriding any evidence of previous human activity such as coppicing of the woodlands.

The Exe, Mole, Bray and numerous small rivers drain off Exmoor. They also start life as moorland streams, which cut down through the bedrock and become fringed with ferns and woodland. On the north coast of Exmoor the rivers form short deep branching combes clothed in ancient woodland. The tree cover is interrupted by scree slopes and rock falls. The rivers reach the rocky coast at small coves, inlets and other smugglers' haunts now transformed into holiday locations. Further west, in the Hartland area, similar streams tumble over the cliffs as waterfalls.

Where some of the streams become major rivers the valleys broaden and the meandering rivers create open flood plains. Other rivers retain a strong element of enclosure and are flanked by steep wooded slopes. These distinctive landform features and tranquil valley landscapes, which dissect the County, contribute strongly to the essence of Devon's landscape character. Their importance has historically been recognised by County landscape designations such as Areas of Great Landscape Value, many of which focus on valley systems (e.g. Exe, Taw, Torridge). The undeveloped nature of many of Devon's valley floors, despite a lack of flat land elsewhere, is a major achievement for landscape conservation that adds greatly to Devon's character and needs to be perpetuated.

It should be mentioned that the wildlife value and natural attraction of these river valleys contributes greatly to the landscape quality and character. Hence issues such as water quality and land use, which reflect on the wildlife integrity, become more than simply an ecological concern.

Apart from the natural assets that these river landscapes contain, they also often host a wealth of man-made features which, through their design, materials and scale, enhance the landscape. Bridges, mills, weirs, stepping stones, boathouses, ferries, can all make a positive contribution to the character of river-based areas. More modern activities, especially recreational ones such as fishing, sailing or canoeing, are less permanent and their landscape impact varies greatly according to the detail of the location. The impact is usually more on the character of an area than on the purely physical aspects.

In East Devon the broad flood plains of the Axe and Otter provide rich agricultural soils, hence they have a long history of cultivation and contain relatively high concentrations of archaeological evidence of past settlement. They also provide a landscape type quite unusual in Devon.

Where development has grown up around a river to form a large village or town, the river often provides a valuable link and potential recreational corridor between town and country. Equally, there may be strong historical links between the river, the origin of the town, and the town's prosperity, even if any river trade has now ceased. Associated riverside features such as wharves, merchants' houses, river crossing points, navigational features, warehouses and street names are all vital to conserve that historic link and add to the landscape appeal of the river feature.

Hoar Oak Water cuts a wooded combe on the Exmoor coast.

2(B) ESTUARIES AND RIAS

The South West has a great attraction to sailors, both modern recreational sailors and also the historic ones who made Devon such a byword for maritime activity. Much of this attraction is explained by the extent of inshore waters which can be used for practice and exploration via Devon's estuaries and drowned river valleys, or rias. It is also from the water that their associated landscapes are perhaps best appreciated. Part of the charm of Devon's estuaries, rias and their creeks lies in their timeless quality, especially where steep waterside woods or tree belts obscure all traces of roads, development and modern farming practices.

The advantages of these waterways and their natural harbours have provided Devon with some of its most distinctive maritime settlements and a strong association with British naval history, most especially at Dartmouth and Plymouth. The historic shape and setting of the maritime settlements and their associated features such as quays, harbours and forts represent vital components of these water landscapes.

Apart from their considerable landscape, cultural and recreational value, Devon's estuaries and rias support significant ecological resources, some of international importance. Devon County Council and other local and national organisations recognise the need for the best possible management of the estuaries, in addition to the special planning policies and designations which already protect these vitally important landscapes and habitats. As a result, management plans for all of Devon's major estuaries have been produced. They aim to promote sustainability, having regard for the present and future needs of nature conservation, recreation, commercial activity and other users, as well as the requirements of landscape conservation.

The role of *The Devon Landscape* is to highlight the landscape importance of the whole of the estuary environment; to show that it is not just the water and its immediate environs, or the woodlands, or the surrounding skylines that are important, but that they all relate to each other to form a distinctive landscape character.

The Avon remains largely undeveloped.

Ferry crossing, Dartmouth.

Map 7.
Major Inland Bodies of Water

1. Wistlandpound
2. Tamar Lakes
3. Bude Canal
4. Grand Western Canal
5. Roadford Reservoir
6. Meldon Reservoir
7. Fernworthy Reservoir
8. Kennick Reservoir
9. Tottiford Reservoir
10. Trenchford Reservoir
11. Bovey Basin
12. Stover Canal
13. Venford Reservoir
14. Burrator Reservoir
15. Avon Dam
16. Slapton Ley
17. Widdicombe Ley
18. South Milton Ley
19. Exeter Canal

2(C) OTHER BODIES OF WATER

While Devon is rich in rivers, streams and tidal water landscapes, it contains relatively few natural areas of still water.

Slapton Ley is perhaps the most important water body, being the largest natural lake in the South West. There are, however, several reservoirs in Devon of similar or even larger size. The majority are on or around Dartmoor, but there are others on the upper Tamar, at Wistlandpound on the fringe of Exmoor and, most recently built, at Roadford in the west of the County between Okehampton and Launceston. Other man-made water bodies include ponds in the former clay pits of the Bovey Tracey and Newton Abbot area and in a few former quarry sites. More unusual are the historic features of the Grand Western, Bude and Stover Canals which, to a greater or lesser extent, comprise water landscapes in their own right.

Slapton Ley with its shingle bar is a particularly unusual landscape and geomorphological feature. It is also an ecologically important wetland site and forms a National Nature Reserve. The low-lying coast, lagoons and reeds provide an attractive contrast to the typically high cliff coastline and, as an additional feature, it has its 'little brother' of Widdicombe Ley just down the coast.

The numerous artificial ponds filling the old clay pits of the Bovey Basin have created their own vegetation and, while relatively unobtrusive, they contribute to the landscape distinctiveness of the area. Some of these have also become features of nature conservation importance.

The much frequented lake at Stover Country Park, near Newton Abbot, illustrates the popularity of such still water landscapes and their accompanying wildlife. This lake also has national recognition for its wildlife importance, primarily for its

dragonfly population. In addition, it is of historic importance, being created as an ornamental landscape feature for the surrounding parkland in the late eighteenth century. It thus combines a range of levels of attraction, in common with many other such wider bodies.

Of similar popularity is the Grand Western Canal, another Country Park, which offers continuous waterside access along its towpath for over 11 miles between Tiverton and the Somerset boundary. Again, its landscape attraction is combined with its wildlife and historic associations, being one of the few canals in Devon.

The County's reservoirs also enjoy the advantage of management which provides for recreation and access, including safe paths, car parking and visitor information. It may be that consequently their popularity in terms of visitor numbers may reflect their convenience of access rather than their intrinsic landscape qualities. Some of Devon's reservoirs integrate more naturally into the surrounding countryside than others. Generally, however, they represent new landscapes with their own distinctive character, rather than contributing to the local landscape as a whole. That does not mean that they are necessarily unattractive; rather that their appearance in the landscape is an unexpected surprise when encountered.

Finally, at the most local level are farm ponds. Very few such now remain in Devon, although they were once very common. However, the construction of ponds is now becoming increasingly popular again. These should ultimately increase the freshwater wildlife resource of the County and may also contribute to the local landscape, so long as they are sensitively designed.

Stover Lake is an important wildlife, recreation and landscape amenity.

THEME 3: FARMED LANDSCAPES AND WOODLAND

BACKGROUND

The previous themes have indicated how Devon's shape has been determined by physical factors. Initially, the land cover was equally the product of natural forces but, over the centuries, the hand of man has shaped this aspect of the landscape and agricultural practices have provided the land-use pattern which now clothes most of Devon. Over 80 per cent of Devon is currently agricultural land, the appearance of all of it the result of human action.

The relationship between the agricultural landscape and the woodland pattern is closely linked, and this has been the case since the first attempts to clear the land from virgin forest for farming. Consequently those ancient woodlands which remain in Devon tend to be concentrated on land unsuitable for agriculture. Typical locations are steep coastal cliffs and combes, the rocky flanks of Dartmoor and the poor thin soils found on many of Devon's steep valley slopes. The well-drained areas of Mid Devon were particularly suited to cultivation and so today this intensively farmed area corresponds with the most sparsely wooded part of Devon. Here, much of the area contains only a few isolated farm woods and amenity plantations.

Hedgerows are a dominant component of Devon's farmed landscape and, like woodland, the hedgerow pattern reveals how the landscape was tamed, cleared and improved over time. The importance of the field boundaries and the patterns they form is so crucial to the essence of the Devon landscape that they have been dealt with as a separate theme.

Further, farm buildings and early settlement patterns provide a record of the process of cultivation and agricultural change, thereby representing an integral part of the rural landscape. However, many other factors have come into play in determining settlement patterns and the nature of buildings in Devon. In more recent times this has become especially true and most of the landscape issues affecting the character of settlements today are unrelated to agriculture. Consequently it is the case that settlements and individual buildings make a crucial and separate contribution to the landscape and are therefore discussed as an individual theme.

While it is important to understand how the landscape has changed over time it is not the intention of *The Devon Landscape* to go into a detailed history of how the farming landscape and woodlands evolved in Devon. A brief résumé is set out, but the discussion of this theme concentrates on the changes and issues facing agriculture and forestry, particularly the economic need to find alternative sources of rural income, the character and land use pattern that currently pertains and the landscape implications of the potential changes.

A mix of woodland, fields and hedgerows in the Axe Valley of East Devon.

3(A) CHANGING AGRICULTURAL LANDSCAPES

The agricultural landscape of Devon has been changing, at a varying rate, for the last 6000 years. It is possible that a knowledge of agriculture was brought into Devon by parties of immigrants who sailed across the Channel from northern France as early as 4500 BC, or as a result of an increasing transmission of ideas through expanding populations. This knowledge will have included corn growing and stock rearing, and the technology through axes to be able to clear forest areas. Their actions may well have increased previous clearances by fire undertaken by the earlier inhabitants and, indeed, areas of open land occurring naturally. It is likely that the thinner soils of the hill tops of East Devon and Dartmoor fringes were the first to be exploited.

As time continued, settlement grew denser. Evidence is especially noticeable on Dartmoor, but other areas almost certainly also experienced population growth. By the first millennium BC quite large areas of the Devon landscape will have begun to take on a pattern of fields, tracks and boundaries, a movement which continued into the Christian era.

The long period commonly known as the Dark Ages, broadly between the end of the Romano-British civilisation and the Norman Conquest, were perhaps the time when land exploitation took on a form recognisable as the ancestor of today's landscape. Although much is unknown of the development of agriculture and land use during this long period, it does seem that the earliest field pattern we would recognise had been established by the time of the Domesday Book at the end of the eleventh century.

Nevertheless, the agricultural landscape would have been very different. Around many of the villages and hamlets would have stretched open fields, cultivated jointly and with intermixed personal holdings. But there would also have been single farmsteads carved out of the wilder, previously uncultivated land, surrounded by small fields of irregular shape often enclosed by massive hedgebanks. Beyond these areas of cultivation would have stretched large areas of unenclosed land – woodland, high moorland, wet lowland areas and marshes, sandy heaths.

The changing agricultural landscape of the following centuries includes a history of enclosure and cultivation of the 'waste'. The result was a landscape of small, enclosed fields, surrounded by hedgebanks and divided by a network of narrow tracks and lanes. This movement encouraged the relatively early enclosure in Devon of the open fields around the villages. However, the landscape resulting from this change was different, with larger fields divided by straighter hedges, often giving a characteristic reversed – S shape. Other, piecemeal, enclosure was also taking place, again resulting in a largely irregular pattern. This enclosure often incorporated field boundaries from earlier periods into the system.

Later enclosure of open fields or 'waste' tends to result in straight boundaries, often the result of Enclosure Acts of the 18th and 19th centuries. It is noticeable, however, that in most of Devon areas with very straight boundaries are more commonly former pasture rather than former open strip field.

The net outcome of this history of agricultural land-use development is what we see as the modern agricultural landscape of Devon. It is a countryside largely dependent on small-scale farming, with a relatively 'intact' hedgerow and

Low intensity agricultural use in the South Hams.

woodland pattern and one which, as we have seen, is deemed to have great aesthetic appeal. Large estates with parklands are also found throughout the countryside. Modern perception is that it is a 'timeless' rural scene, but as has been noted it is the culmination of a long history of change. Not surprisingly, these changes are ongoing and the effects of modern farming practices and policies on pasture and arable land and on nearby features such as streams and small 'unproductive' patches of land, as well as on the more visually obvious features like woodlands and hedgerows, continue to impact on the agricultural landscape.

Devon has, and probably always has had, a predominantly pastoral farming landscape dictated by the steep undulating land and large areas of relatively poor soil. One result has been that, in contrast to many other English counties, it has tended not to see large-scale hedgerow removal or the conversion of pasture to arable land. Devon also retains substantial pockets of 'unproductive' land, including marsh, scrub, heath and grass moorland or coastal and lowland heath.

Nevertheless, there are considerable differences in the scale and intensity of the agricultural resource throughout Devon. On the agriculturally rich soils of Mid Devon, South Devon and the Lower Exe, the land is intensively cultivated, hedgerows are closely cut and only the steepest slopes retain isolated woodlands or small pockets of unimproved grass or scrub. In contrast, the poorer and wetter soils of the high moors, Culm Measures and the exposed greensand ridges in the east of the County contain a high percentage of unimproved or semi-improved farmland, as well as remnants of unproductive land. These remnants include spring line flushes, carr woodland, Culm grassland and uncultivated field margins.

They provide valuable wildlife habitats and also offer great variety and interest to the rural scene, often contributing strongly to local landscape character. In this context it should be emphasised that landscape quality may not only be expressed in grand vistas or panoramas or aesthetic compositions; details such as wild flowers in the hedgebanks, dragonflies over a boggy field corner, the changing colours of rough grassland or heather, the smell of wild garlic in woodlands, the sight and sound of unpolluted streams, are all a precious part of Devon's landscape.

Finally, the contribution that the actual cultivated land makes to the overall landscape composition should not be underestimated. Ploughlines emphasising landform, the changing colours and textures of arable crops through the seasons, the 'wave effect' of wind in crops or long grass all make a positive contribution to the landscape character.

Changing agricultural landscape: grassland to trees, near Blackmoor Gate.

Intensive agricultural landscape in Mid Devon.

3(B) AGRICULTURAL DIVERSIFICATION

During the 1980s the European agricultural industry was forced to face up to the problem of massive over-production. The UK Government announced that five million acres of farmland would need to be taken out of production and put to alternative use, including recreation, tourism, forestry and various rural enterprises. Various Government schemes and grant packages were launched to reduce food surpluses and to encourage alternative uses of farmland. These schemes have subsequently undergone numerous alterations, or are no longer available. However, what was lacking, and is still unresolved, is a clear vision of the future role of the countryside and the potential landscape implications which arise from this. If anything, this need is now even more acute, and is likely to be a major subject of debate following the foot and mouth disease outbreak of 2001.

In Devon, diversification into non-agricultural land-use activities has been happening since before the current concerns began in the 1980s. This is perhaps not unexpected in a county with a highly valued landscape which is the basis of a major tourism industry. However, European policies and economic uncertainties concerning agriculture have accelerated this process of diversification. Even though Devon has less arable land to 'set aside' than some counties, its mix of small farms, characterised by traditional farm buildings, attractive countryside, superb coastline and two National Parks has resulted in a generally tourism-oriented form of farm diversification and rural development. Examples of such diversification include caravan and camping sites, holiday cottages, farm bed and breakfast, cream teas and golf courses. The potential threats and benefits to the rural landscape, as well as the survival of a viable rural economy and environment, are therefore heavily involved with tourism and recreation and its role as an alternative land-use.

Other diversification options have occurred, but tend to be primarily temporary activities. However, such activities can still have a significant effect on the landscape and its character, in particular resulting in a suburbanising effect. Examples of such activities include the development of 'horsiculture', car boot sales, rallying, clay pigeon shooting, scrambling and caravan sites.

New use for an old barn, near Salcombe.

Small-scale camping, Teign Valley.

Barn conversions to holiday use, South Hams.

3(C) WOODLAND

Devon can often appear a very wooded county, but the distribution of woodland is very uneven. It is also a fact that the South West is actually one of England's least wooded areas. This is partly a reflection of the windy climate but also of centuries of felling for boatbuilding and, indeed, agriculture.

The contribution that woodland landscapes and their patterns make to the character of individual areas is discussed in detail in Chapter 6, but a brief overview is useful here to describe how and why Devon's woodlands contribute so strongly to the character of Devon's landscape as a whole.

The majority of Devon's ancient semi-natural woodlands are situated on steep, well-drained slopes. Acid soils are typically dominated by oak with birch, ash, hazel and rowan; calcareous soils, typically those derived from limestones in South Devon and chalk in East Devon, are dominated by oak or ash and occasionally small-leafed lime. Devon's mild maritime climate and relatively unpolluted atmosphere result in the survival of rich bryophyte communities. These characterise the ancient woodlands, particularly those in the valleys.

Management of woodland on a coppice with standards basis occurred over a long period for fuel, charcoal, tannery and timber purposes. Coppiced woodland was particularly prevalent, and is still noticeable in the landscape, around the mineral rich edges of Dartmoor where mining props were needed, around Exmoor where tannery bark was produced and near the naval dockyards of Plymouth and Dartmouth where there were demands for shipbuilding. Such demands led to large estate planting, typically of oak or sweet chestnut, but also beech. Today, woodland retains a practical value, but now primarily for access, recreation, nature conservation and wood for fuel.

On a strategic level, areas in Devon where woodland has a major effect on the landscape character include:

(i) the major 'structural' woodland networks which emphasise the deep valley systems, for example the Taw, Torridge and Exe;

(ii) the distinctive 'primeval' wooded combes on the North Devon coast;

(iii) the luxuriant wooded backdrops to the estuaries and rias of South Devon;

(iv) the unique charm of the lichen-and-moss covered broadleaved trees between the rocks of the fast flowing streams on the fringes of Dartmoor and Exmoor;

(v) the more extensive Dartmoor fringe woodland in the Teign Valley, complemented by its wild daffodils.

Taw Valley woodlands at Eggesford.

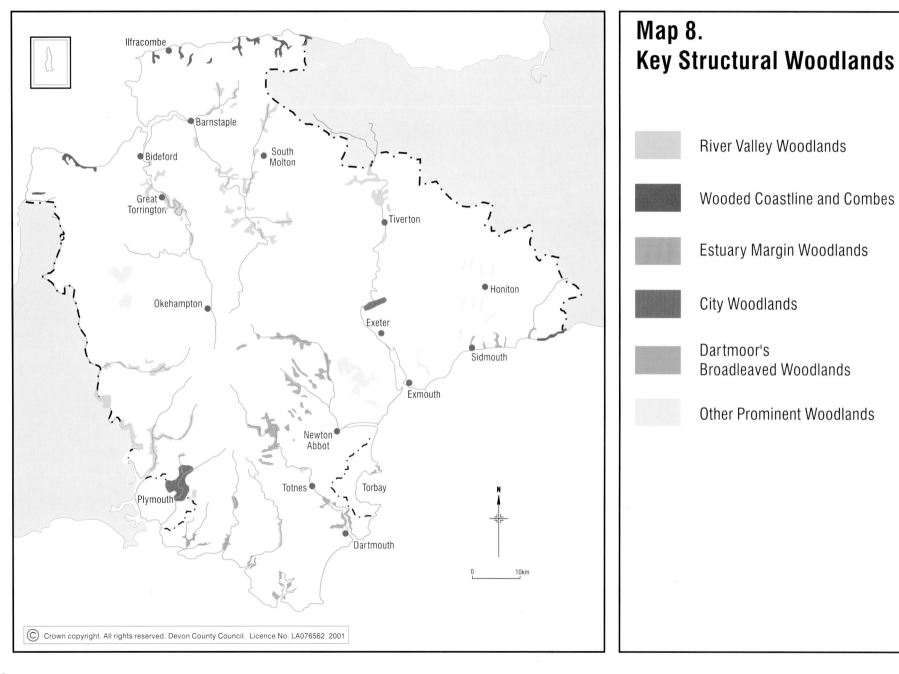

Map 8.
Key Structural Woodlands

River Valley Woodlands

Wooded Coastline and Combes

Estuary Margin Woodlands

City Woodlands

Dartmoor's
Broadleaved Woodlands

Other Prominent Woodlands

Ilfracombe
Barnstaple
Bideford
South Molton
Great Torrington
Tiverton
Honiton
Okehampton
Exeter
Sidmouth
Exmouth
Newton Abbot
Totnes
Torbay
Plymouth
Dartmouth

N

0   10km

The lack of timber in the First World War led to the creation of the Forestry Commission in 1919. This had a considerable effect on the landscape of rural Britain, including that of Devon where the first Commission plantation was established in the Taw Valley. The introduction of fast-growing conifers created new woodland landscapes, not always perceived as a landscape asset. Some were also seen as a threat to wildlife where they replaced more valuable habitats, such as semi-natural ancient woodlands or heath.

While great improvements in the aesthetic design of commercial forestry have occurred since the end of the Second World War, the legacy of some less well designed conifer plantations still remains. Examples include plantations on some of the steep valleys on the southern flanks of Exmoor with prominent straight sides visible for many miles. Visually intrusive plantations may be found on the wild upland landscape of Dartmoor and in places on the north-west coast tall blocks of

Broadleaved woodland in the Mole Valley.

conifers intrude on an otherwise open coastal landscape where natural vegetation is bent and wind-trimmed by Atlantic gales.

However, some large-scale coniferous woodlands have established themselves as 'new', distinctive landscapes, valued in their own right. For example, Haldon Forest dominates the Exeter skyline, the extensive plantations along the East Devon greensand scarps emphasise the grain of the land and planting in the Taw Valley has imparted a character more reminiscent of continental Europe. In addition, a greater recognition of the value of planting woodlands for multiple objectives, including timber production, amenity, nature conservation and game, has led to a greater emphasis on broadleaved woodland planting.

An additional relevant factor is the establishment of South West Forest. This is a 'facilitating' body that works with a range of partners with an aim of using new woodland planting, management and utilisation as a means of regenerating its area of operation, which is North and North-west Devon and across the border into North Cornwall. Woodland currently covers nine per cent of this area, and it is the aim of South West Forest to double this area to provide a mosaic of land uses of which woodland will form an integral part. Clearly, this gives rise to landscape implications, although South West Forest has recognised the importance and vulnerability of the special landscape of the area in its Development Plan.

A potential new demand for timber might be for biomass fuels. This could introduce a series of new landscape issues, such as the introduction of fast growing coppice crops such as willow or poplar and the visual implications of the

Part of Devon's 'structural' woodland in the Torridge Valley

homogeneous crop or of plantings suitable for mechanical cropping.

A further issue is the lack of management of some existing woodland. Many are in a serious state of decline, some, especially former coppice, are single age stands, others have not been thinned or have been colonised by species such as fast seeding sycamore and invasive rhododendron. Elsewhere, uncontrolled grazing has suppressed the regeneration of woodland. However, there are costs and constraints associated with management and carrying out environmental improvements. With grants available to encourage the planting of new woodland, a critical challenge is how to promote tree planting which conserves and enhances local landscape distinctiveness, but which also provides a planned timber resource which will act as a financial motivator for sustainable woodland management.

3(D) TREE FEATURES

In areas where woodland cover is less extensive, the small woods, tree groups and isolated trees take on a special, more enhanced landscape importance. In the absence of an intimate landscape pattern of fields, hedgerows and woodlands, any tree can become a key landscape feature. This further contributes towards the variety and distinctiveness of the Devon landscape.

Examples of such dominant tree features can be wide-ranging; they include wind-trimmed beech plantations and shelter belts on the North Devon Downs and Exmoor fringe; the twisted and stunted trees of the Atlantic coast and interior; Monterey pine shelter belts on the East Devon coastal plateaux and around South Devon coastal settlements; the trees providing shelter around farm buildings on Dartmoor and Exmoor; 'veteran' trees, eg ancient oaks, etc found throughout the landscape and the beech avenues of the Blackdown Hills and, more occasionally, elsewhere.

Many of the more exposed tree features have suffered storm damage, while small isolated woodlands or shelter belts are often threatened by neglect. Replacement of these features is often seen as purely an amenity or landscape measure. While there is clearly a landscape implication there may nevertheless be a functional or commercial element. For example, the trees may provide valuable shelter or screening, or provide a local timber resource for fencing or fuel, or may even enhance the value of a land holding or property for the future.

Another valuable tree feature which has played an important role in Devon's landscape history and rural culture is the orchard. Today, traditional standard orchards are still distinctive and attractive features of Devon, but one only needs to look at old Ordnance Survey maps to realise how many small village and farm orchards have been lost. Orchards were particularly concentrated in sheltered areas such as the Tamar Valley and South and East Devon, but relic or surviving orchards can be found near many villages or farms throughout the County.

Tree features within urban areas are another critical element in Devon's landscape. Discussion of these is included within the section relating to townscapes in Theme 5.

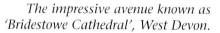

The impressive avenue known as 'Bridestowe Cathedral', West Devon.

An old orchard in South Devon.

THEME 4: FIELD BOUNDARIES

BACKGROUND

Throughout Devon a unifying feature of the landscape is the strong field boundary pattern. Whether the field boundaries are earth or stone-faced banks with hedges on top, hedges alone or stone walls, everywhere they are substantial features. These boundaries influence the local landscape character not only in their physical appearance, but also in the impact they have on the road system. Devon's country lanes are particularly characterised by these distinctive field boundaries which obscure views until a sudden glimpse of a hitherto hidden countryside emerges through a farm gate or where the lane suddenly rises or falls to reveal a steep intimate valley or a panoramic view.

The generally undulating landform is ideal for displaying the extent and intricacy of the field pattern and the associated dense network of lanes. This visual historic record of how the land was cleared and enclosed is relatively well preserved compared with other parts of England where modern farming methods have taken a greater toll on the hedgerows and field boundary pattern. Thus, while the boundaries are clearly an integral part of the farmed landscape generally, they have been identified as a separate theme because of their great significance in contributing to what is distinctive about Devon as a whole.

Devon's field patterns provide a record of the dynamic nature of human activity in the countryside over hundreds or thousands of years. A brief historical overview of this process is set out above in the discussion of Changing Agricultural Landscapes in Theme 3. As indicated in that discussion, some of Devon's historic field patterns are particularly ancient, possibly representing a continuous working landscape dating back several millennia. If we wish to conserve this historic and cultural link and provide a stimulus for future generations to wonder at the taming, enclosure and cultivation of the land, then we need to conserve the visual evidence contained within the surviving pattern, and to prevent the gradual but persistent loss of the boundaries through deliberate removal, neglect or mismanagement.

It is not just the historic pattern of field boundaries which makes them important landscape features but the variety of those boundaries and the individual characteristics resulting from each. In some places the characteristics of the boundaries can almost define the area as a whole; for example, avenues of beech on the Blackdown Hills, stunted and wind-shaped trees near the Atlantic coastline, massive granite boulder boundaries on Dartmoor, high stone-faced beech hedgebanks on Exmoor and its fringes. Hedges and banks are replaced by ditches (or 'drains') in the wet and low-lying

The undulating landform of South Devon near Shaldon shows the hedgerow pattern to advantage.

grazing marshes which adjoin the lower reaches of rivers such as the Exe, Taw or Axe, so creating a very different form of landscape.

The style and character of the hedgerows and other boundaries is strongly dependent on their past and present level of management. This is important not just for stock proofing, shelter or aesthetic reasons but also for the existing and potential wildlife resource that this vast network can support. Boundaries, as can be seen, have a profound influence on Devon's landscape in its widest definition.

Above: *New wall as field boundary, near Bratton Fleming.*

Above: *Stone wall boundary in need of repair, Denbury.*

Below: *Stone walls are typical of parts of South Devon; this is at Bolt Head.*

4(A) LAND-USE PATTERN AND ENCLOSURE

While there are some parts of Devon where a particular style of hedgebank or wall predominates, it is often difficult to generalise about field patterns on a geographical basis, probably because of the complicated historic processes which have gone to produce such patterns.

It may be true to say that there are distinct broad differences between, for example, the field pattern found on the high ground of the Culm Measures (a regular enclosure pattern) and the small irregular fields in the valleys of the Blackdown Hills; or between the small square fields on Exmoor's western fringe and the dense network of winding hedgebanks and lanes in central Devon around Tedburn St Mary. On the other hand, there are often significant differences within the same parish between, for example, valley floor and ridge top, or between areas next to and distant from the central village.

The field patterns around settlements may also differ. There may be long narrow fields around a village, perhaps once part of an open field system but now divided by more recent hedgerows, or fossilised remains of medieval burgage plots. Elsewhere, there may be small irregular fields around a settlement, a legacy perhaps of piecemeal medieval woodland clearance. The regular rectangular fields over much of Devon's high land illustrates a later phase of taming the 'waste', sometimes facilitated by enclosure Acts of Parliament. These various patterns all indicate different phases of the development of agriculture in Devon.

In Chapter 6 discussion of the various Landscape Character Zones of the County will attempt to identify areas where the field pattern is particularly distinctive of an area. However, because of the complex history of land-use development in Devon it is often difficult to say that a given land-use pattern is characteristic of a specific historical period of enclosure. The historic layers are overlain and interwoven, sometimes reinforcing, sometimes obliterating, what was there before. More archaeological and historical research is crucial to help develop our understanding and appreciation of the landscape and its development.

Today we have the potential to obliterate many of these layers through development, rapidly changing agricultural practices, large-scale forestry or even neglect. Devon's landscape distinctiveness as a whole, as well as that of its individual parts, requires that a way be found to slow down the rate of change and conserve the historic field pattern while rebutting claims that such an approach 'fossilises' the landscape.

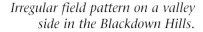

Irregular field pattern on a valley side in the Blackdown Hills.

Lost field boundary near Exeter.

4(B) HEDGEROW MANAGEMENT

The distinctive hedgebank field boundary characterises the Devon countryside probably more than any other single feature. However, while the hedgebank is typical of many parts of the County it varies greatly in the detail of its construction and management.

As an illustration of this diversity, whereas many parts of the South Hams are characterised by vegetated earth banks with hedges on top, in North Devon, especially towards the coast, the hedgebanks are typically more vertical, wall-like structures, stone-faced and topped with a beech hedge.

Through the latter half of the twentieth century hedgerow removal has been a particular issue. It may be, however, that now the most significant problems facing Devon's hedgerows concern management practices.

At one end of the spectrum of management concern are those hedges which have received no management for many years. These are characteristically tall with thick stemmed shrubs and trees, becoming increasingly gappy over time and thus less stockproof. They eventually grow beyond laying or even recoppicing and finally develop into a row of mature trees. As gaps develop in the hedge, stock can break through and their trampling accelerates the more gradual deterioration of the bank which results from the combined forces of weather and gravity.

There are a number of management options, or combination of options, which can be adopted in the earlier stages of such decline to restore the hedge to a stockproof state. These include coppicing, laying, thinning and leaving standards. However, it must be admitted that overgrown hedges do often provide shelter, ecological habitats and fine landscape features and it may be that, in some instances, this stage in the development of the hedgerow is beneficial for the Devon landscape. Indeed, in some parts of Devon lines of overgrown coppice trees determine the landscape character of the area, as around Rackenford, where the Culm Measures meet the Exmoor fringe. In such areas there may be a strong case for a no management 'solution' to be adopted, leaving some hedgerows, e.g. on skylines, to grow out 'gracefully', as long as management efforts to prolong the life of other hedges in the area are taken.

At the other end of the management spectrum are those hedgerows which have been repeatedly flailed to a low height. This often forces new growth to develop from the same growing point each year and progressively weakens the plant. Unless their management is varied, these hedges can become gappy and thin and may decline to such a level that only a bank remains, which will then itself become vulnerable to soil erosion.

It should be emphasised that most hedges were originally planted as stockproof barriers and where they have not been deliberately removed, they usually retain that role. Since either extreme of management, as set out above, leads to the hedge losing this stockproof quality it could be made clear that good management benefits not only the landscape and wildlife, but also agricultural practice, and is good economics.

The Hedgerow Regulations, introduced in 1997, have added a statutory layer of protection for some hedges that did not hitherto exist. Agri-environment schemes, such as Countryside Stewardship, provide much-needed funding to assist in the restoration of hedges. Advice on hedgerow management is readily available through a whole range of organisations and farm advisors and the Devon Hedge Group was set up in the mid 1990s specifically to promote the conservation of Devon's hedge network. All these factors provide hope for the future, although of key importance is the willingness and ability of the land-owning and farming community to continue their management of this fine resource.

Poor hedgerow management; flailed hedge in the Dart Valley.

Management of a new avenue, near Tavistock.

4(C) FIELD BOUNDARIES AS NATURAL CORRIDORS

Hedgerow trees, banks, verges, ditches and field headlands all represent a potentially huge and valuable wildlife habitat and network. However, the wildlife value is dependent on the type of boundary and its management, as well as the intensity and nature of farming on the adjacent land.

Devon's hedgebanks comprise a very special habitat for wildflowers. The flower-rich hedges make a significant contribution to the aesthetic appeal not only of the fields but of Devon's characteristic country lanes, colourfully emphasising the changing seasons. Springtime displays of primroses, bluebells and orchids soon give way to stitchwort, campion and other species. In summer, foxgloves and honeysuckle add odour and scent and in winter, if the hedge has escaped an early flailing, berries and nuts will flourish, providing a valuable food source for birds and small mammals.

The hedgerow plants also contribute to local distinctiveness, varying as they do with soil type, the type of stone in the wall or other factors such as species dispersal. An example of such a distinctive characteristic is formed by the white flowers of common scurvy grass, which cover the inland roadsides of North-west Devon in the spring.

A dense hedgerow network with flowering shrubs and berries is also a valuable resource for notable species such as Cirl bunting, dormice and brown hairstreak butterfly. Further, the role of this network in enabling species which rely on woody cover, shade or lack of disturbance to move around the countryside from place to place is important; for example, hedges are now known to form important navigational flight lines for horseshoe bats.

A further consideration is the role of hedgerow trees. These are more important as wildlife habitats, shelter and food supplies than is often realised, especially in areas where tree cover is otherwise limited. Descriptions of the Landscape Character Zones in Chapter 6 will highlight some such areas, most often towards the north and west of the County.

The contribution that these often isolated trees make to the local landscape is also frequently considerable, even, or perhaps especially, if they are stunted or wind-trimmed as in many locations around the coast or on higher land.

Small woodlands and copses are also an essential and integral part of the hedgerow network. These features are also very important for both visual and wildlife reasons.

Hedgerows as corridors of flowers:

Near Totnes.

Violets near Brixham.

On the south coast.

4(D) HISTORIC LANDSCAPE

The discussion under Theme 3(a) of Changing Agricultural Landscapes includes a brief overview of how the agricultural landscape of Devon has changed and developed over the last 6000 years. The results of this development can now be read, with a greater or lesser degree of difficulty, in the modern landscape.

As has been indicated earlier, it is largely within the field boundaries, their pattern, construction and, in hedges, their species, that this history manifests itself. In different parts of Devon evidence of almost all the stages of agricultural development may be seen, sometimes in close proximity.

Most notable, perhaps, is the continuing existence of Braunton Great Field in North Devon, one of the few remaining examples in England of a medieval open field. More typical of Devon, perhaps, are the small, irregular fields surrounded by substantial boundaries, as a result of the clearance of the 'waste' or subdivision of arable land in medieval times. It is this type of landscape which contributes so strongly to the landscape character of Devon.

Despite this perception of the characteristic Devon field boundary pattern, it is probably the case that it only covers a minority of the County. Further enclosure, probably also in medieval times, occurred, including enclosure of the open field systems around the larger, nucleated settlements, with the obvious exception of Braunton. This movement resulted in a landscape of larger fields divided by straighter hedges. Landscapes characterised by straight hedges resulted from the passing of the Enclosure Acts of the eighteenth and nineteenth centuries, which took in uncultivated land or woodland not previously used or land previously regarded as common. These enclosures are particularly found on the higher parts of the County.

The result of this interplay is that quite different patterns can be found in close proximity. As can be seen, the different ages of enclosure and agricultural use are driven by differences in geography and, in Devon, such differences are themselves in close proximity such is the nature of the landform. Hence in, for example, the Blackdown Hills, the landscape pattern of the field boundaries is quite different in the valley bottoms (generally small, irregular, probably medieval, fields) from the parallel ridge tops (mostly large, rectangular, Enclosure Act fields).

It is not the role of *The Devon Landscape* to undertake a detailed historic examination. This is a matter for the Devon Historic Landscape Characterisation Project. However, it is important to note that the whole modern landscape of field boundaries is a direct result of processes which stretch back for Millennia.

Historic burgage plots, South Zeal.

THEME 5: SETTLEMENT AND BUILDINGS

BACKGROUND

Devon has been settled for several thousand years, at least in places, and evidence of this is found in the landscape. Such archaeological evidence, whether a visible or invisible component, is not just a part of Devon's historic landscape but an important part of both the County's and, indeed, the nation's heritage.

Most tangible are the historic settlements and field patterns which have evolved and remain today as part of the living landscape. Field patterns were discussed as Theme 4. Attempting to understand why and where the surviving settlements were located and the reasons why they might have declined or prospered gives an insight into the process of human landscape change and illustrates

why there is such a diversity of settlement patterns throughout Devon.

In some parts of the County, settlement pattern alone is a strong contributor to the local character. One example might be the distinctive villages located along spring lines under the greensand ridges of East Devon; another, quite different, character is illustrated by the regularly distributed villages of the north-west corner of Devon.

More often it is a combination of such distinctive settlement patterns with a typical town form or layout, or how a settlement sits in its landscape setting, which determines the local landscape character both of the settlement itself and the surrounding countryside.

It is not for *The Devon Landscape* to analyse the details of the historical origins of settlements or their form or appearance. Those who wish to look

into this aspect of the landscape should consult the Devon Historic Landscape Characterisation Project. *The Devon Landscape* addresses these issues only to the extent that they impact on the modern appearance and character of the landscape.

Individual buildings or groups of buildings such as hamlets, farms, barns, estates, individual houses (grand or not so grand) all comprise elements in the landscape too, and often contribute to the local landscape character through the distinctive location, building style, materials or function. Related to this element, parks and gardens can also influence the landscape and its character, sometimes subtly, sometimes more obviously. While originally designed as an escape from the outside world, larger parklands and formal gardens can have an effect on the landscape character of a considerable area while smaller ones, especially if related to urban areas, can impact on a townscape and urban character.

The shape and form of Dartmouth is dictated by the topography.

5(A) SETTLEMENT

To understand the true value of Devon's landscape requires an appreciation which goes beyond aesthetic beauty. Such an appreciation will reflect the richness of the historic heritage and contribute to the 'sense of place' by providing a cultural association with the past.

This perception of the landscape is wider than the recognition of just ancient monuments, settlements or old buildings distributed throughout the countryside. It includes rather an appreciation of the development of human culture, society, economy and land use and how this has affected the physical landscape. This theme has an impact on the wider physical and aesthetic landscape, and this element is addressed in *The Devon Landscape*, but it should not be regarded as the main source of discussion on these issues.

Torquay's appearance is shaped by its origins as a resort.

The earliest visible signs of human activity in Devon include prehistoric settlements, field systems, linear earthwork boundaries, hill forts, burial monuments and ritual sites; some or all may be linked by prehistoric routeways. Many of these visible features are located on high moorland or ridges or preserved amongst heath and common land; however, this does not necessarily mean that these were the only locations of early settlement but rather that modern conditions mean that these areas are least likely to have been subject to more recent changes which may have hidden such evidence.

The process of human colonisation which involved clearing, cultivating and enclosing the land has been briefly described in the discussion of agricultural landscapes in Theme 3. This process to a great extent defined the detail of the rural landscape we have inherited. However, there is a basic settlement pattern which forms the skeleton on which the 'flesh' of agricultural activity hangs. This pattern includes the siting of settlements in sheltered locations, at bridging points or on spring lines; it includes the generally dispersed settlement pattern often associated with Devon and which is largely explained by the agricultural colonisation process referred to above, but also the nucleated settlements established in the Middle Ages in certain parts of the County.

Overlaying this basic settlement pattern are land-uses and historic features which have other origins such as trade, industry or mining. In addition, transport links have always played a strong role in shaping the human landscape from early trackways to turnpike roads, canals and railways and the growth of ports, both on the coast and sometimes far inland via Devon's extensive estuaries.

An indication of the perception of the landscape which was held by earlier inhabitants can also sometimes be obtained by studying place names. Some may indicate the presence of features such as woods where none now obviously exist, others relate to earlier land-use and yet others give an idea of how the physical landscape was viewed by references to features such as 'necks' or 'heels'. They can also help provide evidence for processes of settlement expansion, location of lost settlements and religion, belief and superstition.

Our influence on the landscape continues to lay down new settlement patterns. Some are superimposed on the historic pattern while others are more subtly interwoven with it. The important factor is that our historical heritage is a finite cultural resource and that increasingly we have the potential to obliterate many layers of history through our actions.

The historic city of Exeter does not impose itself on the landscape.

5(B) BUILDINGS AS LANDSCAPE ELEMENTS

The significance of individual buildings, or small groups of buildings, in the Devon landscape cannot be underestimated. A range of buildings contribute to the landscape and character of Devon; lighthouses, forts, estate buildings, follies, solitary chapels and churches, isolated hamlets and grand houses, but one of the most fundamental contributions is provided by farmhouses and other agricultural buildings.

Discussion of previous themes has shown that the nucleated village with several farms concentrated together is relatively rare in Devon, although perhaps not as rare as is sometimes thought. Nevertheless, the more typical pattern is of individual farmsteads fairly evenly scattered throughout the landscape. This traditional pattern is often complemented by traditional building materials – in cob and thatch in some parts of the County, local stone in others, perhaps slate hanging. In addition, site location was often chosen with consideration for the natural surroundings and constraints, for example of shelter, slope or the availability of water. The result is that such buildings seem to sit comfortably in the landscape, to be part of that landscape rather than superimposed upon it.

In addition there are cultural reasons why settlements were located in certain places. People would make choices on what their society regarded as appropriate settlement locations in that culture, which was not always based on environmental considerations.

Constraints of building material and design are no longer the fundamental element they were in earlier times. Advances in building technology, heating, insulation and the availability of cheap, easily transported building materials have also meant that careful choice of site location is no longer the important issue it once was. This gives much more freedom of choice, often at a cost to the integrity of the landscape. Occasionally a building superimposed upon the landscape can enhance it, but this can be as much a matter of luck as of judgement. Today's major constraints are likely to be planning officers' landscape policies rather than natural factors.

As well as new buildings, another landscape issue, perhaps more common, is the conversion of traditional farm buildings to alternative uses. While the rebuilding of barns and outbuildings is often sensitively carried out, there is no escaping the fact that most modern uses, be it residential, holiday accommodation or business, requires modern windows, access roads, parking and possibly advertising. All of this can bring about a change in character despite the use of appropriate materials and design and lead to a perception of suburbanisation, especially at isolated farms in open landscapes. The industrial use of former farm buildings, while important to the rural economy, can often have an especially great impact on the landscape and needs careful handling.

Many of Devon's traditional buildings, including certain types of farm buildings, are 'listed' as being of special architectural and historic interest. Consequently, planning legislation can help to ensure that any changes or improvements are appropriately carried out. However, it must be remembered that the continued occupation of these buildings, and the level of care lavished upon them by their owners, is potentially far more important than statutory protection. In this context, the appropriate 'education' of the owners of historic homes will also play an important role.

In addition, the change of use from farm buildings as a result of the breaking up of agricultural holdings can have an impact; their use as holiday homes, second homes, or for 'hobby farming' or 'horsiculture' can have an effect on the appearance of buildings in the landscape.

Groups of buildings, in the form of hamlets, are also fundamental to the Devon landscape, and indeed are widely regarded as the 'normal' settlement form over much of the County. Many old hamlets have shrunken and then grown again more than once in the course of this history, so often there may be only one house left, perhaps surrounded by earthworks or ruins or old agricultural buildings. Hamlets are fundamental to Devon's settlement pattern and therefore its landscape character.

Castle Drogo is an important element of the dramatic Teign Valley landscape.

5(C) VILLAGE FORM

The layout and three-dimensional form of a settlement and how it relates to the surrounding landscape can make a significant contribution both to the character of the settlement itself and the distinctiveness of the local landscape. Understanding and appreciating the relationship between town and village form and landscape setting is particularly important in Devon.

The variation in slopes and other small-scale differences in local landform plus other features such as individual trees and tree groups result in a great variety and individualism among the County's smaller settlements; in addition, of course, they provide the attractive backdrops, skylines and vistas both into and out of settlements which make them so valued.

Throughout many parts of Devon the village form and its landscape setting represents a key characteristic feature in determining local character. While generally a product of the landscape, village form and setting enhances and accentuates the tendencies found in that landscape and helps to provide the distinctive character. Traditional village forms such as the position of a settlement on a ridge just below the skyline, with the tower of the village church providing a distinctive skyline feature, go a long way to giving Devon its landscape character.

New housing development in Devon has tended to be through additions to existing settlements rather than the creation of new planned villages. However this was not always the case, and in earlier times newly planned villages were 'planted' in the countryside, generally by ambitious landowners who wished to enhance the value of their land. Such settlements are now themselves regarded as traditional and are a valued element in the local landscape. Examples include medieval establishments such as South Zeal on the edge of Dartmoor and Newton Poppleford in East Devon, both centred on important roads, and more recent 'estate' villages like St Giles in the Wood, near Torrington, on the Rolle Estate, or Milton Abbot in West Devon, where the village centre was redesigned by Lutyens in the early 1900s at the instigation of the Duke of Bedford. As we enter the twenty-first century, the issue of new settlements as a means of accommodating population growth is under increasing discussion.

However the expansion of many of Devon's towns and villages has already had an impact on the wider landscape. This has been particularly noticeable where large modern developments have been added to the edges of settlements with little consideration for local distinctiveness. Even using local building styles and materials may not be enough to respect the landscape if the development ignores:

(i) how the existing buildings are adapted to and respect the topography;

(ii) the nature of open space and settlement treescape;

(iii) the overall form of the settlement and balance of the buildings, e.g. around focal points;

(iv) the relevance of the landscape setting, aspect or shelter, including contours and topography, eg geometric additions to settlements are rarely appropriate

(v) appropriate patterns of road layout.

A further traditional aspect of the landscape and its relationship with settlement form is represented by the coastal setting of Devon's maritime towns. The shape of the settlements and their distinctive features, frequently dictated by the geography, often have historic maritime importance. Mariners have used coastal landmarks as navigational features for centuries and they may still be used today by recreational sailors. Insensitive development can thus obscure traditional siting lines for mariners which, for example, may indicate a safe harbour approach.

Finally, as discussed earlier, hamlets are and were much more common than villages in many parts of the County. Over the centuries, many hamlets have grown or shrunk, or both, some perhaps reaching the status of village. The development of hamlets in Devon, despite this frequency, is poorly understood. Research into their history, origins and development, and the effect this has on the landscape, is a priority in understanding their role in the landscape.

Drewsteignton relates well to its surrounding landscape.

5(D) TOWNSCAPES

Once a settlement grows beyond a certain size it becomes harder to examine the town as an overall cohesive landscape unit. While the larger town or city's relationship with the surrounding landscape is important, especially on the urban fringe, the character of the individual townscapes within the urban area provides the crucial landscape elements.

Features which contribute towards creating attractive townscapes in essence mirror those which create attractive rural landscapes, i.e. the result of natural and/or historic factors. They include a town's distinctive history and its natural assets such as a river, proximity to the sea, the presence of woodland or high vantage points; in turn, these factors will result in the presence of a range of built features such as quays, parks and gardens, squares and fine buildings. These will be enhanced by smaller features such as street trees, private gardens and other open spaces.

Devon's larger urban areas display a range of these townscape features. Taking the major settlements as examples:

• Plymouth, while seriously affected by Second World War bombing raids, has sufficient remnants of its maritime past to retain an attractive and historic waterfront with views across one of the finest natural harbours in the world. The city remains fragmented by considerable areas of woodland and other wildlife habitats, especially centred on natural features such as valleys.

• Exeter has a prominent Cathedral, remnants of a Roman city wall and many other fine historic buildings and street features. Its river corridor provides a natural asset for the population as well as a focus of historic industrial activity including the development of one of England's earliest canals.

• The Torbay area has a long history as an elegant seaside resort with distinctive coastal and exotic tree species within the town and a long sea frontage punctuated by beaches and harbours.

Towns and cities, like rural areas, are evolving, living landscapes and many of the changes in Devon's urban areas have the potential to generate both negative issues and positive opportunities. These changes include urban expansion or infill, industrial decline, urban road improvements and bypasses, traffic calming and land-use change on the urban fringe.

Towns can also have an influence on the wider landscape through the effect of their skylines on the surrounding rural areas, and this wider effect needs to be borne in mind in their development.

Many of Devon's urban areas demonstrate the result of good strategic urban planning practice, and there are many good examples of landscape enhancement, conservation of urban wildlife sites and other site specific activities. However, there has been relatively rarely an approach which considers the impact of development on the whole landscape as a strategic landscape planning and management entity.

One example of the lack of co-ordinated management and planning of the entire urban landscape can be illustrated by the issue of trees in towns. The location of street trees in open spaces may be determined by planners or highway engineers but their maintenance and long-term future may be governed by a parks' department. Trees on private land may be under the control of conservation or forestry officers through Tree Preservation Orders or Conservation Area designation. In addition, urban trees may face threats such as the severing of roots during street works which are essentially unpoliced.

Ideally, a holistic approach to the urban landscape is needed. Such an approach would break down the traditional divisions between strategic planning, design and management, include involvement with the community, private business, developers and interest groups and result in the development of comprehensive landscape planning for the whole urban environment.

Plymouth; historic Hoe and post-war development.

THEME 6: DEVELOPMENT ROADS AND PEOPLE

BACKGROUND

Devon is a beautiful county which offers a high-quality environment as a place to live, work and spend leisure time. As a consequence it attracts both new permanent residents and tourists, ironically, perhaps, both groups trying to escape more crowded, overdeveloped areas of the country. To sustain the quality of life that the Devon environment provides, and which helps to underpin the County's economy, it is important that there is a balance between on the one hand, provision of accommodation, facilities and an infrastructure which can adequately serve the economic needs, and, on the other, conservation of Devon's landscape in its widest sense.

The strategic planning of development and transport within Devon, and indeed in the country as a whole, has undergone a significant change in emphasis of recent years. Traditional policies tended to focus on development to provide a stimulus for economic growth, with the improvement of mobility viewed as a benefit to economic activity. Now, however, policies are having to address increasing concerns that the cost of such unfettered development may be too high and that there is a value to be placed on a healthy and attractive environment as a contributor to the quality of life and, indeed, to economic well-being.

The current policies which guide transport and development in Devon were given a special impetus by the Rio Earth Summit and the resulting 'Agenda 21', which set out action to reconcile development with environmental concerns, both locally and globally. The key concept which arises from these concerns is that of sustainability which, in summary, means that short-term progress should not be at the expense of the needs of future generations. In landscape terms this highlights the necessity to ensure that the landscape resource is not diminished to an extent which could be prejudicial to future generations and their quality of life. Taken further, it also implies a need to restore and enhance the existing landscape resource.

Exeter from its Riverside Country Park.

6(A) URBAN FRINGE

Urban fringe areas have traditionally been regarded as something of a problem in landscape terms. They are, by definition, neither truly urban nor truly rural, and can often seem to take on the worst qualities of both areas.

Devon is perhaps luckier than some counties in that, by the nature of its development and the generally relatively modest size of its settlements, the urban fringe is less of an issue than elsewhere. Nevertheless there are landscape implications which need to be addressed and which can impact on the wider area. Issues such as illegal tipping, agricultural degradation as a result of trespass, the impact of 'horsiculture' and the consequent loss of landscape character create obvious problems but it must not be forgotten that there may also be opportunities. Community woodlands, appropriate informal leisure facilities such as walking and cycling routes, picnic sites and viewpoints can all add to the range of opportunities available to the adjacent urban population and heighten the regard in which the urban fringe is held by that population. This can lead to greater care being taken of the urban fringe by its users and, so long as the facilities are in harmony with the landscape character of the wider area, this should enhance Devon's overall landscape.

Examples such as the Valley Parks on the fringes of Exeter, the Plym Valley Cycle and Walkway near Plymouth and Country Parks around Torbay all show that, properly organised, such facilities will be well used and respected and enhance the overall landscape character of the County. They also show that a management presence in such areas is ideally the way forward and that positive approaches involving management measures represent the best way of ensuring that the urban fringe makes a positive contribution to the Devon landscape.

6(B) NEW DEVELOPMENT IN THE COUNTRYSIDE

There has been a policy presumption against new development in the open countryside in Devon for many years. Inevitably, some exceptions have occurred but the County has generally not been subject to wholesale development in its rural areas. Even where development may be permitted under exceptional circumstances, the County policy is that the landscape features which contribute to an area's local distinctiveness should not be adversely affected by that development.

There is, however, an additional aspect which could have an influence on the shape of Devon's future landscape; this is the possibility of absorbing new housing requirements through the creation of new settlements in the countryside.

The option of building new settlements, rather than distributing residential development needs between existing small towns and villages, or allowing further urban expansion of major towns, has been the subject of debate nationally among politicians, developers and planners. In Devon, this issue has been taken up by the County's Structure Plan, which identified that this option was the most viable way of accommodating the level of housing growth required, in conjunction with some increases at existing settlements. The Structure Plan therefore proposes that provision should be made for two new communities, one in the South Hams in the Plymouth area and one in East Devon in the Exeter area. This provision would be within a set of strict criteria. In landscape terms, these criteria include the requirement that the communities should be located where they will be assimilated into the landscape of the area. It will also be a requirement that the open countryside between the new settlements and existing built-up areas are protected from development to prevent coalescence and to maintain the setting of the settlements.

The provisos set out above will help to guide the location and design of any new settlements so that they should have a minimal impact on Devon's landscape. However, it will be important that the appearance and character of the local landscape is not compromised in any way by any such development; depending on the location, there may even be scope for enhancement.

6(C) ROAD AND HIGHWAY IMPROVEMENTS

Road issues probably raise more emotive responses in relation to landscape than do any others with the exception of those relating to development. This is a product both of Devon's high environmental quality and also of the fact that Devon has a greater mileage of roads than any other county in England. It is also partly a result of many roads being seen as integral to the local landscape character and thus road improvements being regarded as an attack on that character.

Given the high mileage of rural roads and the dense network this results in, Devon's roads cover a vast variety of types, including national motorways and trunk roads and major county routes as well as the smaller roads perhaps regarded as more typical of Devon. Even these can show a wide range of appearance, including straight ridge top roads, narrow sinuous and winding lanes enclosed by hedgebanks, switch-back routes with seemingly impossible gradients, open moorland routes or even tidal roads.

In landscape terms, Devon's roads can benefit the landscape in a variety of ways, including the following:

- They provide access to the great variety of distinctive local landscapes, to the advantage of residents and visitors alike.
- The extensive network of verges and embankments provides a range of relatively undisturbed ecological habitats.
- They contribute to the locally distinctive landscape pattern, often to the aesthetic benefit of the area's character.
- They help provide a historical record of how the land was cultivated and settled and how trading and access patterns were established over the centuries.

Today we continue to lay down, modify and improve the road network with the objectives of increasing public accessibility, economic efficiency and public safety. Such road improvements can give rise to conflicting results in landscape and environmental terms. The level of potential impact tends to be a matter of scale, with the motorways and major trunk roads representing the greatest intrusion on the landscape, especially in the matter of the imposition of a new pattern and form on the existing landscape, with consequent implications on its character. Increased and more obvious traffic noise can also affect the character of an area. Other works such as straightening and widening result in similar but generally less extensive impacts. On smaller roads especially, the nature of the road, its hedges and verges, its undulations and its sinuous course, complements or even forms part of the landscape character of the area.

On the other hand, road improvements can give rise to benefits to the landscape in its widest sense; examples include benefits to townscapes resulting

Occasionally, roads dominate the landscape; A30/A38 interchange.

from the establishment of bypasses and, conversely to one of the earlier points, decreases in traffic noise can occur in some places as a result of such works. The net result on the landscape will be very much a matter of detailed design, location and topography.

A great deal of guidance already exists in respect of road design and the County Council already has policies which reflect this. The design of new routes and improvement schemes in a way which minimises the effects on the landscape will remain a challenge for all concerned in these issues.

Road lined by local stone walls, Denbury.

6(D) PEOPLE IN THE LANDSCAPE

Human activity is an element of the landscape often overlooked. Historically, people working on the land were a major feature of the view; it is always a surprise to see how many people are depicted in period paintings or drawings which highlight the landscape. Today, while the presence of people going about their daily lives is a relatively minor element in the rural landscape, they have largely been replaced by human leisure activity. This activity varies between different landscapes.

Despite the special importance of leisure in Devon, much of the landscape nevertheless remains relatively unaffected. There are, however, concentrations. Walkers and cyclists congregate around certain Dartmoor tors and Exmoor viewpoints; estuaries and rivers add sailing boats, fishermen and canoeists to the more traditional scene. On the coast, beaches are dotted with sunbathers, surfers, kite-flyers and youngsters exploring rock pools. Around tourist resorts, coastlines, parts of the National Parks and on major road links, traffic adds a further, if often fleeting element to the scene.

The demands that recreational activities place on Devon's landscapes, especially those with vulnerable ecological habitats, can result in conflict that needs management. Generally, walking and cycling are seen as sustainable activities that benefit the Devon economy without detriment to the landscape or wider environment. However, Devon's variety of landscape does make it an ideal playground for a range of outdoor pursuits some of which (e.g. sailing, climbing, mountain-biking, horse-riding, canoeing) can have an impact on the landscape as a result of the activities themselves or the facilities needed to serve them.

However, countryside recreation must be seen as a vital element in encouraging the health and well-being of society, as well as providing economic benefits and the opportunity for promoting better understanding and appreciation of the landscape.

Traditional salmon netters, Teign Estuary.

Climbers on Baggy Point.

People's activities have an impact on the River Dart.

THEME 7: PANORAMAS, SKYLINES AND LANDMARKS

BACKGROUND

Devon's generally undulating and varied landform provides the opportunity to appreciate a range of visual experiences – panoramic views, framed vistas along valleys, recognisable skylines and landmarks, or whole landscape compositions which remain in the memory and colour our perception of the landscape.

In particular, Devon's two irregular coastlines contain a wealth of distinctive landmarks, from bays and estuaries to sea stacks, rock formations and man-made features such as lighthouses. They also provide memorable opportunities for wide panoramic seascapes, including sunrises and sunsets. Devon's two National Parks of Dartmoor and Exmoor also provide well-known landmarks, skylines and other visual images which have been captured in art, described in literature or presented in travel guides.

However, it would be wrong to over-emphasise the importance of these nationally recognisable landscapes in describing the essence of Devon. Many other such panoramas, skylines and landmarks are found in less well known parts of the County and contribute to the perception of the landscape. In particular, Devon's other areas of high ground are important, not only for their own sake but for the important skylines and backdrops they provide to the areas they overlook and contain.

The importance of these features can often be enhanced by less tangible factors. One example of such a factor is the quality of the air; Devon is fortunate enough to enjoy a relatively unpolluted atmosphere, with weather systems bringing wind, rain and clean air from the Atlantic and this adds to the landscape experience. A further example is the role that the sky plays in providing an ever-changing backdrop of moving cloud, light changes, colour and contrasts. While we cannot, thankfully, control the skies, we can ensure that we can conserve our large-scale open landscapes, with an uninterrupted skyline where the landscape can remain dominated by the sky and air, a place where the forces of nature, a sense of 'wilderness' and a perception of freedom from human intervention can be appreciated.

Finally, it must be emphasised that images of Devon are unique to the individual perceiving them and are often not confined to complete views on a grand scale. Such images may include memorable elements on a very small scale, detail such as the carvings on a ancient stone, the paving texture in a street or the silhouette of a wind-bent tree. While we cannot legislate to protect such features, a recognition and appreciation of locally distinctive small-scale features may go towards ensuring their survival.

The Daymark at Kingswear forms an unplanned skyline landmark from inland.

7(A) PANORAMAS

Devon is a county of superb panoramas, a result of the interplay between high and low land and the generally undeveloped nature of the landscape. Many visitors will return to other parts of the country with their perception of the Devon landscape indelibly branded by some such panorama.

Perhaps most widely known and appreciated are the vast panoramas provided by the high massifs of Dartmoor and Exmoor. Dartmoor's panoramas include wide vistas over surrounding lower, cultivated land from the moorland edge, while 'internal' views are over wild, open moorland where distinctive tors not only provide landmarks but also focal features.

Exmoor is perhaps better known for its coastal panoramas. The characteristics 'hogsback ' cliffs are some of the highest in the country, giving rise to breathtaking coastal panoramas over the Bristol Channel towards Wales, along the coast to distinctive headlands and down the cliff-faces to beaches and bays many hundreds of feet below. However, Exmoor also has its moorland-edge panoramas, especially from the fairly abrupt southern fringe, and its 'internal' moorland vistas, differing from Dartmoor in lacking tors but often having the sea as a distant backdrop.

Not only Exmoor, but much of Devon's coast provides highly valued panoramas. It is a rare location on the Devon coast that fails to provide a stunning panorama of cliff and headland, beach, port, fishing village, estuary or ria, characteristic of one of the best-loved coastlines in the country.

Given the often close association between high and lower land, a considerable variety of ridges, plateaux and hill tops provide a range of panoramas, sometimes very wide, elsewhere more contained and intimate. Examples include the prominent ridge of Great Haldon, where within close proximity contrasting panoramas may be obtained over Exeter and the Exe Estuary in one direction and the high moorland fringe of Dartmoor in another. Elsewhere, perhaps less celebrated but equally superb panoramas are obtained from the edges of almost any of the plateaux or the top of any hill; the East Devon commons and ridges, North Devon Downs, the Broadbury Ridge, Blackdown Hills and ridges of the Culm measures are just some of the locations which provide such panoramas.

Lowland panoramas should not be forgotten. The broad panoramas across Braunton Marsh and Great Field, down the estuaries of the Taw, Torridge, Exe, or Axe to the sea or the length of Slapton Ley offer examples of a relatively uncommon landscape type in Devon, and as such one of considerable importance.

Coastal panorama, East Devon.

7(B) SKYLINES

The often intricate, intimate and enclosed nature of much of Devon's landscape means that skylines are less frequently a prominent feature of the environmental experience than is the case with some other counties. Their importance should not be discounted, however, and there are vast areas of the County where the skyline, if not actually defining the landscape, is certainly a major contributor.

In some instances, skylines are in essence the mirror image of panoramas. Where high, prominent land masses provide panoramas over the adjacent landscape then in turn those high areas provide the characteristic skyline for the lowlands. For example there are few areas of Devon, certainly west of the Exe, which do not have the characteristic skyline of Dartmoor as a backdrop, even if distant. Similarly, the Exmoor fringe provides an equally characteristic skyline through much of North Devon and Great Haldon has a particular importance as the western skyline for Exeter.

Over areas of northern and western Devon the skyline can of itself be the defining characteristic. Although these areas are not flat, the often substantial valleys are frequently hidden from sight on the higher land and the character of the landscape is one of wide, open space and long-range views to a sometimes distant, uninterrupted skyline.

It needs to be remembered that urban areas can sometimes affect skylines, and it is a general planning principle that skyline urban development should be avoided. For the most part, Devon's skylines have not been particularly adversely affected by skyline development. However, peripheral development around some of the larger urban areas has sometimes had an effect on the skyline of adjacent areas, for example to the north and east of Plymouth and in locations to the west of Torbay.

A particular issue is raised by modern technology. Power lines have long been an issue for the landscape, pylons and lines tending to dominate the landscape and undermine its character. More recently, the growth in the use of mobile telephones and similar communications has led to a growth in the number of telecommunication masts, of necessity usually at prominent locations. This has given rise to considerable opposition in some instances.

Sustainable power generation has led to the growth in interest in wind power. To date, Devon has no wind farms, although some applications have been made and considerable interest shown. Experience elsewhere, for example in Mid Wales and Cornwall, has indicated that such developments can have a considerable effect on the landscape and its character. Given the relative suitability in wind terms of much of Devon for such developments, this issue is likely to become subject to increasing debate.

Brentor Church is a skyline feature over much of West Devon.

Skyline pines behind Torbay.

7(C) LANDMARKS

Devon's landscape is not short of landmarks. Some are so characteristic as to almost be a shorthand description either of Devon as a whole or of a specific part of the County. The outline of a tor, for example, will immediately evoke the image of Dartmoor; the statue of Drake on Plymouth Hoe brings to mind images of the Armada, bowls on the Hoe and Devon's maritime history.

Other landmarks are more characteristic of a specific, perhaps quite limited, part of Devon. The stark outline of chimneys of old mines are almost definitive of the Tamar Valley; beech avenues are typical of Exmoor and its fringes and the Blackdown Hills.

The long Devon coastline gives rise to a range of landmarks. These include natural features, particularly headlands and prominent coastal hills, but also man-made features. Some were deliberately placed as landmarks as an aid to shipping; the daymark at the mouth of the Dart is an obvious example, but previously many church towers served the same purpose – Stoke Fleming mirrors the daymark on the opposite side of the Dart for example, and other coastal churches like Wembury in the south and Hartland in the north had a similar function. Lighthouses fall into the same category of distinctive but deliberate landmarks adding to the interest of the coastal scene; coastguard cottages, those characteristic white buildings often found on lonely headlands also tend to add to the landscape value of the coast rather than detract from it.

Many other landmarks have a positive effect on Devon's landscape character; hilltop clumps, church towers or, in more urban settings, features such as clock towers, historic buildings or locally distinctive architecture. On the other hand, some of Devon's landmarks have a less fortunate effect. The impact of power lines, telecommunications masts and, potentially, wind farms has been mentioned earlier in the discussion on skylines. Some modern buildings have also had an unsympathetic effect on the wider landscape, especially industrial or storage premises on urban fringes, where the impact can be considerable on the character of the surrounding rural landscape.

Start Point lighthouse, an important landscape element on the South Devon Coast.

Haytor is a significant landmark on Dartmoor's southern fringe, visible over much of South Devon.

THE ESSENCE OF DEVON – SUMMARY

An examination of the above discussion indicates that a total of seven broad themes will have to be considered in analysing the Essence of Devon in landscape terms. Further, that these may be divided into sub-themes, giving rise to a total of 25 influences on the Devon landscape,

The true picture of Devon and its landscape is one where all these influences are interwoven. Special atmospheres created by a multitude of factors – individual features, sounds, smells, movement, people and nature, the influence of weather and the seasons – combine with visual compositions and all the physical and cultural influences that have created, and continue to shape, the Devon landscape.

Geology, water, trees, field boundaries, development, historic buildings; the mix of influences which creates the superb landscape of Frogmore Creek in the South Hams.

Interplay of land and water – the Salcombe - Kingsbridge Estuary.

The hilltop clump at Denbury – a landscape feature between Dartmoor and Torbay.

CHAPTER 6

LOCAL LANDSCAPE CHARACTER

INTRODUCTION

Chapter 5 sets out the themes which go to make up the character of Devon's landscape. The sum total of all these themes, and the features they give rise to, provides the overall Essence of Devon as a landscape entity. However, the individual mix of the themes and features varies in detail through-out the County and these variations result in a series of different landscape character traits. The outcome is a diversity of landscape types, which can be identified as a range of areas, each with its own local landscape character.

Such areas of local landscape character have been identified at a national level by the Countryside Agency. Within this national analysis Devon is included within all or part of seven such Character Areas, details of which are set out earlier in Chapter 4. However, at a county level, these areas are a little too general to address the more detailed landscape distinctiveness appropriate to this scale. *The Devon Landscape* therefore examines local landscape character at a more detailed, fine-grained level, resulting in a division of the County into a total of 32 areas, referred to as Landscape Character Zones.

LANDSCAPE CHARACTER ZONES

The Countryside Agency has published a set of principles to act as guidance in the assessment of landscape character, and these have been followed in the preparation of Devon's Landscape Character Zones.

No one factor has been used to identify the Landscape Character Zones. Initially a desk study was carried out to look at factors such as geology, soils, landform, existing landscape designations and the influence of some of the more prominent themes discussed in Chapter 5. This was followed by field survey and then finally an appraisal which examined not only the various features in detail on the ground and their objective description but also the subjective response to them and to the landscape character which results.

The dominant factor determining the character of the various zones varies. Certainly, geology has been perhaps the major influence and many of the Landscape Character Zones have been defined largely in response to it, and the resultant landform, soils or drainage pattern it creates. Sometimes the influence of the coast is paramount and this can stretch far inland in places with salt-laden winds creating a distinctive vegetation. Elsewhere, the location and form of settlements may be an important factor in identifying locally distinctive areas. But although it may be possible to identify a dominant influence, the essence of the character typifying each given area is almost invariably an amalgam of different degrees of different elements.

It must also be remembered that the Landscape Character Zones will not be completely uniform within themselves. While the overall character will have an identifiable similarity throughout there will nevertheless be distinctive aspects to the landscape, perhaps peculiar to a parish or a single hill or valley or perhaps as the result of the efforts of a single individual landowner.

While there are occasionally some quite abrupt changes from one landscape character to another, generally the transition is a relatively gentle one. It will often be the case that individual locations in boundary areas will share some character traits with the Landscape Character Zones on both sides. Consequently the boundary lines of the Landscape Character Zones shown on the accompanying maps should not normally be taken too literally, but perhaps be seen more as boundary areas, where one Character Zone gradually phases into the next. Nevertheless, this is not always the case, and examples will be found where quite definite and clear-cut changes do occur.

Whether the boundaries are abrupt or gentle, the important thing to bear in mind is that the definition of the Landscape Character Zones should be seen as a guide or tool to help people to look more closely at the landscape, to become more conscious of what aspects of the landscape are special, to give a 'sense of place' and to lead to a desire to see the defining features survive and prosper. Such features should be seen as a wide definition, and people's cultural and 'spiritual' links to local landscapes can be as important as an appreciation of aesthetic beauty.

GROUPING THE ZONES

The analysis outlined above has resulted in a sub-division of the County into a total of 32 Landscape Character Zones. For convenience, these have been grouped together into six areas which closely reflect the Countryside Agency's Character Areas.

The Agency's Character Areas, with their key features, are set out in Chapter 4.

The six areas of grouped character in the County identified in *The Devon Landscape*, and their corresponding Countryside Agency Character Areas, are as follows: (see table)

THE DEVON LANDSCAPE; CHARACTER ZONE GROUPING		COUNTRYSIDE AGENCY CHARACTER AREA	
(a)	Eastern Devon	147	Blackdowns
(b)	Central Devon	148	Devon Redlands (excluding southern extremity)
(c)	Culm Measures	149	The Culm (excluding coastal area)
(d)	Northern Devon	145	Exmoor
		149	The Culm (coastal area)
		159	Lundy
(e)	South Devon	148	Devon Redlands (southern extremity)
		151	South Devon (excluding Tamar and Tavy Valleys)
(f)	Dartmoor and West Devon	150	Dartmoor
		151	South Devon (Tamar and Tavy Valleys)

PRESENTATION OF THE ZONES

An overview and map of the respective Character Zone grouping precedes the individual discussion of the Landscape Character Zones within that grouping. Discussion of each Zone includes the following issues:

- Location of the Zone.

- Relevant landscape designations.

- Key characteristic features.

- Description of Zone and discussion of boundaries.

- Subjective response.

- Retention of the landscape's character and integrity.

The aim of *The Devon Landscape* is simply to record the situation as it exists at the beginning of the twenty-first century, in particular in relation to the criteria outlined above. It will be the role of a companion document, which together with *The Devon Landscape* goes to make up the Landscape Strategy for Devon, to set out a suite of principles and priorities to help ensure that the characteristics which typify each zone are maintained and enhanced.

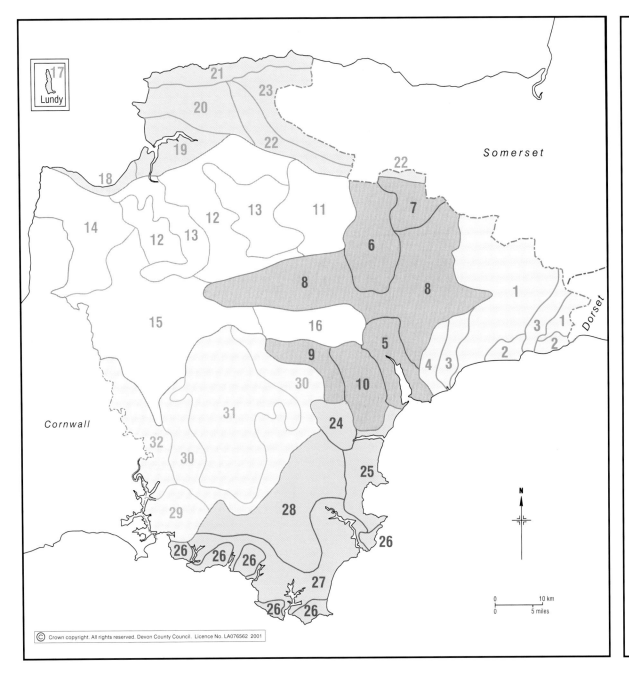

Map 9.
Landscape Character Zones

Eastern Devon
1. Greensand Ridges
2. Coastal Chalk Plateaux
3. Axe and Otter Valleys
4. Pebble Bed Heaths

Central Devon
5. Exeter and Estuary Fringe
6. Exe Valley and Environs
7. Bampton and Beer Downs
8. Mid Devon Farming Belt
9. Teign Valley
10. Haldon Ridge

Culm Measures
11. Witheridge - Rackenford Moor
12. High Culm Ridges
13. Taw and Torridge River Systems
14. Hartland and Atlantic Coast Interior
15. Broadbury and Western Devon Ridges
16. Tedburn St Mary Area

Northern Devon
17. Lundy
18. Clovelly Coast
19. Taw - Torridge Estuary
20. North Devon Downs
21. Exmoor and North Devon High Coast
22. Exmoor Fringe
23. Exmoor Upland

Southern Devon
24. Bovey Basin
25. Tourist Riviera
26. South Devon Coastal Plateaux
27. Ria Coastline
28. Under Dartmoor

Dartmoor and West Devon
29. Plymouth City, Estuary and Environs
30. Dartmoor - Enclosed
31. Dartmoor - High Moor
32. Tamar and Tavy Valleys

EASTERN DEVON

This grouping consists of four Landscape Character Zones in the eastern extremity of the County. While each has its own individual character, they do share an overarching degree of similarity which sets them apart in many ways from Character Zones in the rest of the County.

To a considerable extent, the discernible character in Eastern Devon is a product of the geology. As was described in Chapter 5 under the discussion on Geology (Theme 1), this part of the County is distinguished by being an area of newer, softer rocks than is most of Devon, in particular chalk, sandstones and mudstones. The landscape character this gives rise to is in many ways more reminiscent of neighbouring counties to the east than it is to other parts of Devon.

The area is characterised by a marked north-south trend of rivers, valleys and ridges; the result is a clearly differentiated landscape of high and low land, often in close proximity; at the coast this is manifested in high, often crumbling cliffs, punctuated by steep combe mouths and occasional wider river mouths with sand or pebble ridges backed by marshland.

The East Devon coast backed by a series of greensand ridges.

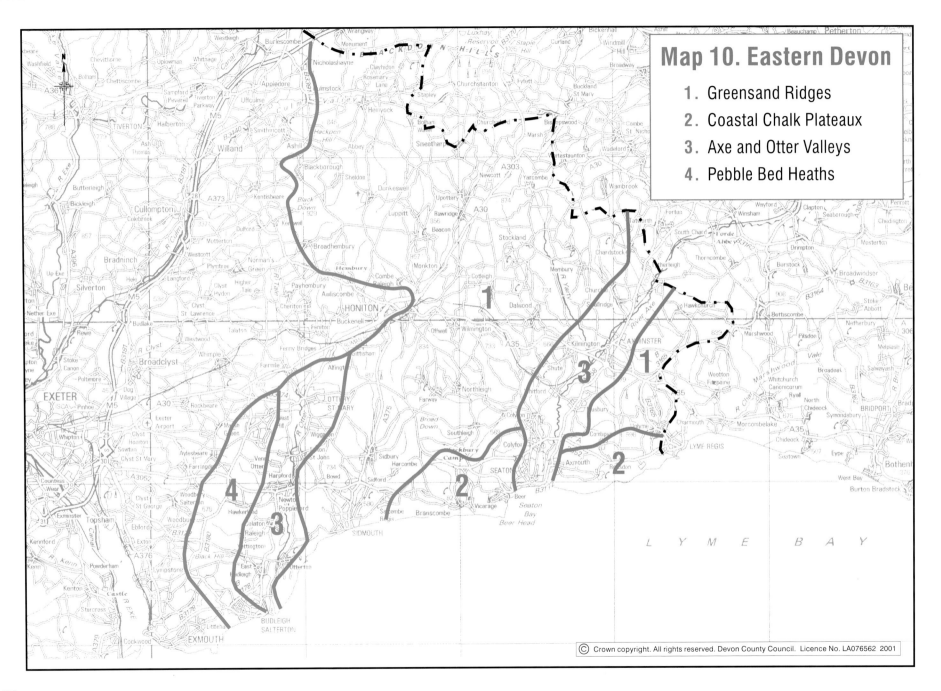

Map 10. Eastern Devon

1. Greensand Ridges
2. Coastal Chalk Plateaux
3. Axe and Otter Valleys
4. Pebble Bed Heaths

1. GREENSAND RIDGES

EASTERN DEVON
1. Greensand Ridges

Crown copyright. All rights reserved. Devon County Council. Licence No. LA076562 2001

LOCATION

The Zone occupies two separate areas in the far south east corner of the County, the two parts being separated by the Axe Valley. The larger, more westerly area stretches from the Somerset boundary in the north to the English Channel coast in the south, bounded on the west by a line between Budleigh Salterton, Ottery St Mary, Honiton and Culmstock and on the east by the Axe Valley. The smaller, eastern area abuts the Dorset boundary and covers an area bounded by Lyme Regis and Axminster but excluding the coast.

DESIGNATIONS

The whole of the western area is covered by the national designation Area of Outstanding Natural Beauty (AONB), with the exception of Sidmouth and its surroundings and a very small area adjacent to Honiton. Two separate but contiguous AONBs are involved, virtually dividing this part of the Zone into two equal halves. The northern half falls within the Blackdown Hills AONB and the southern half within the East Devon AONB, the boundary being the A35 road linking Honiton and Axminster.

The separate, eastern area also falls partly within the East Devon AONB; this designation covers approximately the southern third. The northern part of this area, broadly a stretch of land centred on the village of Hawkchurch, has been designated as an Area of Great Landscape Value (AGLV), indicating a landscape of county importance.

The County's Coastal Preservation Area (CPA) designation covers the coastal area between Budleigh Salterton and Sidmouth. The same area has been defined as Heritage Coast by the Countryside Agency.

The top of the cliffs to the Mean Low Watermark is part of the Dorset and East Devon Coast World Heritage Site.

KEY CHARACTERISTIC FEATURES

- Long greensand ridges including heath and forestry, beech hedges and avenues.

- Plateau landscape on ridge tops which includes common land, parliamentary enclosures, airfields and communications structures.

- Steep valleys between ridges enclosing a varied farming landscape, with woodland, hedgerow trees and springline flushes.

- Historic farm buildings utilising local materials.

- Springline settlements.

Wooded greensand ridge near Sidmouth.

DESCRIPTION

Perhaps the most dominant feature of the entire East Devon landscape is the line of long ridges which runs southwards from the Blackdowns escarpment. These ridges, and the valleys between them, strongly characterise this Zone.

Strictly speaking, the different character of the ridge-top landscape as opposed to that of the valleys could be seen as worthy of being two separate areas. However, so interwoven are these landscapes with each other, the one relying on the other for contrast, background and interplay, that the whole complex can be seen as having an overarching single character when looked at on a county scale.

The ridge lines vary between quite substantial widths, almost plateaux, and much narrower ridges. In all cases the characteristic feature is flatness on the tops, valley sides falling abruptly away on either side. Hedgerows enclose many of the ridge tops, characteristically straight lines resulting from parliamentary enclosure of what was previously 'waste'. Associated with these hedges are long, straight roads running the

length of the ridges, sometimes lined by narrow plantations of trees. In one or two places the ridge tops remain as unenclosed and unimproved land. There are areas of forestry, especially at the ridge edges, which create a wooded appearance seen from afar.

In the more southern part of the Zone, broadly coinciding with the East Devon AONB area, the grain of the land is less obviously north–south, tributary streams creating a more complex and incised landscape. Parts of this area trend east–west as much as north–south. However, the major, most dominant ridges remain north–south and both they and the more complex ridges display virtually identical characteristics to those further north.

The ridges contrast with the valleys between them. These quiet, pastoral valleys offer added variety to the area from the fact that each has been individually carved into the plateau and thus each has its own unique shape. Nevertheless, there are many common features: a strong, complex hedgerow pattern; well-wooded appearance, largely as a result of an abundance of mature hedgerow trees; springline settlements augmented by some valley bottom

villages; very steep valley sides with considerable woodland in places.

The ridge and valley trend continues south to the coast, centred on the town of Sidmouth. The result is a coastal landscape of high red sandstone cliffs punctuated by steep valleys, most obviously by that of the Sid at Sidmouth.

The western boundary of this Zone is relatively well defined, the most westerly ridge falling to the more generally low-lying landscape stretching towards central Devon or the clear feature of the Otter Valley. A similarly clear definition is found on the eastern edge as the landscape descends into the Axe Valley. To the south the Zone's landscape generally terminates in a broad, clear coastal plateau; where this itself ends the Zone reaches the coast. To the north, the Zone reaches the county boundary at Somerset. This area coincides with the high escarpment from which the north–south ridges protrude; almost immediately beyond the boundary the escarpment plunges steeply into the Vale of Taunton Deane.

The separate, smaller, eastern section of the Zone has, over its southern half, a very similar appearance to the main block of the Zone. Further north the ridge and valley landscape is less extreme, less differentiated, the only really distinctive ridge top being on the eastern edge, on the Dorset boundary. The remainder is a complex landscape of valleys and low ridges.

To the west, this landscape falls to the clear feature of the Axe Valley, while the southern boundary of the Zone is marked by another broad, high, flat-topped coastal plateau. The county boundary with Dorset marks the eastern edge, a similar landscape continuing into Dorset.

Ridge top with straight road, near Luppitt.

Cob and thatch is found in the valleys; Gittisham.

SUBJECTIVE RESPONSE

The character of the Zone is defined by the intimate inter-relationship between the ridges and the valleys. Although the major valleys tend to run north–south, many have minor tributary valleys leading into them and in places the valleys themselves trend in different directions. The character of these valleys and the response they evoke are thus quite different from that of the ridges.

The valleys have a confined, intimate character. This character is reinforced by the winding, narrow, often steep lanes which run through them. Their sinuous nature means that a sense of direction is easily lost and can only be retained by reference to the valley sides. The hedges, copses and trees mean that views are generally limited to very close range. In the smaller valleys settlements are generally small, often on the springline, and can occur quite unexpectedly. The houses use local stone, for example chert nodules faced with greensand blocks. The small-scale feel of the landscape is reinforced by a well-retained hedgerow pattern, enclosing generally small, irregular fields. Plantations on the higher valley sides give a wooded feel to the backdrop and add to the intimate, enclosed character. Here and there larger valleys penetrate the area, such as the Culm and the Sid. While less enclosed and intimate, the overall character of such valleys is nevertheless similar if less remote in its feel.

There is a considerable contrast with the ridge tops. Here, a flat, more open landscape creates a quite different response. This is reinforced by the straight lines, of roads, hedges and trees, which characterise the ridges. The dominant trend on the tops is horizontal, both of the tops themselves and the views. Such views are often very extensive, sometimes over considerable areas of lower land to distant high areas. Elsewhere views are merely to the next parallel ridge.

Despite their largely open character, the appearance of the ridge tops can often be quite wooded, as a result of strategically positioned plantations alongside roads or along the rims of the ridges. These plantations can also give a wooded appearance to the ridges as viewed from afar, an important element of the wider East Devon landscape.

Although high and largely open, the ridge tops rarely convey a feeling of remoteness. This is probably the result of the straightness of the roads, added to the not infrequent features such as communications development, airfields and similar sites. Despite these quite different basic characteristics, the ridges and valleys complement each other to form a complex but identifiable overall character, the whole being more than simply the sum of the parts.

INTEGRITY

The landscape character of most of this Zone has been well retained. Some peripheral development has occurred on the outskirts of the larger settlements, especially Sidmouth but also at Honiton on the very edge of the Zone. This development, not especially in local character, does have a limited impact on the character of part of the larger valleys. The smaller, perhaps more characteristic valleys have not been affected.

The ridge tops have been affected by a variety of developments, including telecommunications masts and stations, and industrial development on airfield sites. There is also one relatively large area of residential development near Dunkeswell. So far, however, the scale of the landscape has enabled it to absorb these developments without too much of a negative impact on its character. Nevertheless, such is the wide visibility of these tops that any large-scale development would have an impact not only on this Zone but on a wide area of East Devon.

Maintenance of the essential character of this Zone also depends on the retention of relatively less intensive land-use and farming methods, especially in the valleys, the retention of the distinctive valley settlement pattern and of the tree and hedgerow features.

2. COASTAL CHALK PLATEAUX

EASTERN DEVON
2. Coastal Chalk Plateaux

LOCATION

The Zone occupies two separate areas on the English Channel coast in the south-eastern corner of Devon, the two areas being separated by the Axe Valley. The western area stretches from a little way east of Sidmouth along the coast to Beer; the eastern area occupies the coastal stretch between Axmouth and the Dorset boundary at Lyme Regis. Both areas reach inland between 2 and 4 km (1–2 miles), as far as and just beyond the coastal road A3052.

Coastal landslip at Hooken Undercliff.

DESIGNATIONS

The national designation of the East Devon Area of Outstanding Natural Beauty covers the whole Zone with the exception of a relatively small area between Beer and Colyton at the eastern end of the more westerly element of the Zone. Most of this excepted area has been covered by Devon County Council's Area of Great Landscape Value designation (AGLV), indicating its landscape importance in a county context. A small area, basically the developed area of the settlement of Beer, is excluded from both designations.

The County's Coastal Preservation Area desig-nation covers much of the Zone, with the exception only of the most inland parts; it has also been defined as Heritage Coast by the Countryside Agency.

The top of the cliffs to the Mean Low Water Mark is part of the Dorset and East Devon Coast World Heritage Site.

KEY CHARACTERISTIC FEATURES

- The only chalk outcrop in Devon, and the most westerly in England, giving spectacular cliffs, local building materials (including Beer stone and flint) and chalk grassland.

- Flat plateau, more arable than surrounding Zones, exposed to salt-laden winds.

- Plateau dissected by deep, branching coastal combes with historic settlements.

- Shelterbelts, including species such as Monterey pine and larch.

- Varied underlying geology creating dramatic changes in cliff scenery in close proximity as well as dramatic landslips.

DESCRIPTION

The main characteristic of this Zone is that of a high, flat-topped plateau falling abruptly to the sea at high cliffs. In many places, especially to the east, the plateau displays rolling features typical of chalk scenery, but unique in Devon. There is, per-haps, more arable use of the land on this part of the Zone than in neighbouring Zones. Field boundaries are well retained, enclosing relatively large and generally regularly-shaped fields.

At the coast the plateau falls abruptly to the sea; in places this results in characteristic white chalk cliffs, the most westerly in England, as near Seaton Hole and, especially, Beer Head. However, the geology has also resulted in dramatic landslips at the coast, sometimes on a very large scale. By their nature and topography, these landslips have often remained undisturbed for many years, creating ideal conditions as areas of nature conservation importance. Consequently the two main undercliffs resulting from these landslips, Hooken Undercliff between Branscombe and Beer and the Axmouth–Lyme Regis Undercliffs, are both designated as Sites of Special Scientific Interest and the latter is also a National Nature Reserve. In contrast to the plateau tops, where trees are few and often stunted and wind-shaped, the undercliffs are places of dense and luxuriant growth, largely impenetrable over most of their area.

Cutting into the plateau is a series of small valley systems. These features are narrow, steep-sided, often curving and branching. Pastoral in nature, they display often small and irregular fields, noticeable areas of woodland on their slopes and, in contrast to the sparsely inhabited plateau tops, each contains hamlets or villages.

The two elements of the Zone are both bounded on the south by the sea. To the north, the plateaux break into the ridge and valley landscape, typically north–south in trend, of the greensand ridges. In the west, the plateau falls steeply into the Sid Valley, one of the most prominent valleys in this ridge and valley system, while to the east the Zone ends at the County boundary at Lyme Regis, which also marks a change to a more diverse topography in Dorset. Between the two elements of the Zone lies the Axe Valley, the high plateau lands falling quite abruptly from both east and west into this flat, lowland feature.

SUBJECTIVE RESPONSE

The plateau tops give a general feeling of space and air, a product of the largely level horizons, open aspects and frequent views of the sea. There are few buildings and few trees, those that there

are often being small or bent by the wind, adding to the feel of height and air. On the cliff tops the sea views add their appeal to the senses.

A contrasting experience is provided by the undercliffs. These are areas of dense growth, in places almost primeval in feel, creating probably a unique environment in Devon; shady or even dark, secretive, surprisingly unmaritime in character, in places perhaps almost threatening.

The third landscape constituent, the incised valley systems, result in yet another response. These valleys are intimate, sheltered, steep-sided although never with a feeling of total remoteness. Their wooded or gorse-covered sides and attractive, irregular hedgerows complement the villages and hamlets each valley contains, these often characterised by 'picture-book' houses of cob and thatch, or local materials such as flint.

Buildings in local flint, Beer.

While each landscape has its own characteristics, at a county level the relationship and interplay between them, and the complementary attributes each gives to its neighbour, go together to create an overall unit of landscape character defined by these inter-relationships as much as the individual elements.

INTEGRITY

The Zone has retained its essential character very well. Some hedgerow loss is apparent in places, especially on the plateaux, but this has not been sufficient to have a negative impact on the overall character. The undercliffs remain almost totally untouched and the incised valleys have also generally retained their essential characteristics. Only on the outskirts of Beer, where development has extended up one of the small tributary valleys, has any of these features been greatly affected; here, the development, while post-war, is not immediately recent and does relate to an existing town. It does not adversely affect a very wide area.

Perhaps the most obvious impact on the landscape of this Zone is the car park and holiday park development adjacent to Beer Head. This not only affects the character of the immediate plateau and coastal area but is visible across Seaton Bay from the town of Seaton and the cliffs in the eastern part of this Zone.

Important to the retention of the Zone's character are maintenance and restoration of coastal shelterbelts, the landscape setting of the combe villages and the mosaic of semi-natural habitat types found throughout the area.

3. AXE AND OTTER VALLEYS

EASTERN DEVON
3. Axe and Otter Valleys

LOCATION

The Zone comprises two parallel north–south river valleys in south-east Devon, separated by higher land. The Axe Valley stretches from the Somerset and Dorset boundary to the English Channel coast at Seaton. The Otter Valley element of this Zone occupies the lower part of the valley only, from just south of Honiton to the estuary at Budleigh Salterton.

DESIGNATIONS

Most of the lower Axe Valley, below Axminster, is part of the national designation of the East Devon Area of Outstanding Natural Beauty. At the mouth of the river, however, from just north of Axmouth to the coast, the AONB excludes the river itself as well as the valley floor, which is occupied by the settlement of Seaton. North of Axminster, the western fringes of the valley fall within the boundary of the Blackdown Hills AONB, again giving national recognition. The remainder of the Axe Valley north of Axminster, as well as the estuary itself and the adjacent marshes plus the valley floor of the tributary river Coly, have all been subject to Devon County Council's Area of Great Landscape Value designation.

The lower part of the Otter Valley element of the Zone, south of Tipton St John, falls within the East Devon AONB.

The County's Coastal Preservation Area designation covers the Axe estuary south of the A3052 road, excluding the urban area of Seaton, and also covers the Otter estuary south of Otterton.

The top of the cliffs to the Mean Low Water Mark is part of the Dorset and East Devon Coast World Heritage Site.

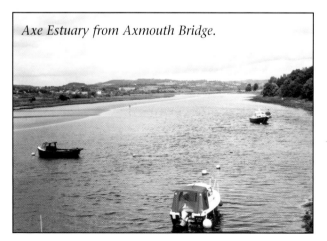

Axe Estuary from Axmouth Bridge.

KEY CHARACTERISTIC FEATURES

- Lowland rivers with noticeable flood plains and tightly meandering courses, unusual in most of Devon's major rivers.

- Shingle or pebble bars across both estuaries, both backed by ecologically important salt marsh.

- Historic settlements sited at old crossing points, just above the flood plain.

- Drainage channels.

DESCRIPTION

The more northerly parts of the Axe Valley have a somewhat undulating valley floor, the actual flood plain being fairly narrow. There is a good, strong hedgerow pattern and the hedgerow trees, augmented by some woodland blocks, make the valley appear well wooded. Further south, the valley opens out to a much wider flood plain, particularly after it becomes fed by major tributaries such as Yarty and the Coly. In this area drainage channels criss-cross the valley floor and, especially south of the A3052 road, there are appreciable areas of estuarine marsh. The western side of the lower valley is occupied by the settlements of Colyton and Seaton.

The Otter Valley has a similar profile, although here, perhaps, the actual flood plain is more marked. The good quality agricultural land has led to the establishment of large estates which have in turn created a parkland landscape in places. South of Newton Poppleford the valley floor is characterised by drainage channels. Marshland occupies the estuarine area. The valley immediately west of the estuary is covered by the settlement of Budleigh Salterton.

Both estuaries are characterised by a course deviation to the east, caused by the build-up of shingle or pebble bars across the river mouths.

Both valleys are quite distinct from the neighbouring land to east and west; in both cases the neighbouring land is much higher, and the boundary between valley and adjacent high land is often quite abrupt. Both have the sea as their southern boundary. The northern boundary of the Axe Valley element of the Zone is at the County boundary with Somerset and Dorset. Over the boundary the landscape remains very similar in character for a while, until the valley becomes more absorbed into its higher surroundings east of Chard. The northern boundary of the Otter Valley element of the Zone occurs to the south-west of Honiton, where the valley becomes less of a distinct feature set aside from its neighbouring high land and more an integral part of the overall landscape.

SUBJECTIVE RESPONSE

The lower parts of both valleys were traditionally a water meadow landscape, later with drainage channels. While changes, including enclosure by hedges and much increased drainage, have altered this landscape to an extent, the essence of domination by water remains, especially in autumn, winter or spring when even modern drainage cannot always cope with the rainfall. The resulting almost quasi-water meadow landscape is very unusual in Devon and can give an almost timeless quality to the scene. This is accentuated by the presence of picturesque cob and thatch buildings and villages which are common in the valleys.

The more inland parts of the valleys are in some ways less distinctive, more typical of lowland valleys elsewhere in lowland Devon or even in lowland England. However, the contrast with the always nearby higher land, the pattern of river meanders, the generally unimproved riverbanks and the cob and thatch buildings and settlements, all create a very favourable impression of both valleys as landscape features, reflecting an almost traditional English scene.

INTEGRITY

The unadulterated water meadow landscape quality of the lower valleys has been lost as a result of drainage improvements and the enclosure of fields. However, at times the element of water remains the dominant theme, and even at other times the essential water-based character of the landscape has been retained.

The estuaries also retain their essential characteristics, despite the proximity of sizeable settlements to both estuaries. Both remain essentially undeveloped and the characteristic features of ridges deflecting the river outflow, backed by marshland, are largely intact.

Budleigh Salterton, at the mouth of the Otter, relates well to the landscape. Seaton, situated next to the Axe estuary, has more of an impact on the landscape. Vertical outlines, uncharacteristic of the generally horizontal trend of the estuary character, impinge somewhat on the view down the estuary and, indeed, some of the sea-front buildings do impact on views from the cliffs to east and west. Seaton has also grown up the valley

sides to an extent. In contrast, the other sizeable settlements in the lower Axe Valley, Colyton and Colyford, relate rather better to the surrounding landscape and affect its integrity much less.

Inland, the generally unspoiled rural valley landscapes largely remain in both Axe and Otter. Axminster generally sits appropriately in its landscape, although it is now somewhat divorced from the lower valley by the A35 Axminster by-pass. To the north the main influence is exerted by the presence of the A358 road. Although not as busy as the A35, it does run along the valley rather than across it, and so brings a 'taming' influence on the valley, resulting in a lack of a feeling of quiet remoteness. The Otter, too, loses any remote character at its northern end, partly because of the presence of Ottery St Mary, although the town does not really straddle the river nor does it particularly detract from the overall scene. North of Ottery, the proximity of the main A30 trunk road just north of the Zone boundary is clearly heard, with a noticeable effect on the character. The remainder of the Otter Valley, however, remains an extremely attractive rural landscape of meandering river in a clearly defined valley dotted with cob and thatch settlements.

In places, the landscape integrity of both valleys is delicate. Maintenance or restoration of the open nature of the lower valleys is important to retain or recreate the water meadow character, while inland the importance of the natural meanders, unimproved waterside habitat and traditional building design and materials must be emphasised.

4. PEBBLE BED HEATHS

EASTERN DEVON
4. Pebble Bed Heaths

LOCATION

The Zone occupies a fairly narrow north–south area of land in the south-eastern part of the County. It stretches from the west of Ottery St Mary south to the English Channel coast between Exmouth and Budleigh Salterton.

DESIGNATIONS

The southern two-thirds of this zone is covered by the East Devon Area of Outstanding Natural Beauty designation, indicating a national significance. The northern third, from West Hill northwards to the Zone boundary, is not subject to a landscape designation. The coastal area is within Devon County Council's Coastal Preservation Area.

The top of the cliffs to the Mean Low Water Mark is part of the Dorset and East Devon Coast World Heritage Site.

KEY CHARACTERISTIC FEATURES

- Extensive area of lowland heath.

- Popular recreational resource with fine panoramic views.

- Distinctive geology of Bunter Pebble Beds influencing vegetation, land-use and building materials.

- Backdrop to the Exe Estuary.

- Important archaeological features.

DESCRIPTION

The Zone comprises a prominent ridge running in a north–south direction. It forms the western flank

of the Otter Valley and, as such, closely mirrors the north–south greensand ridge on the east side of that valley. However, its geology sets it apart from the greensand ridges described under Zone 1, and produces a markedly different landscape.

The pebble bed deposits which form this Zone give rise to a characteristic landscape of dry lowland heath. This open heathland scenery covers most of the Zone and is characterised by gorse vegetation with scattered pines and other distinctive tree groups, of pine, fir or wind-trimmed beech, creating local landmarks. Some of the edge slopes, particularly in the west and south, are well wooded. While some areas of semi-natural ancient woodland remain most has been replaced with conifers or beech. Nevertheless, the resultant almost continuous wooded escarpment performs an important landscape role, both in emphasising the landform and as a backdrop to the Exe Estuary and its lowland farmland.

A combination of its proximity to Exeter and Exmouth, its open nature and the permitted access regime of the Clinton Devon Estate which owns much of the area, means that the area is a well-used recreational resource. Walking and riding are popular activities, and panoramic views over Exeter, estuary and the sea mean that formal and informal car parking occurs widely. The heathland is also used as a resource for Royal Marines training.

To the north, beyond the AONB boundary, the characteristic landscape is less obvious, although the ridge feature and the underlying geology continue. Here the heath is fragmented with irregular blocks of conifers and numerous small-holdings. 'Horsiculture' and enclosed fields become common and the suburban-style settlement of West Hill obscures most of the ridge's characteristics near the northern end of the Zone.

For the most part the boundaries of the Zone are very distinct, again a product of the geology. To the east and west the land falls away quite abruptly, in the west towards the Exe Estuary and the Exeter fringe, in the east to the Otter Valley. The southern boundary is defined by the sea, the Zone forming the highest cliffs in this part of East Devon at West Down Beacon (129m/425ft). Only in the north is the boundary more amorphous, the Zone gradually merging into the lower, less strongly defined land in the Exeter-Honiton corridor.

SUBJECTIVE RESPONSE

This is a relatively high, open area of big skies, extensive views and a feeling of spaciousness. This response is emphasised by the relatively level or undulating nature of most of the Zone. In many locations in the County such a landscape would give rise to a character of remoteness, but here the proximity to the large settlements of Exeter and Exmouth and the popularity of the area as a recreational and military training resource evoke a more 'used' feel.

Despite its popularity, it is still usually possible to find isolated locations within this area, and it is a much-loved and appreciated area for its landscape and panoramic views. It is also important as one of Devon's, and indeed the country's, few remaining lowland heaths, an important ecological resource.

INTEGRITY

The southern two-thirds of this Zone, coinciding with the area within the East Devon AONB, has retained its essential characteristics of open heathland well. The main loss in this area has been to quarrying activity at one location towards the western edge of the Zone (Black Hill). Elsewhere, threats to the landscape integrity come from recreational pressure – path erosion in some locations is now highly visible – and from geometric blocks of conifer plantations.

In the north, the character of the Zone has suffered rather more, and its essential integrity, which should produce a landscape similar to that further south, has been generally lost. Enclosure and reclamation of heathland for smallholdings and paddocks has produced a landscape and character reminiscent of an outer urban fringe. The settlement of West Hill, characterised by large properties within their own grounds, the whole area studded with pines, is more typical of parts of Surrey than of Devon.

It is important that those parts of the Zone which have retained their landscape integrity are not compromised; as such the management and restoration of heathland vegetation is important to the landscape of the Zone, as is the continued management of recreation. Trees are also important to the Zone, especially distinctive individual trees and tree groups which provide local landmarks, complement the heathland and frame views; maintenance of the wooded fringe area is also important, more as a backdrop to the landscape of neighbouring Zones.

Opposite page: *A typical view over the heaths; Peak Hill in the background.*

Right: *Heathland, plantations, scattered pines; typical landscape on Woodbury Common.*

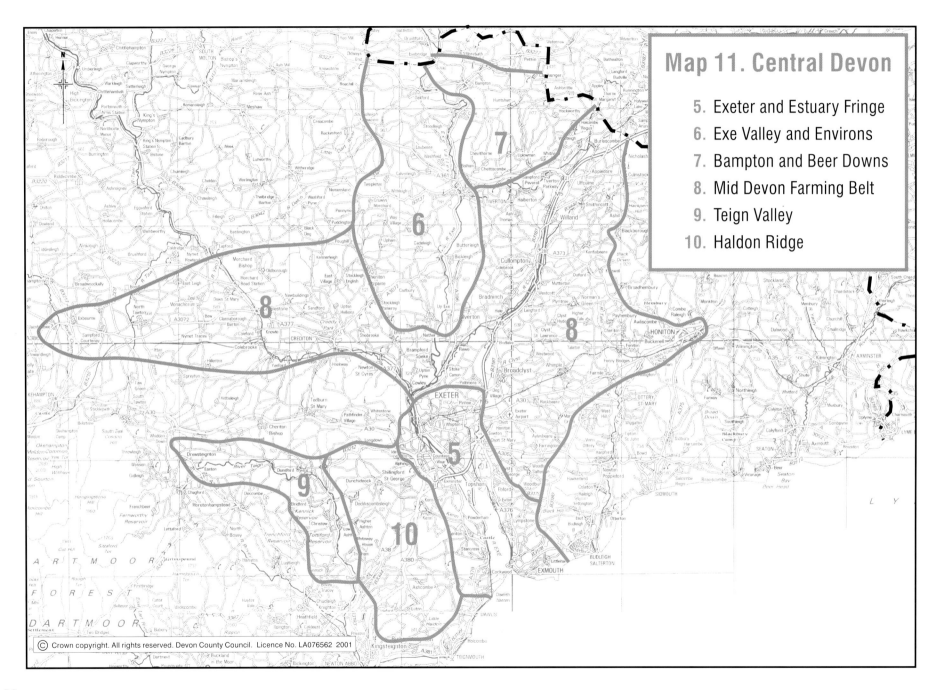

Map 11. Central Devon

5. Exeter and Estuary Fringe
6. Exe Valley and Environs
7. Bampton and Beer Downs
8. Mid Devon Farming Belt
9. Teign Valley
10. Haldon Ridge

CENTRAL DEVON

This grouping consists of six Landscape Character Zones in what is strictly the east-central part of the County. It covers a relatively diverse area, stretching from the fringes of Exmoor in the north to the Exe Estuary in the south, and from the edge of Dartmoor in the west to the Blackdown Hills in the east.

Basic to this part of the County is a large area of relatively fertile soils, the largest continuous area of such in Devon. This generally lowland, fertile area is centred on the north–south axis of the Exe Valley, with important extensions to the east along the Exeter–Honiton corridor and, even more distinctively, to the west through Crediton and on to the north-east of Dartmoor.

On its fringes this part of Devon shows a more diverse character. In the north the Bampton area shows a transition towards Exmoor. In the south-west the north–south Haldon Ridge, parallel to and west of the Exe Estuary, is a major landmark through this part of Devon and marks a fundamental change in geology and landscape character. West of the Ridge, the Teign Valley is also transitional, having elements which relate it to Dartmoor to the west, but included in this grouping because it is an essentially lowland feature with a close landscape inter-relationship with Haldon.

In some ways transition is the hallmark of this grouping of Landscape Character Zones; transition between the essentially newer geology and consequent landscape to the east and older geology with associated higher, less 'soft' landscapes to the west. It reflects the national line of transition between lowland and highland Britain traditionally said to run from the Exe to the Tees.

The Exe Valley, backbone of Central Devon landscapes.

5. EXETER AND ESTUARY FRINGE

CENTRAL DEVON
5. Exeter and Estuary Fringe

LOCATION

The Zone encompasses the City of Exeter, its immediate surroundings and the Exe Estuary and both its flanks to the English Channel.

DESIGNATIONS

Most of the western side of the Estuary below Exminster has been designated as an Area of Great Landscape Value, indicating its County importance as a landscape. A small area to the north of Exmouth on the eastern side of the Estuary has also been so designated.

The County Council's Coastal Preservation Area covers much of the western side of the Estuary, as well as a small area on the eastern bank between Lympstone and Exmouth and also the short coastal element of the Zone, at Dawlish Warren and immediately east of Exmouth.

KEY CHARACTERISTIC FEATURES

- Internationally important estuary for waders, wildfowl and sea birds, with associated dunes, marshes, mud and sand flats and a landscape which changes with the tides and seasons.

- Intensively farmed landscape with good quality soils and large fields.

- Few hedgerow trees, farm woods or shelterbelts.

- Glimpsed views of estuary or city of Exeter.

- Historic settlements associated with the estuary.

- Parkland and estate planting.

- The historic city of Exeter, marked by green corridors and inter-relationship with its countryside, especially along the Exe corridor.

DESCRIPTION

The topography of this Zone is predominately flat or gently undulating. This reduces the impact of the numerous scattered dwellings, farms and villages, although this becomes more obvious when viewed from the higher ground which characteristically flanks both sides of the Zone, i.e. Woodbury Common to the east and Great Haldon to the west.

The Zone is characterised by good quality soils which have led to intensive farming. This has resulted in generally large fields often with neglected boundaries of gappy hedges and bare earth banks. Hedgerow trees are few and fields are ploughed close to shelterbelts. In many parts of the Zone there is evidence of hedgerow loss.

The north of the Zone is dominated by the city of Exeter, best viewed from the flanking high ground or from the river corridor, which provides a link between city and countryside. The historic core and its immediate surroundings sit quite well in the overall landscape but peripheral developments, especially towards the M5 to the east, make more of an unfortunate impact. The M5 itself, crossing the head of the estuary just below Exeter, is also a major landscape feature.

Below Exeter the western bank of the estuary is marked by areas of marshland and, at Dawlish Warren at the mouth of the estuary, a dune system. The eastern bank is more developed, dominated by the sizeable town of Exmouth at the mouth.

The western border of this Zone is clearly delineated by the abruptly rising high land of the Haldon Ridge. In the east, the equally clear slopes to the pebble bed heaths of Woodbury Common mark the boundary from the coast to Topsham. East of Exeter the Zone includes the urban fringe developments west of the M5; east of the motorway is the farming zone of the Exeter–Honiton corridor. The Zone's northern boundary includes the woodland of Stoke Hill, long associated with Exeter, excluding the farmland beyond.

SUBJECTIVE RESPONSE

The estuary is the dominant landscape feature of the Zone, dwarfing even the impact of Exeter. The estuary, and especially the western bank, represents a landscape type unusual in Devon; although the County has a number of estuaries, few are as extensive as that of the Exe. This is an area of open skies, the sound of seabirds, the masts of boats, of mud and dunes at Dawlish Warren; of views over the river, its details changing according to tide and season, the whole scene framed by the high ground of Woodbury Common and Haldon.

The feel of the eastern bank is different, although similar characteristics are experienced at some riverside locations. Generally, however, the eastern bank has much more development, based on Exmouth and the historic settlements at Lympstone and Topsham. These settlements show an attractive face to the estuary. Less attractive in traditional terms is the prominent development of the Royal Marine Barracks near Lympstone.

The M5 bridge across the estuary head cuts off Exeter from the lower estuary in visual terms, although views out of Exeter down the estuary, certainly from higher locations within the City, are relatively unaffected. The road is, nevertheless, something of an emotional dividing line.

Most of the inland rural area is intensive farmland, well populated and closely related to main roads, although some parts west of the estuary do have more of a remote feel. Always, however, the estuary, roads and frequently Exeter, influence the character of the landscape.

For a city of its size, Exeter sits very well in the landscape, marking the top of the tidal estuary. Even seen from high vantage points it never dominates the landscape. On the ground it inevitably has more of an impact, although only comparatively recently has this begun to have its effect on a wider area. Some peripheral developments now have probably more of an impact on the wider scene, especially as viewed from surrounding high land, than does the whole remainder of the city.

INTEGRITY

This Zone is under considerable pressure, both from development and from agricultural trends. Although it still presents a generally attractive face, these pressures are becoming more apparent.

Perhaps the major loss of integrity has occurred as a result of the building of the M5 across the estuary. Although within the Zone itself, its impact is relatively limited, it does psychologically cut off the lower estuary from Exeter, and has a considerable landscape effect on the higher estuary.

Developments around Exeter are also beginning to affect a wider area of the Zone. This is particularly true of those towards the M5, which have an impact on visitors' introduction to the city. These developments are also highly visible from the high land which flanks the Zone, having possibly more of an adverse impact than the whole of the older parts of the city.

At the other end of the Zone, Exmouth has been one of the fastest growing settlements in Devon. Although there has been no real adverse impact on the estuary element of the Zone, development has considerably eaten into the hinterland landscape, especially to the north.

The agricultural value of the Zone is reflected in hedgerow loss, lack of appropriate field boundary maintenance, the absence of hedgerow trees and, especially on the eastern bank, of woodlands and shelterbelts.

It is unlikely that any of these pressures will diminish. Consequently this is a Zone where much vigilance will be needed to maintain and, preferably, enhance its distinctive character.

The middle Exe Estuary, the dominant feature of the local landscape.

6. EXE VALLEY AND ENVIRONS

CENTRAL DEVON
6. Exe Valley and Environs

LOCATION

The Zone comprises the middle Exe valley, in the east-central part of the County, from the Somerset boundary in the north to a few miles north of Exeter in the south.

DESIGNATIONS

Much of the Zone has been designated as an Area of Great Landscape Value, indicating its importance as a landscape of County significance. This designation covers most of the valley itself as well as two western tributaries. It excludes the town of Tiverton, in the middle of the valley, and some of the flanking high land to the west which is included within the Zone.

KEY CHARACTERISTIC FEATURES

- Landscape dominated by dramatic topography.

- Extensive woodlands flanking the valley, contrasting with the flat and open valley floor.

- Tree-lined River Exe, fast-flowing in the north, weirs and wide tranquil stretches in the south.

- Picturesque historic villages on or near the river; thatched cottages hidden in side valleys.

- Surrounding hilly terrain.

DESCRIPTION

The Exe Valley forms a very distinctive element in the landscape of Central Devon. North of Tiverton it forms a very clearly defined valley feature, flat-bottomed, flanked by generally steep sides, largely wooded, these being complemented by copses on the valley floor and by the generally tree-lined nature of the Exe itself. In the north there are numerous steep and deep-sided valleys, appearing as distinctive clefts in the valley sides, also generally well wooded. The further up the valley, the less flat land on the valley bottom and the more enclosed is the appearance of the valley, this being especially marked as it narrows above Holmingham.

South of Tiverton the valley widens. The floor is broader, flatter and less wooded. The flanks become less steep and present more of a patchwork of woods, pasture and hedges than the more generally wooded flanks north of Tiverton. The valley remains a noticeable feature in the landscape, however, even if it is less enclosed.

The Zone also includes flanking high land, especially to the west, where the high land often forms 'fingers' between side valleys. This area is characterised by more open, pastoral, hedged land with copses and trees, irregular in trend.

Exe Valley near Thorverton; flat floor with patchwork pattern on flanks.

In the centre of the Zone sits the town of Tiverton, the service centre for the Exe Valley and its environs. Sited on the Exe itself, the town mostly relates well to the surrounding landscape.

The Zone is characterised by attractive villages which display 'typical' Devon features, especially cob and thatch cottages. Villages such as Bickleigh and Thorverton add to the valley's obvious attractions.

The northern boundary of the Zone is marked by the Somerset border, beyond which the Exe continues in a similar landscape to Exmoor. The southern boundary occurs where the Exe widens to an extent that it has lost its identity as a definable feature; at this point its valley is joined by that of a major tributary from the east, the River Culm. The eastern flanks of the valley form a fairly recognisable boundary in this direction, although the Zone does include those parts of the neighbouring land which relate to the valley itself. In the west, two major tributaries with similar, or even more marked, characteristics to the Exe itself are included, (the Iron Mill stream and the Dart) together with neighbouring high land. The boundary marks the change to the more uniform landform of the Culm Measures along the northern part of the Zone, and to the westward and southward-oriented valleys further south.

SUBJECTIVE RESPONSE

The dramatic topography of the Exe Valley is its most characteristic feature. The deepness and distinctiveness of the valley, the fact that it is rarely uniform, never straight and that the river swings across the valley floor, the presence of woodlands, the contrast with the open hilltops surrounding, the views from those hilltops, all combine to give rise to a response that this is a landscape of great aesthetic appeal.

Response to the experience of the major side valleys is similar, but added to this is the feel of a quiet, secretive, remote, almost isolated area. This contrasts with the high, airy, spacious pasture above, with the long range views in all directions, Exmoor especially catching the eye, and the feel of being close to the elements.

INTEGRITY

The landscape characteristics of the Exe Valley have been well retained. The distractions, such as they are, include the noise and sight of traffic on the A396 road, most noticeable in the south, and on the A361 North Devon Link. Quarry workings have had an impact, especially at Holmingham near Bampton, although some may claim that such features add an element to the landscape.

Further south there is some, largely sporadic, valley bottom development, especially farm buildings. The tributary valleys and intervening high land remain largely unaffected.

The high quality and integrity of the landscape will need some attention to ensure its maintenance, certainly in the longer term. The landscape importance of the woodland is especially noteworthy and it will be important that regeneration and management measures are in place to ensure its continuation. Similarly, the conservation and replacement of the riparian trees, copses and hedgerow trees will need addressing, while it will be important to maintain the essentially open nature of the valley floor. The landscape quality may also be enhanced by appropriate road screening on the major roads in one or two locations.

'Chocolate box' Devon; Bickleigh on the middle Exe.

95

7. BAMPTON AND BEER DOWNS

CENTRAL DEVON
7. Bampton and Beer Downs

LOCATION

This Zone is towards the east of the County with, indeed, its eastern edge forming the border of Somerset. It lies to the north of the A361 North Devon Link and M5, east of the Exe Valley and south of the B3227 which links Bampton and Wiveliscombe.

DESIGNATIONS

In the west of the Zone is a small area which has been designated as an Area of Great Landscape Value, indicating its County importance as a landscape. This part of the Zone is peripheral to the Exe Valley, to which the designation primarily relates.

KEY CHARACTERISTICS FEATURES

- Relatively flat hilltop areas dominated by large farms with modern barns.

- Few trees on the hilltops but dense beech and holly hedges.

- Some isolated beech plantations in the higher areas.

- Woodland on fringe areas, especially in the valleys.

- Remote area unaffected by through routes.

DESCRIPTION

Much of the Zone comprises a large-scale open farming landscape on a relatively flat, hilltop area. These hilltop stretches have few trees but there are quite dense holly and beech hedges. Because these are generally closely trimmed there have been few opportunities for hedgerow trees to grow up.

However, in the northern and western peripheries, where the high land falls away, there are plantations and hedgerow trees; their landscape effect is perhaps more on the outside areas than on the landscape of the Zone itself.

The high, flat-topped hills are interspersed with slightly lower, more undulating land, often formed by small rivers and tributaries flowing off the high land. There are, in addition, some quite marked river valleys, in particular those of the River Lowman and Town Leat. Both flow out of the high land in a southerly direction, their steep-sided, deep and often wooded valleys contrasting with the higher tabular hills surrounding them.

The hedgerow pattern generally varies between the hills and the intervening lower land. On the hilltops the fields tend to be large, with a regular, often rectangular hedgerow pattern. Lower down, and especially in the valley bottoms, fields are small and hedgerows much more random in pattern.

Undulating landscape near Huntsham.

There are few settlements on the hilltop areas other than some relatively large, sometimes quite prominent farms. Villages occur on the lower land around the edges but in the heart of the Zone there is only the small village of Huntsham, in the highest part of the Lowman Valley.

The western boundary of the Zone is marked by the quite abrupt drop into the Exe Valley. To the north another abrupt drop, into the valley used by the B3227 Bampton–Wiveliscombe road, marks the edge of the Zone. To the east the Zone is bounded by the Somerset border; an area of similar landscape continues beyond the border as far as the valley of the River Tone. On the south the Zone's edge is again marked by a clear fall in height, to the flood plain of the lower part of the River Lowman and to valleys of tributaries of the River Tone.

SUBJECTIVE RESPONSE

The Zone's most noteworthy characteristic is its remoteness and absence of traffic noise. There are no through routes, the only traffic on the generally narrow roads being that with business there. This pervading characteristic is augmented by the fine long-distance views obtained from the hilltops. Those to the west over the Exe Valley are notable for their almost aerial aspect, while those to the south and east are more marked for their long range, over intervening low land to distant heights in the Blackdown Hills.

Some of the hilltops add to these characteristics by their feel of being airy, subject only to the wind, which accentuates the remoteness. On the other hand, this remoteness is also accentuated by the quiet, enclosed, cut-off-from-the-world character of the valley lands.

However, the Zone is a relatively small one so, although noteworthy enough, the remote feel is somewhat limited in its scope. Nevertheless, the general response to this little-known landscape is enhanced by the overall characteristics which define it, with the interplay between high, usually flat-topped but sometimes rounded hills and intervening, often unexpected valleys particularly appealing.

INTEGRITY

The remoteness and lack of through roads has meant that pressure for development in this Zone has been minimal. However, there is a concern that over-management of hedges could weaken the hedgerow pattern, and there is some evidence of deliberate hedgerow loss. The landscape would also benefit from the retention of hedgerow trees, both to enhance it in its own right and to reduce the impact of artificial elements such as telegraph poles.

Modern farm buildings are prominent in some locations and, occupying as they often do hilltop sites, they have an impact on the landscape which would be enhanced by appropriate screening.

Bampton, the only settlement of any size in the area.

Typical landscape of the Beer Downs.

Huntsham Church, at the centre of a relatively remote landscape.

8. MID DEVON FARMING BELT

CENTRAL DEVON

8. Mid Devon Farming Belt

LOCATION

This Zone occupies the lowland heart of Devon. It stretches from the Blackdown Hills in the east to the valley of the River Okement, north of Okehampton, in the west. To the north, the Zone wraps itself around the middle Exe Valley. It skirts the northern edge of Exeter and includes the Exeter–Honiton corridor as well as the historic routeways to the rest of the country between Exeter and the Somerset border near Wellington.

DESIGNATIONS

None of this Zone is subject to any landscape designation.

KEY CHARACTERISTIC FEATURES

- Flat or rolling mixed farmland with distinctive red soils.

- Relatively few woodlands, meaning hedgerow trees are an important landscape element.

- Major road and rail corridors: also the route of transmission lines.

- Heavily settled, by Devon standards, with many villages and scattered farms and a number of large towns.

- Cob and thatch buildings.

DESCRIPTION

The unifying factor of this Zone is the distinctive red sandstone which has produced good, fertile, well-drained soils. This combined with the relatively level topography has resulted in an intensive agricultural 'heartland' of the County.

Most of the Zone is relatively level or moderately undulating; extremes of slope are rare. The valleys and tributaries of the Rivers Exe, Culm and Clyst are perhaps the most level, but similar topography extends east along the corridor to Honiton and north to the Somerset border. This topography has created a relatively easy access into the County which has been traditionally used by main communication routes with the rest of the country; this continues today with the routes of the M5 and the main London rail line, and also the A30 and the other rail line to London via Salisbury. The main power lines also enter the County along these routes.

The red soil geology continues in a long narrow band to the west of the Exe. As it does so it becomes perhaps rather less level, and the landscape of the western end of the Zone is perhaps less uniform. This is especially marked where the Zone flanks the west of the middle of the Exe Valley, the landscape of the area north of Shobrooke (near Crediton) being quite diverse. Irregular, often rounded hills, dissected by small but well-marked valleys, give this part of the Zone a somewhat different, smaller scale and more intimate appearance.

The Zone often appears well wooded, but large areas of woodland are actually rare. The appearance arises from numerous mature hedgerow trees, thin remnants of woodland and small coppices on steeper slopes. Hedgerows are typical of the Zone. Over such a large area the detailed pattern varies but fields tend to be medium in size with straight edges. As a result of agricultural intensification there is considerable evidence of hedgerow loss.

The Zone is a heavily populated one by Devon standards, with hamlets and villages as well as a considerable number of sizeable towns. Most of these towns and villages sit appropriately in the landscape. The larger settlements generally are former market towns, many of which are now seeing residential expansion with peripheral developments not always as appropriate in landscape terms.

The eastern edge of the Zone is marked by the abruptly rising ground of the Blackdown Hills north of Honiton and the Pebble Bed Heaths south of Honiton. In the north, the high land flanking the Exe Valley marks the Zone boundary as it wraps around the Valley, while the start of the narrow part of the Exe Valley as a distinctive feature north of Thorverton ends the Zone in the valley itself. To the south the Exe Estuary fringe, while similar in appearance, has a distinctive alignment setting it aside from this Zone and the woodland of Stoke Hill marks the Zone boundary on the Exe.

The western arm of the Zone has boundaries marked by a transition to less uniform topography, more pastoral, generally higher land and a characteristic lack of red soil. On the western flank of the Exe Valley the Zone boundary marks the appearance of the Exe tributaries with their intervening high lands which fade, often imperceptibly, into the Zone's landscape.

SUBJECTIVE RESPONSE

While never dramatic, the landscape does evoke what for many is the traditional English lowland landscape, with the added distinctiveness of the relatively unusual red soil. The hedged fields, the wooded appearance, the cob and thatch villages and individual buildings all go towards reinforcing this reaction. Even the lack of dramatic steep slopes gives weight to the Zone's 'traditional' feeling and appeal.

In places the feel of the Zone reflects its role as a communications corridor. The sight and sound of the M5 and A30 roads in particular make it obvious how important this communication role is. The good road network generally, the ease of access to Exeter and to other parts of the country, all give this Zone, and especially the eastern part of it, one of the least remote characters of any in Devon.

Further west in the Zone a combination of distance from communications and slightly more dissected topography reduces this character, although rarely does it display an aura of quietness or solitude. Just occasionally, in one of the small valleys or along the maze of lanes north of Crediton, such a feeling may be experienced.

Perhaps the main visual feature of the Zone is provided by the red soil; indeed, red soil has sometimes been used as a shorthand descriptive of Devon, although outside this Zone it is actually quite rare. The red soil combined with the more open and undulating topography in the west of the Zone gives quite a startling appearance to this area, especially in comparison with the neighbouring landscapes.

INTEGRITY

The Zone is under considerable pressure, both from development and agriculture. This has begun to have an effect; already the M5 has had a considerable impact on the local character, and most of the former market towns have experienced peripheral growth which does not particularly relate to local styles.

In the more rural areas the appearance is that the integrity of the landscape has been retained. However, trees and woodlands are in decline throughout the Zone and there is a danger that once these have died the Zone will become just another English farming landscape, almost an agricultural 'desert' lacking any distinction save its trademark red soil. This fear is exacerbated by the loss of hedgerows, already very marked in some parts of the Zone.

Undulating farming belt landscape north of Crediton.

9. TEIGN VALLEY

CENTRAL DEVON
9. Teign Valley

LOCATION

The Zone covers the middle Teign Valley, in the south-central part of the County. It abuts the eastern edge of Dartmoor and is centred on the Teign from near Chagford downstream to the neighbourhood of Chudleigh. The course of the river results in the Zone trending west–east between Chagford and Dunsford and north–south between Dunsford and Chudleigh.

DESIGNATIONS

Almost the whole of the west–east element of the Zone falls within the Dartmoor National Park. The Teign itself forms the National Park boundary in most of the north–south element, the west bank being included. The designation highlights the national landscape importance of much of this Zone.

The remainder of the Zone, primarily the east bank of the Teign, but both sides of the Valley in the south, have been designated as an Area of Great Landscape Value, indicating that this area also has a County significance.

KEY CHARACTERISTIC FEATURES

- Distinctive, often intimate valley sandwiched between the highlands of Dartmoor and Great Haldon.

- Valley dominated by woodland on steep, sometimes rocky flanks.

- Small-scale, irregular field pattern with strong hedgebanks.

- Small villages tucked into side valleys away from the main valley.

- Tree-lined river course with stone bridges, weirs, mills and daffodil woods.

DESCRIPTION

The middle Teign Valley is perhaps the most dramatically steep and consistently wooded valley in Devon. As well as this landscape significance in its own right, the valley also provides a steep,

wooded, often rocky flank for much of the eastern boundary of Dartmoor National Park.

Despite its proximity, the high moor is invisible from within the valley and access up on to the high moor appears impossible. The granite influence of the moor intrudes here and there but is not a major factor.

Over the north–south section, the valley is relatively narrow, the steepness of the flanks emphasised by the height of the land on both sides, Haldon to the east and Dartmoor to the west. In turn, the flanks emphasise the valley's depth and give it a distinctive appearance in the landscape. The valley floor is relatively narrow, even in the south, flat-bottomed and marked by the tree-lined course of the river. Although it has a heavily wooded appearance many of the flanks are in fact pastoral, marked by small, irregular fields with good hedges.

Further north the valley deepens and as the Zone reaches the east–west section the Teign Valley

Stone bridge and valley woodlands, Ashton.

has achieved gorge-like proportions of highly dramatic appearance, with rocky outcrops emphasising the steepness and scale of the valley sides. Both sides of the valley are clothed in extensive oak woodlands, many of them of ancient origin. The valley floor here is very narrow and the river is fast-flowing and rocky.

The river is marked by numerous historic stone bridges which give the valley scale, and there are riverside pubs, mills, and weirs. Picturesque villages are found in the side valleys; these are primarily cob or thatched but in the west the granite of Dartmoor begins to make an appearance.

In the south is an area of old metalliferous mines, now largely hidden in the woodland. The same part of the Zone is also home to modern quarry working, although the landscape impact remains generally quite limited.

The 'top' end of the Zone is marked by the change from deep and dramatic valley to the more diffuse landscape of the enclosed Dartmoor fringe. The 'bottom' boundary occurs where the valley widens out into a considerable flood plain immediately below Chudleigh. The Zone being focussed on the valley, the 'side' boundaries are parallel to the river and are designed to include the main side valleys and slopes which are oriented towards the Teign.

SUBJECTIVE RESPONSE

The valley forms a significant element in the landscape of south-central Devon, impacting on the senses not only within the valley itself but over a wider area. The valley and its associated woodland are visible from considerable areas of the neighbouring landscape and form an element throughout much of these surrounding areas.

Within the valley the steep wooded slopes, interspersed with hedged pastoral areas, contrast with a flat-bottomed, open valley floor punctuated by the tree-lined river. Along the valley bottom itself the presence of traffic on the B3193 road means that some of the expected sensual effects, e.g. quietness, remoteness, are lacking. However, paths and lanes up the side valleys soon give rise to these reactions.

In the highest part of the valley, the road leaves the river, which here is lined only by footpaths, and the sights and sounds of the river become paramount. The landscape of the Teign Gorge is as dramatic as any in Devon, or possibly the country, the combination of steep, deep, narrow valley, twisting course, woodlands and nearby moor being awe-inspiring; to cap it, the granite bulk of Lutyens' modern Castle Drogo adds further drama for the senses. Not surprisingly this is a popular recreational area and despite the grandeur of the landscape an 'away-from-it all' feel is hard to achieve, except perhaps during the depths of the winter.

INTEGRITY

The landscape integrity of the Zone has been well retained. Any loss of character is due more to other factors, principally the presence and use of the B3193 road and the popularity of the Teign Gorge area for recreation.

The main landscape impact has arisen from quarrying activities towards the south of the Zone. Here, extensions to quarry workings have occurred which have resulted in realignment and rebuilding of the B3193. Although well screened, the modern standards required do not enhance the local landscape character. However, associated with the quarry extensions and new road, considerable areas of new tree planting will in time help to soften the impact in a locally appropriate way.

The importance of the valley and Gorge woodlands mean that the continuance of this land cover is fundamental to the integrity of the Zone's landscape, so continuing management and appropriate felling regimes are vital to maintain the woodland and thus the landscape character in the longer term.

Built development has been relatively limited. The valley itself is not suitable for development but very limited development has occurred in some of the peripheral villages. Generally, this has not had an impact on the landscape character of the Zone. However, in places development is visible across the valley, e.g. development at Christow visible from the more remote slopes on the east side of the Teign, and care will be needed to ensure that these impacts do not grow to more intrusive levels.

River Teign and ancient oak woodlands, Steps Bridge.

10. HALDON RIDGE

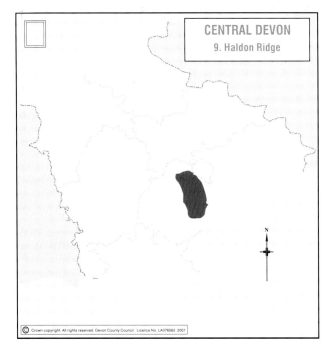

CENTRAL DEVON
9. Haldon Ridge

© Crown copyright. All rights reserved. Devon County Council. Licence No. LA076562 2001

LOCATION

The Zone encompasses the north–south ridge of Great Haldon and Little Haldon, in the south-central part of Devon between the Exe Estuary to the east and the Teign Valley to the west.

DESIGNATIONS

The whole of the Zone has been designated an Area of Great Landscape Value, signifying its landscape importance in a County context.

KEY CHARACTERISTIC FEATURES

- Isolated high ridge forming a dominant back-drop to the Exe Estuary and Exeter, but also to the eastern edge of Dartmoor.

- Extensive coniferous forest area covering former lowland heath.

- Important areas of broad leaved woodland on ridge flanks.

- Forest, open glades, heathland and pasture providing a combination of valuable habitats.

- Major trunk roads dissect the area.

DESCRIPTION

The Haldon Ridge forms a distinctive north–south feature stretching from west of Exeter virtually to the Teign Estuary. Most of the ridge is a relatively narrow feature, falling quite abruptly on the east towards the Exe Estuary and on the west towards the Teign Valley. Fingers of high land reach out east from the main ridge towards the Exe, where they meet and mingle with the landscape of the Exe Estuary lands.

Towards the south the ridge widens very slightly to the area known as Little Haldon, from where it falls abruptly towards the Teign Estuary. The flanks of Little Haldon send their fingers east towards the coastal lands around Dawlish and Teignmouth and west towards the developed area of the Teign flood plain occupied by Newton Abbot and Kingsteignton.

The top of the ridge, especially Great Haldon, the more distinctive northern area, is generally perceived as being an area of coniferous wood-land, although this hides the fact that there is also much mixed woodland and heathland on the generally flat ridge top. The contrasting steep flanks, often cut by side valleys, are also very wooded. Here, however, broad leaved woodland is more common and on much of the ridge side the character is one of often small pastoral fields, patterned by often random hedges.

In the south, Little Haldon is much more open in character with more heathland. The eastern flanks in particular are marked by considerable areas of mixed and broad leaved woodland, especially in one of the major side valleys.

The Zone is crossed by two major roads linking Exeter with the south and west of the County, the A38 to Plymouth and the A380 to Torbay. The roads

The eastern flanks of the Haldon Ridge fall abruptly to the Exe lowlands.

effectively mark the boundary between Great Haldon in the north and Little Haldon in the south and have the effect of cutting the Zone in two. The Zone is also crossed by a major power transmission line.

Not surprisingly there is little settlement within the Zone, this being found only in the form of individual buildings or small hamlets in some of the side valleys. One sizeable settlement, the town of Chudleigh, is situated on the very periphery of the Zone and relates closely to the western flanks of the ridge.

Haldon has a landscape significance not only in its own right but as a backdrop to the landscape of a considerable surrounding area. It provides the characteristic western skyline for Exeter, helping to give the city its rural aspect. It also provides the

The A380 is a significant dividing line over Haldon.

western frame to the Exe Estuary and, distantly, the western skyline from considerable areas of East Devon. In addition it forms a significant skyline for the eastern edge of Dartmoor, almost prolonging the highland feel of the moor to the east.

The eastern, southern and western boundaries of the Zone are very clear, as the ridge lands fall steeply towards the Exe Estuary, the coastal area, the Teign Estuary and the middle Teign Valley. In the north the boundary is less obvious, the landscape merging gradually and almost imperceptibly with a more diffuse, upland pastoral landscape. The Zone boundary reflects the widening of the ridge into this more diffuse landscape and the change of emphasis from woodland and heathland to pasture.

SUBJECTIVE RESPONSE

One of the most defining features of the Haldon Ridge is the range of spectacular views offered over the surrounding landscape. Often, given the relative narrowness of the ridge, views to the east and west are in close proximity. These views, of the contrast between the very steep higher slopes, often forested, and the more pastoral and less obviously aligned lower slopes reaching to estuary, valley or sea, create a very positive impression. The Zone is probably unique in Devon for its range of views and ridge scenery.

On the ridge itself the combination of woodland, heathland and views create a highly individual and remarkable character. Much of the area is popular as a recreational area and certain locations can be well used as a result of its landscape attractions, but it is possible to experience the character of the area allied to quietness away from the 'honey-pots'.

To the south, Little Haldon offers a different character as a result of its more open aspect. It is also more obviously aligned to the sea, with long-range views along the coastline. This creates a less enclosed, more airy, open character. However, it also means that a feeling of seclusion is more difficult to experience than in the more wooded areas to the north.

In the centre of the Zone, the A38 and the A380 roads have created a corridor of fast-moving traffic crossing the ridge. This has resulted in Great Haldon and Little Haldon being almost divorced from each other physically and psychologically. There is also intrusion into the character of the Zone as a result of traffic noise. However, given the thickly wooded nature of the Zone here, the sights and sounds of the roads have been considerably masked, and intrusion is very limited.

Heathland on Little Haldon.

The ridge is an important landscape feature viewed from most directions, adding to the landscape attraction of neighbouring areas, including the Exe and Teign estuaries, the East Devon pebble bed commons and the eastern and south-eastern flanks of Dartmoor. It also helps to define the landscape setting of Exeter as well as other settlements such as Dawlish and Teignmouth. In this context, the ridge top and flanking woodlands are especially important, and the significant skyline landmark of Haldon Belvedere is a defining feature.

In a Devon-wide sense, Haldon marks the divide between essentially lowland landscapes to the east and highland areas to the west, creating both a physical and psychological boundary. As such, it forms the southern-most end of a national boundary between highland and lowland Britain, traditionally said to stretch from Exe to Tees.

INTEGRITY

It must be acknowledged that the original landscape character of the Zone was essentially heathland, and that this now constitutes a fairly small proportion of the landscape, certainly on Great Haldon. However, the quality of the current prevailing landscape cover, commercial forest, does seem well suited to the topography both in internal Zone terms and as viewed from afar. In conjunction with such heathland as does exist, as well as broad leaved woodland, the essentials of the ridge scenery remain in good condition. Little Haldon has remained more typical of the traditional landscape, Teignmouth Golf Course excepted.

Although the landscape character can probably sustain the loss of heathland which has occurred,

it will be important to maintain the balance which has been achieved and to consider the balance in any future land-use regimes.

The character of the flanks remains in good condition. The major loss of integrity has been the removal of hedges, especially on the eastern boundary of the Zone, which has created a more open, hedgeless landscape in a few places, less in tune with its surroundings.

As discussed above, the presence of the A38 and A380 has affected the landscape integrity. Although largely hidden by the topography, as well as being screened by woodland, there are nevertheless areas where the sight and sound of these roads is to the detriment of the landscape's character, as is the existence of prominent ancillary facilities such as filling stations.

Forestry and heath, the main landscape constituents on the Haldon summit.

CULM MEASURES

The name 'Culm Measures' is a term based on geological usage. The greatest thickness of rocks of Carboniferous age in Devon is made up of an alternating sequence of shales, sandstones and mudstones generally referred to by this local name. Within this rock sequence there are occasional areas of harder slates and schists and rocks of igneous origin formed as a result of later volcanic activity.

Not surprisingly, the landscape will also vary along with the variation in the geological detail.

However, there is enough similarity to include the six Landscape Character Zones found on the Culm Measures in one overall grouping.

The Culm Measures cover an enormous area of Devon, at least a quarter of the County's surface. From east to west they stretch from the outskirts of Exeter to the Cornish border while from north to south they reach between Exmoor and Dartmoor. Within such an area the landscape details will obviously show considerable variation, and this grouping includes wild, wind-battered coastlines, secretive wooded valleys, areas of high semi-moorland and swathes of coniferous forestry.

Despite these variations, the overall character of the Culm Measure landscapes is held together by the factors of relative height, levelness, a pastoral agricultural economy and sparse population. These factors mean that the boundaries between the Culm Measure Zones are more subtle than many, often forming a zone of transition rather than a clear-cut line. Although incorporating some of the least known parts of the County, the area is in some ways the most archetypal landscape in Devon, more than red cliffs, tors or sandy beaches.

Over a Culm Measures landscape towards Dartmoor.

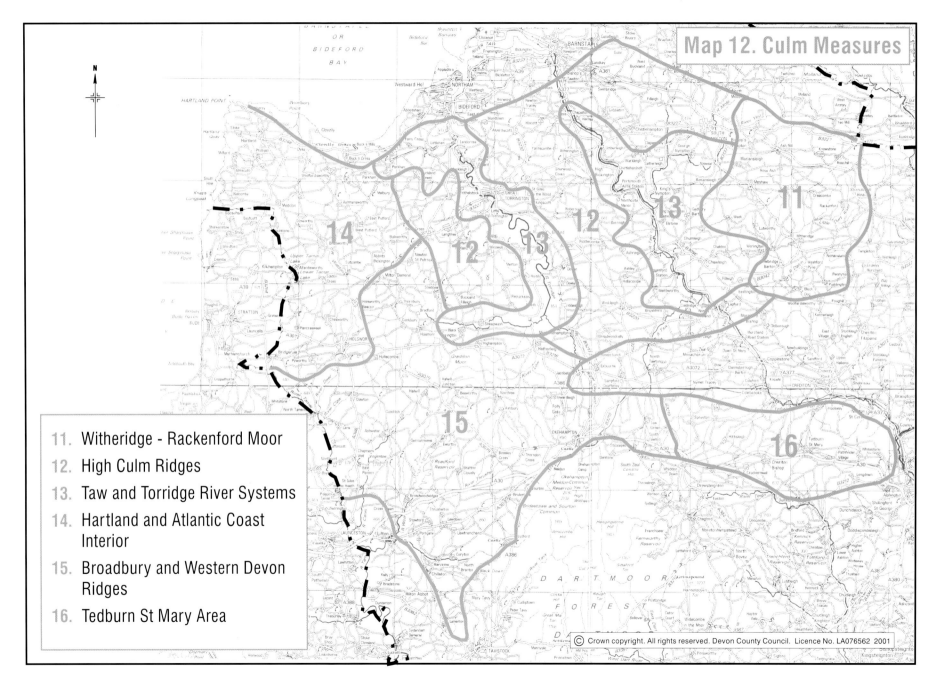

Map 12. Culm Measures

11. Witheridge - Rackenford Moor
12. High Culm Ridges
13. Taw and Torridge River Systems
14. Hartland and Atlantic Coast Interior
15. Broadbury and Western Devon Ridges
16. Tedburn St Mary Area

11. WITHERIDGE – RACKENFORD MOOR

CULM MEASURES
11. Witheridge - Rackenford Moor

LOCATION

This Zone is situated in the north-eastern part of the County, to the south of Exmoor. It is flanked by the upper Exe Valley to the east and the valley systems of the Taw and its tributary the Mole to the west.

DESIGNATIONS

The north-eastern part of the Zone has been designated as an Area of Great Landscape Value (AGLV), indicating a County landscape significance. Although the bulk of this AGLV covers the Exe Valley, the extension into this Zone reflects the importance of the major areas of unimproved Culm grassland, centered on Knowstone and Rackenford Moors and Hares Down.

KEY CHARACTERISTIC FEATURES

- High, undulating series of ridges.

- Extensive views north and south.

- Mosaic of improved and unimproved grassland with generally straight-edged fields, often with beech hedges.

- Distinctive tree groups, generally beech and pine.

- Outgrown hedgerows often forming skyline features.

- Some small woodlands in sheltered locations and larger conifer plantations.

- North Devon Link A361 cuts across the Zone.

Unimproved grassland, Hares Down.

DESCRIPTION

The Zone is generally high, over 200m in height. While part of the Zone appears to have a plateau-like character, it is formed by a series of ridges, some more clear-cut than others. Cutting into this highland area are a number of rivers, mostly flowing east or west into the neighbouring major valley systems. These rivers, such as the Little Dart, the Dalch and the Crooked Oak, form quite significant valleys somewhat different in appearance and character to the bulk of the Zone.

The geology has created poor soils and drainage problems which have strongly influenced the landscape of the Zone. The overall appearance is something of a patchwork of unimproved Culm grassland interspersed with improved pasture. The former gives something of a bleak, rough, moorland quality and is found primarily in the northern part of the Zone. Here, on areas such as Hares Down, Knowstone Moor, Rackenford Moor, Luckett Moor and Paul's Moor is a landscape reminiscent of some of the higher parts of Exmoor. Hedges are few but, where they exist, are typically beech. Many have grown out to form attractive skyline tree features. Occasional wind-trimmed beech and pine groups add to the landscape, whose moorland quality is emphasised by the views to Exmoor.

Further south, improved grassland becomes more the norm. Hedgerows are more common, often severely trimmed, and form large, straight-edged fields. Hedgerow trees are also a feature here, especially on roadsides. The contrast with the north of the Zone is heightened by the views, which here are characteristically towards Dartmoor rather than Exmoor.

Throughout the Zone are a number of valleys, marked landscape features characterised by valley woodlands, and smaller, sometimes more irregular, fields. For the most part the valley bottoms are narrow, but they tend to be much more populated than the heights.

The Zone generally carries a sparse population. There are few settlements through the bulk of the Zone, but a few villages are found on the margins and in the occasional lower locations. Some of the smaller villages seem almost to huddle in a valley or hollow and, with cob and thatch frequent building materials, they can present an attractive face in contrast to the open landscapes on the higher areas. However, Witheridge, the main settlement of the Zone, stands relatively high, above the neighbouring valleys, its church tower making something of a landmark.

While settlements have not impinged on the landscape, one development feature has. The A361 North Devon Link road crosses the Zone from east to west, bisecting Knowstone Moor, Hares Down and Rackenford Moor, the three largest areas of unimproved Culm grassland, with an inevitable landscape effect.

The northern boundary of the Zone largely coincides with the valley of one of Devon's many Rivers Yeo, this Yeo being a tributary of the Mole and effectively marking the edge of the Exmoor fringe area. To the east the Zone excludes the tributaries of the Exe as they become significant features, although on the higher land the Zone boundary is more amorphous. A similar situation exists on the western boundary with the Taw and the Mole and their tributaries. The southern boundary marks the transition to a lower, more complex topography and the more fertile red soils of Devon's farming belt.

SUBJECTIVE RESPONSE

Over most of the Zone the character is determined by the height and by the ever-present views of Exmoor or Dartmoor, and occasionally both. This creates a feeling of airy openness, accentuated where the Culm grassland is unimproved and the hedges less obvious. Often, a feeling of remoteness is experienced, resulting from these open characteristics and the lack of settlements. Only where the A361 is an obvious factor is this experience lost.

A different experience occurs in the more significant river valleys, although remoteness is also a factor here. The more enclosed nature, accentuated by the narrow valley bottoms, generates a secluded character. In many cases this may be quite literally true, some of the valleys having no roads or public paths.

INTEGRITY

The unimproved Culm grasslands of this Zone give some idea of how large areas of Devon would have looked in the past, before agricultural developments, drainage, ploughing and fertilisers. It is therefore perhaps ironic that it is the more extensive such grasslands of the Zone whose landscape integrity has been compromised by the building of the A361.

The road and its consequent sight and sound, together with the service area at Beaple's Moor, are perhaps the most significant impacts on the integrity of this Zone. It has not in the past been a part of Devon under particular pressure and this is perhaps the reason why it continues to exhibit a face of Devon's past. It is, however, important that no further incursions are made on the landscape and character of this Zone, so that what does remain can be retained.

The A361 has an impact on the landscape of Rackenford Moor.

12. HIGH CULM RIDGES

CULM MEASURES
12. High Culm Ridges

© Crown copyright. All rights reserved. Devon County Council. Licence No. LA076562 2001

LOCATION

This Zone comprises two separate areas in north-central Devon, separated by the Torridge Valley. The more easterly occupies an area between the valleys of the Taw and the Torridge, crossing the Taw in its higher course towards the River Dalch. In the north this part of the Zone also crosses the Taw to include the prominent landmark of Codden Hill as well as the valley of the Venn Brook and its headwaters which flow though Swimbridge and Landkey.

The westerly element of the Zone is found immediately to the west of the Torridge Valley in its middle course.

DESIGNATIONS

Most of the Zone is uncovered by any landscape designation. However, in the north-east an area has been designated as an Area of Great landscape Value (AGLV), indicating its importance as a County landscape. This designation covers the high land on the northern side of the east–west tributary valley in this part of the Zone, effectively the 'foreland' of the inter-valley high lands east of Barnstaple. It also covers Codden Hill, a prominent landscape feature adjacent to the same valley.

A very small section of AGLV is also found to the north-east of Winkleigh, where it spills over from the Taw Valley.

Atherington Church forms a landmark for the adjacent valley.

KEY CHARACTERISTIC FEATURES

- Exposed broad ridges with few trees except for isolated trees and clumps and some conifer plantations.

- Pastoral landscape with regular, rectangular fields and hedges.

- Scattered farmsteads, hamlets and high villages.

- Prominent landmarks of churches and chapels, also aerials, pylons and hilltop farm buildings.

- High concentrations of species-rich grasslands.

- Wide views.

DESCRIPTION

The two elements of the Zone have very similar characteristics. Both are essentially high, but rather than an undifferentiated plateau, both represent a series of broad, high ridges, interspersed with noticeable, although never dominant, valleys. The geology of the Culm has resulted in an area of generally poor drainage, dominated by grassland. Most has been improved, although there are remnant areas of unimproved pasture, the texture of which has an impact on the landscape. This is more obvious in the western element of the Zone, the eastern area having a more intensive improved pastoral system. The fields tend to be rectangular in shape with a fairly strong hedgerow pattern. Smaller fields are found in the shallow valleys.

The Zone has few trees, although some isolated trees and clumps on skylines form strong landscape elements. There are some small plantations of conifers.

Settlement is generally sparse, especially on the higher ridges. However, such settlements as do exist are often prominent, be they individual farms, hamlets or villages. Some such hilltop villages, and especially their church towers, are particularly important as skyline features over a wide area. This tendency is strengthened by the frequent occurrence of such settlements towards the edge of the Zone, overlooking lower land. Less welcome features can also be prominent, including power lines, pylons and aerials.

The height of the Zone results in extensive views in most directions, especially from the Zone's margins. The most impressive are in the north, where views encompass elements of the North Devon coast from Hartland Point to Baggy Point. Dartmoor and, in the north and east, Exmoor, also feature prominently in the views.

The topography of this part of Devon means that the Zone frames the setting of neighbouring, lower Zones, especially that of the Taw and Torridge river valleys.

In the north-east the Zone is a little different in character and appearance. Here it takes in the east–west valley of a tributary of the Taw, a more marked valley than is included elsewhere, with noticeable valley sides patterned with hedges and copses and a clear, if narrow, valley bottom. Next to the valley it also includes the landmark of Codden Hill, a large hogsback feature very prominent in the landscape of a large area of North Devon.

The eastern element of the Zone has boundaries largely dictated by the adjacent Taw and Torridge valleys. To the north its boundary respectively marks the fall to the lower lands backing the Taw and Torridge estuaries, the northern edge of the east-west valley between Barnstaple and Filleigh, and the more dissected Exmoor fringe area. In the south, the lower, more fertile redlands of central Devon mark the boundary.

The western element of the Zone is clearly differentiated from the Torridge Valley to its east, but the western boundary is less clear, fading gradually into the high, maritime-influenced and increasingly windswept high lands of the Atlantic interior or the remote, infertile areas to the south-west.

SUBJECTIVE RESPONSE

A combination of height and often impressive views gives the Zone its character. Views towards the north are especially noteworthy, giving the feeling of having a bird's eye view over the coast. Elsewhere, the presence of Dartmoor can seem dominant, especially in the southern parts of the Zone.

The character is open rather than intimate, and the response is one of being impressed rather than charmed. A generally remote character is also encountered, although this can sometimes be reduced by the fairly frequent hilltop farms, aerials and power lines.

The north-east of the Zone is different, and the valley east of Landkey is more reminiscent of the Taw and Torridge valley systems. The presence of the A361 North Devon Link also adds a different dimension to this part of the Zone. Codden Hill also is different, a hogsback feature of great importance to the landscape of a wide area of North Devon. Views from, and perhaps even more important, views of Codden Hill have a great impact over a wide area.

Hill top farm on High Culm near Torrington.

INTEGRITY

A lack of development pressure has meant that the general integrity of the landscape of the area is largely intact. There are, however, some developments which have had an effect. These include the building of the A361 North Devon Link east of Barnstaple, which has altered the character of this valley. The hilltop aerials and power lines found in a number of locations reduce the sense of remoteness and impact not only on the Zone itself but on views to it from surrounding lower land. Hilltop farms can have a similar, if lesser, impact although here there may be more historic validity for their existence; nevertheless modern materials do not enhance the effect.

One area of substantial impact occurs in the clay quarrying activity based on the Petrockstowe area in the western element of the Zone. This has an effect on the local landscape integrity; restoration measures have helped lessen the effect, but the essential shape and character of the landscape is adversely affected. In addition, the quiet and remote nature of the area is affected by noise and by heavy vehicle movements associated with the quarrying.

The Zone is one where trees are not common and it may be that the restoration and/or maintenance of tree groups, clumps and shelterbelts would help the integrity of the landscape by off-setting their gradual loss by age and disease. However, the essence of the landscape's character is such that large-scale tree planting would need to be very carefully positioned. The Zone lies within the area of the South West Forest and it would be important that any planting associated with the Forest did not adversely affect the integrity of the Zone's character.

Further, the nature of the Zone could well make it attractive for such developments as wind farms. The loss of character such developments would cause must give rise to caution.

Wide views to the North Devon coast from near Alverdiscott.

13. TAW AND TORRIDGE RIVER SYSTEMS

CULM MEASURES

13. Taw and Torridge River Systems

LOCATION

This Zone is in the north-central part of the County, comprising the middle and lower valleys of the Taw and Torridge rivers and the valleys of some of their most notable tributaries, including the Mole, the lower Little Dart and the Mully Brook (tributaries of the Taw), and the Yeo, Duntz and Langtree Lake (tributaries of the Torridge). The Zone comprises two discrete parts, centred on the two major rivers, separated by an area of High Culm ridges.

DESIGNATIONS

The majority of the Zone has been designated as an Area of Great Landscape Value, reflecting its landscape importance in the County context. Some of the peripheral flanking land which has been included in this Zone has not been part of the designated area, neither has the highest part of the Torridge Valley which is within this Zone, between Huish and Black Torrington.

KEY CHARACTERISTIC FEATURES

- Natural river form, tree-lined banks and associated water features.

- Substantial woodland, broadleaved and coniferous, emphasising the distinctive landform and creating enclosure.

- Open valley floor with pastoral and sometimes parkland character.

- Roads, railways and bridges along the length of the valleys, few routes across the valley floors, steep wooded winding routes out of the valleys.

- High villages and farms overlooking the valleys.

DESCRIPTION

The Taw and the Torridge, together with their major tributaries, comprise two important valley systems which deeply dissect the predominantly high land of the Culm Measures of this part of Devon. The pronounced valleys which these two rivers and their tributaries have formed provide a dramatically different landscape to the more exposed open ridges which flank them.

The Taw flows northwards across Devon from Dartmoor, while the Torridge follows a strange U-shaped course with its source not a great distance from its estuary. However, the characteristic landscape which marks this Zone begins where the rivers and their tributaries start to carve a distinctive landform feature in their middle and lower courses.

The Zone is characterised by the steep, wooded landscape of the valley sides. Broadleaved and coniferous woodland merges quite naturally in these valleys and, although the valleys in reality are less wooded than appears at first sight, woodland remains the characteristic landscape type. Nevertheless, many valley sides are pastoral, with clear hedgerows marking the flanks. Fields are usually straight-edged, but in certain locations knots of small, irregular fields occur.

The Torridge valley near Torrington.

The valley-bottom flood plains are relatively open pasture land with few field boundaries. The valley floor is punctuated by the sinuous course of the tree-lined river and in a number of places in both valleys large estates have created parkland scenery which is especially visible on the valley floor.

In both valleys settlement is more likely to be found on the valley side, or in a side valley, than on the floor, although examples of riverside settlements are found, especially on the Torridge. Notable in landscape terms are the prominent settlements on the edge of the flanking high land, actually situated outside this Zone. The settlements, and especially such features as their church towers, form an important backdrop in long-range views over the Zone.

The lateral boundaries of both parts of the Zone naturally occur at the brow of the flanking highland, although here and there some overlap does occur between the tributaries. The northern end of the Zone occurs where the respective valleys open out into their higher estuaries at a wide flood plain, between Chapelton and Bishop's Tawton on the Taw and just above Bideford on the Torridge. The 'upstream' boundary occurs where the valleys cease to be a distinctive element in the landscape but rather an integral part of it. This occurs near Lapford on the Taw and Black Torrington on the Torridge.

SUBJECTIVE RESPONSE

The valleys provide an intricate, complex and varied landscape, especially compared to the landscape of the wider area in this part of Devon. The woodland and the slopes combine with bends and spurs in the valleys hiding views onward. Bridges, mills and even major tributaries are hidden until the very last moment. Tightly wooded sections unexpectedly open out to display quite wide vistas across broad valley bottoms. In places, the mixture of broadleaved and coniferous woodland gives rise to a character reminiscent of continental Europe, a feature especially noticeable at Eggesford on the Taw. Elsewhere, tranquil parkland provides the valleys with a soothing atmosphere.

Roads run the length of the Taw Valley as well as along the lower part of the Torridge, so seclusion is not totally part of the character of these parts of the Zone. Even here, however, it is possible to escape from the influence of the roads, helped by the masking effect of the woodland and the character of neither valley could be described as busy. An even quieter character is evident in some of the tributary valleys and in the higher part of the Torridge Valley.

The valleys have their impact on neighbouring areas. A characteristic experience is to see the tops of trees in one of the valleys while on the neighbouring heights, a view inviting curiosity and exploration.

Above: *The valley system cuts into the surrounding higher land near Umberleigh.*

Below: *One of the intimate tributary valleys, near King's Nympton*

INTEGRITY

The characteristics of this Zone have been well maintained. The essential complex mix of woodland, pasture and hedgerow, interspersed with parkland features, all within a dramatic and distinctive valley setting, remains in basically good heart. Such valleys contribute to the overall essence of Devon and their integrity is to be valued.

It is to be hoped that management of the characteristic valley woodlands remains ongoing to produce the aesthetically pleasing land cover typical of the Zone; there is no reason to suppose this will not continue, but so fundamental is it to the character of the Zone that it is to be emphasised.

Otherwise, the only factor to raise is the impact of the major roads. The Taw Valley road, once a major link between Exeter and Barnstaple, has now been superseded and no longer exerts an overriding influence on the character of its valley. In the Torridge Valley, the A386 road between Bideford and Torrington is well used and can impact on the valley's character in places, although it is usually possible to escape its sight and sounds. Nevertheless, any measures which helped screen these roads from the bulk of the valleys, and especially the rivers themselves, would add to the overall integrity of the Zone.

The Taw also has its railway line, the Tarka Line, between Exeter and Barnstaple. Although frequently raised on an embankment, the railway is not intrusive and arguably adds character to the scene, emphasised by the small settlements gathered around the stations and level crossings. The railway can also help maintain the integrity of the valley's character offering an ideal way to experience its landscape.

The Torridge's railway, between Bideford and Torrington and then up the valley of the tributary Langtree Lake, now forms part of the Tarka Trail footpath and cycle route and as such also provides a means of appreciating the landscape while maintaining its integrity.

As it becomes tidal, the Torridge Valley opens out at Landcross.

14. HARTLAND AND ATLANTIC COAST INTERIOR

CULM MEASURES
14. Hartland and Atlantic Coast Interior

LOCATION

The Zone occupies the north western corner of Devon, from Hartland Point to the Cornwall border, then south to Bridgerule, east to Holsworthy, north-east to Stibb Cross and north to Parkham.

DESIGNATIONS

The north-western corner of the Zone, between the A39 and the coast, is designated as part of the North Devon Area of Outstanding Natural Beauty (AONB). This reflects the national importance of the landscape in this area, particularly in relation to its coastal scenery. Within the AONB, a narrower coastal strip has the Devon County Council designation of Coastal Preservation Area, and has also been defined as Heritage Coast by the Countryside Agency.

KEY CHARACTERISTIC FEATURES

- Storm-lashed coastline with salt-laden winds influencing vegetation far inland.

- Spectacular geological cliff formations, including coastal waterfalls.

- Severely deformed hedgerow trees and stunted woodlands in coastal valleys.

- Clustered hamlets and regularly spaced sizeable historic villages.

- Rectilinear field pattern.

- Poorly drained rough pasture, commons and conifer blocks.

DESCRIPTION

The coast of this Zone is arguably the most dramatic in Devon. The rugged scenery of spectacular geological cliff formations with characteristic jagged fingers of rock reaching seawards faces the full fury of the Atlantic swell. This coastal landscape is backed by a generally flat clifftop area of gorse, low scrub and stunted trees. Narrow sheltered coastal combes contain ivy-covered ancient woodlands.

Inland, the predominant appearance of the landscape is of a gently undulating tableland. The landscape is dominated by the sky, with occasional long-range views to the coast to the west, including the Cornish coast over the county boundary. There are few trees but wind-trimmed hedgerow trees and tree groups add to the landscape's coastal influence. Small woods occur in sheltered locations and especially towards the north of the Zone there are some coniferous plantations.

The Zone is crossed by river valleys, of the higher Tamar in the west, the Waldon in the centre and the higher Torridge in the east. The valleys become less noticeable as individual features as they approach their respective sources but within this Zone are rarely especially distinct from the wider landscape in which they sit, other than as relatively wide and shallow elements in the overall plateau, with perhaps a reduced coastal influence.

Unimproved grassland in the upper Torridge Valley.

Towards the east the coastal influences also diminish. More shelterbelts are found and there are roadside tree lines and these more general inland Culm Measure features increase towards and over the Zone boundary.

Settlement is clustered in hamlets, occasionally in lone, often whitewashed cottages, which add to the coastal atmosphere. There are also quite characteristic clustered larger villages, often gathered round a village square, as at Hartland, Bradworthy or Woolfardisworthy, or a village that has grown to become the local centre, Holsworthy. The church towers of these villages are visible over a long distance in this open landscape, and at Hartland the tower is also an historic daymark for mariners.

The field pattern tends to be rectilinear and the fields relatively large. Around some of the settle-

Knife-edged rock stretches into the Atlantic, near Hartland Quay.

ments smaller rectilinear fields reflect an historic pattern as at Bradworthy, Woolfardisworthy and Hartland, and also on some of the 'moors' south of Hartland. Here and elsewhere in the Zone are areas of unimproved grassland, whose colour and texture has an impact on the landscape.

The eastern and southern boundaries of the Zone are relatively imprecise, marking the area where coastal influences become less obvious than those of the inland Culm Measures. In the east the high ridges take over from the more general tableland of this Zone while to the south coniferous plantations and views of Dartmoor and Bodmin Moor become more dominant landscape features.

In the north the boundary of the Zone is more abrupt, generally coinciding with the edge of the tableland feature, beyond which the broken coastal landscape of Bideford Bay shows a markedly different character.

SUBJECTIVE RESPONSE

The drama of the coastal landscape leaves an indelible impression. The rugged cliffs marked by geological features at seemingly impossible angles, the knife-edged rock fingers stretching into the Atlantic, the coastal waterfalls, the almost invariable wind and swell, make this not only Devon's most impressive coastal landscape but one of England's. Add to this the contrast of the narrow, secretive coastal combes, with small stunted woodlands huddled for shelter, and the character produced is truly remarkable.

Inland, the generally level nature of the terrain, dominated by the wind and the sky, adds to the unfettered, coastal feel. This is often emphasised by the appearance of individual wind-shaped trees

and lonely, whitewashed cottages. Even the larger settlements seem to gather together for shelter from the elements. The colours and textures of unimproved grassland further emphasise the character.

The Zone inland also offers occasional distant coastal views, again adding to the wild, 'end-of-the-earth' atmosphere. Even where the sea is not actually visible its proximity seems to add a distinctive, almost luminous, light to the landscape.

INTEGRITY

This Zone displays a highly distinctive landscape character which has retained this individuality very well. However, given its open nature, and the importance this very nature has to the character of the landscape, there is a vulnerability.

In the north of the Zone there are blocks of coniferous plantations, and these tend to intrude on the open nature of the Zone's landscape. These sound a warning on the impact of such developments. The Zone lies within the South West Forest area and it is important that if any planting is envisaged under this project it does not have an adverse effect on the essential landscape.

In similar vein, the Zone is probably attractive in principle to developments such as wild farms. Again, the impact on the character of this landscape would be immense.

The presence of unimproved grassland also adds to the wild and almost untamed character, and any large-scale loss of this feature would also have a detrimental effect on the landscape.

15. BROADBURY AND WESTERN DEVON RIDGES

CULM MEASURES
15. Broadbury and Western Devon Ridges

Crown copyright. All rights reserved. Devon County Council. Licence No. LA076562 2001

LOCATION

This very large Zone covers an extensive area from the north-western edge of Dartmoor to the Cornwall border, with extensions east along Dartmoor's northern fringe and north along the upper Torridge. It thus comprises a large proportion of west-central Devon.

DESIGNATIONS

There is an area in the south of the Zone which has been designated as an Area of Great Landscape Value, recognising its County landscape importance. This area reflects the Lyd and Lew Valleys which cross this part of the Zone.

KEY CHARACTERISTIC FEATURES

- Vast catchment area of streams and rivers, including Roadford Reservoir.

- High rainfall, heavy soils, wet pastures, unimproved grassland.

- High land dominated by views of Dartmoor and, more distantly, Bodmin Moor.

- Extensive coniferous plantations with pockets of wet pasture and secondary woodland.

- Individual hedgerow trees and oak-lined field boundaries.

- Sparsely populated 'frontier' area.

- General features interrupted by softer, lusher river valleys.

DESCRIPTION

The Zone is centred on the watershed ridge of Broadbury, a high, flat-topped area flanked by relatively gentle sides. The edge trends in a north-west to south-east direction and rivers flow from this broad ridgeland east and north towards the Torridge on one side, or south and west towards the Tamar on the other. Broadbury is flanked by a series of wide, gentle ridges between more marked valleys, and it is this series of high, undulating ridges which characterises the Zone.

Forestry plantations near Clawton.

The poor wet soil of these uplands, combined with the high rainfall sweeping in from the west, has given rise to a agricultural economy based on sheep farming. Over the centuries the pasture has been drained and improved in many areas, although the essential wetness and heaviness of the land remains. The improved pasture gives rise to a clear hedgerow pattern, generally of straight-edged fields which tend towards the larger size. The hedges are characterised by frequent and prominent hedgerow trees, sometimes giving rise to lines of field-edge trees. This creates a relatively wooded appearance over much of the Zone. The pattern is interspersed with areas of unimproved grassland and wet scrubby woodland which emphasise the wet and exposed nature of the Zone.

In some places large estates have been established and these give rise to more extensive woodland areas and features such as hilltop clumps. Limited areas of parkland landscape may also be associated with these estates.

To the north of the Zone especially, the landscape has been affected by extensive coniferous forestry plantations. These, sometimes quite large, blocks can give an appearance of continuous dark woodland, although the forestry is actually interspersed with pockets of rush-covered grassland and wet scrubby woodland.

The Zone is crossed by a number of river valleys which create a contrasting landscape to the high, wet and open character of the ridges. The Tamar marks the western boundary, both of the Zone and of the County, and with its tributaries the Claw and the Deer, forms a distinctive feature of flat-bottomed, tree-lined valley, quite wooded and with a much more intimate scale than the mostly open character of the ridges. Other valleys, of the Carey, Thrushel and Wolf are similar in character, although the Wolf Valley is distinguished by the presence of the extensive water body of Roadford Reservoir. In the south, the valleys of the Lyd and Lew are even more distinctive, forming clearly defined and often quite dramatic features cut into the surrounding higher land. The slopes of these valleys are relatively steep and often thickly wooded, the valley floors flat and pastoral, the landscape intimate and small-scale.

Settlement is sparse and generally confined to hamlets or individual farms. Some have grown into small villages, but the only sizeable towns are on the very edges of the Zone, Okehampton at one end and Holsworthy just over the Zone boundary at the opposite end.

The Lyd Valley near Sydenham, a contrasting landscape to the high ridges.

Everywhere in the Zone the landscape is overlooked by Dartmoor, emphasising its open, almost undeveloped nature, and in many places Bodmin Moor forms the western horizon, adding to this atmosphere.

The western boundary of the Zone coincides with the County boundary with Cornwall at the Tamar Valley. The valley landscape of the Zone is mirrored on the Cornish side. To the north the Zone's boundary marks the gradual transition to the slightly lower landscape, more obviously maritime affected and less marked by ridges, of the Atlantic Coast interior. The Torridge Valley and the drier, more definite ridges of the northern Culm limit the Zone to the north-east. In the east the boundaries are dictated by the fertile red lands and the wooded, dissected landscape towards Tedburn St Mary, and in the south by the abrupt edge of the high moorland of Dartmoor and the lusher valley lands of the Tamar.

SUBJECTIVE RESPONSE

The high ridges form the backbone of the Zone's landscape character. Here the landscape is dominated by height, by the wind and rain and infertile soils. It is a character shaped by the huge source of water draining off Dartmoor and by the vast catchment lands of the Tamar and the Torridge.

The topography, the climate, the wide views, the brooding presence of Dartmoor and, to an extent, Bodmin Moor on the skyline combine with the dark coniferous woodlands and the lack of settlement to create the atmosphere of a 'frontier' area, heightened by the actual frontier between Saxon Devon and Celtic Cornwall on the western edge of the Zone. The frequently straight roads add to this impression. It is further emphasised by the colour and texture of the unimproved grassland and by the frequent wet, often unmanaged, scrubby woodland which is found throughout the mosaic of land cover.

This almost undeveloped atmosphere diminishes to the east, as the Zone becomes gradually more intensively farmed, and in the valleys, whose more intimate landscape and more human scale are perhaps less forbidding. In most of the valleys however, the influence of the character of the heights is never completely absent. At Roadford Reservoir, in the Wolf Valley, the wide waterscape forms an especially close link between the two elements.

Only in the Lyd and Lew Valleys in the south of the Zone does the character so markedly vary that the fundamental subjective response is different. Here the more complex, wooded valley landscape with flat pastoral floors creates a real contrast to the heights, emphasising the respective very different attractions of both landscapes.

INTEGRITY

The generally open character of the Zone is an important part of the essence of Devon, the area covering such a large part of the County. It is, by its nature, relatively vulnerable. Already, impacts have occurred as a result of the coniferous woodland planting although so far this has tendered to complement the 'frontier' landscape rather than threaten it. It is important that such developments do not destroy the mosaic-like character that typifies this part of the Zone. Although further forestry planting is possibly not out of character in certain locations, it is necessary that this only occurs where it would be in sympathy with the landscape mosaic, and South West Forest proposals should reflect this.

The influence of the wind on the essence of the Zone would be attractive to developments such as wind farms. Again, the essential character of the Zone is vulnerable to such development, which would not be in sympathy with the remote, open feel.

The valleys have largely retained their essential integrity of character. As a foil to the more austere ridges it is important that this continues and that management of the valley woodlands is an activity which receives appropriate backing.

16. TEDBURN ST MARY AREA

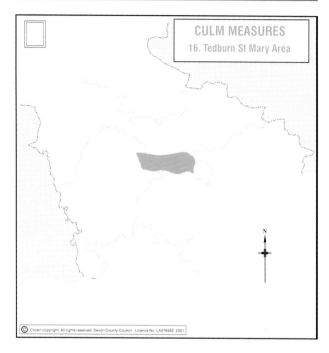

CULM MEASURES
16. Tedburn St Mary Area

LOCATION

The Zone comprises an area in the centre of Devon, stretching from the outskirts of Exeter west to a line between North Tawton and Whiddon Down. It is relatively narrow in a north–south direction.

DESIGNATIONS

Most of the Zone has been designated as an Area of Great Landscape Value, indicating a County landscape importance. South-west of Cheriton Bishop a small part of the Zone falls within the Dartmoor National Park boundary. A few parts of the north of the Zone, south of Crediton, have not received a landscape designation.

KEY CHARACTERISTIC FEATURES

- Panoramic views north over red Devon, south over the Teign, Haldon and the Exe Estuary and east over Exeter.

- Hilly landform backed by Dartmoor skyline.

- Dense network of narrow winding lanes with high hedgebanks.

- Secluded thatched cottages hidden in wooded valleys.

- Numerous small woodland and hedgerow trees.

DESCRIPTION

The main feature of the Zone is height, certainly relative to the surrounding land. The essence is elevated pasture, well dotted with woodland and hedges and scattered settlements. The hedgerow pattern is often irregular, but tends more towards the rectangular on the higher slopes. The presence of Dartmoor on the skyline is integral to the Zone, especially in the west.

The Zone is shaped by a series of valleys, mostly small, narrow and winding, generally with fast-flowing streams lined with woodland at their bottoms. The valleys tend to be quite random in pattern, although the area is also crossed by one or two slightly larger valleys, generally in a south to north direction, which display similar characteristics on a slightly larger scale.

The result of the extensive valley woodlands and the hedgerow trees and woodland blocks on the higher land is to create a strong woodland network which helps to retain a small-scale landscape over the whole Zone. The landscape character is thus far more intimate than that of other essentially high Character Zones.

The Zone has a maze of narrow winding lanes, following ridgelines or the sinuous valleys and linking isolated farmsteads. Many are lined by high hedgebanks but where views are possible from the ridges they are often very panoramic. The ridgetop roads often have wide verges supporting wild flowers and unimproved grassland. Some of the lanes dropping into the valleys cut through the crumbling rock to display the yellow clayey soil.

In contrast to the minor roads, the A30 carves its way across the Zone in an east–west direction, numerous shallow cuttings being necessary in the

Hills and valleys, woodland and hedges; near Whitestone.

undulating landform. To a considerable extent however, the design of the A30 has succeeded in achieving a very limited effect on the landscape.

Large villages are rare, although Tedburn St Mary acts as a local focus. Cheriton Bishop in the south and Spreyton in the west are the only other villages, a settlement pattern of scattered isolated farmsteads being typical. These are often hidden away in the wooded valleys, but sometimes more prominent, almost hilltop farms are found. However, because of the relatively complex topography and presence of woodland these farms rarely impinge greatly on the landscape.

In the north the complex highland topography falls abruptly to the valley of the Crediton Yeo and the flat redlands from Colebrooke through Bow to North Tawton, and this line marks the Zone's boundary. In the south-west the dramatic gorge of the Teign Valley marks the boundary while to the south-east a less definite boundary is marked by the gradual transition to the narrow north–south Haldon Ridge. To the west the landscape is much less dissected and also generally lower, while the eastern end of the Zone ends abruptly on the outskirts of Exeter.

SUBJECTIVE RESPONSE

The two major landscape elements of this Zone, the pastoral highlands and the intimate valleys, complement each other to create the essential character of the Zone. On the heights the feel is open and airy, augmented by the frequent wide views to Dartmoor, Exeter or the Exe Estuary. However, the character is always 'civilised', never totally remote, in contrast to some of the other Culm Measure Zones further west. Partly this is because of the presence in almost every view of

some settlement, however small, partly because of the human, intimate scale of the topography and the small-scale woodlands. Views to Exeter and the Exe Estuary also tend to minimise any feelings of remoteness.

In the valleys the character is a contrast. The valleys are generally very narrow, sinuous and steep. It is easy to lose a sense of direction, especially as there is rarely a general trend in their orientation. The well-wooded appearance adds to the isolated, secretive nature of these valleys. Tiny road bridges crossing the valley bottom streams add to the character, as does the appearance of an unexpected thatched cottage hidden away in a valley bottom.

Either element alone would have interest and attraction, but a combination of height and valley forms a complementary partnership which gives the Zone its distinctive character.

INTEGRITY

The essential characteristics of both highland and valley systems are well retained. The major impact on the Zone's character has been caused by the presence of the A30 road. This results in a loss of some ambience of remoteness, as a result of both sight and sound. In terms of sight, the road has been well designed, with a very limited effect on the landscape, although there is evidence of cuttings in a number of locations. Traffic noise is intrusive over a wider area, as is light pollution from the well-lit road junctions.

Tree cover is very important to the character of the Zone, helping to maintain its small-scale character. A continuing management regime to retain this element of the landscape is central to maintaining the Zone's landscape character.

Tedburn St Mary, the focus for this part of Devon, in a typical local landscape.

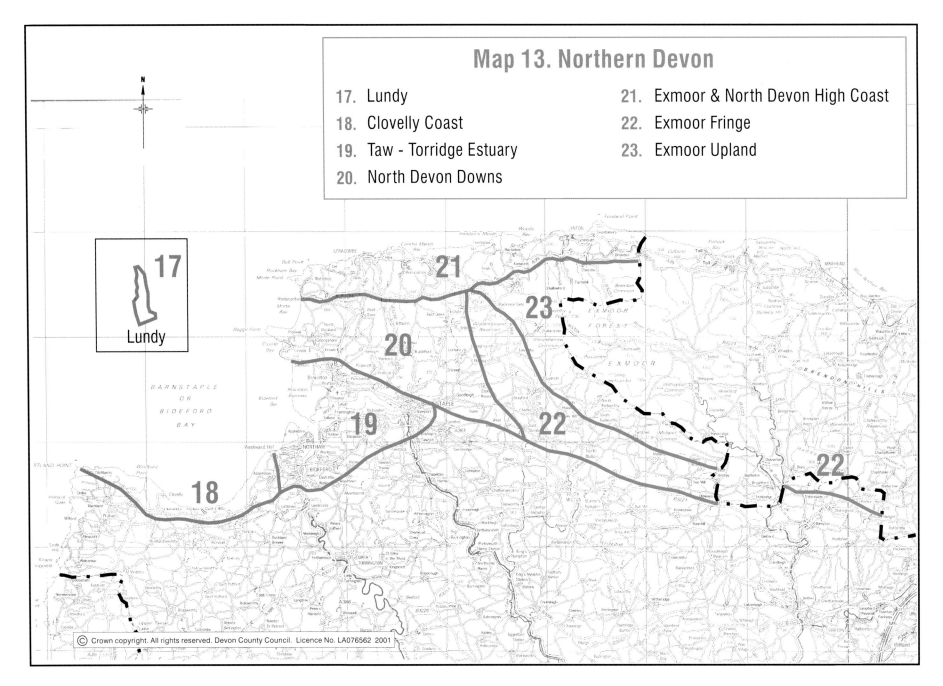

Map 13. Northern Devon

17. Lundy
18. Clovelly Coast
19. Taw - Torridge Estuary
20. North Devon Downs
21. Exmoor & North Devon High Coast
22. Exmoor Fringe
23. Exmoor Upland

NORTHERN DEVON

This grouping consists of six Landscape Character Zones which stretch across the northern extremes of Devon from Hartland Point in the west to the heights of Exmoor in the east, plus the separate Zone of the offshore island of Lundy.

The Zones are very much oriented northwards in their character, away from the heartland of Devon and towards the Bristol Channel coast. This is largely true even of the uplands of Exmoor, where the eye is automatically drawn towards views over the sea. Only in the southern part of Exmoor, and the higher parts of its fringe, is the obvious landscape relationship with the south. Here Exmoor forms an important backdrop skyline for the landscapes to the south and, in turn, views from the heights are across a vast area of lower land to the rim of Dartmoor on the horizon.

The coast is an important unifying factor to this part of Devon, comprising generally high cliffs with few natural harbours. The coast of northern Devon centres on its great natural gap, the combined estuary of the Taw and Torridge rivers. Here is found the bulk of the area's population, the economic and social heartland of the area.

North and east of the estuary rise the area's highlands, culminating in the far north-eastern corner of the County on high Exmoor. Yet although two-thirds of Exmoor lies within the neighbouring county of Somerset, the Devon element nevertheless relates closely to the remainder of this grouping of Character Zones, either by its relationship with the coast or by its links with and reliance on Barnstaple and the estuary.

This is a diverse grouping of Zones, yet one which does hang together. Even Lundy, that lonely outpost of Devon in the middle of the Bristol Channel, relates to the mainland Zones, forming as it does a focal reference point out to sea in the views from so much of the coastline.

A dramatic coastal landscape in North Devon; Lynmouth and Countisbury Hill.

17. LUNDY

NORTHERN DEVON
17. Lundy

N

LOCATION

An offshore island in the middle of the Bristol Channel, 11 miles/18km north-north-west of Hartland Point and 22 miles/35km west of Mortehoe.

DESIGNATIONS

Lundy is designated by Devon County Council as a Coastal Preservation Area.

*The weather-beaten Marisco Tavern,
in Lundy's only settlement.*

KEY CHARACTERISTIC FEATURES

- Mostly granite tableland towering high above the sea.

- Exposed and open rolling heathland.

- Stone walls and wire fences.

- Immense seascapes.

- Lack of tree cover.

- Wind and sea swell.

DESCRIPTION

Lundy is small in size, some 3 miles/5km north–south and less than a mile/1.3km east–west

at its widest point. Largely comprised of granite, it forms a tableland some 400ft/120m above the sea. There may have been trees at some time in its history but they seem to have been cleared at an early date. The south-westerly winds which drive a constant swell on to the west coast and sweep salt spray across the width of the island have made it difficult for any tree cover to re-establish.

The result is an open heathland landscape of little value other than as rough grazing for livestock, a landscape reminiscent of an area of high Dartmoor marooned at sea. The impression is heightened by the existence of stone walls crossing the island from east to west. In the south some pasture has been enclosed by stone walls and wire fences and this has been improved or semi-improved, but the area involved is small compared with the rest of the island.

The granite cliffs are spectacular, rearing almost vertically out of the sea to the tableland. In places, relics of gun batteries and stone quarries may be seen.

There is one small settlement, in the south of the island, and this is also the location of the landing stage for visitors. Archaeological remains indicate that settlement did exist elsewhere in earlier times, and there are remains of more recent cottages here and there.

Lundy has no fewer than three lighthouses, one at either end and one at the highest point. This latter was the earliest one, but had to be replaced as it was frequently obscured by fog.

The word 'unique' is probably over-used as a landscape description, but in the case of Lundy as a location anywhere in England, the word is justified.

SUBJECTIVE RESPONSE

The approach to Lundy by ship from Bideford or Ilfracombe is awe-inspiring for the effect of the cliffs rising sheer out of the water. Until relatively recently, this effect was heightened by the need to disembark to a tender to reach the shore. This is no longer necessary, at least not during reasonable sea conditions.

The climb to the top of the island gives a good idea of the scale of the cliffs and on reaching the tableland, the scale and effect of the rolling treeless plateau, crossed by stone walls, sitting in the sea like a giant ship, is truly impressive. The sight of the single stone-built settlement, trying to huddle down out of the wind, adds to the character. Further atmosphere is provided, if needed, by the vast number of sea-birds, (although sadly, few puffins any more), and seals in the waters around the island.

INTEGRITY

Not suprisingly, the integrity of Lundy's landscape is largely intact. Even the sometimes slightly untidy wire fences seem right in this rough and ready place. Concerns were raised about the building of the current landing jetty, but this does not seem to have had an adverse effect on the character.

Given its uncompromising location, and the sheer economics of development which would impinge on the landscape, the integrity of the landscape character of Lundy is likely to be intact for some time.

Above: *The harsh cliffs of the west coast of Lundy.*

Left: *Lundy's South Light in a typical moorland landscape.*

18. CLOVELLY COAST

NORTHERN DEVON
18. Clovelly Coast

LOCATION

This Zone comprises a narrow coastal strip in the far north western corner of Devon, from Westward Ho! and Abbotsham in the east to Hartland Point in the west. In the south it follows the A39 road, or just south of it, as far west as Clovelly Dykes, beyond which it continues parallel to the coast to Hartland Point.

DESIGNATIONS

Most of the Zone falls within the North Devon Area of Outstanding Natural Beauty (AONB), reflecting a landscape of national significance.

Only the easternmost extreme of the Zone, plus those few parts within the Zone south of the A39, are excluded from the AONB.

The AONB's boundaries coincide with those for the County Council's Coastal Preservation Area designation and also the area defined by the Countryside Agency as Heritage Coast.

KEY CHARACTERISTIC FEATURES

- High cliffs, sometimes unstable, blanketed by woodland and scrub.

- Narrow combes, thickly wooded; the woodland of ecological importance, spilling out over the adjacent farmland.

- Undulating mixed farmland on cliff tops.

- Picturesque settlements in larger combes.

- Wide seascapes over an extensive bay.

DESCRIPTION

The bulk of the Zone comprises an undulating coastal foreland of hedged fields. These vary over the Zone between quite large, regular fields and relatively small fields of irregular pattern. In some locations, especially towards the east and in the centre of the Zone, there is evidence of hedgerow loss which has an adverse effect on the landscape character.

This coastal farmland backs a line of cliffs. The cliffs are rarely sheer, tending to lean back at the top and there is clear evidence of instability in some places. In the central section, between Peppercombe and Brownsham, the cliff-faces are

clothed in woodland or scrub, giving rise to a valuable ecological habitat as well as adding variety to the appearance of the cliff line.

The cliffs are broken by a series of deep combes, each one cut by an often quite small but fast-flowing stream. The combes are thickly wooded, largely with ancient semi-natural woodland, creating further landscape variety. Inland the combes often branch out, each branch also being wooded, and the woodland spills out of the combes on to the coastal foreland, adding to its character. The combes are quite short, their heads generally coinciding with the southern boundary of the Zone.

A further element to the Zone's character is provided by parkland landscape created by existing or former estates. The relatively exposed nature of the location has meant that a strictly formal, 'tamed'

High cliffs blanketed by woodland, typical of the Clovelly Coast.

landscape does not exist, but elements including parkland trees, fences, gates and drives add a further variety without subduing the essential character.

The most distinctive settlement feature of the Zone is the existence of very picturesque villages in two of the combes, at Clovelly and Bucks Mills. The former, largely the creation of an Elizabethan landowner, is especially distinctive in form and has achieved a national, if not international, reputation for its quirky but picturesque location. Both Clovelly and Bucks Mills are also seen from other vantage points on the coast, as well as from offshore, adding to the appeal of this coastline.

The only other village in the Zone is at Abbotsham, virtually on the eastern boundary. Elsewhere, settlement is found only at individual farmsteads, except for a string of whitewashed

Bucks Mills occupies one of the coastal combes.

hamlets along the line of the A39. These originally grew up at crossroads locations, or at the head of the coastal combes.

In the east, the Zone's boundary marks the change from a coastal-oriented landscape to that of the wider landscape associated with the Torridge Estuary. Moving west, the Zone's southern boundary marks the abrupt drop into the adjacent valley of the Torridge's tributary, the Yeo; further west still, it marks the change from northwards facing coastal land to a wider, more open landscape trending more to the Atlantic coast to the west. In the far west of the Zone, approaching Hartland Point, this boundary becomes quite blurred, elements of both types of landscape occurring on both sides of the boundary.

SUBJECTIVE RESPONSE

Over most of the Zone the most powerful response is probably evoked by the sight and proximity of the sea. While not everywhere in the Zone is within sight of the sea, nowhere is far from it, with its effect on the light and the wind. Wherever it is visible, the seascapes are impressive, encompassing the wide sweep of the bay framed by Lundy and Baggy Point.

The landscape character changes, or progresses, subtly from east to west. Primarily, this is to do with the perception of the greater remoteness in the west. The A39 becomes less busy and, indeed is lost after Clovelly Dykes; the woodlands and combes become more extensive in the Brownsham area; the influence of the population in the Torridge Estuary area becomes less; the impact of the Atlantic becomes stronger. This characterisation seems somehow to be emphasised by passing through the succession of hamlets on the

A39, their whitewashed, almost squat appearance having a maritime air.

Certainly, a sensation of increasing remoteness is encountered moving westwards along the coast on foot, although in this mode it manifests itself very soon. By the time the extensive wooded cleaves of Brownsham are reached, the essence of a quiet, peaceful, almost unchanging landscape is persuasive.

INTEGRITY

The Clovelly Coast is still a relatively far-flung part of Devon and relatively inaccessible, and this has helped maintain its integrity as a landscape.

Perhaps the major influence on the character of the landscape has come from the A39 road. While the line of this road is long-standing it is obviously used far more than was once the case, and indeed it has been branded the Atlantic Highway presumably to encourage its use. However, its level of use still does not generally intrude too drastically on the character of the landscape and, indeed, it is quite easy to escape its impact over most of the Zone.

The A39 has encouraged tourist development along the road in one or two locations which have also had some impact on the character. Again, so far this has not had unacceptable results, but such is the delicate nature of this landscape and its character that it would be easy for further intensification of such developments to have a seriously adverse effect. Otherwise, the only concern is that, such is the importance of the cliff-face-and combe woodland to the Zone, every effort should be made to maintain and manage these resources. There is no evidence that this is not the case.

19. TAW – TORRIDGE ESTUARY

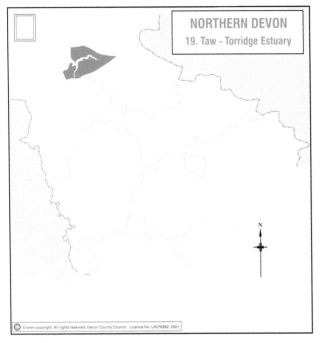

NORTHERN DEVON
19. Taw - Torridge Estuary

© Crown copyright. All rights reserved. Devon County Council. Licence No. LA076562 2001

LOCATION

The Zone occupies the central part of the coast of northern Devon centred on the two towns of Bideford to the west and Barnstaple to the east and encompassing the estuaries of the Taw and Torridge rivers, including their joint outflow to the sea.

DESIGNATIONS

The coastal strip of the Zone, effectively confined to the marsh and dune systems of Northam Burrows and Braunton Burrows, is part of the North Devon Area of Outstanding Natural Beauty, indicating the national landscape importance of this area. A rather wider coastal area, stretching inland around Appledore and Instow and including Braunton Marsh and Great Field, is within the County Council's designated Coastal Preservation Area. This same area is defined by the Countryside Agency as Heritage Coast.

KEY CHARACTERISTIC FEATURES

- Vast estuary of two river systems.

- Extensive flat land including salt marshes, sand and mudflats, dune systems and slacks, historic open field, beaches.

- Urban waterfronts and historic estuary settlements.

- Important ecological habitats.

DESCRIPTION

The importance of the Taw-Torridge estuary system in terms of landscape, ecology and archaeology cannot be overestimated. It is the only major estuary on the north coast of the entire region between Bridgwater Bay in Somerset and the Camel Estuary in Cornwall. It is internationally recognised for its bird populations and associated habitats and is home to a variety of rare species of flora and fauna. It also contains a very rare example of an extensive open field system which has been a working agricultural landscape since medieval times.

However, this landscape also provides a home to the largest human population concentration in northern Devon. This combination of ecological habitat and human settlement, dominated by the presence of the estuary, gives the Zone its character.

The Zone is essentially an area of lowland surrounding the two major arms of the estuary, the whole being surrounded by a ring of land at a higher level, creating almost a saucer-like effect. The two estuary elements themselves tie the Zone together and dominate its character, creating a landscape which can change remarkably with the state of the tide. The features associated with the estuary add to this effect. Dune systems dominate the outermost parts of the estuary, backed by dune slacks and marshes. Further upstream are sandy beaches with sand and mud flats, appearing and disappearing with the ebb and flow of the tide. Around the mouth of the estuary the sea also makes itself felt in the landscape, this effect heightened by the almost ever-present surf.

A quiet corner of the Taw Estuary.

The result is a very horizontal trend to the landscape, a trend heightened by the saucer effect created by the surrounding rim of higher land.

Mixed agriculture is practised in a landscape of small to medium sized irregular fields with a hedgerow pattern showing some signs of loss. Most remarkable is the survival of Braunton Great Field on the north side of the Taw Estuary, the open strip system almost a piece of living history, in landscape terms being very complementary to the marshland systems it abuts.

Over much of the Zone, however, it is development and settlement which is the dominant landscape feature. Where this urban landscape fronts the estuaries the waterfront development often complements its setting but in other areas development has not had such a happy effect on the Zone's landscape. Urban development is the dominant feature over much of the Zone; the largest settlements of Barnstaple, Bideford and Braunton all impose themselves to one extent or another, but so do smaller settlements and other locations such as Chivenor Royal Marines base and industrial buildings of one sort or another, spreading over the floor of the Zone or climbing the outer rim.

Roads are also an important element in the landscape of this Zone, perhaps especially the A39. The building of the Torridge Bridge just north of Bideford to carry the A39 over the estuary has resulted in a major new feature in the landscape of the area, perhaps soon to be mirrored in a new bridge over the Taw downstream of Barnstaple. The old road between Barnstaple and Bideford is almost lined with ribbon development, creating a major impact on the local landscape and there are lines of development on other roads, especially out of Barnstaple and at Braunton.

The 'inland' boundary of the Zone, to south, east and north, is marked by the fairly clear rise to the higher land forming a rim around the edge of the estuary lands. To the west the Zone ends at the sea.

SUBJECTIVE RESPONSE

The two major landscape elements of the Zone are, on the one hand, the open, spacious character created by the estuary, the dunes, beaches, marshes, the Great Field and the surf-fringed sea, and on the other hand, development. While almost diametrically opposed character elements they perversely hang together surprisingly well here. It is perhaps their close proximity which helps. Wherever you are in the Zone, even in an urban area, almost any turn will bring a view of the estuary or sand or the sea. Conversely, and perhaps less happily, even in the middle of one of the dune systems, any clear view will bring the sight of a town or some other evidence of development.

The response does therefore very much depend on the location of the observer. Since most observers will probably be within a developed area, the feeling generated by the landscape is likely to be mostly favourable. However, in an overall landscape context the situation is different, with a danger in certain locations of the essential estuary character being submerged by the development.

Little of the Zone can claim to have a remote character, but the one area that could perhaps

The historic port of Bideford with old and new bridges.

claim that until relatively recently, the area in the extreme south, has lost that status as a result of the building of the A39. The road has been engineered to be largely inconspicuous in the landscape, but the noise of the traffic and, indeed, its very presence, even if unseen, has changed the character of this part of the Zone.

The other, perhaps more contentious, result of the A39 on the landscape derives from the building of the Torridge Bridge. Some claim it adds to the landscape drama and ties the two sides of the estuary together, others that it dwarfs the landscape and imposes itself on the setting of the estuary and Bideford. Whichever the personal reaction, there is little doubt that

it is an important landscape element. Proposals for a bridge downstream of Barnstaple on the Taw will doubtless provoke similar debate.

INTEGRITY

The discussions above clearly indicate that the landscape integrity of this Zone is highly vulnerable and is probably approaching a position where it could be irrevocably changed. The major towns continue to expand – Barnstaple away from the estuary up the slopes fringing the Zone, Bideford beginning to climb the slopes at East the Water; ribbon development is in danger of joining up further; industrial development continues lower down the estuary;

suburbanisation of the approaches to towns continues; development climbs hills behind the smaller settlements, including examples of skyline development.

Despite this, the essence of the Zone's landscape remains. The estuary system continues to provide its heartbeat; the dunes, marshes and sands continue to reflect the sky and give a sense of space; most of the downland rim continues free of development. If these features can be retained, together with a softening of the urban developments perhaps though appropriate tree planting, then perhaps the Zone's integrity will not be lost.

Appledore and the Torridge Estuary,
the essence of the local landscape character.

20. NORTH DEVON DOWNS

NORTHERN DEVON
20. North Devon Downs

N

Crown copyright. All rights reserved. Devon County Council. Licence No. LA076562 2001

LOCATION

The Zone meets the sea at Morte Bay and Croyde Bay and runs eastwards towards the edge of Exmoor as far as a line approximately between Kentisbury and East Buckland. Its northern edge is parallel to the north coast but inland, largely following the line of the A3123 road, while in the south it keeps north of the Taw Estuary and the A361 road.

DESIGNATIONS

The coastal area in the west of the Zone falls within the North Devon Area of Outstanding Natural Beauty, a designation reflecting its national landscape importance. The same area has been designated as a Coastal Preservation Area by Devon County Council and defined as Heritage Coast by the Countryside Agency. In addition, areas based on the valley of Bradiford Water and that of the River Yeo which flows into Barnstaple, plus its tributaries, have been designated Areas of Great Landscape Value by the County Council, indicating a county importance.

KEY CHARACTERISTIC FEATURES

- Rounded, open downland, divided by three significant wooded river valleys.

- Large fields, closely trimmed hedgebanks.

- Wind-trimmed tree groups and occasional stunted hedgerow trees.

- Parkland scenery, especially in the east.

- Secluded hamlets and farms in valley bottoms.

- Coastal down headlands in the west enclosing broad sandy bays.

- Picturesque cob and thatch coastal villages.

DESCRIPTION

The essence of the landscape of this Zone is an area of relatively high, broad, rounded profile hills. Most of the area is patterned by a largely rectilinear field pattern, the fields tending to decrease in size to the east. Beech hedges are common in the east, gorse-topped banks and, in places, wire fences, being more the norm elsewhere. The relatively large fields and more open aspect resulting from the presence of the fences gives quite an open appearance to much of this Zone.

There are areas of parkland landscape in the east particularly, and these are marked by hilltop tree features and clumps. Elsewhere, tree features are confined to occasional wind-bent tree groups or hedgerow trees.

At the western end of the Zone the landscape becomes more like traditional downland, open sheep pasture with very few hedgerows. The downland extends to the headlands of Baggy

Open, rolling downland and wooded valley, near Marwood.

Point and Saunton Down and these, together with Woolacombe Down to the north, enclose and give a backdrop to the wide sandy beaches enclosed in bays at Woolacombe and Croyde which provide the scenic meeting between the Zone and the sea.

The Zone is crossed in a north–south direction by three fairly substantial valleys. These represent quite deep clefts through the rounded hills, contrasting with the heights not only in their topography but in the fact that they are typically well-wooded, mostly with mixed or broadleaved woodland. The valley floors are quite narrow, sinuous, pastoral with few hedges. The woodland on the steep valley sides spills over the rims onto the edge of the downland, and the wooded pattern created by these valleys

and their woodlands adds a distinctive element to the Zone's landscape. There are few locations on the downs where the shape of the valleys as reflected by their woodlands cannot be seen, this interplay between open downland and wooded valley being characteristic of the Zone.

As well as the major valleys, smaller tributary valleys also exist, narrower and even steeper. Also wooded, the fast-flowing streams on the valley bottoms add a further feature and these side valleys extend the influence of the wooded valleys further into the downland.

There is little settlement on the downland heights. Settlement is concentrated in the valleys although even here it is in the form of farms

or hamlets rather than anything more substantial. Only in the far west of the Zone, as it nears the sea, are villages found. Here Croyde and Georgeham in particular add to the attraction of the landscape with their picturesque cob and thatch appearance.

The Zone ends abruptly to the north, where it meets the distinctive ridge running east–west parallel to the north coast. Similarly, there is a clear Zone boundary to the south, the complex mix of downs and valleys falling obviously to the lowlands of the Taw-Torridge estuary lands and the valley extending east of Barnstaple. Its eastern boundary is more gradual, but is marked by the change from rolling downland and valleys to the rising foreground to Exmoor gradually climbing eastwards.

Opposite page: *Saunton Down, where the downlands meet the sea at Croyde Bay.*

Left: *The pattern of woodland of the valley of the River Caen marks the rounded downs.*

SUBJECTIVE RESPONSE

The high, rounded downlands evoke a feeling of airy spaciousness, almost of being up in the clouds. This feeling is emphasised by the lack of settlement and the consequent character of remoteness that arises, and also by the views over the tops of the valleys cut through the downs. Towards the west, views over Bideford Bay add to the appeal and perhaps reinforce the feeling of being apart from the rest of the world.

A rather different character is evoked where the downlands meet the sea. The picturesque villages and the extensive, popular beaches give a bustle to the area in the summer although even here it is relatively easy to find peace and quiet away from the most popular locations.

The valleys have an atmosphere that is different again. Each of the three major valleys contains a road; one the main road between Barnstaple and Ilfracombe, the second a secondary road between the same towns and the third a local road. The consequent character varies with the degree of busyness of the road, although it is also largely true the busier the road the larger the valley. Nevertheless, the impact of the roads in their respective valleys is fairly limited. Away from the immediate influence of the main roads, and more particularly in the tributary valleys where there are no roads or only steep, winding local roads, the complex shape of the valleys, the wooded environment and the frequent appearance of running water all give rise to a remote, almost secretive character. Occasional unexpected cottages or hamlets heighten rather than dispel this reaction. The character of the valleys and of the downlands, although quite different in detail, are remarkably similar in appeal, their proximity and inter-relationship helping to complement each other.

INTEGRITY

The complex appeal of downland and valley has been well retained throughout the Zone. The nature of the topography has meant that pressures for change have been limited.

Pressures relating to development have been largely confined to the western end of the Zone, where tourism and recreation pressures have particularly occurred. Woolacombe, on the fringe of the Zone, spreads up its hill somewhat, a contrast to the open downland immediately adjacent. Croyde has also spread from its original picturesque centre, but here adjacent holiday camps, caravan sites and seasonal markets have a negative effect on the landscape of the downland at Baggy Point.

The roads have had something of a 'taming' influence on the valley systems, in particular the A361 road between Braunton and Mullacott Cross.

Nevertheless, as indicated earlier, it is easy to escape the effect of the road and certainly the landscape essence of the valleys, including this one, remains intact.

On the downlands, pressures have been agricultural rather than for development. Some loss of hedges has occurred in places, and wire fences are now evident elsewhere, but the essential character remains. The character includes the transition east to west from small hedged fields, through large banked or fenced fields to open downland, and this pattern is very effective as a landscape element.

Woodland, although confined to the valleys, is important to the overall character of the Zone, and its management and retention is important. The individual trees and groups of the downs, especially in the east, are also important and require ongoing management.

21. EXMOOR AND NORTH DEVON HIGH COAST

NORTHERN DEVON

21. Exmoor and North Devon High Coast

LOCATION

The Zone occupies a relatively narrow coastal fringe along the northernmost coast of Devon from Woolacombe and Morte Point in the west to Exmoor and beyond to the county boundary with Somerset in the east. It has an average depth of only 3 to 5km/1–3 miles.

DESIGNATIONS

The whole Zone west of Combe Martin, with the exception of the town of Ilfracombe and its immediate hinterland, lies within the North Devon Area of Outstanding Natural Beauty. East of Combe Martin the Zone is within Exmoor National Park. Both these designations reflect a landscape of national importance.

In addition, the whole Zone, with the exception only of the developed areas of Ilfracombe, Combe Martin and Lynton/Lynmouth, is designated by Devon County Council as a Coastal Preservation Area. In the west, most of the Zone except Ilfracombe and its hinterland, and in the east a narrow coastal strip, have all been defined as Heritage Coast by the Countryside Agency.

KEY CHARACTERISTIC FEATURES

- Geological strata shaping distinctive jagged features and headland landmarks.

- High cliffs rising in height to 'hogsback' formations to the east.

- Hidden inlets and rocky coves.

- Steep, dramatic wooded combes with waterfalls and scree.

- Distinctive settlement pattern in sheltered combes – linear forms.

- Archaeological interest.

- Valuable ecological habitats.

DESCRIPTION

The north-facing coastline is dominated by rugged cliff scenery with impressive sloping rock strata forming distinctive headlands sheltering small rocky coves. The cliffs increase in height to the east where they take on a classic 'hogsback' shape, rising to some of the highest cliffs in England east of Lynmouth. In one or two locations the cliff-faces are clothed with broad leaved woodland.

Contrasting with the exposed cliff tops, steep branching combe systems cut deep into the highlands. The sheltered combes, each with its fast-flowing stream, are clothed on their steep sides with extensive broad leaved woodland, often semi-ancient. These combes are important landscape features both in their own right and as viewed from the high cliffs surrounding them.

In the west especially the cliffs are backed by farmland dominated by generally rectangular hedged fields. These also create a contrast with the cliffs and the combes. Elsewhere, in the centre and the east, the moorland character of Exmoor extends virtually to the clifftops and the open rough pasture of Holdstone Down, east of Combe Martin, and the Valley of Rocks and Foreland Point, respectively west and east of Lynton, make a fine backdrop for the impressive cliff scenery.

Hogsback-shaped cliffs near Trentishoe.

The nature of the coastline gives rise to fine views, over the Bristol Channel to Wales but also lengthwise along the coast. Fine viewpoints are afforded by the rugged and prominent headlands, giving rise to dramatic panoramas over the rocky coves far below or over the spectacular wooded 'cleaves'.

Development is very much confined to the valleys and bays. The topography gives rise to linear town form, perhaps most spectacularly at Combe Martin, alleged to be 'the longest village in England'. Similar, if less spectacular, fingers of development snake along the valleys out of Ilfracombe, the main settlement on the coast, and characterise the inland settlement of Berrynarbor. The Zone also accommodates the unusual feature of the 'double-decker' twin settlement of Lynton and Lynmouth, linked by their trademark cliff railway.

Archaeological features also add to the landscape drama: these include numerous prehistoric hilltop settlements overlooking the cleaves, evidence of medieval mining and narrow, elongated fields climbing the slopes around Combe Martin, remains of a medieval farming landscape.

The Zone's only landscape boundary is to the south. In the west this is marked by a prominent ridge parallel to the coast beyond which the rolling downland landscape of the North Devon Downs extends southwards. Further east the boundary marks the change from the coastal-dominated landscape of this Zone to the more typical Exmoor Upland scenery. In the east the county boundary with Somerset ends the Zone, but the landscape continues eastwards in much the same vein as far as Porlock.

SUBJECTIVE RESPONSE

The Zone probably represents one of the most dramatic coastal landscapes in the country. A combination of prominent headlands, folded geological strata, rocky coves, steep and deep wooded cleaves, coastal moorland and some of the highest cliffs in England results in a landscape which must be described as spectacular.

Given its landscape, not surprisingly much of the Zone is an important recreational resource. Ilfracombe, Lynmouth and Combe Martin are popular tourist locations and, especially in summer, smaller locations on the coast or inland are very popular. Such locations are very concentrated however, and the character of the Zone has been very little affected by such popularity.

The range of individual landscapes in the Zone evokes a comparable range of responses. High, airy cliff tops and headlands dominated by sea and sky; open, rolling moorland still with an ever-present sea; deep, steep, lush wooded valleys, marked here and there by scree, narrow, dominated by birdsong and the sound of the fast-flowing streams; grassy sheep pastures overlooking the dramatic valleys; all these constituents create their own response, in each case invariably positive, but in addition the response is to the sum total of all these elements, again positive.

On some of the less visited cliff tops, or in some of the least frequented cleaves, a feeling of solitude and remoteness is experienced. In winter, this character is evoked over a surprisingly large area. Only around the larger settlements is this reaction entirely absent.

INTEGRITY

The essence of this spectacular landscape is intact. Threats to it are limited, found only around the main settlements. Ilfracombe has experienced development pressures, and it has begun to climb some of its backing hills. Generally, however, the topography has managed to contain this expansion visually and the integrity of the wider landscape remains intact.

Elsewhere, settlements are perhaps more vulnerable. The special character of Combe Martin needs to be retained by keeping its valley bottom, linear form, and other valley settlements need similar protection. The woodlands which provide such an important element of the local landscape character must be managed for the future to ensure the continuation of the distinctive scenery, while the open character of the clifftops, conversely, requires similar attention. In neither case, it must be said, is there any evidence that the essential character of the landscape is under any real threat, but the landscape of this Zone is such that it must remain uncompromised.

The rugged headland of Rillage Point.

135

22. EXMOOR FRINGE

NORTHERN DEVON
22. Exmoor Fringe

LOCATION

Situated in the north-eastern part of Devon, as its name suggests the Zone wraps around Exmoor from a northern point some 5km/3 miles inland of the Bristol Channel coast, south and then east to the county boundary with Somerset at Oldways End. A small addition continues further east, to the north of Morebath, also adjacent to the Somerset border.

DESIGNATIONS

The vast majority of this Zone has been designated as an Area of Great Landscape Value, reflecting its importance as a landscape in a County context.

KEY CHARACTERISTIC FEATURES

- Foreground landscape to high lands of Exmoor.

- Beech hedges, occasionally grown out.

- Crossed by steep, wooded valleys.

- Drove roads and tracks leading to and from the high moor.

- Patchwork of fields.

- Individual hilltop tree features.

DESCRIPTION

The eastern part of the Zone, between East Anstey and North Molton, comprises land rising to the north towards the moorland rim of Exmoor. The general appearance is pastoral, patterned by hedges, mostly beech, these being largely straight but never regimented. Tree features and hilltop

Exmoor Fringe; pastoral landscape with well-wooded valleys near West Anstey, a foreground to the moorland beyond.

clumps, most notably Bampfylde Clump near North Molton, add to the scene.

The area is crossed by a number of north–south valleys. These form quite deep clefts and are mostly wooded, adding variety to the overall scene. The landscape is dotted with scattered farmsteads and occasional hamlets or small villages.

This part of the Zone acts as the foreground to Exmoor behind. In views over the area from the south the Zone appears as the introductory 'lead-in' to the open moor which is just in view above the Zone. Conversely, views 'out' over the Zone from the moorland above are very extensive, reaching well into the heart of Devon, and the patchwork of fields crossed by wooded valleys forms a superb foreground to these wide views.

Further west, from North Molton to Brayford, the landscape detail is more complex. The land still rises towards the moorland rim, here to the north-east, but this general trend is often difficult to discern internally as the landscape consists of a series of steeply undulating landforms, irregular in alignment. This part of the Zone is also punctuated by a large number of valleys, shallower and often less wooded and less dramatic than those to the east but nevertheless important in the landscape. The only settlement comprises scattered farmsteads.

North of Brayford the landscape trend comprising a rise in height to the Exmoor rim, now to the east, becomes obvious again, although punctuated not only by valleys cutting across the area but, more noteworthy, by the Bray Valley which forms a major deep wooded feature parallel to the Exmoor boundary and running lengthways through the Zone. Again, the settlement pattern is characterised by individual farmsteads or small hamlets, other than the one village of Brayford, itself quite small, in the Bray Valley. As with the more easterly part of the Zone, the area forms an introductory foreground to the open moorland above.

The northern boundary of the Zone coincides with the change in landscape from primarily improved pasture and woodland to primarily moorland, although there are examples of features being on the 'wrong' side of the boundary. To the west, the landscape falls to the valley and downland complex of the North Devon Downs while to the south the less differentiated landscape of the Culm Measures indicates a change in character.

The small separate element of this Zone to the east of Exebridge has a similar appearance and character to the more easterly parts of the main Zone. An area of high pasture land is cut by some very marked valleys, often steep and wooded, but with a less obvious north–south trend. Here also, spectacular views may be obtained, but more focussed here on the Batherm and Exe Valleys. The landscape falls quite markedly to the Batherm and its tributaries, and this marks the Zone's southern boundary. West, north and east the landscape continues similar in appearance over the county boundary into Somerset.

SUBJECTIVE RESPONSE

This is a quiet, remote Zone, where the sensory reaction is a product both of its location adjacent to Exmoor, with its moorland acting as a psychological and visual backdrop, and also of the area itself with its open pastoral landscapes, often unpredictable in shape, alternating with deep, sometimes quite spectacular, wooded valleys.

The interplay of these elements is impressive, especially when added to other senses. Factors such as the sound and feel of the wind, the sensation of being high above the world, of being very much in the elements aid a positive reaction; in contrast in the valleys characteristic is the sight and sound of fast running streams, a feeling of enclosure, of being in a lost world.

Different again, but complementary, is the Bray Valley. While it carries the road between the A361 and the north coast, the landscape character of the Bray Valley continues to convey a sensation of quietness and seclusion. The major landscape feature within the valley is provided by the stone quarries. Fairly limited in their impact and typical perhaps of one kind of productive use of the landscape, they also include examples of positive restoration. Nevertheless, that they have an impact on the landscape is undeniable, and factors such as sounds of plant and machinery and flashing lights are perhaps as intrusive as the landform itself.

In the north of the Zone, the reservoir of Wistlandpound adds a further dimension, and a different response, perhaps one of surprise. It is an unexpected landform to find in its setting, and also is associated with a fairly substantial area of coniferous woodland which, while not unique in the Zone, is relatively uncommon. If anything, the reservoir probably adds to the remote feel of the area rather than detracting from it, its use being generally very low-key.

INTEGRITY

Views in both directions across this Zone will reinforce the general impression that the landscape integrity of the area is largely intact.

Farmstead overlooked by moorland, near Blackmoor Gate.

Settlement is scattered and has not had an impact; development pressures are limited in an essentially remote area. The integrity is generally threatened only by any gradual deterioration which might occur. It is therefore important that the characteristic elements – beech hedges, field pattern, historic drove roads on to the moor, valley woodlands, hilltop trees and clumps – are maintained as viable features in the landscape by positive management.

Quarrying has had an effect on parts of the Bray Valley, but not enough to jeopardise its integrity. Some might argue that the existence of this traditional industry is positive in landscape terms. This may well be so, but it is nevertheless important to the integrity of the valley that the scale of development does not become inappropriate in the landscape as a whole. This has not yet happened, but may be a potential danger.

137

23. EXMOOR UPLAND

NORTHERN DEVON
23. Exmoor Upland

LOCATION

The Zone occupies the north-eastern corner of the County, comprising the highest parts of Exmoor in Devon, adjacent to the Somerset boundary.

DESIGNATIONS

The Zone falls almost entirely within Exmoor National Park, a landscape of national significance. The one or two peripheral areas which are excluded from the National Park have been designated by the County Council as an Area of Great Landscape Value, reflecting its County importance.

KEY CHARACTERISTIC FEATURES

- Extensive grass and heather moorland.

- Broad, sweeping landforms.

- Distinctive beech hedgebanks, some stone faced.

- Old oak coppice woodlands, especially associated with valleys, rivers and upland streams.

- Fast-flowing upland streams cutting across open moorland.

- Extensive views.

DESCRIPTION

The most characteristic feature of the Exmoor Upland is the extensive range of grass and heather moorland giving rise to wide, sweeping landforms and broad horizons. The moorland is cut through by a series of upland streams flowing off the highest land, approximately the area around the

Old beech hedge grown out into a line of trees, near Twitchen.

county boundary, and thus the streams radiate out over the Devon element of the moor, to the north, west and south. In a few locations, especially on the county boundary around the area known as the Chains, the moorland is wet and boggy, contrasting with the generally dry grassland found over most of the Zone.

However, although the billowing grass moorland is the most characteristic element, away from the very highest areas the appearance is perhaps more typically a mosaic, an intricate mix not only of grass and heather moorland but of improved pasture, enclosing hedges and woodland. Trees are not common individually, the odd ones existing being even more remarkable landscape features for their rarity. However, examples exist of old beech hedges which have grown out to leave a line of trees, often on the skyline, adding a distinctive element to the landscape.

As the upland streams radiating across the moorland reach slightly lower levels, the valleys they cut become more pronounced features in the landscape, often well-wooded, and the contrast between the open uplands and the enclosed valleys becomes quite marked. The streams are fast-flowing, often cascading over minor rapids.

Wide views are characteristic of the Exmoor Uplands. Even from the heart of the Zone it is not infrequent for views to extend as far as the more prominent coastal features to the north, or well into Devon to the south. It is perhaps the mixture of moorland and coastal backdrop which gives Exmoor such a distinctive character.

The rim of Exmoor is an important landscape feature to other parts of Devon, stretching over large areas of the northern half of the County. As such, its landscape influence extends far beyond its own borders.

There is little or no settlement on the Exmoor Uplands in Devon, settlement being confined to individual farms and hamlets in some of the valleys flowing off the moor. One or two peripheral hamlets have expanded into small villages, Challacombe and Parracombe in particular.

The eastern edge of the Zone is the Somerset boundary, the typical Upland landscape continuing unchanged over the border. To the south and west the boundary marks the transition to the Exmoor Fringe, reflecting more improved and enclosed land, a general slope away from the heights and a greater area of woodland. To the north, the boundary marks the transition to the area of coastal influence. As such, it excludes one of the major coastal combes, the valley of the East Lyn.

SUBJECTIVE RESPONSE

A character of wide-open space is the distinctive feature of high Exmoor. The heather and grass moorland creates a skyline of wide, billowing expanses where sharp angles are a rarity. This sweeping landform accentuates the influence of the wind and sky, the rippling of the wind through the moorland grass being a feature of some of the higher areas.

This atmosphere of openness is emphasised by the frequent wide views. On clear days coastal features such as Great Hangman and Countisbury Hill stand out to the north, and from some vantage points the sea itself is a background feature. Elsewhere far-flung views across the Exmoor mosaic or off the moor over the patchwork of Devon fields give an extra feeling of height and airiness.

It is not an infrequent occurrence in the Devon landscape for areas of lofty space to be closely interrelated with enclosed valleys, each complementing and accentuating the effect of the other. High Exmoor is another example of this counter-balance, the contrast being supplied by the narrow upland valleys radiating off the highest part of the moor. Shallow, almost imperceptible features at first, they soon carve substantial clefts into the moorland. Initially still moorland features, as they tumble off the very highest areas woodland appears, the valleys take on a secretive, enclosed nature, the only sounds those of fast-flowing water and moorland and river birds. It was a valley such as this which inspired R.D. Blackmore to write of the secret Doone Valley in his classic book 'Lorna Doone'.

Exmoor as a whole is a deservedly popular recreational area, but the Exmoor Uplands in Devon probably represent among the least frequented parts of the National Park. The B3223 road linking Lynton with Simonsbath in Somerset and the B3358 between Blackmoor Gate and Simonsbath are the main accesses and the former in particular is well served with car parking provision which is much used as a base for exploring the moor. It is, however, very easy to escape this influence and it is perfectly possible to spend an entire day on this part of the moor and meet virtually nobody. The open topography does not make for seclusion exactly, or even perhaps remoteness, but the area does engender a feeling of being away from it all, of being alone, secure in the knowledge that a path or a track or a road will easily be encountered to lead back to civilisation.

The valleys do give more feeling of seclusion, aided by the enclosed atmosphere and steep sides. Again, however, it is not a threatening seclusion, but one which gives the impression that it could be escaped wherever the need arose. This is essentially a moorland with a friendly face.

INTEGRITY

As befits a National Park, the landscape integrity is uncompromised. Development is too small-scale to pose a great threat and even recreation pressures are relatively subdued here. Small informal car parks flank the Lynton-Simonsbath road, and the presence of cars in the landscape on the road and in these car parks has a minor effect. It is scarcely enough to threaten the overall integrity.

In the longer term, it is the pattern of land use which has greatest potential to threaten the integrity of the landscape. It is actually quite a fragile and vulnerable mix which goes to make up the distinctive character and a significant shift in any of the constituents could have a marked effect. As such, continuing lack of ploughing of the grassland and heather moorland, continuing management of the woodlands, management and maintenance of the beech hedgerows and maintenance of the vernacular architecture of farms and hamlets and of features such as gate-posts and bridges, will all contribute to the well-being of the complex mix which forms the essence of the landscape's character.

Heather and grass moorland plus patchwork of fields; Exmoor above Barbrook.

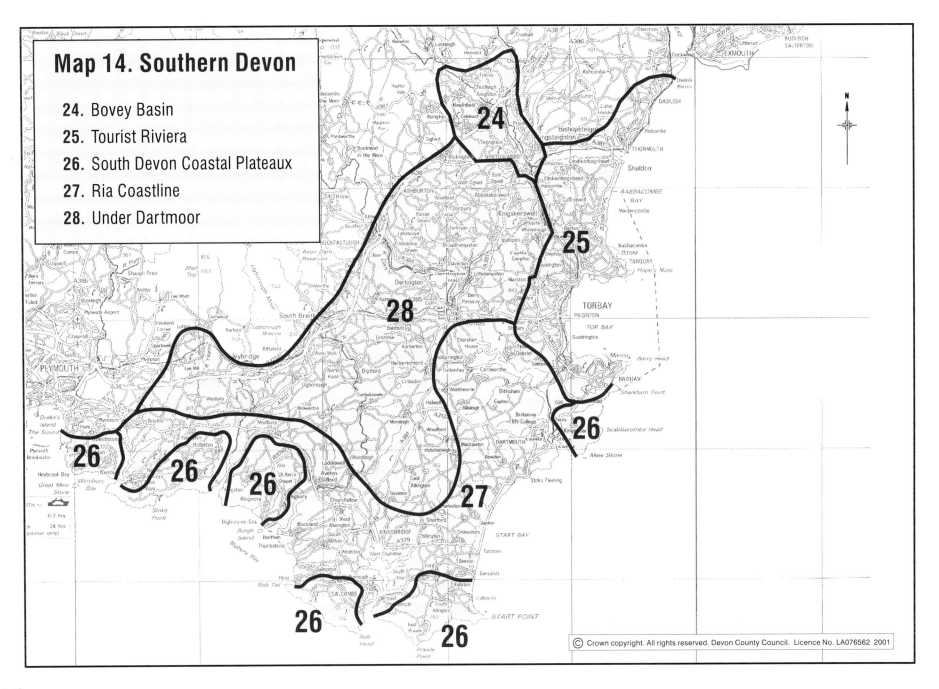

Map 14. Southern Devon

24. Bovey Basin
25. Tourist Riviera
26. South Devon Coastal Plateaux
27. Ria Coastline
28. Under Dartmoor

SOUTHERN DEVON

This is a group of five Character Zones encompassing the area between Dartmoor and the south coast. It stretches from the very edge of the Exe Estuary in the east to the outskirts of Plymouth in the west.

To a greater or lesser extent, the landscapes of these Zones are influenced by the two boundaries of Dartmoor to the north and the sea to the south. Except on the beaches themselves, there are few parts of South Devon where Dartmoor is not visible on the horizon, be it nearer or further. By the same token the sea has its impact over most of the area too, be it the main constituent of the character, a silvery line on the horizon or simply the quality of the light.

The two factors have also combined to make the area the most popular tourist destination in the County, and among the most popular in the country. This popularity has itself had an impact on the landscape. Sometimes this has been benign, more often it has been unfortunate. Indeed, even where the physical impact on the landscape has been negligible, sheer numbers of visitors may have an influence on the character, or feel, of the landscape, certainly in high summer.

This should not be taken as indicating that the landscape of this part of Devon is suffering. These Zones contain among the most scenically outstanding, and certainly among the best loved, coastal landscapes nationally and even at the beginning of the twenty-first century in high summer, it is possible to experience a profound character of remoteness in parts of South Devon.

Sandy beaches, wooded estuaries and creeks, quiet coves, sophisticated resorts, historic buildings and castles, preserved steam railways, lagoons, lighthouses; all this and more makes this part of the County perhaps the landscape that springs to mind more immediately than any other when Devon is mentioned to the public at large.

Southern Devon; cliffs, beaches, hills, valleys, woods, hedges, sea, sailing boats; Hallsands and Beesands.

24. BOVEY BASIN

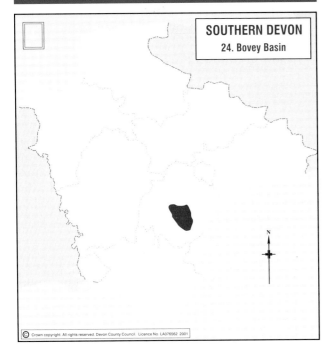

SOUTHERN DEVON
24. Bovey Basin

LOCATION

At the head of the Teign Estuary, just to the east of Dartmoor, the main river is joined by a major tributary, the River Bovey. The Zone represents the flood plain of the two rivers, stretching between Bovey Tracey and Newton Abbot and east to Kingsteignton and Chudleigh.

DESIGNATIONS

A small area on the northern fringe of the Zone has been designated an Area of Great Landscape Value, indicating a County significance; it is, however, more of a backdrop to the Zone than an integral part of it. There are no other designations.

KEY CHARACTERISTIC FEATURES

- Largely flat river basin ringed by hills, often wooded, including the rim of Dartmoor.

- Vast open-cast ball clay quarrying, spoil pits, settling lakes and associated buildings.

- Artificial lakes and ponds from past quarrying activity.

- Conifer plantations, other woodland belts and scrub.

- Open heathland areas.

- Expanding urban areas, scattered residential development, industrial estates, main roads, power lines.

DESCRIPTION

The basic topography comprises a fairly extensive flat-bottomed river valley, the flood plain of the middle Teign and its major tributary, the Bovey. The resulting basin is ringed by hills, these generally having a wooded aspect. On its western side the flanks of Dartmoor form these hills, but this edge of Dartmoor is rather gentler than some and the appearance is not dissimilar to the remainder of the Basin's rim.

The landscape of the Zone has been much affected by open-cast ball clay quarrying activity. Clay working has a long history in the Bovey Basin, and is the basis of a number of historical features such as early clay-drying cellars, pottery works and the Stover Canal. However, the scale of modern industrial extraction is such that its impact on the landscape is now very substantial.

Pits, spoil heaps, settling lakes, loading bays and other associated buildings all have an impact; safety features such as flashing lights and warning sirens add to this impact. Despite the best efforts, dust settles over neighbouring vegetation and the presence of heavy vehicles on the roads has a further impact. Considerable restoration works have been undertaken on former spoil heaps in order to disguise them. These have had an ameliorating effect, but the presence of large, unnaturally regular-shaped hills in an otherwise level river basin does have an impact on the landscape.

General development has been the other main factor with an effect on the landscape. In the south of the Zone the large town of Newton Abbot is expanding and has now all but merged with its smaller neighbour Kingsteignton. Around both are suburban developments, shopping warehouses and industrial buildings, covering the original form of the landscape.

Elsewhere in the Zone suburban and industrial development is creeping across the basin floor, as at Heathfield and Liverton. The result of all this is that areas of typical urban fringe activity occur, for example uncontrolled motor-bike scrambling on rough ground, trespass, fly-tipping, advertising and unmanaged agricultural land.

On the positive side, there are areas of heathland, valuable as an ecological resource and as an unusual landscape feature. Areas exist on the north and east of the Basin, although it is undoubtedly true that these were formerly much more extensive and are now ringed by main roads, development and quarries.

A further feature of the Basin's landscape is its extensive coniferous and mixed plantations. Some of these are of considerable antiquity as landscape features, if not as woodlands, those at Great Plantation and Stover dating back to the end of the eighteenth century. Their effect, aided by other narrow belts of woodland, is to help screen, soften and absorb the impact of development and quarrying.

In addition, around the northern and western edges of the Zone are areas of mixed farming interspersed with blocks of woodland, which give a rural aspect to the landscape.

The heart of the Zone is the course of the Teign and its tributary Bovey, meandering over its flood plain. In places the rivers display typical features – water meadows, drainage ditches, large straight-edged fields with hedges – and this helps preserve a degree of the essence of the Basin's landscape. Elsewhere, however, clay quarrying has progressed to the very course of the river and on reaching Newton Abbot it is lined by industrial development.

The Zone's boundaries are fairly clear cut, reflecting the topography of the river basin. Only to the south are there no hills to mark the edge of the Zone; here the transition to the Teign Estuary, and to the higher, dissected landscape west of Newton Abbot, marks the boundary.

SUBJECTIVE RESPONSE

The reaction over most of the Zone is that the landscape is no longer a major factor in the environment. Various developments – quarrying, residential, industrial – have so greatly reshaped the look and feel of the area that a response to the landscape itself is difficult. The presence of major road corridors which cross both axes of the Zone add to the effect.

The immediate response is thus that the Zone represents an urban or quasi-urban environment,

Opposite page: *Old clay pit in the Bovey Basin.*

Right: *Heathland in the eastern Bovey Basin, overlooked by power lines.*

that it is uniformly 'busy' – everywhere there is movement, noise. The essence of the Basin – its flat-bottomed shape – has been diluted by quarrying, spoil heaps and various developments. Even as viewed from surrounding land, the developments that have occurred do not always make good visual neighbours.

Yet all is not doom and gloom. Over a surprisingly large area the essential wooded rim of the Basin is still visible, keeping a contact with the original essential landform. Further, on some of the edges of the Zone in particular, the blocks of woodland, plantations, hedgerows and trees make for a surprisingly rural appearance; with the proximity of the neighbouring highlands the effect is very positive. The landscape here has an unexpectedly enclosed feel and the presence of Dartmoor nearby has a positive effect, not giving the 'brooding' atmosphere found in some other areas with a Dartmoor skyline.

Heathlands and ponds add to the mix and give the Basin a considerable importance in ecological terms. The heathland also helps keep a degree of 'wildness' in visual terms. The ponds are artificial, mostly drowned clay pits, but the largest, Stover Lake, was designed as an artificial landscape feature from the outset in the eighteenth century. Another, Pottery Pond, also has a long history and is now an informal recreational resource.

INTEGRITY

The general description of the Bovey Basin indicates the extent to which various forms of development have had an impact on the landscape and how the integrity of its essential character has been severely eroded. However, it also indicates that the entire integrity has not been destroyed. As such, it is important that what remains is retained and that efforts are made to lessen the impact of development on the Zone, as befits an area which is justifiably billed a 'Gateway to Dartmoor', through which large numbers of visitors pass travelling between the moor and the coastal area of Torbay.

In effect, this means retention of the largely undeveloped Zone fringes, retention of the wooded rim, of the wooded blocks and strips and management of the plantations, further screening of roads, development and operational areas and the retention of as much of the integrity as is possible of the central river corridor.

An attractive face of the Basin; Bovey Tracey beneath wooded hills.

25. TOURIST RIVIERA

SOUTHERN DEVON
25. Tourist Riviera

LOCATION

The Zone stretches along the English Channel coast from Dawlish Warren at the mouth of the Exe to Berry Head, the southern limit of Tor Bay. It includes the resorts of Dawlish and Teignmouth, the Teign Estuary and the urban development of Torbay – Torquay, Paignton and Brixham – and its immediate hinterland.

DESIGNATIONS

With the exception of the developed areas, most of the Zone has been designated as an Area of Great Landscape Value, indicating a landscape of County importance. The County Council's Coastal Preservation Area designation covers the undeveloped coastal areas and the Teign Estuary.

KEY CHARACTERISTIC FEATURES

- Extensive coastal development of resorts and associated tourist infrastructure.

- Elegant seafront parks, promenades, palms, pines, white 'riviera' buildings.

- Small-scale, dissected, hilly landscape in hinterland.

- Tidal Teign Estuary, largely undeveloped.

- Coastal cliffs, ranging from red sandstone to limestone headlands.

- Steep urban areas overlooking bay, estuary and harbours.

DESCRIPTION

This Zone comprises a very narrow coastal lowland area backed by a frequently steeply rising hinterland. It is characterised by considerable coastal development. Most of the actual coastal frontage is developed, with the exception of the length between the Teign Estuary and Maidencombe. The resorts of Dawlish and Teignmouth occupy most of the coastline north of the Teign, while to the south Torquay reaches the coast north of Hope's Nose and, together the virtually continuous development at Paignton and Brixham, takes up the coastline of Tor Bay.

The coastal development is very tourist orientated. The atmosphere is relatively sophisticated, formal and elegant, with seafront parks and promenades, palm trees and pines and white 'riviera' type buildings. Brixham is something of an exception, its image as a traditional fishing port acting as a tourist attraction and thus being less formal in appearance.

While the coast is largely developed, the Zone does include some impressive cliff scenery. Red sandstone cliffs, complete with stacks and arches, are found in the Dawlish and Teignmouth areas and through parts of Torquay. In contrast, the southern end is marked by the imposing limestone headland of Berry Head.

There is a break in the cliff-line at Teignmouth, where the Teign Estuary meets the sea, framed by Teignmouth and its sandy spit on one side and the red headland of the Ness on the other. The estuary also marks the only break in the line of hillier land forming the hinterland of the Zone. The broad estuary is largely undeveloped, especially on its southern bank, and forms a gap enabling views between Dartmoor and the sea.

The resorts climb steeply inland, giving views over the sea, the Teign Estuary, Tor Bay and the resorts' harbours, and they themselves provide a backdrop to views inland from the sea. However, behind the resorts, and in the gap between the Teign Estuary and the Torbay developed area, the Zone displays a much more rural appearance. South of the Teign Estuary, especially, is a deeply dissected area characterised by deep, narrow valleys and a maze of sinuous lanes. The steep slopes show to advantage the plentiful hedges surrounding relatively small fields and the distinctively red soil. Villages and hamlets of cob and thatch, of 'typical' Devon appearance, contrast with the formality of the coastal resorts.

The inland boundary of the Zone is marked by a series of landscape transitions; to the higher, obvious feature of Little Haldon, to the developed area of Newton Abbot at the head of the Teign Estuary, and to the crest of the rim of high land which backs Tor Bay.

SUBJECTIVE RESPONSE

The formal, elegant townscapes of the Riviera resorts have a distinctiveness and an attraction of their own, and one which very much typifies this part of the Devon coast. The appeal is added to by the impressive cliff features which punctuate the coastline, by the Teign Estuary, by the surrounding areas of undeveloped land and by the frequent and often abrupt changes of slopes in the resorts themselves. This latter also helps the appeal by offering a range of views over town and sea.

The formal, elegant appearance of Torquay.

The near proximity of surprisingly undeveloped land adds to the appeal. In Torbay fingers of green follow steep valleys between development towards the sea, creating welcome contrasts. The area between the Teign Estuary and Torbay is especially undeveloped and the narrow valleys with their sinuous roads and tracks, sometimes soaring steeply up a valley side, can bring a surprising character of remoteness. The terrain, the hedges and small fields, red soil and cob and thatch villages all create an unexpected atmosphere so close to busy resort areas. The area's undeveloped nature is also important as a backdrop to the Teign Estuary. Only on the very top of the ridges, where views encompass the higher parts of Teignmouth and Torquay, is the relationship with the rest of the Zone seen.

Similarly surprising reactions can be obtained in the hinterland of Torbay. Here also is a steeply dissected landscape of small farms, orchards, small fields and red soils, but here rather more interspersed with caravan sites and industrial estates. The proximity of the A380 Torbay Ring Road and its sights and sounds further impinge on this area.

INTEGRITY

The formal townscapes are much cherished and considerable efforts are made to maintain and enhance them. Threats to the integrity of the landscape of this Zone relate more to the surrounding rural areas.

In particular, the integrity of the urban fringe to the west of Torbay is fragile. Its position on a rim of highland, passed through by the A380 Ring Road, punctuated by industrial premises, caravan sites, and seasonal tourist markets, make it especially vulnerable, to the possible detriment both of this Zone and its neighbours to the west. Conservation and strengthening of existing features such as the hedgerow network could help maintain the integrity here, and development on the Ring Road needs careful attention.

Other rural areas seem less vulnerable, but vigilance will be required to ensure that the integrity of the area south of the Teign Estuary is not encroached upon. Given its topography, this area should be relatively safe, but ribbon development along the valleys or on the ridges would shatter its character. The estuary itself may also be vulnerable, for example to expansion from existing settlements, and this would also have an impact on the Zone.

The urban areas, as mentioned, have less of a threat to their integrity but the tree and woodland networks throughout the resorts will need maintenance and, in particular, the tree features which give the Zone its character, especially formal palms and Monterey pines, will need maintenance and replacement as appropriate.

The old fishing port of Brixham; a more informal scene.

26. SOUTH DEVON COASTAL PLATEAUX

SOUTHERN DEVON

26. South Devon Coastal Plateaux

LOCATION

This Zone consists of six separate plateaux on the southernmost coast of Devon between Torbay and Plymouth. From east to west they are:

- the area between Brixham and the Dart Estuary;

- Start Point to the Kingsbridge-Salcombe Estuary;

- Bolt Head to Bolt Tail;

- the area between the Avon and Erme Estuaries;

- the area between the Erme and Yealm Estuaries;

- the area between the Yealm Estuary and Plymouth Sound.

DESIGNATIONS

All the separate parts of the Zone have national recognition as part of the South Devon Area of Outstanding Natural Beauty. The most coastal parts are also designated by Devon County Council as Coastal Preservation Area and have been defined as Heritage Coast by the Countryside Agency.

KEY CHARACTERISTIC FEATURES

- Unconnected areas of relatively flat coastal plateaux cut by narrow, steep combes which are sometimes wooded.

- Arable or mixed farming landscape with exposed character of windswept, stunted trees.

- Distinctive geological coastal features.

- Historic coastal features – lighthouses, daymarks, coastguard cottages, forts, wrecks.

- No through roads creating 'cut-off' character.

- Popular recreation locations.

DESCRIPTION

While there are subtle differences between each of the six individual elements the overall appearance of each has much in common. Each element consists of an area of relatively flat plateau land, undulating to a greater or lesser extent, deeply cut through by narrow, steep combes, some of which are wooded. Land-use is mixed farming, but arable land is the most common individual use. The plateaux are divided into medium-to-large sized fields. Most field boundaries are hedges, but stone walls, using local hard schists, are found in some locations, notably around Prawle and between Bolt Head and Bolt Tail. Trees are relatively rare on the plateaux, but there arc examples of hedgerow trees in particular which are wind-beaten, emphasising the coastal character.

The plateaux reach the coast at an impressive line of cliffs, the geology giving rise to stark headlands, hidden coves, raised beaches, offshore rocks and caves. There are some notable headlands, including Bolt Head, Bolt Tail, Start Point, Froward Point and Prawle Point, the most southerly point in Devon. Only in the most western element, between the Yealm and Plymouth Sound, is the line of cliffs relatively low, although here is the most note-worthy offshore island, the Great Mew Stone.

The plateau fronted by a raised beach at Prawle.

The importance of the sea as a means of communication along this once very remote coastline has resulted in a number of man-made features distinctive in the landscape. Lighthouses at Berry Head, the eastern extremity, and Start Point; coastguard cottages at Dartmouth and Prawle Point; the daymark at Dartmouth; forts fringing Plymouth Sound.

Settlement has been generally sparse on the plateau tops, being mostly confined to valleys, especially in peripheral areas where they relate more to the neighbouring estuaries. There are exceptions, however; Bigbury and Malborough are two examples of plateau villages, the latter especially a landmark with its church spire visible over a wide area. In the westernmost element also, between the Yealm and Plymouth Sound, plateau top settlement is relatively common.

The boundaries of the Zone's separate elements are generally clear-cut, marking the transition between the high plateau area and the neighbouring estuary lands or sandy bays.

The plateau character of the inland landscape between the Avon and the Erme.

SUBJECTIVE RESPONSE

Although a plateau area, it is the coast which defines and characterises the various elements of this Zone and gives it its distinctive character. The natural and man-made coastal features are particularly impressive and have resulted in the area being popular for recreation. In addition, views of the sea are possible from large areas of the plateaux, sometimes in more than one direction and this, together with the general lack of visible development, adds to the popular recreational appeal.

Road access throughout the Zone remains relatively poor, especially to the coastline itself, and consequently it is possible to experience a sense of isolation and remoteness along various parts of the coast, except perhaps in high summer. However, the very popularity of the coast plus the narrow winding roads can give rise to very busy locations and mini-traffic jams at one or two places in high summer, dispelling the remote feel for a time. This is most likely in the two elements either side of the Salcombe Estuary.

The Zone's character is further defined by the geography. Each element forms virtually a peninsula, a large cul-de-sac. There is, as a result, something of an 'end-of-the-line' feel to some parts of the Zone, a feeling that the end of Devon has been reached and it is impossible to go any further. It is perhaps most strongly felt at East Prawle but locations such as Bolberry and Soar (between Bolt Head and Bolt Tail), Coleton (near Kingswear) and Kingston can provoke a similar reaction.

The secluded character is probably least obvious in the two extreme elements, east and west, where urban influences from nearby Torbay and Plymouth are felt. East of Kingswear the impact of

Torbay is minimal, but west of the Yealm, Plymouth exerts a pressure on the character of the plateau. Here plateau top semi-suburban development has occurred in places, there is an extensive wirescape and views over the Sound feature the urban area of Plymouth, with a consequent sense of being almost an appendage to the urban area.

INTEGRITY

This impressive coastline is a gem both in County and national terms. Other than west of the Yealm its integrity in landscape terms is well preserved, but such is its importance that its retention must be a high priority. Of importance is the need to retain a sympathetic appearance to the many examples of farm building conversion which occur here; also a sympathetic appearance to areas of amenity land, golf courses, caravan sites and MOD land; a retention of the open appearance of the plateaux; maintenance and repair of the field boundaries in traditional style; and the maximisation of ecological habitats.

Coastguard cottages add to the character of the landscape at Mansands.

27. RIA COASTLINE

SOUTHERN DEVON
27. Ria Coastline

© Crown copyright. All rights reserved. Devon County Council. Licence No. LA076562 2001

LOCATION

This Zone occupies the coast of South Devon between Torbay and Plymouth, enfolding the six separate elements of the Coastal Plateaux Zone. It includes the estuaries of the major South Devon rivers, including that of the Dart upstream as far as Totnes.

DESIGNATIONS

The major part of the Zone has national landscape recognition as part of the South Devon Area of Outstanding Natural Beauty. Some of the most inland parts of the Zone are excluded from this,

but have been designated as Areas of Great Landscape Value as a landscape of County importance. The coastal fringe has been designated by Devon County Council as Coastal Preservation Area and defined by the Countryside Agency as Heritage Coast.

KEY CHARACTERISTIC FEATURES

- Major estuaries and rias (drowned river valleys) forming large expanses of inland tidal water and mudflats.

- Sudden landform variations adjacent to estuaries and rias.

- Plateau areas between rivers cut by streams and creeks with steeply undulating farmland and woodland.

- Historic settlements.

- Waterside features and water activities.

- Dense network of hedgebanks, green lanes, coastal tree groups, orchards.

- Freshwater coastal lagoons.

DESCRIPTION

The essence of the Zone is a waterside landscape, typically of an estuary or a ria, this being steeply flanked by wooded sides. Branching off the main waterways is an intricate network of tidal creeks, each generally ending abruptly at its head with a disproportionately small stream. Each creek is itself steeply flanked by hedge-patterned farmland or woodland. The waterway networks penetrate far inland, forming an historic means of transport

and, conversely, making land communications difficult. They enable maritime climatic influences to penetrate inland, bringing an associated landscape with them.

The tidal systems result in a very characteristic landscape, which can change markedly between wide expanses of water and shimmering mud flats. Frequently, however, the topography is such that views of the estuaries and creeks are tantalisingly fleeting, usually from one of the high sides.

The estuaries and rias have long been important areas of settlement, especially when land transport was difficult, and Devon's maritime heritage has much to do with such settlements in these sheltered estuaries. Settlements such as Dartmouth, Kingsbridge and Salcombe, each on an estuary or ria, add positively to the Zone's

The stone bridge over Bowcombe Creek, off the Kingsbridge Estuary.

landscape as a result of their setting and architecture. The presence of maritime trees such as Monterey pine adds to their appearance. In addition, the historic features associated with many of these waterways – dams, weirs, mills, boat houses, lime kilns, ferries, quays — now provide local 'colour' and, not infrequently, tourist facilities.

The Zone also includes major lowland coastline areas between the rias occupied by reed-fringed freshwater lagoons. Most noteworthy is Slapton Ley, separated from the sea by a shingle and sand bar, but similar smaller features exist nearby at Widdicombe Ley and South Milton Ley. These features are important ecological habitats.

The flanking high farmlands create a considerable contrast to the estuaries, rias and lagoons. Typically they occupy a limited area of high land before plunging steeply into a neighbouring valley. Farming is mixed, with substantial field boundaries of hedgebanks. Often these are low,

with few hedgerow trees, more as a result of exposure to salt-laden winds than over-enthusiastic maintenance. Occasional tree groups, including pine and holm oak, occur in roadside hedges or on the edges of villages, and they add a distinctive feature to the landscape.

The Zone is crossed by a dense network of lanes, including many unmetalled green lanes, historically linking villages and hamlets. These settlements are typically located in the sheltered fold of a side valley off an estuary, or at the head of a creek or ria. Even those at the mouth of an estuary, such as Dartmouth and Salcombe, are hidden away from the excesses of the prevailing winds or potentially unfriendly prying eyes. In places, villages are more prominent, such as West Alvington or Churchstow, the church tower of the latter prominent over a wide area. Some of the settlements retain vestiges of their orchards, once common in the valleys and even now still an element in the landscape in places.

The Zone's boundaries reflect the rise in height to the coastal plateaux on the one hand, and to the inland plateau lands less affected by the maritime estuary influences on the other.

SUBJECTIVE RESPONSE

The combination of an extensive network of tidal creeks allied to enfolding high land, often incorporating woodland, is a powerful one. Oak woodlands fringing the estuaries and creeks bring a secluded, almost secretive character to these parts of the Zone, some of which are virtually only accessible by water. The effect is heightened by the contrast in character between high and low tide.

Views of the ria systems are often from neighbouring high land, and frustrating glimpses rather than expansive views. This adds to the secretive nature of the waterways, giving almost an air of mystery. Where paths and roads do

Slapton Ley, enclosed behind its shingle bar.

Newton Ferrers and Noss Mayo, on the sheltered inlet of Newton Creek.

Historic settlement on the Dart Estuary.

fringe one of the estuary shores they are usually low-key and their limited use has not intruded on the estuary's character.

Neighbouring high farmland has quite a different feel, as benefits its lofty height, but the proximity to the rias and more minor stream valleys and steep slopes mean that the influence of the character of the water features is still felt here. The often-wooded slopes have a particular impact.

Different again, if related, is the impact of the lagoons. These are very unusual features nationally as well as in Devon and form a landscape much admired and wondered at.

The Zone's settlement and other historic features seem to complement the topographic environment. The appearance of settlements such as Dartmouth, Salcombe and Kingsbridge, with their architecture of merchants' and seafarers' properties and coastal trees, of estuary-side parklands and estates, of historic defensive forts, all enhance the environment, and the estuary villages and smaller features such as bridges over creeks, mills and lime kilns add further interest. It is a landscape with a very human scale, a very obvious human influence and yet still with a natural appearance and pockets of seclusion.

INTEGRITY

The landscape integrity of this much-loved area is generally intact, but pressures exist. Such a popular area clearly gives rise to development pressure, and expansion is occurring at some of the larger settlements, especially Dartmouth and Kingsbridge. Because of the topography, expansion can generally only occur on to high land, where it can be seen over a wide area, to the visual detriment of the landscape character, or along valleys, where it erodes part of the essence of the Zone's landscape character. Some extensions have already had a visual effect on parts of the estuaries.

Recreation pressures also exist. The Zone has not been badly affected by developments such as caravan sites, although in the summer touring sites and camping sites can alter the landscape character of some areas to a surprising degree. Water-borne recreation has had a particular effect in some areas, for example the marina development on the Dart Estuary.

Trees are important to the character of the Zone. The wooded flanks of the rias and creeks are fundamental in giving the atmosphere of seclusion and loss of these, be it deliberate or through lack of replacement and management, would considerably alter the landscape character. Town trees are also significant, the Monterey pines at the mouths of some estuaries being particularly important to the character. Further up the estuaries, parkland trees, and indeed the actual formal parklands themselves, add a dimension which would be missed.

The coastal rias penetrate far inland; here, from Salcombe towards Kingsbridge.

151

28. UNDER DARTMOOR

SOUTHERN DEVON
28. Under Dartmoor

LOCATION

The slightly ambiguous Zone title refers to the area of South Devon immediately to the south of Dartmoor. It stretches from Newton Abbot and Totnes in the east to the outskirts of Plymouth in the west, extending south towards Kingsbridge.

DESIGNATIONS

An area in the centre, where the valley of the River Avon crosses the Zone, is part of the South Devon Area of Outstanding Natural Beauty, a designation indicating national landscape significance. Large areas of the remainder of the Zone have been designated an Area of Great Landscape Value, indicative of a landscape of County significance. Parts of the western end of the Zone, the area between the Avon and Dart valleys and that to the north-east of the Dart Valley have no designations.

KEY CHARACTERISTIC FEATURES

- A plateau surface dissected by major rivers flowing off Dartmoor.

- Complex, steeply undulating landform shaping the overall plateau, the result of a network of streams and valleys.

- Farming landscape dominated by Dartmoor on the northern skyline.

- Patchwork of fields, small woodlands and hedgerows with some estate planting, including hilltop clumps.

- Scattered settlement of dispersed farmsteads and villages.

- Elements of limestone scenery in the north east.

- Influence of the A38 road along the northern edge.

DESCRIPTION

The basic landform consists of a plateau surface, highest generally in the area between the Dart and the Avon and immediately west of the Avon, but never as high as the coastal plateaux to the south. This plateau surface is cut through by a series of major rivers flowing generally south off Dartmoor to the sea. The Dart, the easternmost of these, is the largest in scale, while the Avon is perhaps the most dramatic. To the west, the valleys of the Erme and the Yealm are wider, shallower and more an integral part of the overall landscape which is, in any event, lower here.

As well as the major north–south river valleys, the plateau is further dissected by a large number of smaller valleys, each quite steep, deeply cutting into the landform, each with a stream. There is no definite grain to these valleys, creating a complex detailed pattern superimposed on the overall plateau form.

The essence of the land-use pattern is a patchwork of some arable land and much improved pasture, small scale woodlands and some forestry. On the higher, flatter land the fields tend to be larger and relatively regular in shape, whereas on the flanks of the valleys there is a more intimate pattern of smaller fields. North-east of the Dart there is a slightly different pattern with perhaps more woodland and areas of formal parkland, including hilltop clumps. This part of the Zone also includes an area where an outcrop of limestone occurs, in the neighbourhood of Woodland and Denbury. Here is a distinctively flatter area, less dissected, with calcareous grassland. Unusually for this Zone, the limestone area is characterised by stone walls rather than hedges.

The Dart Valley forms a major feature through the Zone, well defined although complicated by prominent hill features within the valley. The river is generally lined with trees, and there are substantial woodland areas at Dartington.

Equally well defined is the Avon Valley. Less wide than the Dart Valley, arguably less a factor in the landscape as a whole, it is very important as a deep and narrow wooded cleft cut through the heart of the Zone. The steep wooded sides, flat floor and secretive tree-lined river set it apart from most of the Zone.

To the west the general height of the Zone falls somewhat so that the Erme and Yealm Valleys, although still distinct features, are far more integral to the overall landscape than are the Dart and Avon.

Settlement in the Zone is scattered, perhaps more common in the valleys but not uncommon on the plateau. It is perhaps most dense in the east, especially north-east of the Dart.

The whole Zone is overlooked by the rim of Dartmoor, defining its character and giving it its name. The influence of Dartmoor is clearly strongest in the north, but even in the south never entirely absent. North-east of the Dart the high

moorland recedes to the north, lessening the impact somewhat but again, never entirely absent.

The northern boundary of the Zone is very much defined by the Dartmoor fringe, and by the A38 which effectively cuts Dartmoor and its fringe off from these Under Dartmoor lands. East and west more urban influences define the boundary, Newton Abbot and Torbay to the east, Plymouth to the west. Only to the south is the landscape transition more subtle, the boundary indicating the line of the more maritime influences coming from the rias.

SUBJECTIVE RESPONSE

Although there are areas of exception, most of the Zone is characterised by a character of remoteness. Away from the few main roads, access is via a network of narrow lanes, following ridgelines or valleys, more frequently plunging and rearing between the two, making any sense of direction

very difficult. The landscape types add to this character, be it high and airy farmland, Dartmoor on the horizon, or secretive narrow valley, stream running along the bottom, crossed perhaps by an old stone bridge. The fact that the two types are generally so intimately inter-related adds to the overall appeal.

Of the larger valleys, the Avon is similar in character and appeal to the smaller valleys – wooded, secretive and remote. The Dart is less remote, especially as it carries an important road linking Totnes with the A38, but the self-contained nature of the valley, contrasting with the surrounding landscape, its unpredictability within the context of the obvious valley and its 'starting' and 'finishing' point of Dartmoor and the handsome historic town of Totnes give the valley great visual appeal.

The character of remoteness is perhaps less obvious to the north of the Dart, where settlement

Over Diptford to the ever-present rim of Dartmoor.

153

is more dense, the influence of Newton Abbot and Torbay begins to pervade the countryside, the dissected nature of the topography is less intense and the influence of Dartmoor more distant. In the far west, beyond the Yealm, urban influences of Plymouth, developments along the A38, more central to the Zone here, and the sight and sound of the road itself, all begin to draw this part of the Zone into the embrace of the urban fringe.

The influence of the A38 is a potent one along the northern edge of the Zone, although rarely as strong as in the west. The road itself is not a great visual intruder, but its sound is, the distant hum of traffic impinging on an otherwise remote and peaceful location along much of the northern part of the area.

INTEGRITY

As discussed above, much of the Zone has a remote character and this is reflected by a high level of retention of the landscape integrity over the bulk of the area. Efforts to safeguard some character elements might be worthwhile however, especially those which are integral to the landscape, including small-scale woodlands, clumps, hedgerow trees and lines of grown-out hedgerow trees which are characteristic of the skyline in some parts of the Zone, also small areas of unimproved land in valley bottoms or on steep slopes, which add to the landscape mosaic.

Generally, however, the pressure on the integrity of the landscape character comes from a variety of development sources. Here and there modern farm buildings are found on the plateau, intruding somewhat into its open aspects. Around the edges of the Zone residential expansion is occurring at

the larger settlements, including Totnes, the Newton Abbot area and Ivybridge, and the effect is to eat away at the essential character of the landscape in these areas. More insidiously, the impact of the major urban areas of Torbay and Plymouth also affects the landscape, the latter more particularly. Views of suburbs, industrial buildings, busy roads, playing fields and the like bring a totally alien character to the fringe of the Zone, exacerbated by urban fringe effects such as fly-tipping, lack of care of agricultural land and neglect of hedges and gates.

The effect of the A38 along the northern edge of the Zone has been the remaining noteworthy factor. This has created a corridor quite different in character to that found over most of the area. In fact, except in parts of the west of the Zone the visual envelope is not very wide, views of the road being quite narrowly confined other than from occasional vantage points. For the most part, the impact is on the more intangible character of the

Zone, particularly as a result of traffic noise, but also as a psychological reminder that maybe these northern parts of this Zone are not so remote as they seem at first sight.

Above: *The Erme Valley cuts through the wider local landscape.*

Much of the 'Under Dartmoor' area is a rolling patchwork landscape, as here north of Totnes.

DARTMOOR AND WEST DEVON

This grouping of four Landscape Character Zones represents quite a diverse range of landscapes, from some of the remotest areas in southern England to the centre of a city of over a quarter of a million inhabitants.

The area is dominated by the highland massif of Dartmoor, a remarkable landscape in its own right but also one which influences most of the surrounding landscapes. The Dartmoor-enclosed fringes have an especially close landscape relationship with the high moor, and to the west the lower Tavy Valley represents part of the continuum of landscape whose end is those same moorland heights. The Tamar is closely integrated with the Tavy at the estuary, although it does not itself flow off the moor. To a greater or lesser extent however, the Tamar Valley is overlooked by Dartmoor; in many paces, indeed, the valley can seem almost sandwiched between its high neighbours where Bodmin Moor approaches the County boundary from the west.

Plymouth, at first sight, seems more to turn its back on Dartmoor. The city very much faces the sea, and its history and wider relationships have always been very much closer to the sea than the moor. Approach Plymouth Sound from the sea, however, and the proximity of the moor overlooking the city is more obvious. Plymouth also has its historical relationships with Dartmoor, not least its series of leats which have supplied the city with fresh water since Drake's time and which can still be seen in the landscape today.

Thus while representing a diverse group of landscapes, this part of Devon also represents much of the County's landscape essence, not only visual but historic.

The south-west edge of Dartmoor overlooks Plymouth and its river valleys.

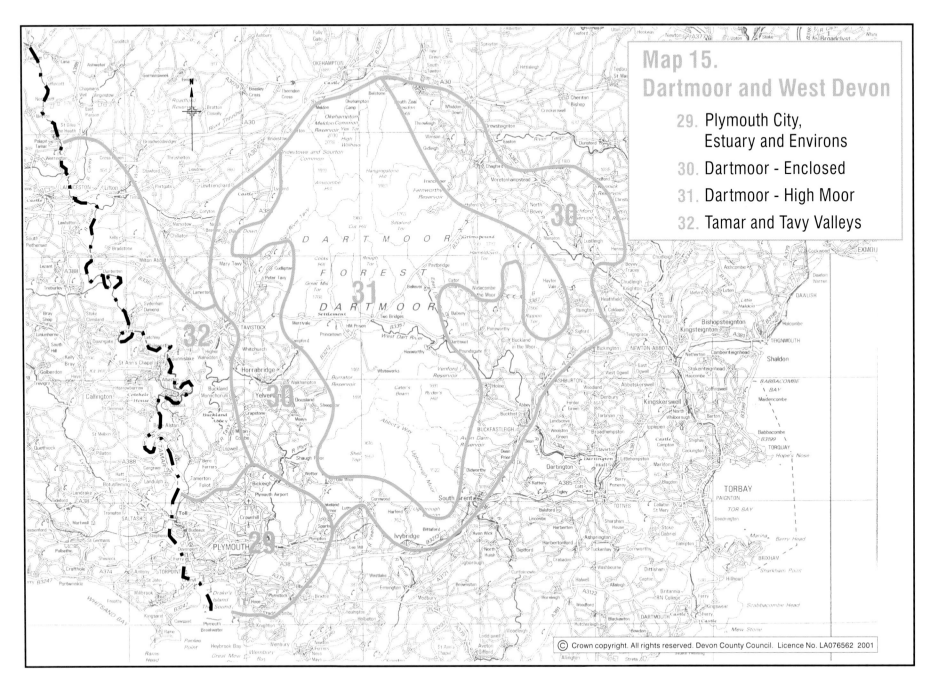

Map 15.
Dartmoor and West Devon

29. Plymouth City, Estuary and Environs
30. Dartmoor - Enclosed
31. Dartmoor - High Moor
32. Tamar and Tavy Valleys

29. PLYMOUTH CITY, ESTUARY AND ENVIRONS

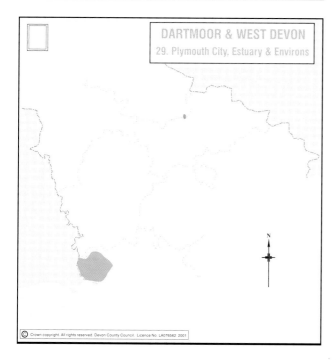

DARTMOOR & WEST DEVON
29. Plymouth City, Estuary & Environs

LOCATION

The Zone is located in the extreme south-west corner of Devon, based on the City of Plymouth. It includes the lower estuary of the Tamar, which is Plymouth's western frontage and shared with Cornwall, as well as the immediate hinterland of the City to its east, north east and south east.

DESIGNATIONS

To the north-east of Plymouth is an area which has the County designation of an Area of Great Landscape Value indicating its County landscape significance. This reflects the landscape of the Plym Valley and its surroundings. A very small strip of land on the eastern side of Plymouth Sound is within the national designation of the South Devon Area of Outstanding Natural Beauty. This same area has been designated as Coastal Preservation Area by the County Council.

KEY CHARACTERISTIC FEATURES

- Historic waterfronts and dockyards surrounding a vast natural harbour.

- Water-based features – quays, marinas, dockyards, breakwaters, buoys, naval installations, Tamar Bridges.

- Water activity – ferries, yachts, dinghies, warships, sightseeing boats, fishing vessels, commercial shipping.

- Parkland, hilltop planting, tree features, steep wooded slopes, ridges and valleys.

- Skyline of Dartmoor as a backdrop.

- Variety of ecological habitats – cliffs, tidal estuaries, wooded valleys.

- Housing estates with regimented layouts often unsympathetic to landform.

DESCRIPTION

Plymouth owes its origins to the sea and it is a city dominated, appropriately, by its waterfront. It is blessed with what must surely be one of the most impressive natural environments of any major city in the country. It fronts a superb natural harbour which itself is framed by imposing cliffs, it sits between the estuaries of two rivers, Tamar and Plym, and is backed by the skyline of Dartmoor.

As a result of redevelopment following Plymouth's large-scale war damage during 1939–45, the current city centre layout differs considerably from that which had originally grown up as Plymouth grew inland from the coast. Nevertheless, this central area is on relatively flat land and its landscape impact does not have wide repercussions. Further north, however, the terrain becomes much more broken by increasingly steep slopes, valleys and ridges; a topography reflecting tributary streams feeding the Tamar or the Plym. Once development reached these areas its relationship to the difficult terrain became very important. To a large extent, the steep ridges and wooded valleys have been retained as part of the developed area, and these features have a great effect in breaking up the visual impact of the urban environment and in retaining the original

The rebuilt city centre of Plymouth looking towards the Hoe.

pattern of the topography. However, considerable areas of housing, both pre- and post-war, do comprise long lines with straight roofscapes and can then often appear very unsympathetic to the landform.

As Plymouth continues to expand, it encounters continuing steep slopes and ever higher terrain. As a result, more modern developments can become visible over quite wide areas both within the Zone and beyond it, a situation which the retention of natural breaks or the provision of screening can never quite overcome. Some of the larger peripheral developments, particularly industrial buildings, are quite prominent features in the landscape.

While water (the Sound and the estuaries) and development are perhaps the main defining features of the Zone, other factors also have an impact. The influence of woodland is particularly important. Its role in breaking up the visual impact of development internally has been highlighted, but to the north of the City especially it is an important landscape feature in its own right. Here the River Plym has carved a substantial valley prior to opening out into its estuary, and the valley is lined with mixed woodland. This, and neighbouring woodlands both broadleaved and coniferous, help contain the urban effect of the City and soften the sight of it as viewed from the slopes of Dartmoor.

The northern and eastern edges of the City are also home to areas of parkland, remnants of grand estates established over many centuries. In addition, the fine parkland of Mount Edgcumbe, while situated over the Tamar in Cornwall, has an important visual effect on Plymouth's setting.

Around the northern rim of the Zone the land rises towards Dartmoor, providing a superb backdrop to the City although here and there spoiled by the bright white of china clay workings. The change to a more open, moorland-orientated landscape from the mixed pastoral and arable fields, hedges and woodland of the outer urban area marks the edge of the Zone here. Further west it is defined by Tamerton Lake, a tidal creek containing the urban area while to the south the boundary marks the transition to the rural landscapes of the coastal plateau east of the Sound and the wooded ria creeks.

SUBJECTIVE REACTION

Plymouth Hoe has been described as affording the finest vista from a major urban area any-where in the country. Together with the nearby Barbican and Sutton Harbour, the true origins of Plymouth, these waterfronts create and reflect a landscape full of visual and historic interest.

Mount Batten, the Citadel and the mouth of the Plym.

Plymouth Sound as seen from the edge of Dartmoor.

If views from the waterfront are spectacular, views to it from the Sound or the cliffs which line it are equally full of interest. The Hoe, the Citadel, the various harbours and dockyards all create a scene of great impact, albeit a very urban scene. But although a scene of impact, it never overawes the senses nor, indeed, the natural harbour of the Sound and the estuaries on which it sits. There is a surprising harmony.

Inland, however, the reaction can be less positive. Retention of the natural valleys and ridges in the terrain has been mentioned, but this cannot always hide the regimented appearance of some areas of the City. The impact of large industrial buildings on the wider landscape of the Zone and its surroundings is likewise not always happy.

This is a busy, bustling, developed Zone containing over a quarter of the population of the historic County. From that perspective, even if there are some inevitable landscape concerns, they are, so far, relatively confined.

INTEGRITY

It is perhaps difficult to discuss the integrity of the landscape in a Zone which is largely developed, since it is not the role of *The Devon Landscape* to go into detail of urban design. Suffice it to say that the urban waterfront vistas, both to and from the City, are of very high quality; that the ridges and valleys which shape inland development are necessary to soften the already sometimes overpowering regimented impact, as well as offering a glimpse of the original topography; that the

woodlands and valleys of the Plym, Tamerton Lake, Tory Brook and their estuaries are vital to the integrity of the overall landscape setting as well as in softening the urban impact as viewed from afar.

There are, of course, concerns for the landscape integrity of the surroundings of Plymouth. The urban fringe influences including neglect of hedgerows, trees and agricultural land, piecemeal informal development, traffic, the ever-present faint urban noise, light pollution, all spread slowly north and east from the urban area over the Zone and into neighbouring areas. While specific actions can help stem the detailed visual landscape integrity concerns highlighted, it is more difficult to deal with the more diffuse, 'creeping' deterioration of the landscape's character resulting from these fringe activities.

Sutton Harbour; historic origin of Plymouth and waterfront landscape of great character and attraction.

159

30. DARTMOOR – ENCLOSED

DARTMOOR & WEST DEVON
30. Dartmoor - Enclosed

LOCATION

The Zone is a horseshoe-shaped area of land cupped around the eastern, southern and western sides of Dartmoor. It is a generally fairly narrow band stretching from South Zeal in the north-east all the way round to Bridestowe in the north-west, with a significantly expanded area towards Widecombe in the south.

DESIGNATIONS

Most of the Zone falls within the Dartmoor National Park, reflecting a landscape of national significance. Parts of the outer edges of the Zone in the west are excluded from the National Park. Here, a small area near Yelverton is included within another landscape of national importance, the Tamar Valley Area of Outstanding Natural Beauty. Other outer edges have been designated within the County's Areas of Great Landscape Value, including the fringes of the Lyd Valley in the north-west, the Plym Valley in the south-west and Crownhill Down further east.

KEY CHARACTERISTIC FEATURES

- Strongly undulating landscape underlain by granite geology.

- Cut by distinctive wooded valleys.

- Strong field pattern, characterised both by hedges and stone walls.

- Enclosed, wooded appearance deriving from the valley woodlands, bushy hedgerows and hedgerow trees.

- Close visual relationship with adjacent high moor.

- Granite buildings, especially farmhouses.

- China clay works.

DESCRIPTION

The essence of the Zone is a strongly undulating landscape, in places positively hilly. Land-use is generally pasture, fields tending towards the small to medium size and irregular in shape, but becoming larger and more rectilinear on some of the higher slopes, especially in the southern and western parts of the Zone. Field boundaries vary between hedgerows, stone-faced hedgebanks and drystone walls. In general, hedgerows are found at lower heights, walls at higher levels.

The Zone is cut by a number of significant river valleys, carved by rivers flowing off the high moor. These tend to be steep sided and are generally wooded. The wooded slopes comprise broadleaved woodland, often oak of semi-natural origin, and are of considerable ecological as well as visual importance.

Here and there throughout the Zone are areas of coniferous plantation. Generally they are relatively small in size, often on slopes and frequently intermixed with broadleaved woodland so that the landscape impact is reasonably limited. The greatest impact is probably found in the far north east of the Zone, where a small plateau area has been planted with coniferous trees, creating a less characteristic landscape. Generally, however, the Zone displays a well-wooded appearance of broadleaved character, this resulting from the combination of the valley woodlands, bushy hedgerows, hedgerow trees and hilly landform.

To the west of the Zone are areas of uncharacteristically open appearance, principally Crownhill Down, Roborough Down and Whitchurch Down. To an extent these areas have as much in common with the landscapes of the high moor as with the enclosed area, but their size, location and character places them more appropriately in this Zone. These are generally close-grazed areas of improved grass moorland, plateau-like in appearance, much used for recreation. Crownhill Down is slightly different to the others; an area of unimproved moorland but much affected by former quarrying activity and cut off from the remainder of the high moor by workings.

The china clay workings of the Lee Moor area are the other main landscape variation. Large open pits, settling lagoons and associated industrial buildings impact on the local landscape. A wider impact arises from the large spoil heaps, as a result of their size, shape and bright white colour. These impacts occur over a wider area than this Zone alone, although restoration provisions help to ameliorate the worst effects, at least from a distance.

Development over most of the Zone is fairly scattered, typically of individual farmsteads, often constructed of granite. Villages occur in the valleys, and are occasionally found in more prominent locations, especially hillsides, as at Shaugh Prior and Holne.

The 'outer' boundary of the Zone is largely marked by the geology, reflecting a change from the granite of this Zone. This also tends to reflect the change to the lower levels and generally less hilly landscapes of the neighbouring Zones. 'Inland', the boundary reflects the change to open moor and the generally higher levels associated with that area.

SUBJECTIVE RESPONSE

The topography and land cover of most of the Zone creates a generally enclosed atmosphere. This is emphasised by the maze of twisting, often steep lanes which cross the area, resulting in an easily lost sense of direction but also giving unexpected and often quite impressive views over valleys or up on to moorland. This, together with the dense valley woodlands, can result in an atmosphere of remoteness over much of the Zone. To an extent, the popularity of the area for recreation in the summer can reduce this atmosphere but it is never completely dispelled.

The role the Zone has as a foil to the high moorland above adds to the character of both areas and to the positive response evoked. This contrast, together with the intimate mix of landscape and habitats which typify the Zone, make it valuable scenically and ecologically.

The downs of the west do display a quite different character. These downs are high, open, airy, very popular as places of recreation, usually quite busy, never remote. However, they are relatively limited in size, are surrounded by the more typical landscape and character of the Zone and to an extent rely on these very surroundings for their appeal.

The china clay area evokes a quite different response. The character of the landscape is influenced not only by the visual impact of the workings and their plant and machinery, but by the noise, flashing lights, dust over the vegetation and heavy traffic, creating almost an urban fringe character in this part of the Zone.

INTEGRITY

Pressures do exist on the integrity of the Zone's landscape. These include pressures for hedgerow removal, most strongly at lower levels, pressures on the woodlands as a result of the lack of a commercial basis for their management, recreational pressures on the general landscape character, especially near Plymouth and Tavistock, and pressures from china clay quarrying.

Despite this, taking the landscape of the Zone as a whole, its integrity and character remain largely unspoiled and an important asset to the essence of Devon's landscape character as a whole.

Characteristic Dartmoor fringe landscape closely linked to the adjacent high moor.

31. DARTMOOR – HIGH MOOR

DARTMOOR & WEST DEVON
31. Dartmoor - High Moor

LOCATION

Dartmoor is situated in the west-central part of Devon, west of Exeter and north-east of Plymouth. The high moorland part of Dartmoor occupies the central part of Dartmoor.

DESIGNATIONS

The whole Zone is within Dartmoor National Park, a landscape of national importance.

KEY CHARACTERISTIC FEATURES

- Extensive high moorland of blanket bog, heath and grass moor.

- Natural granite features providing characteristic landmarks.

- Archaeological features, remnants of quarrying and other extractive workings.

- Visual skyline element of many Devon land scapes.

- Broad, sweeping skylines punctuated by tors; panoramic views and wild 'internal' vistas.

- Exposure to the elements.

- Recreational use.

- Ponies, cattle, sheep, walkers, cyclists, horse riders, kite-flyers, paragliders, parked cars.

DESCRIPTION

Dartmoor represents the largest upland landscape in southern England. It rises to over 600m/2000ft. towards its northern edge, the highest land in England south of the Peak District. The granite geology has created poor soils which, combined with the height and consequent exposure to the elements, give a characteristic land cover of blanket bog, heather and grass moorland.

The very highest and most exposed parts of the moor are the areas of blanket bog. These areas are in the north and south central parts of the high moor, separated by the main cross-moor roads between Tavistock and Yelverton in the west and

Moretonhampstead in the east. The area of blanket bog has been described as similar to a giant sponge, and from here radiate out many of Devon's rivers – the Plym, Yealm, Erme and Avon from the south, the Tavy, East and West Okement, Taw, East and West Dart, North and South Teign and Bovey from the north. These are areas of broad, sweeping horizons, virtually uninterrupted by any skyline features, completely uncultivated, no field boundaries visible for great distances.

Surrounding these very highest moors are areas of heathland and grass moor. Again characterised by broad, sweeping horizons, these moors also contain perhaps the most recognisable feature of the Dartmoor scene – granite tors on hilltops, surrounded by a scattering of surface rock or 'clitter'. These areas are grazed by cattle, sheep and ponies and in the valleys and around

A typical view of Dartmoor, here near Fernworthy.

settlements are enclosures taken in from the moor, these often small fields surrounded by drystone walls.

As the rivers radiate out of the areas of blanket bog they cut initially quite shallow valleys, barely perceptible as distinctive features in the landscape. By the time they reach the grass and heather moors they are beginning to become noticeable elements, and this is accentuated by the presence of the enclosures in the valleys. Initially fast-flowing, they slow down as they cut ever more incised valleys, these becoming quite major, often wooded features where they cross into the enclosed Dartmoor zone.

Other than in the valleys, woodland is rare on the high moor. Stunted ancient woodlands occur in one or two sheltered locations, but most noticeable in the landscape are the large areas of coniferous plantations found on the moorland at Bellever and Soussons near the centre of the Zone. The dark colour and straight edges of these areas are immediately recognisable and appear unsympathetic in the context of the moorland landscape.

Settlement is very sparse, and indeed is non-existent in the areas of blanket bog. On the heather and grass moorland it is confined to small settlements in the valleys. Only the largest moorland settlement, Princetown, is an exception, and this is an artificial settlement deliberately positioned in its exposed location.

Dartmoor is also very important as a skyline backdrop to many parts of Devon and in some areas in its immediate neighbourhood its presence almost defines the character of the landscape.

The Zone boundary is defined by the transition from high granite moorland, generally to the hilly, dissected, enclosed granite farming landscape which fringes it, but in the north the high moor ends abruptly at the shallow ridge landscape which rolls on towards the upper Tamar.

SUBJECTIVE RESPONSE

High Dartmoor has perhaps been subjected to more of a cliché landscape description than any comparable area in the country – swirling mists, rain, moonlit tors, treacherous bogs, archaeological remains – yet there is an element of truth in all these. It is indeed an area exposed to the elements with all that this implies – high rainfall, poor visibility – and an area of poor soils giving rise to the bogs. There are tors and there is much visible archaeology and a combination of these features and the relevant literature goes far towards defining the character of the landscape.

Nevertheless, vast areas are never experienced by more than a handful of people. These, the areas of blanket bog, are truly remote, possibly among the most remote in the country, certainly in southern England. Commonly described as a 'wilderness', the purist will say that this is not so, that the hand of mankind, albeit with a light touch here, maintains it. While true, it is as near a wilderness as this crowded and long-settled country can provide.

Outside the areas of blanket bog, the moor presents a slightly less austere face. The natural elements are still paramount, the broad horizons enfold the visitor, but here the landscape is broken up by the tors, archaeological features, rivers, settlements and clapper bridges and, although it is still very easy to experience a character of remoteness, it is less guaranteed. This is especially the

Sourton Tors, on the north west edge of the moor, forms a skyline backdrop over a wide landscape.

163

case in summer, when Dartmoor's recreational potential is maximised and walkers, cyclists and horse-riders may be encountered almost anywhere outside the blanket bog and every road, however minor, will carry its quota of cars. Mist and rain, however, is not unknown on Dartmoor even in summer, when the character will quickly change.

INTEGRITY

As a National Park, much effort is expended on maintaining the integrity of Dartmoor's landscape. A number of factors are of particular importance, covering both land use and human activity in a wider sense.

Although the open moorland appears unchanging, some areas of heathland and grass moorland are becoming invaded by bracken and ferns. In the short term this will not have a great impact on the landscape, but it affects the fragile ecology and will, in time, adversely affect the visual integrity of these moorlands if unchecked.

A feature which has already had an impact is the presence of the coniferous woodland plantations. The dark, unchanging face they present, straight-edged and uncompromising, represent an unsympathetic element in the landscape. However, many plantations are reaching the end of their current commercial rotation and it may be

possible to adjust the details of the replanting regimes to take more account of visual impact.

Concerns also exist regarding the impact on the landscape of visitor numbers, particularly in regard to erosion and to the visual impact of people and cars. Visitor management regimes are intended to address this, for the benefit of the integrity of the landscape character.

Another major issue regards the presence of the military. This impacts on character, access and appearance, with reference to lookout posts and the like. This is a national issue which has run for a long while and which continues to give rise to debate.

Soussons Plantations; unsympathetic to the moorland landscape.

Grimspound; an older face of Dartmoor.

32. TAMAR AND TAVY VALLEYS

DARTMOOR & WEST DEVON
32. Tamar and Tavy Valleys

LOCATION

The Tamar Valley is in the far west of the County, forming the majority of the length of the border with Cornwall. That part of the valley within this Zone is essentially the lower half, but excluding the lower estuary at Plymouth. The Zone thus stretches from just north of the A30 near Launceston to the northern edge of Plymouth. The Tavy is a major tributary of the Tamar, joining it at its estuary, and the Tavy Valley part of the Zone links the Tamar to the fringe of Dartmoor to the east.

DESIGNATIONS

Most of the Zone lies within the Tamar Valley Area of Outstanding Natural Beauty (AONB), a designation of national significance, which also covers the Cornish side of the valley. A small finger of Dartmoor National Park extends to the Tavy. North of Greystone Bridge on the Tavistock – Launceston road and the area around Tavistock and Lamerton are outside the AONB. However, an area between Greystone Bridge and Lifton has been designated as an Area of Great Landscape Value to reflect its County landscape importance.

KEY CHARACTERISTIC FEATURES

- Historic transport route, with quays, lime kilns, old ferry points, stone bridges.

- Wide estuary landscape lined with wetlands.

- Tidal middle valley with creeks, wetlands and wooded sides.

- Granite ridge giving gorge-like qualities.

- Mining heritage, including chimneys.

- Market gardens and orchards.

- Landscaped estates.

DESCRIPTION

The Tamar Valley displays a gradual, almost classic progression of river landscape types. In the south the estuary is broad, lined with low hills and tidal, with mudbanks and wetlands lining the main channel. The surrounding hillsides are mostly pastoral with hedgerows, often with substantial trees. The lowest part of the Tavy is of similar appearance.

Moving north the river begins to narrow and meander more. Creeks feed the main river; the whole system is still tidal with mudbanks and wetlands but the surrounding valley sides are steeper and more wooded, the valley more enclosed. There is still much valley-side pasture but here and there remnants of the formerly important market garden strips are seen. Most of the Tavy is of this appearance, minus the market gardening.

North again and the valley is crossed by a granite ridge resulting in a virtually gorge-like landscape north and south of Gunnislake New Bridge. The gorge sides are thickly wooded and rocky outcrops on the sides add further to the landscape. In this section the river ceases to be tidal.

Finally, north of the ridge the valley opens out again. While still a clear feature in the wider landscape the valley is much wider and shallower here. The river is lined with trees and twists over the valley floor. The general appearance of the landscape is still quite wooded and steeper and narrower side valleys, also wooded, add further variety. Estate parkland occurs as a landscape feature.

The Zone also includes the Bere Peninsula, the area between the estuaries of the Tamar and Tavy. Closely related to both rivers, the peninsula itself forms something of a plateau. The land-use is mixed farming, fields divided by substantial hedges, sometimes stone-banked.

The various parts of the Zone are bound together by a number of key features. Firstly, it is a route of historic importance, and the whole valley is lined by landscape features reflecting this – quays and

165

old ferry points, the access lanes leading to them, lime kilns, medieval stone bridges crossing the river and old fords.

Secondly, the historic importance of human activities has had a landscape impact. The valley has been important for mining since medieval times, with a great burst during the 19th century, and this has had its effect on the landscape with old mine chimneys in particular being characteristic. In addition, horticulture in the form of market gardens and orchards was also a characteristic land use. Largely gone now, remnants remain as reminders in the landscape.

Settlement tends to be scattered, individual farms being most common with one or two small villages. On the plateau of its peninsula, Bere Alston sits as the largest settlement fully within the Zone, although

the town of Tavistock, on the edge, is shared with the neighbouring enclosed Dartmoor Zone.

While the river marks the county boundary with Cornwall, it is clearly not the landscape boundary, so in this Zone the importance of the landscape impact of the neighbouring county must be borne in mind. It is often the Cornish valley landscape which is the main element of the view in the Devon Zone and, of course, the opposite is also true.

To the north, and the east above Lamerton, the Zone boundary marks the transition from a landscape inclined towards the Tamar to one which is part of the great line of shallow ridges stretching north. Below Lamerton the change is to downland outliers of Dartmoor and an intricate, enclosed landscape which is clearly the foreland to

the high moor. The southern boundary marks the abrupt change to the urban dominated area of Plymouth. To the west the Tamar marks the county boundary, with the valley landscapes of the Devon side replicated in Cornwall.

SUBJECTIVE RESPONSE

For an area which would have been a hub of industrial activity over much of its length just over a hundred years ago, the change to the current quiet, remote, almost secretive character is remarkable. The valley's historic role as a transport route meant that no roads were ever built along its length, and it remains remarkably inaccessible. Despite its proximity to the large urban population at Plymouth, there is no direct or easy road access, a factor which helps to maintain the area's character.

The Lower Tamar Valley has a broad, expansive character; Weir Quay.

Upstream, the valley is more intimate as here at Horsebridge.

Roads in the valley tend to be steep, winding and lined with often massive hedgebanks, rarely parallel to the river, but offering sudden and unexpected spectacular views of river and valley. Paths line part of the river but even these do not reach some lengths, adding to the atmosphere of seclusion.

Over and above this atmosphere, which helps define the valley's character, each element of the gradual succession of landscape types has its own individual character, which in turn helps form the composite. Tidal mudbanks and wetlands, secretive wooded creeks, broad meanders, old mine chimneys, ancient quays, steep wooded valley sides, stone bridges, parkland, pastoral banks – all are characteristic of part of the Tamar, all add an important element to its character, all evoke a positive reaction individually and collectively. Add to that the constants – principally the river itself, but also the skyline views of Dartmoor and Bodmin Moor from the higher valley sides and the feature of the chimney on Kit Hill, visible from most parts of the Zone, and the result is an area with a highly distinctive, highly recognisable and much valued appearance and character.

INTEGRITY

As has been indicated, the loss over the last century or less of substantial areas of market gardens and orchards has already resulted in a considerable change in the character and appearance of the landscape. Yet, as also mentioned, the current landscape is much loved and valued, but remains vulnerable to further change.

Development pressures are inevitably felt, despite the general inaccessibility referred to. Plymouth is close to the southern edge of the Zone and, although it is unlikely that large-scale development will occur actually within the Tamar Valley itself, skyline views of Plymouth intrude at some locations and the effect of light pollution from the city is considerable. In addition, some of the larger settlements receive pressure as a result of their desirable location.

At Bere Alston in particular, the plateau location of the settlement is prominent in the landscape and there could be implications for the wider character if expansion occurred.

Some of the main features of the valley landscape could also be vulnerable. The woodlands on the steeper slopes characterise the area, but to be viable need to have a commercial foundation. Another feature, the tidal wetland, has declined from its former extent as a result of the erection of flood embankments. It seems unlikely this would recur but may be possible. Proposals for marinas could also threaten the valley's character, although here the road inaccessibility would still be a negative factor.

One feature of land-use which is already having an impact in parts of the Zone is resulting from changing farming practice and land ownership. The popularity of horse-riding is giving rise to an increase in the number of horse paddocks as farms are sold off. While there is nothing inherently undesirable in this, the resulting landscape of wooden fences and stabling is not sympathetic to the more traditional appearance.

It has already been indicated that the mining legacy is important to the Zone's landscape. Many buildings and chimneys, important in the landscape, have become semi-derelict and in danger of disappearing. Luckily, funds are currently available specifically to address this concern so it should be that this vulnerability will no longer be the case.

Finally, almost a reverse concern of the last point, the Tamar Valley is home to two large quarries, at Hingston Down and Greystone. Both are on the Cornish side but the landscape impact of both is greatest in Devon. Extractive industry is traditional to the valley, as seen, and is important economically, but it is important that the delicate landscape of the valley is not overwhelmed by large-scale extensions to these workings.

It might appear that the Zone has completely lost its landscape integrity from this list, but nothing could be further from the truth. It is an outstanding landscape of visual charm and historic interest, yet still little known to the wider public.

Old mine chimneys are characteristic of parts of the Tamar Valley.

The Tamar Valley is shared between Devon and Cornwall; the viaduct of Calstock is a unifying landscape element.

CHAPTER 7

SUMMARY AND CONCLUSIONS

SUMMARY

'Devon's landscape is a valued inheritance'. This statement opens this appraisal of the landscape of Devon at the beginning of the twenty-first century, and a close inspection of the appraisal will bear out the truth of this assertion. However, such an inspection will also indicate that the landscape is characterised by change, and probably always has been. Such change may be for the better or the worse, may heighten locally distinctive characteristics or minimise them, but in any event should not give cause for complacency.

The landscape of Devon is part of a constantly evolving process. It has changed, and will continue to change, in response to social and economic needs and circumstances. The issues that contribute to this change are numerous, but the forces that lie behind them tend to fall principally into three categories: agricultural change, tourism pressures and development pressures.

Historically it has been the change in farming practices and land use that have had the greatest impact on Devon's predominately rural landscape. The appearance and character of Devon's countryside has been forged by individual efforts of farmers and landowners over the centuries, influenced by outside factors such as economics, scientific advances, policy and incentives. This situation remains the case today, but now the potential speed and scale of change, arising from factors such as mechanisation, the use of chemicals and rapidly changing national and European Union priorities, is greater than ever.

Other visual intrusions can have an impact on the landscape and its distinctiveness; examples include mobile telephone and other masts which break up the historic skyline, lighting in rural areas which can 'destroy' the night skies, proliferations of road signs which have to follow national guidelines, derelict machinery, insensitive farm buildings.

It is therefore necessary that wherever possible the outcomes of the impacts are assessed to ensure that future changes benefit all aspects of the countryside – the rural economy, ecology and the landscape. We should also try to ensure that change avoids obliterating layers of history contained in the landscape which provide evidence of how the countryside has evolved and also provide cultural links with the past; also to ensure that it retains much-loved distinctive features particular to an area.

Discussion earlier in *The Devon Landscape* on the various themes which go to make up the essence of Devon's landscape character, as well as on the distinctive character traits of the individual parts of Devon, has indicated some of the main potential changes. These include:

• Loss of semi-improved or unimproved habitats which, as well as being of ecological value, provide an immense variety within the Devon landscape. Such habitats include lowland heath, heather moorland, coastal heath and species-rich grassland. Generally speaking, the rate of loss of these features has slowed and current concerns often relate as much to inappropriate management, or lack of management, rather than deliberate removal.

• Loss of woodland which, if ancient or semi-ancient, also falls into the previous category. Local landscape character is strongly dependent on trees and woodland features so their conservation, enhancement and restoration is an especially key landscape issue. Storm damage can be an additional factor here, and the County still bears the scars of the unusually severe storms of 1990. Lack of management of woodlands is often exacerbated by the lack of suitable markets for the products of small woodlands particularly. The development of coniferous forestry has been an especially contentious issue in landscape terms, dependent at least partly on the availability of grant incentives and the future of this type of forestry and its appearance in the countryside will doubtless continue to be influenced by broader policy considerations.

• The vast network of hedgebanks, walls and hedgerows is one of Devon's distinctive and major landscape assets. The loss of such field boundaries is thus always likely to be a landscape issue. However, of as much concern as the deliberate removal of field boundaries, possibly more concern currently, is the issue of management regimes. In some areas the problem is one of neglect; elsewhere over-management is potentially damaging hedgerows as an ecological resource, removing the functional qualities of shelter and stockproofing and reducing the landscape value.

• Related to the previous issue, the future of hedgerow trees, shelter belts and copses associated with hedgerows is an important landscape issue in Devon. In exposed areas particularly, such features are often key landscape components characterising the area.

• Farm diversification which, in Devon, tends to be primarily into tourism. The future of historic farm buildings in many parts of the County is becoming dependent on conversion to non-agricultural uses, introducing both threats and opportunities for the landscape. Associated with this is the impact of new land-uses such as golf courses, caravan and camping sites and, elsewhere, industrial uses. In their different ways, all of these tendencies introduce the danger of 'surbanising the countryside' and having an adverse impact on its character.

• Increased development pressures, particularly on the edges of Devon's larger settlements. Devon's cities, towns and villages generally enjoy a special and individual relationship with their landscape setting. This is often due to the undulating terrain and steep slopes which characterise much of the County. The contribution which Devon's historic settlements make as valuable features in the local landscape can be degraded or enhanced by new development. Typical urban fringe concerns include supermarkets, ribbon development on ring roads or bypasses, non-agricultural temporary land uses and neglect arising from potential future development use. However, the problem can also arise at smaller locations where town or village form, roofscapes or subtle relationships with the landform or the surrounding historic landform can easily be destroyed by quite small-scale development if inappropriate.

• Alternative means of dealing with Devon's development pressures are emerging at the beginning of the twenty-first century, in particular the establishment of new, planned, free-standing settlements. National and local guidelines limit the areas of the County where such an approach could be adopted, but currently debate is underway considering the possibility of new settlements to the east of Plymouth and to the east of Exeter. Detailed assessment and planning will be needed before proposals for any such settlements are finalised so that they can be assimilated into the local landscape and to ensure that the landscape character of the area is not jeopardised.

• The future development of Devon's road network, which has the potential to affect the landscape and, more particularly, the character of the areas through which it passes. By its very nature, however, it also has the potential to influence the ease of access to other areas, with consequent implications for development and tourism pressures.

• The impact of vertical structures such as wind farms, pylons, microwave towers, communication dishes and aerials on Devon's skyline, particularly on its high land. Many of Devon's skylines, and especially its high ground, provide valuable backdrops to other valued landscapes. They also provide opportunities to enjoy open landscapes with panoramic views, often with few signs of human settlement, which are assets in their own right.

Not all the issues giving rise to landscape changes are negative. Many forces for change have the potential to offer positive benefits for the landscape. In some instances, policy deliberately proposes landscape enhancement as an objective, and proposals arising from schemes such as Countryside Stewardship, Woodland Grants Schemes, Environmentally Sensitive Areas and Management Plans relating to National Parks and Areas of Outstanding Natural Beauty have great potential to benefit the landscape.

The unspoiled landscape of the Avon Estuary; being within an Area of Outstanding Natural Beauty offers positive benefits to the landscape.

CONCLUSIONS

The Devon Landscape forms the basis for a landscape strategy for Devon. However, it also has a role in its own right, that of setting out the condition of the landscape of Devon at the beginning of the twenty-first century. This role includes an evaluation of the overall essence of the Devon landscape and the major themes which go towards shaping it, a breakdown of the overall essence into a series of Landscape Character Zones, an identification of the main forces for landscape change and promotion of an understanding and appreciation of the Devon landscape in all its forms.

The prime role of *The Devon Landscape* is to foster and support a vision for the future of the landscape of Devon where:

• The value of the landscape in its widest sense is acknowledged – not simply its aesthetic beauty, but recognising that it reflects the richness of Devon's ecology and historic heritage; that it contributes to our quality of life through providing a cultural association with the past and an affinity with nature as well as visual pleasure and a recreational resource.

• The character and quality of the Devon landscape is appreciated in its entirety, cherishing the typical and the commonplace as well as the rare and special; recognising the subtle variations in landscape character and understanding the role of local distinctiveness in giving a 'sense of place'.

• The potentially conflicting forces of conservation and social/economic change have been harmonised to create a sustainable and living landscape for the benefit of local communities, visitors and future generations.

• Everyone appreciates that they can have a role to play, or a responsibility to act, to shape the Devon landscape, through creative planning and design, conscious thought about how the land is managed or learning to respect and understand the environment.

Heathland, pasture, woodland, estuary; the Lower Exe.

GLOSSARY

Area of Great Landscape Value (AGLV)

An area of land designated for its landscape quality at a County level. As well as a definable landscape quality and character AGLVs are also of a sufficient scale to reflect a County significance. AGLVs are a Devon County Council designation, but the detailed boundaries are defined within the Local Plans prepared by the various District Councils.

Area of Outstanding Natural Beauty (AONB)*

An area of land designated nationally for its landscape quality. The primary purpose is to conserve and enhance its natural beauty. In pursuing this primary purpose account must be taken of the needs of agriculture, forestry and other rural industries and of the economic and social needs of local communities.

Coastal Preservation Area (CPA)

An area of land designated to safeguard Devon's unspoiled stretches of coastline and estuary. CPAs are a Devon County Council designation but the detailed boundaries are defined within the Local Plans prepared by the various District Councils on the basis of two criteria carried in the County Structure Plan, i.e.

1. The area should be substantially un-affected by development, and

2. the area should be generally visible from cliff top, beach, sea or estuary, or form part of the view from significant lengths of an access road, public footpath or bridleway leading to the coast from the long-distance coastal footpath.

Council for the Protection of Rural England (CPRE)

An environmental pressure group whose aim is 'to work for a beautiful and living countryside and to campaign for the more sustainable use of land and other resources in town and country'. Involved with the then Countryside Commission in the preparation of maps of Tranquil Areas, i.e. areas undisturbed by visual or noise intrusion by traffic or development.

Countryside Agency (CA)

The statutory body which works to

- conserve and enhance England's countryside;
- spread social and economic opportunity for the people who live there;
- help everyone to enjoy the countryside.

The CA was formed in 1999 from the Countryside Commission and parts of the Rural Development Agency.

Countryside Commission

The statutory body which was the Government's official advisor on countryside matters until absorption into the Countryside Agency in 1999.

Heritage Coast

An area of coastal land defined by the Countryside Agency nationally as being appropriate for positive management measures to be undertaken to maintain and enhance its qualities.

National Park*

An area of land designated nationally for its landscape quality. The statutory purposes of National Parks are:

- to conserve and enhance the natural beauty, wildlife and cultural heritage, and

- to promote opportunities for the understanding and enjoyment of their special qualities.

Where conflicts arise between these two primary purposes, then the conservation purpose should be given greater weight.

It is also a statutory requirement to seek to foster the economic and social well-being of the local communities in the National Parks.

*It should be noted that, under the original 1949 legislation, AONBs and National Parks should be recognised as of equal importance nationally in landscape terms. This position was formally reiterated by the Government in 2000.

RECAP OF THE APPRAISAL

This document constitutes an overview of the Devon landscape at a point in time, the beginning of the twenty-first century. As such, it provides a useful academic landmark on the state of Devon's landscape as well as acting as a reference point to monitor landscape change. In this sense, it has an identity of its own.

However, it also forms part of Devon's Landscape Strategy. For this, it provides the fundamental groundwork, the body of information on which the actions of the overall strategy will impact. Other documents, comprising an examination in more detail of some of the issues raised and policies and proposals to address them, together with a Role and Action Plan for the County Council, arise from this Appraisal and go together with it to form Devon's Landscape Strategy.

INDEX

The wild coastline near Welcombe; conservation of unspoiled landscapes such as this has a high priority.

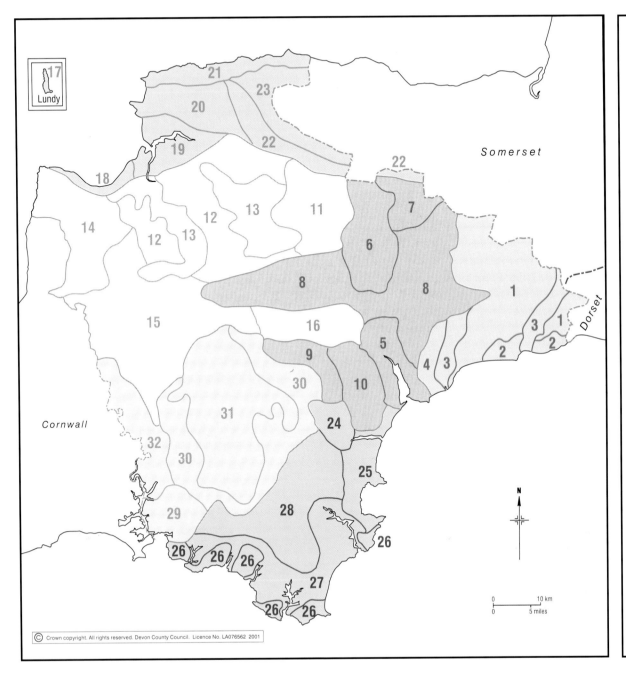

Map 9.
Landscape Character Zones

Eastern Devon

1. Greensand Ridges
2. Coastal Chalk Plateaux
3. Axe and Otter Valleys
4. Pebble Bed Heaths

Central Devon

5. Exeter and Estuary Fringe
6. Exe Valley and Environs
7. Bampton and Beer Downs
8. Mid Devon Farming Belt
9. Teign Valley
10. Haldon Ridge

Culm Measures

11. Witheridge - Rackenford Moor
12. High Culm Ridges
13. Taw and Torridge River Systems
14. Hartland and Atlantic Coast Interior
15. Broadbury and Western Devon Ridges
16. Tedburn St Mary Area

Northern Devon

17. Lundy
18. Clovelly Coast
19. Taw - Torridge Estuary
20. North Devon Downs
21. Exmoor and North Devon High Coast
22. Exmoor Fringe
23. Exmoor Upland

Southern Devon

24. Bovey Basin
25. Tourist Riviera
26. South Devon Coastal Plateaux
27. Ria Coastline
28. Under Dartmoor

Dartmoor and West Devon

29. Plymouth City, Estuary and Environs
30. Dartmoor - Enclosed
31. Dartmoor - High Moor
32. Tamar and Tavy Valleys

Humphry Repton in Norfolk

Edited by

Sally Bate, Rachel Savage and Tom Williamson

Norfolk Gardens Trust

This book is available direct from:

Norfolk Gardens Trust

via the 'Get in Touch' page on our website:

www.norfolkgt.org.uk

Printed and bound in Great Britain by
Barnwell Print Ltd, Aylsham, Norfolk, NR11 6SU
www.barnwellprint.co.uk

WORLD LAND TRUST™

www.carbonbalancedpaper.com
Barnwell Print Reg. No. 2102
CBP00018961904185408

By using Carbon Balanced Paper through the World Land Trust on this publication we have offset 1080kg of Carbon & preserved 750sqm of critically threatened tropical forests.

Carbon Balanced Paper. One of the most sustainable forms of communication that will reduce your carbon foot print and promote CSR. www.carbonbalancedpaper.com

CONTENTS

PREFACE

This book has been produced to coincide with the 200th anniversary of the death of Humphry Repton, who died on 24 March 1818 and is buried in the graveyard of St Michael's Church at Aylsham. One of the first self-proclaimed 'Landscape Gardeners', Repton started his career in Norfolk, and remained passionate about the county throughout his life, describing it in his Red Book for Sheringham as the 'Prophet's own country'. Together with his son John Adey Repton, he is connected with more than twenty sites in Norfolk, for which seven Red Books remain. This study explores all of his known commissions across the county and is illustrated with over 280 beautiful illustrations.

In 2013 members of the Norfolk Gardens Trust formed a research group with shared interests in gardens, landscape and history, and with the help of Professor Tom Williamson at the University of East Anglia, went on to research Lancelot 'Capability' Brown's work in their county. Their book, *Capability Brown in Norfolk*, was published in 2016 to coincide with the celebrations taking place across the country to mark the 300th anniversary of Brown's birth. Despite the time and commitment required to produce the Brown book, but perhaps buoyed up by the praise it had received, the research group met in the autumn of 2016 and agreed to produce another volume exploring Humphry Repton's work in Norfolk. Once again, the support of Professor Williamson has been invaluable. Not only has he continued to host meetings and provide advice and information, but most importantly he undertook the giant task of weaving together all the reports, images and surveys sent in by the individual researchers, to produce a cohesive, chronological text.

The Norfolk Garden's Trust Research Group is excited to be publishing this book to coincide with the bicentenary of Repton's death and to be contributing to the wider reappraisal of Repton's work taking place across the country. This book takes the reader through the different stages of Repton's career from the early days of his first commissions at Catton Park and Hanworth Hall, through the development of his Red Book approach with commissions such as Bracondale Lodge and Northrepps Hall, to his work with his son John Adey Repton and his final commissions at Hoveton House and Sheringham Park. The book concludes with studies of some of the commissions of Repton's contemporaries, shedding light on the similarities and differences of approach – putting Repton's work in the wider context of Regency landscapes.

To produce this book, visits to houses and parks took place, alongside archival research in private and public collections, as well as the Norfolk Record Office Norfolk Heritage Centre and Norfolk Museums Service. Much of this research would not have been possible without the generosity and hospitality of the various individuals, who allowed us to view their Red Books, watercolours, letters and sketches in their possession, as well as explore and record the landscapes featured in them. Although full acknowledgements are given in the next section, special mention must be made to David Clarke of City Bookshop, Norwich, who very kindly made available a significant number of items to be photographed and included in the book. Roger Last has again been invaluable to the project, by producing wonderful photographic images of Red Book illustrations, maps, paintings and documents, often achieving a clarity of which we thought we could only dream. Special thanks must also be given to the Centre for East Anglian Studies, based at the University of East Anglia, for a substantial subvention towards the costs of publication.

The editors and many authors of this book would like to pay tribute to their families and friends for their patience and support during such an absorbing time, especially one coming so hot on the heels of Brown! Without their support the commitment needed to gather information, produce drafts, track down images and gain their reproduction permissions would not have been possible. Also, they would like to convey their thanks and appreciation to their copy editor Mary Worthington, their indexer Sarah Harrison, cover designer Karen Roseberry and to the staff at Barnwell Print in Aylsham.

The Norfolk Gardens Trust currently has over 500 members and promotes the conservation, restoration, knowledge and enjoyment of gardens and designed landscapes. The year 2018 sees the Trust celebrate its 30th anniversary and we are delighted to publish this book about such a renowned landscape gardener, who considered himself a Norfolk man, as part of our milestone year.

ACKNOWLEDGEMENTS

The Norfolk Gardens Trust would like to thank the following organisations, and their respective staff, for their help with archive material, images and information for this book.

Norfolk Record Office, The Norfolk Heritage Centre, Norfolk County Council Library Service, Norfolk Museums Service (Norwich Castle Museum and Thetford Ancient House Museum), City Bookshop (Norwich), University of East Anglia, Environmental Arts at the Norfolk and Norwich Hospital, Royal Institute of British Architects, Barclays Bank Archives, The Holkham Estate, The University of Florida, Broadland District Council, The National Trust and the National Trust Image Archive, British Library, Francis Frith Collection, Ordnance Survey.

The following individual people have in many ways enabled this book to go ahead, by the generous sharing of their personal archives, maps, paintings, documents, information and Repton material.

The Earl and Countess of Leicester, Lord and Lady Walpole, Dr Geoffrey and Professor Katy Cubitt, Major General Sir William and Lady Cubitt, Sir Jeremy and Lady Bagge, Mr and Mrs A. Bagge, Lady Rose Hare, Mr and Mrs Henry McDougall, Mr and Mrs Brian Charlesworth, Mr and Mrs Tom Blofeld, Mr and Mrs Thomas Courtauld, Mr and Mrs Andrew Buxton, Mr and Mrs Harry Buxton, Mr and Mrs Simon Gurney, Mr and Mrs Robbie Buxton, Mr David Clarke, Mr Kit Martin, Mr and Mrs Rupert Stretton-Derham, Mr George Carter, Mrs Elizabeth de Longh, Mrs Marion Folkes, Mrs Daphne Warham, Dr Giorgio Bottinelli, Mrs Charlotte Crawley, Mr Paul Underwood, Mr Malcolm Fisher, Mr Keith Zealand, Mrs Sally Owles, Mr Ray Jones, Mr Cecil Pond, Ms Emma Jarvis, Ms Clare Agate, Ms Clare Everitt, Ms Lucy Purvis, Mr Anthony Bate, Dr Andrew Macnair, Ms Chloe Griffin, Mr Roger Lloyd and members of the Norfolk Gardens Trust.

A special thank you to the Centre for East Anglian Studies at the University of East Anglia for their generous contribution towards production costs.

The Norfolk Gardens Trust would like to thank the members of their Research Group (all volunteers) for their invaluable contribution in the sites researched and other roles below:

Sally Bate:	Co-editor, book internal design, image co-ordinator, Sustead Hall, Blickling Hall, Bracondale Lodge, Mergate Hall (Bracon Ash).
Anita Delf:	Felbrigg Hall.
Janet Ede:	Worstead Hall, Brooke Hall, Middleton Hall, Earsham Hall, Buckenham Tofts Hall and West Tofts Hall.
Marcia Fenwick:	Hoveton House and Hoveton Hall.
Bob Greef:	Wood Hall.
Roger Last:	Photography.
Kate Minnis:	Hanworth Hall, Stradsett Hall and Stow Hall.
Rachel Savage:	Co-editor, Bawburgh Hall, Barningham Hall, Lyng Rectory, Gillingham Hall, Sheringham Hall.
Tom Williamson:	Co-editor, main text author, Catton Hall, Holkham Hall, Honing Hall, Northrepps Hall, Witton Hall.
Judith Wilson:	Blickling Hall and Gunton Hall.
Peter Woodrow:	The Repton Family, financial administrator.

Chapter 1

Repton in Context

Humphry Repton is, after Lancelot 'Capability' Brown, the most famous of English landscape designers. This book is about his work in Norfolk, a county with which he was particularly closely associated. Much of his early life was spent here, and he lies buried in the churchyard of the market town of Aylsham. But to appreciate and to understand the character of his style, and the scale of his achievement, we must first examine, very briefly, how styles of landscape and garden design had developed in England in the decades leading up to the start of his career.

Figure 1. *Miniature painting of Humphry Repton (John Downman ARA. 1750–1824).*

Up until the 1730s, and at many places for much later than this, the grounds of country houses had been 'formal' or geometric in character (Figure 2). The garden areas were enclosed by walls or fences and mainly comprised displays of topiary, and areas of planting incorporating inert material like gravel often arranged in symmetrical and complex patterns, known as knots or parterres.[1] These displays usually occupied only some of the courts arranged around a house: the others contained more practical facilities, such as farmyards and stable yards, or features which were at once both useful and ornamental, such as fish ponds, orchards and dovecotes. Many high-status residences also had parks attached but while many of these were, by the late seventeenth century, crossed by one or more avenues (usually focused on the mansion itself) they were otherwise only minimally designed. Parks at this time were essentially areas of pasture and grazed woodland in which deer were kept, partly for the chase but mainly to supply the owner's table.

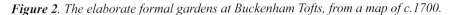

Figure 2. The elaborate formal gardens at Buckenham Tofts, from a map of c.1700.

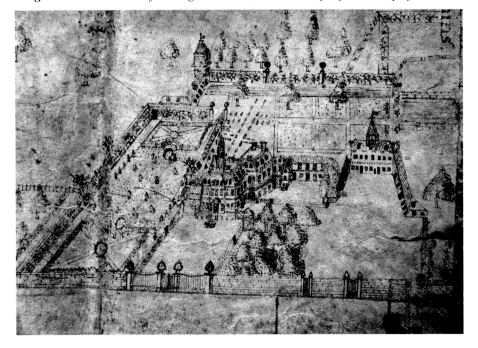

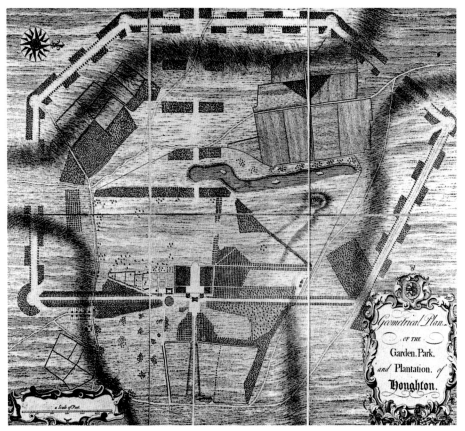

Figure 3. Ware's 1735 plan of Houghton Park, showing extensive, geometric layout.

In the 1720s and 30s, under the influence of men like Charles Bridgeman, the grounds of many country houses became simpler, and in many cases grander, in design, as for example at Houghton in Norfolk (Figure 3). Geometry still governed their overall layout, but walls were often taken down (sometimes replaced by a ha-ha or sunken fence) and parterres were steadily replaced by expanses of closely clipped lawn ('plats') and by large areas of ornamental woodland, or 'wildernesses'.[2] Within the latter, through the 1730s and 40s, straight paths or walks were supplemented or even replaced by serpentine ones; but more dramatic was the tendency, at the more fashionable residences, for whole areas within the gardens to be laid out in an irregular and asymmetrical manner, with winding paths, areas of shrubbery and ornamental buildings and structures of various kinds.[3] To begin with, under designers like William Kent, Roman temples and obelisks were dominant features but by the 1740s more eclectic collections became fashionable, and some gardens were filled with dense clutters of inscriptions, gothic ruins, Islamic mosques and Chinese pagodas. These, and their irregular, serpentine settings, were intended to encourage political or philosophical musing, thoughts of exotic countries, and emotions – whether of surprise, melancholy, or delight.

It is important to emphasise that such evocative gardens usually formed only one part of landscapes which were still organised on geometric lines, with avenues and straight vistas.[4] In more rural areas, lying at a distance from fashionable London, the grounds of the local gentry usually remained entirely geometric in character, and enclosed by walls. The real change in garden fashions came in the 1750s and 60s. Under Capability Brown, and a number of other less famous designers, all signs of geometry and formality – all straight lines and avenues – were ruthlessly removed from around fashionable residences, and walled gardens and other enclosed courts were removed.[5] The main setting for the mansion became the 'landscape park', a kind of tidied-up version of the deer park, comprising extensive areas of turf, lightly scattered with trees; carefully placed clumps of woodland; and, where the topography was suitable and the money available, a lake of serpentine or irregular form (Figure 4). The complete ensemble was surrounded, in whole or part, by a perimeter woodland belt which served to separate the private landscape of pleasure from the wider working world. Ornamental buildings – classical temples, gothic ruins – continued to be important, but they were now fewer in number and scattered more thinly across the landscape of the park, serving as eye-catchers and as places of resort, where tea might be taken and distant glimpses of the mansion enjoyed. For in these rather simple, almost minimalist landscapes, the house became, in effect, the main garden building, viewed to best advantage from the approach drives and from the other rides and carriage drives which wound their way through the landscape, passing in and out of the woodland belts.

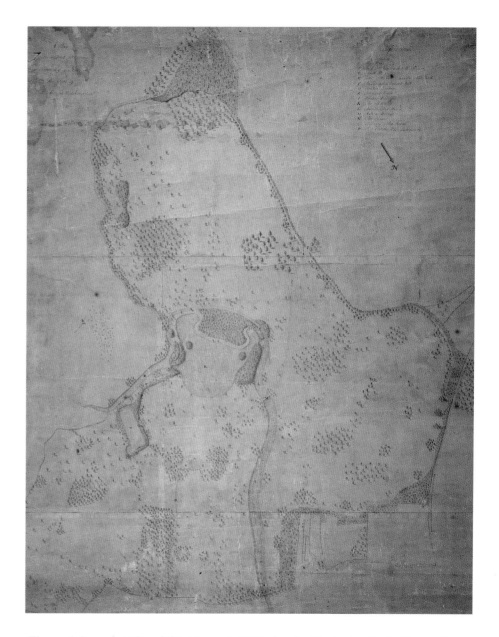

Figure 4. Lancelot 'Capability' Brown's 1762 plan for Kimberley Park, Wymondham.

13

The reasons why landscapes of this kind became so fashionable in England in the second half of the eighteenth century need not detain us here. What is important is that these supposedly 'natural' compositions were not all the work of Capability Brown. True, even in the eighteenth century his leading role as 'the great Arbiter of British Taste'[6] was widely acknowledged, and the many other 'improvers' working in the same general manner were already being characterised as his 'followers' or 'imitators'. In part this was because Brown was the style's most financially successful practitioner, and because he worked on the properties of the greatest aristocrats, and the wealthiest merchants, in the land. In all, he may have undertaken around 250 commissions, but by the time of his death in 1783 there were several thousand landscape parks in the country. In Norfolk, for example, Brown worked at Langley, Kimberley and Melton Constable; perhaps at Holkham; and possibly at one or two other places.[7] Yet the map of Norfolk published by William Faden in 1797, but which was surveyed between 1790 and 1794 – within a decade of Brown's death – shows nearly 200 reasonably sized parks.[8]

Some of the other landscape parks in England were designed by their owners, working perhaps with their head gardeners; others by local nurserymen and surveyors – in Norfolk, such men as Samuel Gooch or Joseph Rumball. But some were the work of men who, while not as famous or successful as Brown, operated nevertheless on a national scale. Richard Woods, Thomas White, Samuel Driver, William Emes or Nathaniel Richmond all had successful careers in the middle and later decades of the eighteenth century. Richmond, for example, who designed the park and pleasure ground at Beeston St Lawrence in Norfolk in the 1770s, originally worked with Brown but set up on his own in 1759 and designed more than 35 known landscapes in England, in a style which it is very hard to distinguish from that of Brown himself. How far, in fact, 'Brown's style' was simply copied by his contemporary designers, how far it was developed by a number of individuals and was simply the 'style of the times' continues to be a subject for debate amongst garden historians.[9]

Either way, this kind of landscape, while everywhere dominant by the 1770s, was not without its critics. Some considered it too boring, bland and stereotyped, and thought that it was imposed on places without any real regard for their true character. Others bemoaned the manner in which, with their perimeter belts and wide expanses of turf, landscape parks served to isolate local landowners from the wider community: they were expressions not just of privacy, but of social exclusivity. Joseph Craddock lampooned 'Mr Layout' – 'a designer in taste in gardening' – and his fellows, who 'talk of taste just as if it was to be brought down in a broad-wheeled wagon, and they had nothing to do but scatter it at random'.[10] William Chambers thought Brown's parklands 'smooth and green as a billiard table', containing 'little to flatter the senses, and less to touch the passions'.[11] One particular problem was that Brown's style worked best on a large scale, and most of Brown's own clients were immensely wealthy landowners. Applied to smaller properties, those of the local gentry, it was less effective. A small park (or 'lawn') looked little different from a pasture field, and when surrounded by near-continuous perimeter belts seemed restricted and claustrophobic. This form of landscaping could not really be applied at all to the 'villas' – the residences of wealthy merchants and financiers, without any real estate attached. Houses of this kind were proliferating on the margins of major cities, and in manufacturing areas, as England industrialised, and its economy became more complex, through the second half of the eighteenth century.

When Brown died in 1783 the style with which we now so closely associate him did not come to a sudden end. Nathaniel Richmond, 'many years known among the gentlemen of landed property, as an eminent improver of parks and gardens', died the following year.[12] But Richard Woods was still preparing new designs when he died in 1793 and Thomas White was producing landscapes in a broadly 'Brownian' style well into the 1790s, as was William Emes.[13] Nevertheless, the time was ripe for something new.

Repton's Early Years

Humphry Repton came from a moderately wealthy middle-class background. His father John was a Collector of Excise, his mother Martha the daughter of a minor Suffolk landowner, John Fitch of Moor Hall.[14] Humphry was born in Bury St Edmunds in the same county in 1752, but moved to Norwich, with his parents, when still young. He had an elder sister Dorothy and a younger brother John; eight other siblings died in infancy. Until he was twelve Humphry was educated at the grammar school at Norwich. His father then decided to send him to Holland, where he remained for four years. The intention was to prepare him for a career in business, and to make him fluent in Dutch, as at this time the textile trade with the Low Countries was still of some considerable economic importance in East Anglia. Repton's Dutch sojourn can also be seen in more general terms – as a manifestation of the wider economic and cultural ties between East Anglia and Holland. These include the involvement of Dutch engineers in fen drainage, the use of pantiles as a roofing material, and the remarkable resemblance of the works of the 'Norwich School' artists, such as John Crome or Joseph Stannard, to those of Dutch artists like Hobbema, Hondecoeter or Cuyp.[15]

Repton attended a boarding school run by a man called Ægidius Tinnerman at a place, according to his *Memoirs*, called *Workum*. This is the name of a city in north Holland, but it has recently been suggested that his real place of education was a town called Woudrichem – locally pronounced *Woerkum* – in the south.[16] Either way, after two years he moved to a school in Rotterdam, where he lived with Zachary Hope, a wealthy merchant banker, and his French-speaking family. He later recalled how he had viewed the gardens in Holland, mainly the properties of merchants rather than great landowners, which were still geometric and 'formal' in character, with parterres, avenues and carefully clipped shrubs.

> Nature was never consulted, they were works of art; the lofty clipped hedges, and close over-arching trees, were as carefully kept by the shears, as the walks were by the scythes and rollers. All was neatness; the effect of incessant labour. A Dutch merchant's

accounts and his garden were kept with the same degree of accuracy and attention.[17]

Repton, in his formative years, was thus exposed on a daily basis to a very different tradition of garden design than that which had emerged in England in the course of the eighteenth century. He also had the experience of a much wider European culture than he could possibly have received had he remained in East Anglia.

On his return to England he was apprenticed for five years to a textile merchant. As soon as he was 21, in May 1773, he married Mary Clarke at the church of St Mary in the Marsh in Norwich, and the couple settled in the parish of St Giles. Immediately afterwards Repton was provided by his father with the capital necessary to start up his own textile business dealing – in the words of John Claudius Loudon, writing in 1840 – in 'calimancoes, Mecklenburgs, worsted satins, and other articles which fashion has now discarded from the list of modern dress and furniture'.[18] But in his leisure hours Repton indulged his real passions, for drawing, music and other artistic pursuits (Figure 5).[19]

Figure 5. Two sketches 'Concerto Spirituale' and 'Susannah and the two Yonkers.'

Figure 6. Repton's watercolour looking north across Aylsham Market Place, 1814.

The first of his sixteen children, Martha, was born on 5 March 1774 but survived for only a few days; his second child, John Adey Repton, was born in May the following year, followed by Humphry (Jnr) on 3 June 1776.[20] His family was growing, but he was losing whatever interest in business he had possessed, and then began to lose money. In 1778, following a serious business failure and the death in rapid succession of both his parents, he became (to quote Loudon again) 'more disgusted with a pursuit so little in accordance with his natural taste and inclination'.[21] Accordingly, and with the benefit of an inheritance,

16

Figure 7. *Repton's second view looking south across the same market place, 1814.*

Repton – still only 26 years old – moved with his young family to Sustead Old Hall, a manor house not far from the market town of Aylsham in north-east Norfolk (Figures 6 and 7). Here he farmed on a small scale and in general lived a congenial rural life, cultivating friendships with local landowners, and especially with William Windham of Felbrigg Hall, who became a personal friend (the two men were of similar age). Little has been written of his time at Sustead, but it is likely that these years saw a steady development in his artistic abilities, and in his ideas on gardening and landscape improvement.

Life at Sustead

Repton's choice of Sustead, a few miles to the north of Aylsham, as a place of 'rural retirement' was probably dictated in large part by family connections. His father had moved to the district after retirement, managing property in the town and farming at Oxnead Hall, a short distance to the south-east.[22] His sister was also in Aylsham, having married John Adey, a solicitor of that town, who had been known to the family for several years, and had leased a house in Hungate Street from Humphry's father since 1764.[23] Humphry's younger brother John, moreover, took over at Oxnead from his father. It was an obvious place to settle.

Sustead Hall, which Repton rented from William Windham, is a brick and flint building which stands on the brow of a hill with far-reaching views south towards Hanworth and Thurgaton, and north towards Aylmerton and Felbrigg. It had previously functioned as a parsonage. The last clergyman to live there was the Reverend Theophilus Lowe and his wife Elizabeth (daughter of the Reverend Patrick St Clair, another previous incumbent).[24] It was a homely building, more like a prosperous farmhouse than a mansion – Repton described in a letter to an old friend how his more exalted neighbour, William Windham, liked 'my snug study at Sustead better than the old rambling library at Felbrigg'.[25] The house continues to exude this atmosphere two hundred and thirty years later, and it is easy to imagine Repton working in his study or sketching in the garden. He would certainly recognise the house today, as the panelling, oak staircase and fireplaces all remain in place.

For eight years Repton lived here, with a growing family. Another son, Edward, was born in 1782, followed by William on 14 October 1783, George Stanley and Mary Dorothy on 30 January 1786, and Elizabeth in 1791 (eight other children were born at various times, but none survived infancy). Repton supervised his small farm, 'gardened and planted, sketched and botanised', and undertook a range of local offices, explaining to a friend how Sustead was 'so small a parish that I am obliged to enact the various parts of churchwarden, overseer, surveyor of high-ways and esquire'.[26] He followed, if in a small way, the current fashion for agricultural 'improvement', describing in a letter how 'The wet hazy meadows, which were deemed incorrigible, have been drained and transformed into flowery meads . . . come and see how happy we are!'[27] A cottage on the property, in view of the hall, was embellished with a new gothic-style window.[28] He worked in 1780 as Windham's election agent (Windham was not elected). A keen reader, Repton enjoyed the privilege of being able to visit and borrow titles from Wyndham's library at Felbrigg, particularly books on natural history but also on poetry, classical literature and world affairs. In one letter written to Mr Cobb, Windham's steward at Felbrigg, he described how he had

> returned all the books I have borrowed belonging to the library – the 2nd Vol. of Beaumont Sketches I suppose you observed was missing. I thank you to send me Dodsley's Poems.[29]

And in another, noted that he had

> sent home all the books I have – I will thank you to send me Advis aux Veritables Hollandois [*Advice to the True Dutch*]. Mrs Repton will thank you to send her from the Class of Plays, 2 Vols. of either Congreves, Wycherley's or Beaumont Fletcher's works.[30]

While in a third he requests Cobb to send him a copy of Dryden's Translation of Virgil's *Aeneid*.[31]

Some idea of the character and appearance of Repton's home can be obtained from a map which Repton himself drew up c.1782, based on a survey of 1732 (Figure 8); from two watercolours by Repton, dated 1782, showing the rear (south) of the hall (Figures 9 and 10); and from a second watercolour, now almost monochrome with age, showing the northern entrance front (Figure 11). The map shows the lands in the parish belonging to Edward Chamberlayne (of Sustead), William Windham (of Felbrigg) and Robert Lee Doughty (of Hanworth Hall, where Repton was later to propose improvements to the landscape (below, p.45).[32] It includes a vignette of the hall, viewed from the south over a gothic-style painted gate and fence pales. To the left (west) of the house a long fence is shown, at the south end of which stands a summerhouse (it is unclear whether this is tiled or thatched). The fence corresponds with a rectangular feature which Repton shows on the map, which was probably an enclosed kitchen or flower garden. It is shown more clearly on one of the two watercolours (that depicting the rear of the house: Figure 9), with shrubs or climbing plants planted against it.[33] A painted white bench is placed in front, facing east across a lawn towards a circular seat which surrounds the base of a conifer of some kind – probably a spruce or possibly a young cedar. Some of the details of the grounds shown in these representations may well have been added by Repton, especially the shrub planting around the base of the groups of trees, the seats, and possibly the painted fence and gate shown on the map: tree-seats in particular were later to feature in a number of his designs. But much of what they depict must have been long established, especially the trees growing in groups and in an avenue to east of the house. In a letter to the Rector of Sustead, Edward Chamberlayne, Repton referred back to Elizabeth Lowe's time at Sustead Hall, and described how

> her old home contains the staircase, the panelling, the fireplaces which she and her father knew, and in its garden a grove of beeches which must surely be the remnant of the plantations which were her pleasure and her modest pride.[34]

Armstrong's *History and Antiquities of the County of Norfolk* of 1781 similarly states that

> the house in which she lived is small but convenient, and pleasantly situated in the middle of a small farm, which she has ornamented with several small plantations. It is now in the occupation of Mr Humphry Repton, to whom we are obliged for many drawings with which this work is embellished.[35]

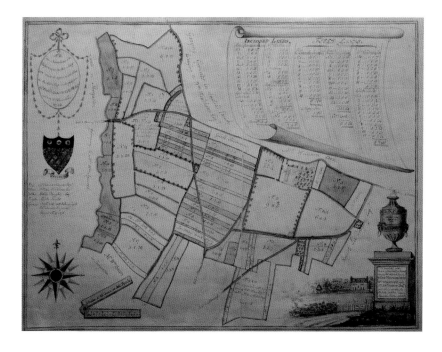

Figure 8. *Repton's 1782 version of the Sustead map with detail of his home, below.*

Figure 9. Watercolour dated 1782 by Humphry Repton, showing the garden south of Sustead Hall.

Note at page 101 of MS.

Figure 10. *Grape picking on the south wall of Sustead Hall c.1782 by Humphry Repton.*

The avenue, which looks on the painting in Figure 10 to have been perhaps fifty or sixty years old at the time, was a striking feature (the remains of a beech avenue still survive here but the trees are of twentieth-century vintage). It is a useful reminder that not all geometric features were swept away by fashionable 'improvement', especially from provincial manor houses. At its far end another painted bench can be seen, while a distant figure walking towards it provides a sense of perspective and seems to entice the viewer to follow. Other features included in the view seem intended to evoke the impression of a relaxed rural lifestyle: a wheelbarrow in the foreground, loaded with gardening tools; a dog looking up at a gentleman in a red frockcoat, who is picking and handing down bunches of grapes to a lady, pastorally attired to receive them. In both watercolours a figure in a red outfit appears, Repton here anticipating by some thirty years John Constable's device of using a red highlight to bring his paintings alive, but also perhaps drawing attention to himself at the centre of this little world. A note written in pencil on the back of the painting in Figure 9 says: 'The boy tossing the ball is J. A. Repton who is still living aged 84½ years, September 1859.' John Adey Repton (1775–1860), Repton's eldest son, would have been seven years old when the painting was made.

The monochrome painting by Repton (Figure 11) shows the front elevation of the house, with its shaped gables with iron clamps proclaiming its construction in 1663.[36] The hall in fact had much earlier origins. Brick mullion windows on the west and east wall date from the sixteenth century.[37] On this, as on the other paintings, the hall is immediately recognisable as the house which stands here today. The only significant difference is that the shaped gables were remodelled into a stepped design following the collapse of the front façade in 1888,[38] a photograph taken just before this happened, shows a large area of missing flints to the left of the door – a precursor of what was about to take place! The painting shows that the front court was defined by a pair of parallel walls with opposing gates. The view is from the west and shows the farming side of the property, with black turkeys, chickens, guinea fowl, and ducks. The identities of the women shown are unknown: the one wearing the hat might be Mary Repton, the other with a bonnet, possibly a servant or nursemaid. While the three paintings appear to be a private record of an idyllic rural life, it is very likely that they were

intended for publication. At the top of the painting illustrated as Figure 10 Repton has written the words: 'Note at page 101 of M.S.'. This note, along with the collection of Repton's drawings in Appendix 1, appears to confirm this.

Repton's life as a rural squire, whether or not as idyllic as the paintings suggest, was not in itself sufficient to maintain his growing family, and he was obliged to seek other work. In the late 1770s he was commissioned to prepare much of the text for Volume III of Mostyn John Armstrong's *History and Antiquities of the County of Norfolk*, published in 1781, which deals with the hundreds of North and South Erpingham and Eynsford. He also supplied sketches, turned into engravings, to illustrate it. These are all of country seats located in the area around Sustead, namely the halls at: Felbrigg, Hanworth, Heydon, Irmingland, Barningham, Wolterton and Wood Dalling, as well as Gunton Park and Baconsthorpe Castle.[39] In addition, he provided illustrations of Stiffkey Hall, Great Walsingham Priory and Little Walsingham Friery (*sic*) for Volume VI, Melton Constable Hall for Volume VII and views at Sheringham and Cromer for Volume III (Figure 12). It is unlikely that Repton received much money from this project, but it provided an opportunity to further familiarise himself with the varied landscapes surrounding the houses and mansions of the Norfolk elite, a knowledge of which no doubt stood him in good stead when he later launched his career as a landscape gardener. A few years later a more lucrative opportunity presented itself. In 1783 William Windham was appointed chief secretary to the Lord Lieutenant of Ireland, and Repton accompanied him to Dublin as his assistant. Unfortunately, Windham resigned after only a few weeks in post, and Repton remained in Ireland for little more than two months. The following year he became involved in anther enterprise, assisting John Palmer in his scheme to establish a system of coaches to transport the royal mail. But this seems to have brought him little money, and John Claudius Loudon later described the 'utter failure of all his schemes to make his country pursuits profitable, in a pecuniary point of view'.[40] As a result, Repton was eventually obliged to leave Sustead, in 1786, and move to a much smaller house in Hare Street, Essex, thirteen miles north-east of London. A less remote location would allow him to pursue interests in and around London and, in particular, to develop a career in writing and publishing. His play, *Odd*

Figure 11. *Watercolour dated 1782 by Humphry Repton, showing the north garden and farmyard of Sustead Hall.*

Key:
1. Irmingland.
2. Heydon.
3. Wood Dalling.
4. Beeston and Runton villages seen from Sheringham Heath.
5. Walsingham Priory.
6. Baconsthorpe.
7. S. W. view of Grey Friers (sic) at Walsingham.

Key: 8. Stiffkey.

9. Gunton Church.

10. Melton Constable.

11. Wolterton.

12. S. W. view of Cromer.

13. Barningham.

Figure 12. Previous page and this page (along with Figures 13 and 37). Illustrations from Mostyn John Armstrong's: History and Antiquities of the County of Norfolk, (1781), based on drawings by Humphry Repton. (See Appendix One)

Whims; Or, Two at a Time, appeared in 1786 (and was staged in Yarmouth and Aylsham by the Norfolk and Suffolk Company);[41] and *The Bee: a critique on the exhibition at Somerset House* was published in 1788.[42]

Felbrigg

In the same year, as we shall see, he began to work as a professional landscape designer, or 'landscape gardener' to use the term which he himself appears to have invented. But while living at Sustead, with his circle of landowning friends, he was already offering informal advice on landscapes and gardens. In the Memoir which he wrote for his children shortly before his death he describes how he had been determined 'to make that pursuit his profession which had hitherto been only his amusement', sentiments echoed in the circular letter which he sent out to friends and acquaintants at the start of his career in 1788.[43] It is possible that his engagement at nearby Hanworth Hall in 1790, recorded in his account book, may have come after several years of offering advice gratis to his friend Robert Lee Doughty. But more important is his possible involvement in the grounds at Felbrigg, where the garden historian John Phibbs has suggested he may have had a significant influence.[44]

Figure 13. Repton's illustration of Felbrigg from Armstrong's History and Antiquities of the County of Norfolk (1781).

The grounds at Felbrigg, which had been the property of the Windhams since the fifteenth century, had been laid out on grand geometric lines by William Windham I in the later seventeenth century and remained largely unchanged into the 1760s when one visitor – Lady Beauchamp-Proctor – described how 'The park is walled around, and capable of great improvement, but the owner being a minor, nothing can yet be done'.[45] Walled gardens still survived around the house and a long axial walk extended through the woods to the north, leading to an oval clearing which Repton described admiringly in the section on Felbrigg which he

Figure 14. Humphry Repton's sketch of William Windham.

penned for Armstrong's *History*.[46] As William Windham III (who inherited in 1761) matured, the grounds were gradually brought more up-to-date (Figure 14). The woods were extended, and belts planted around part of the park's boundary; new drives were laid out; the planting within the garden altered (although most of the walls remained); and various other changes effected. Some of these additions and alterations appear rather 'Reptonian' in character. Phibbs has drawn attention, in particular, to the line taken by the Marble Hill Drive, and the Cromer and Sexton's drives, as well as to the clearings made within the Great Wood, which follow the bottoms of the valleys cutting through it. There are, moreover, references in Repton's letters to conversations about landscaping between him and Windham, while in October 1779 Windham required his steward Cobb to 'go to Mr Repton with my compliments and say that I shall be much obliged to him if he will send me by any great opportunity that offers, the drawing which he promised of Felbrigg: or two, of different views, if he can spare so many'. [47]

It would, perhaps, be surprising if Repton had not had an involvement here, but Windham's land agent, the famous 'improver' and writer on forestry, Nathaniel Kent, was almost certainly also advising on how the Felbrigg landscape might be developed. In Kent's *Hints to Gentlemen of Landed Property*, published in 1775, he describes how Windham adopted his plan for forestry at Felbrigg with enthusiasm, and had 'empowered me to carry it on upon such a vigorous scale, as will gradually swell the quantity and value of his timbers, notwithstanding his falls will be considerable every year'.[48] Many of the additions made under Windham, moreover, pre-date Repton's time at Sustead, or came so soon after his arrival there, that it is hard to believe that he had a major influence on their form or character. The western belt of the park, for example, seems to have been established in 1777, when planting was undertaken 'next Sexton's Gate' (the west lodge)[49] and the south belt was planted in 1778.[50] Round Wood, which Phibbs tentatively suggested may have been designed by Repton, appears to have been planted in 1779.[51] Nathaniel Kent was unquestionably responsible for many of the areas of woodland planted in and around the park between 1770 and 1786.[52] Repton certainly prepared two illustrations of Felbrigg while resident at Sustead; one for Armstrong's *History* in 1781; the other published in 1787 by William Walker (Figures 13 and 15); but there is no evidence that either was intended to illustrate the results of proposed changes.[53] The ornamental cottage in the Great Wood, which was planned in the 1780s, does sound rather 'Reptonian'. In short, Repton may well have advised William Windham and Nathaniel Kent on the gardens and park at Felbrigg, but to date, hard evidence is lacking.

As well as influencing the gardening activities of friends and neighbours, Repton was himself influenced in his approaches to landscape by contacts with other East Anglian residents. He became friends not only with Nathaniel Kent; but also with Robert Marsham, owner of the Stratton Strawless estate, a famous naturalist and arboriculturalist, whose method of planting deciduous trees intermixed with thorns to give them protection he much admired and utilised later at Sheringham. Another important friendship was with the Rev. Norton Nichols of Blundeston in Suffolk, an amateur garden designer who advised on the grounds of Costessey Hall in Norfolk, as well as having a fine garden of his own.[54] More importantly, Repton's landscaping style was perhaps more generally influenced by his time at Sustead. Although north-east Norfolk included the homes of some large landowners, it was quintessentially a land of small squires, with

manor houses rather than great palaces. The terrain was rolling, gentle, cultivated, rather than wild and rugged. Repton himself, commenting on the landscape of the area in which Sustead lay, described how

> The county of *Norfolk is by no means so flat* a country as it is generally described to be, and this is chiefly owing to the hasty manner in which itinerant writers view it. Every part (the fens and marsh lands excepted) is strongly marked with rising grounds, which, though they ascend with an almost imperceptible egravity, terminate with a prospect of twenty, some thirty miles distant.[55]

All this perhaps contributed to the rather homely, practical, domestic feel of Repton's designs, suited to an elegant and comfortable, but not necessarily extravagant, life in the countryside.

Figure 15. Walker's engraving of Felbrigg, taken from a drawing by Repton, 1798.

Repton's Career

It was in 1788, two years after moving to Essex, that Repton began his career as a professional landscape gardener. He sent out a circular letter to acquaintances and friends, informing them that he was available for business.

> H. REPTON having for many years (merely as an amusement) studied the picturesque effect resulting from the act of LAYING OUT GROUNDS, has lately been advised by many respectable friends (to who he has occasionally given sketches for the improvement of their own places) to enlarge his plan, and practise professionally his skill as a LANDSCAPE GARDENER.[56]

He went on to lament the fact that gardening had been neglected 'since the loss of Brown and Richmond', stating that 'Mason, Gilpin, Whately and Girardin have been of late my breviary, and the works of Kent, Brown and Richmond have been the places of my worship'. Mason and Whately were English writers on landscape design, advocates of the mainstream 'natural' landscape style, who published important texts in 1777 and 1770 respectively.[57] René de Girardin, in contrast, was a French designer whose book *De la Composition des Paysages* was published in 1777.[58] While he designed gardens which were heavily influenced by the English tradition, they harked back to the somewhat cluttered designs of the early eighteenth century – pleasure grounds full of features and buildings, intended to stimulate the emotions and the intellect – rather than emulating the somewhat 'minimalist' simplicity of Brown, Richmond or their contemporaries. His own garden at d'Ermenonville was a shrine to the philosopher Rousseau, who died there, and contained a number of buildings and other features including a ruined temple, a grotto, and the tomb of Rousseau himself, on the Isle of Poplars. 'Picturesque gardens in France were often eclectic spaces of emblems, symbols and conceits, more cluttered than their English counterparts. Girardin's garden was a space of ideas as well as sensation.'[59] The Rev. William Gilpin is also an interesting name to appear in a list of Repton's stylistic mentors. He was an immensely successful writer on landscape representation and appreciation who, in a number of popular books written in the 1780s and 90s, had propagated the notion of Picturesque beauty.[60] He looked at real landscapes with a painter's eye and believed that the best examples should – like the classic compositions of Poussin and Claude Lorraine, whom he so greatly admired – be organised into 'three distances', with a clearly defined foreground, middle ground and distance. More importantly, he encouraged the appreciation of rougher and wilder scenery than had hitherto been fashionable: not only upland mountains but also forests, and such things as ancient trees, exposed roots and rock strata. He was keenly aware of the particular qualities of places and districts, and viewed Brown's style of landscape as bland and repetitive. 'How flat, and insipid is often the garden scene, how puerile, how absurd! The banks of the river, how smooth and parallel! The lawn, and its boundaries, how unlike nature.'[61] As we shall see, his followers Richard Payne Knight and Uvedale Price advocated, from the 1790s, that gardens should be designed on similar Picturesque principles and were to be highly critical of Repton's style.

Figure 16. *Repton's view of Beeston Hall, Norfolk, the seat of Jacob Preston Esq.*

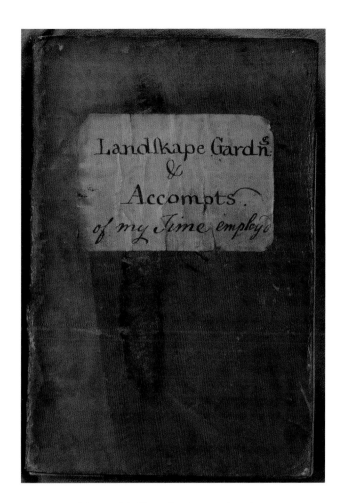

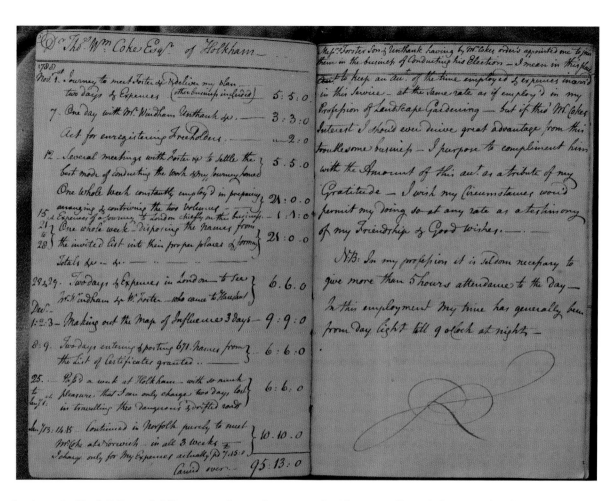

Figure 17. Humphry Repton's only surviving account book, in the Norfolk Record Office, page shown: his entries for Thomas William Coke Esq. of Holkham.

Repton's account book – a vital source of information about his first years in practice, and which survives in the Norfolk Record Office – records on its first few pages the expenses incurred in visiting some of the 'works of Kent, Brown and Richmond' (Figure 17).[62] In June 1788 he travelled to Beeston St Lawrence (Norfolk, Figure 16) and Wolverton (Suffolk), both designed by Richmond, and to Redgrave (Suffolk), designed by Brown. In July of the same year he visited Oatlands (Suffolk), partly designed by William Kent and in the October, he journeyed to the famous Stowe in Buckinghamshire, where both Kent and Brown had worked. His visit to Brockett Park in Hertfordshire, however, shows him attending to the work of another of Brown's contemporaries, Richard Woods, a designer of parks but more importantly widely known as the 'Master of the Pleasure Ground'.[63]

Repton's career took off rapidly and we shall examine it, in the pages that follow, through the prism of his Norfolk commissions, something which – as we shall see – throws a distinctive light on his work and his art. In very general terms, we might say that, just as Repton's career spanned the cusp of the eighteenth and nineteenth centuries, so his style represented a bridge between the naturalistic landscape parks of Brown and his contemporaries, and the more structured and formal gardens of the Victorian period.[64] Initially, Repton's landscapes broadly resembled those of Brown, and indeed he was criticised in 1794 by Knight and Price for creating landscapes 'designed and executed exactly after Mr Brown's receipt, without any attention to the natural or artificial character of a place'.[65] But from the start there were significant differences, born in part of the fact that Repton tended to deal with much smaller properties than Brown, with the grounds of local gentry, or of wealthy businessmen, rather than with the extensive demesnes of great aristocrats. He thus criticised, from an early date, Brown's meandering drives, much less suitable for smaller park landscapes than for large, and in general terms relied on subtlety of planting or building, rather than scale, to produce required effects. Where Brown would hide an unpleasant feature in the prospect with massed planting at a distance, Repton tended to use a few carefully placed trees in the foreground. Repton was also highly sensitive to the social aspirations of the moderately wealthy, to their particular concern to dominate, or at least appear to dominate, the countryside around them. At Livermere in Suffolk in 1790, for example, he proposed that all the fences in the village should be painted the same colour, to demonstrate that they were all the property of the owners of Livermere Hall.[66] And in other ways he manipulated the landscape to emphasise status and dominance, even if in reality the owner did not have quite the status implied, a practice which Repton referred to as 'appropriation', a subject to which we shall return in Chapter 3.[67]

The suitability of Repton's style for the design of relatively restricted properties needs to be viewed in terms of wider contemporary changes in society and economy. In particular, this was a period in which the local gentry flourished, and in which the rising numbers and increasing wealth of merchants and financiers led to the building of numerous wealthy 'villas' with elaborate grounds, but often without a significant estate attached, on the fringes of major cities. Indeed, in spite of the economic dislocations of the Napoleonic Wars, industrialisation and agricultural prosperity focused wealth at ever lower social levels. Repton explained in 1816 that the setting of smaller properties could not in general be improved by 'adding field to field, or by taking away hedges, or by removing roads to a distance', but instead by exploiting 'every circumstance of interest or beauty within our reach, and by hiding such objects as cannot be viewed with pleasure'.[68] He continued:

> It seldom falls to the lot of the improver to be called upon for his opinion on places of great extent . . . while in the neighbourhood of every city or manufacturing town, new places as villas are daily springing up, and these, with a few acres, require all the conveniences, comforts and appendages, of larger and more sumptuous, if not more expensive places. And . . . these have of late had the greatest claim to my attention.[69]

This in part explains why, in the later stages of his career, he began to create increasingly structured and formal gardens, with flower beds, terraces and even parterres. These could look impressive even when they occupied a restricted area of ground. This said, we should also note that from his earliest commissions, Repton was as much concerned with pleasure grounds (albeit of a less formal and structured character) as with parklands. His designs often show flowers planted informally in the area around the mansion, on trelliswork against its walls, or in special Hardenberg baskets, although it is usually hard to say what species these are supposed to represent. Repton was no plantsman!

There were other reasons why Repton, in the later stages of his career, came to concentrate on structured gardens. For most of the eighteenth century, country houses had usually been built in a broadly classical style – first Palladian, and then Neoclassical. Such buildings sat well within sweeping open parkland, and Neoclassical houses in particular shared a number of key characteristics with the parklands of Brown. Both displayed a certain simplicity, and were characterised by distinct, continuous outlines, rather

Figure 18. Repton's trade card from his Red Book for Honing, Norfolk.

made it a reality.[71] Repton, with a few exceptions, supplied only the design. He sometimes staked out the line of an approach, or the precise boundaries of an area of planting, on the ground, and he occasionally supervised the activities of a nurseryman or other contractor. But his main and often only contribution were his proposals for improvement. These were usually, although by no means invariably, presented in the form of a Red Book, so called because it was generally bound in red Moroccan leather (with marbled end-papers and his trade card, Figure 18). A text, written by Repton or a member of his family, analysed the appearance and character of the landscape as it was and explained how it could be best improved. This was accompanied by a series of watercolours, many of which were provided with flaps which could be lifted to reveal the changes in question.[72] Writing in *Sketches and Hints* Repton explained the need for his method.

> To make my designs intelligible, I found that a mere map was insufficient; as being no more capable of conveying an idea of the landscape than the ground-plan of a house does of its elevation. To remedy this deficiency, I delivered my opinions in writing, that they might not be misconceived or misrepresented; and I invented the peculiar kind of slides to my sketches . . .[73]

His Red Books, and particularly his innovative 'before and after' illustrations, remain a significant part of his legacy, so it is with some irony that whilst they were key to his self-promotion, he also recognised their limitations, perhaps knowing that this clever device would become what he was best known for.

> Such drawings, to shew the proposed effects, can be useful but in a very few instances; yet I have often remarked, with some mortification, that it is the only part of my labours which the common observer has time or leisure to examine . . .[74]

On receipt of a Red Book, clients would then use their own estate workers, or employ some professional nurseryman, to implement the suggested changes. The red books were thus, in effect, the product purchased by clients, and were a clever and beguiling device, although some contemporaries were

than by complex, fussy forms.[70] The overwhelming dominance of classical styles did not outlast the century. As Repton's career was taking off, other forms of architecture were becoming popular, and country houses based on medieval gothic and Elizabethan models, or in 'Italianate' style, began to be erected. For these a more structured setting seemed appropriate. In time, avenues, topiary, and even formal parterres came back into fashion, for they seemed to fit in well with the antiquarian style of many of these houses. In fact, one of the themes of this book is the more general importance of architecture in Repton's life and career, and particularly in the work which he did after 1800 in association with his son, the architect John Adey Repton.

From the start Repton's style thus differed from that of Brown, and it became more distinct with the passing years. But an equally sharp contrast can be seen in the working methods of the two men. Brown usually provided not only a design for his clients but a team of subcontractors and labourers who

sceptical. William Mason for example commented on how Repton

> alters places on paper and makes them so picturesque that fine folks think that all the oaks etc he draws will grow exactly in the shape and fashion in which he delineated them, so they employ him at great price; so much the better on both sides, for they might lay out their money worse, and he has a numerous family of children to bring up.[75]

Red Books provide our best evidence of Repton's activities at particular places. But there are often questions about how many of the proposals they contained were actually executed, or were subsequently altered by Repton, following discussions with the client, before being implemented. It is also likely that in many cases Repton made further suggestions for 'improvement', in addition to those prescribed in the text. The Red Books are certainly of immense importance to garden historians in that they explain the reasoning behind Repton's design proposals – they allow us to understand, to some extent at least, precisely what he was trying to achieve. Further light on his attitudes to design, and to landscape and society more generally, are provided by his published books, for, unlike Brown – who wrote little and published nothing – Repton authored a number of books, including *Sketches and Hints on Landscape Gardening* (1794), *Observations on the Theory and Practice of Landscape Gardening* (1803), *An Inquiry into the Changes in Taste in Landscape Gardening* (1806) and *Fragments on the Theory and Practice of Landscape Gardening* (1816). We should note, however, that Repton's proposals were not always presented in the form of a Red Book. Sometimes, for small commissions, they were simply communicated verbally; in other cases, one or more watercolours were supplied, but without a written text.

There are seven places in Norfolk for which a Red Book survives: Holkham (1789), Honing (1792), Bracondale (1792), Northrepps (1792), Witton (1801), Wood Hall in Hilgay (1806) and Sheringham (1812). Repton's first account book, which is kept at the Norfolk Record Office and which covers the years 1788 to 1790, suggests a further five places where he worked, in addition to Holkham.[76] They are 'Baber' (probably Bawburgh), Buckenham Tofts, Catton, Hanworth and West Tofts. For Catton and Hanworth we also

have surviving paintings by Repton, showing proposed improvements, none of which appear to have been cut from a Red Book. The work he later undertook at Gunton and Blickling is known only from drawings, supplemented in the latter case with the text of an accompanying letter. The evidence for Repton's activities at Barningham is entirely graphic in character – a series of watercolours drawn up in 1809 showing suggested changes to the hall and its immediate setting – together with a number of architects plans and elevations, and designs for new lodges.

Several of these places – Barningham, Catton, Holkham, Bracondale and Sheringham – are also discussed in one of Repton's published books, while seven – Barningham, Bracon (Bracon Ash), Bracondale, Buckenham Tofts, Catton, Hanworth and Witton – appeared as illustrations in a publication called *The Polite Repository, or Pocket Companion*, a diary-cum-almanack which was published annually by William Peacock between 1790 and 1811. Between 1793 and 1795 the text of this publication explicitly stated that the places illustrated were ones which had been 'improved' under Repton's direction (although even in these years some of the places pictured may not in fact fall into this category).[77] It is less certain whether the illustrations published before and after this period were also, for the most part, places where he worked, but most probably were. This suggests another three possible Norfolk commissions – Bracon Hall (illustrated in 1804), Worstead House (in 1803) and Lyng Rectory (in 1806). For the last of these there is also a watercolour painting made by John Adey Repton;[78] for Worstead and Bracon Ash no other evidence survives, and in none of these cases do we have any real idea of the scale or character of Repton's activities. Felbrigg, which we have already discussed, also made an appearance in Peacock's *Polite Repository* in 1795, perhaps indicating further advice received by William Windham (Figure 19). Lastly, Repton's involvement at Hoveton Hall is indicated by architectural drawings, and a reference in a letter; and at Hoveton House by letters, an architectural drawing and watercolours; and at Stradsett by a note in the estate accounts.

In all, there are thus 21 places in Norfolk where Repton appears to have been employed in some capacity (22 if we include Felbrigg). In terms of absolute numbers, this would place the county second in rank order, behind

Figure 19. Repton's image of Felbrigg for Peacock's Polite Repository, 1795.

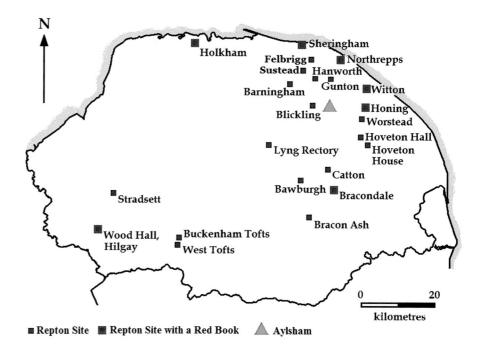

■ Repton Site   ■ Repton Site with a Red Book   ▲ Aylsham

Figure 20. Distribution map of Repton's sites in Norfolk.

Essex with 37 known commissions, equal to Surrey with 21 and just ahead of Suffolk with 20 and Hertfordshire with 18 or 19.[79] Superficially, this suggests that Repton was most active, or most appreciated, in the counties in which he was born (Suffolk), spent much of his early life (Norfolk) and began his professional career (Essex). However, when the differing *sizes* of the various counties is taken into account, this order of importance is changed. Middlesex now comes first, with around one Repton commission for every 49 square kilometres of land; Hertfordshire second, with one for each 91 square kilometres; and Surrey third, with one for every 93 square kilometres; just ahead of Essex, with one for every 107. Norfolk, in contrast, a large county, has only one Repton site for each 240 square kilometres. Repton's commissions were, not surprisingly, noticeably clustered around London, in the Home Counties, where wealthy clients were present in large numbers. They were significantly sparser in Norfolk, and Repton bemoaned on a number of occasions a lack of recognition in 'the prophet's own country'. It is noteworthy that most were located in the north-eastern part of the county, in part a reflection of Norwich's role as a major regional centre (ringed with the homes of successful merchants and bankers), and in part indicating the importance of social networks forged while living at Sustead (Figure 20).

We should also note, however, the likelihood that Repton worked at some places – in Norfolk as elsewhere – for which no evidence has survived. It is noticeable that six of his known Norfolk commissions date from the first three years of his career, with the other eleven being spread out across the subsequent two decades. But the high numbers known from the period 1788–1790 may reflect in part the fact that his only surviving account book spans these years and seems to contain references to all his work. After this the picture is partial, the evidence patchier. Several other possible Repton sites are suggested by local tradition, such as Bolwick near Aylsham, but with little or no supporting evidence. Conversely, a pair of unlabelled 'before and after' sketches with a lift-up flap by Repton, apparently showing somewhere in Norfolk, survive in the Colman collection at the Millennium Library in Norwich. They may illustrate proposed changes to the park at Hanworth, but this is far from certain (Figures 21 and 22). One problem is that it remains unclear how different Repton's gardens and parks really were from those of contemporary designers working at a local or national scale – whether he was a great innovator, or the most successful and prolific practitioner in a more widely shared style – an issue to which we return in Chapter 6. This follows three chapters in which Repton's work in Norfolk is divided in a broadly chronological fashion. The first covers the commissions undertaken in the first three years of his career – those recorded in his account book. The second deals with three well-documented sites dating from the early 1790s – Honing, Northrepps, and Bracondale. The third is devoted to the period after 1800, when – in Norfolk in particular – Repton worked closely with his son, John Adey Repton, on projects which were increasingly architectural in character. It also covers the years after 1811 when – following a serious carriage accident – Repton's health deteriorated markedly, leading to a noticeable decline in the number of his commissions. In Norfolk there was only one – Sheringham – although this he was able to

describe as his 'most favourite work'.[80] It was among his last commissions. In 1818 he died at Hare Street, but was brought back to Norfolk, his 'own country', to be buried in Aylsham churchyard.

Figure 21. *Repton's 'before' image of an unknown Norfolk landscape.*

Figure 22. *Repton's 'after' image of the same unknown landscape.*

Chapter 2

Starting Out

Having briefly summarised the character of Repton's career and the development of his style, we can now look in more detail at his work in Norfolk. We are particularly fortunate that his first account book, which covers the years 1788 to 1790, has survived, and, as already noted, seems to provide a complete list of his commissions in this period.[81] It is, nevertheless, a problematic source for two reasons. Firstly, it gives few indications of the character of the work carried out by Repton, in most cases merely detailing how long it took and what he charged for it. Secondly, for a number of places it gives only a partial picture even of these, for the entries indicate that the work continued beyond 1790, with later payments for particular commissions being carried over to the 'New Ledger 1791' since lost. The account book is a priceless survival, but has to be combined with other archival information, where this is available, to provide a clear indication of what Repton actually did. This can involve some particularly complex detective work.

Catton Park

Catton Park, now embedded in the suburbs of north Norwich, was Repton's first paid commission. The account book records that he began work here in September 1788, but payments continued through 1789 and into 1790 and the account was carried over to the following ledger, showing that activity was even then still continuing. It had presumably been completed by 1792, when

Figure 23. *Catton Park illustration from Peacock's Polite Repository, 1792.*

an engraving of the south front of Catton Hall, based on a drawing by Repton, was published in Peacock's *Polite Repository* (Figure 23). Repton's client was Jeremiah Ives, a member of one of Norwich's leading merchant families, a wealthy businessman and banker, and mayor of the city in 1769 and 1786.[82]

Repton appears to have been acquainted with him for many years, probably through his friend William Windham. No Red Book survives for Catton and whether one ever existed is hotly debated. The two paintings by Repton of Catton Park, which still survive in Norwich Castle Museum, are of a different shape to the usual Red Books and do not seem to have been cut from one (Figures 24 and 25). However, Cecil Pond, a young architect in the early 1950s, remembers seeing a red Morocco-bound book about 15 inches in length in the County Architect's Office. He recalls that it had a gold border with the words 'Catton Park' or similar in gold Roman lettering: some of the letters were upright and others slightly sloping. The book's contents were line and colour-wash panoramas entitled 'vista from . . .' and showed landscape scenes spread across both pages.[83] If this was Repton's first Red Book, it was not passed on with the title deeds and has now disappeared from public record. Repton also refers briefly to his work at Catton in his book *Observations on the Theory and Practice of Landscape Gardening*, published in 1803. According to most published interpretations of these sources, Repton created Catton Park to accompany a new house for Ives, built on a virgin site, which was designed by

Figure 24.
View of Catton Park
looking south-west by
Humphry Repton.

Figure 25.
View of Catton Park
looking south-east by
Humphry Repton.

36

his associate and friend, the architect William Wilkins the elder. Repton may himself have decided the site for the house, close to the northern boundary of the park.[84] In fact there is no doubt that all this is incorrect. Both Catton Hall and its park had been in existence for over a decade when Repton was commissioned to make 'improvements'. His work involved making additions or alterations to an *existing* landscape, rather than creating one *de novo*.

Ten years before Repton was employed here, in 1779, a road closure order had diverted a road running south from Catton village, through what is now the western part of the park, some way further to the west.[85] The map accompanying the order shows elaborate entrance gates already positioned on the eastern side of this road, apparently giving access to a house of some pretensions, presumably Catton Hall itself (Figure 26). There seems little doubt that the road was diverted either to create a new parkland setting for this mansion, or to expand a diminutive landscape park which already existed around it. The road closure was carried out for Charles Buckle, and the attached map indicates that the hall and surrounding land were his property. The new road was to run through land that was partly owned by Buckle, and partly by Edward Lincoln. Edward Lincoln's father, also Edward, already held an extensive estate in Catton in 1748, which is shown on a map of that date preserved in the Norfolk Record Office.[86] Much of it comprised scattered parcels, many of them strips in Catton's open fields, or small bundles of former strips, enclosed with hedges. These lay interspersed with the property of other proprietors. The same map indicates that the land later owned by Buckle was then owned by one Mr Marjoram, and formed a more compact although rather smaller holding, apparently concentrated in the area of what was to become Catton Park. Charles Buckle was a prominent local businessman and steward of Norwich in 1752, a post he still held in 1774.[87] He seems to have acquired the Marjoram property around the same time, building his new house a few years later. He acquired further property in Catton in 1779, the year following the road diversion, a move probably also connected with the creation or expansion of a park around the house.[88]

Buckle died around 1784 and his Catton property passed to his daughter, Frances, the wife of Jeremiah Ives.[89] The latter (Figure 27) already had a number

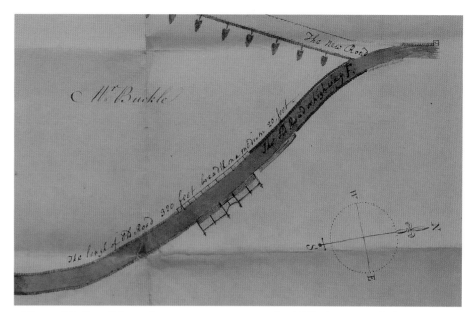

Figure 26. *Detail from the map accompanying the 1779 Catton road closure order showing the ornate gates (upside down) to the existing Catton Hall and the new road at the top.*

of connections with Catton. His brother-in-law Robert Harvey and his nephew Jeremiah Ives Harvey both lived in the parish, which was in effect already becoming suburbanised – a favoured residence for the city elite. As Armstrong's *History* put it in 1781:

> Catton is a very pleasant village, and the residence of many opulent manufacturers, who have retired from Norwich, and built elegant houses. The air is reckoned very healthful, and many invalids resort thither for the benefit of it . . . . The late Robert Rogers, esq. and Robert Harvey, esq. both aldermen of Norwich, have erected handsome seats in the village; as also Jeremiah Ives Harvey and Mr Suffield.[90]

It is likely that Ives and his wife took up residence at Catton Hall soon after Buckle's death. Three years later, in 1787, Ives' own father, Jeremiah, also died, and the following year he purchased the bulk of Edward Lincoln's property in Catton, a total of 120 acres together with a number of houses and gardens.[91] Most of this land, and a number of other parcels acquired around the same time by Ives, lay in the area to the south-west of the existing park, on the far side of the new road created by the 1778 diversion. Almost certainly, Repton's commission was associated directly with Ives' acquisition of this additional land in the parish.

Repton charged for five days' work in September 1788, one day in October and two and a half days in November (one in the company of Ives, one with the surveyor James North and one with both Ives and the architect William Wilkins), as well as for unspecified time spent mapping and making drawings of a proposed ha-ha.[92] In the spring and summer of 1789 Repton worked a further day and a half at Catton, again with unspecified additional time drawing and mapping; and he charged for yet more days in November and December of that year. Two further days were spent at Catton in June 1790, bringing the total bill to £54 15s. 6d. This was a large sum: for visiting Shrubland Park in Suffolk around the same time, and for producing a Red Book, he only charged £24 9s. 0d. It should, in addition, be noted again that the commission was still at this point ongoing, the sum owed by Ives being carried over to another, now lost, ledger starting in 1791. Some indication of the improvements made under Repton's direction can be gleaned from the two watercolours of Catton that he produced, and by comparing the way the park is depicted on a number of maps: William Faden's county map, surveyed between 1790 and 1794 (Figure 28); the drawings made by the Ordnance Survey, but never published, in 1817 (Figure 29); an estate map surveyed in 1819, the year of Ives' death; and a sale map of 1835 (Figure 30).[93]

Faden's map clearly shows the landscape before any of Repton's changes were carried out, or at least before they had made any significant visual impact. It depicts, rather schematically, a small (c.50-acre, 20-hectare) park, marked as the property of Jeremiah Ives, which is bounded to the south and east by woodland belts. The main approach to the hall ran in from the west, from an entrance on the road created in 1778. The Ordnance Survey drawings of 1817, and the maps of 1819 and 1835, all show another drive, running in from the north-east from an entrance on Church Street

Figure 27. *Jeremiah Ives (1728/9–1805) by Charles Catton junior.*

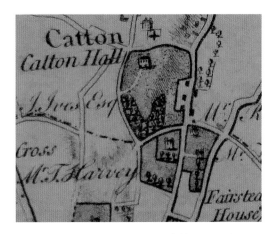

Figure 28. *Detail from Faden's Map of Norfolk, 1797 showing Catton Park.*

38

Figure 29. Detail from Ordnance Survey Drawing, Norwich Sheet, date 1817.

– effectively, the main street of Catton village. This appears to have been created by Repton. In *Observations* he describes how

> the real importance of a place might be distinguished by the number of cottages, or rather, substantial houses, appropriated to the residence of those belonging to the place; this would truly enrich the entrance to every park. . . . Various specimens of this attention may be seen at the roads near the following places . . . CATTON.[94]

Catton thus represents the first clear example of the way in which Repton was keen to provide an approach to a mansion which served to emphasise the status of the owner, the extent of his ownership and his importance in the local community.

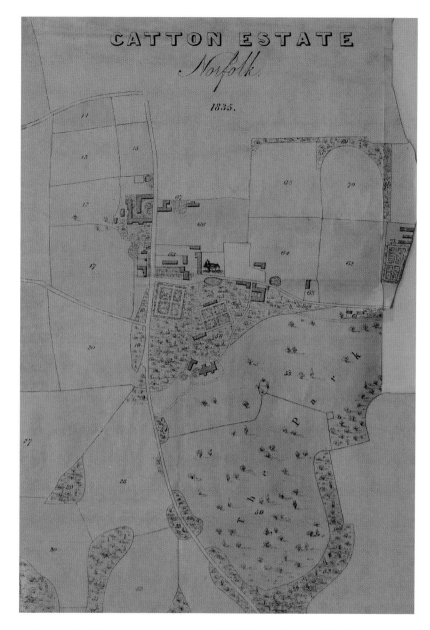

Figure 30. Map accompanying the 1835 Catton Estate Sale Particulars.

A more important difference between the landscape shown of Faden's map of 1797, and that depicted on these later maps, concerns the area to the south-west of the park, where Ives had purchased significant amounts of land in 1787. The Ordnance Survey drawings show an extensive area here which is shaded as parkland, but which was clearly separated from the park proper by the public road created in 1778. This contained three large woodland blocks – named on later maps as Fiddle Plantation, Scarecrow Plantation and Night Plantation – as well as a number of smaller clumps. The drawings show a drive running through its northern section, beginning at a point almost opposite where the main western drive from the hall met the public road. The sale map of 1835 also depicts the clumps and plantations but shows them now set within arable fields. In addition, the Ordnance Survey drawings, and more clearly the maps of 1819 and 1835, suggest that the western belt of the park, running beside the public road, was less solid and continuous than when surveyed for Faden's map, with gaps allowing glimpses across the road into this area. In this context, it is striking that Repton's painting of the view to the south-west in Catton Park (Figure 24) appears to show a much more extensive area of parkland than exists today, with grass extending continuously as far as these same new plantations. The key difference between the landscape shown on the maps, and that depicted by Repton, is that the latter does not show the road running along the western margins of the park, nor the perimeter belt running along it – both of which should be clearly visible in the middle distance.

The Ordnance Survey drawings of 1817 also show another 'detached' area of parkland, separated from the park proper by a public road, this time lying to the east, on the far side of the Spixworth Road. This is the area later known as the Deer Park, but then as 'Till's Pasture'. That both these areas were planned and designed by Repton is strongly suggested by the fact that in November 1788 he charged Ives for surveying 112 acres, work that he had subcontracted to James North.[95] The area of Catton Park shown on Faden's map amounts to only around 50 acres (c.20 hectares), including the belts; around 60 acres if the site of the house and the pleasure grounds are included. However, the combined area of the park, the 'Deer Park', and the detached area of park and plantations to the west of St Faith's Road (shown on the Ordnance Survey drawings) comes to around 110 acres (c.45

hectares), which seems to indicate that Repton was preparing a plan which embraced all these areas.

The 'Deer Park' (Till's Pasture) was probably always intended to lie outside the park, and to form a distant backdrop to the view from the house. It occupied sloping ground, at the only point where the road to Spixworth was not lined by a string of houses, mostly in the ownership of others. These properties were hidden by the perimeter belt of the park, but there was a gap in this opposite the slope, and an illusion was thus created: the park appeared to extend onto the rising ground beyond the public road. In contrast, it seems likely that the rather larger area of parkland and plantation designed by Repton to the south-west of the park *was* originally intended to form part of it – that is, the park was to be expanded in this direction, and the intervening road and perimeter belt removed. As noted, Repton's painting showing the view towards the south-west does not include any sign of either: the new area of parkland appears continuous with the old. Of particular significance in this context is the entry in Repton's account book (not previously commented on by garden historians), which records how he 'made a sketch from the map of the roads to be turn'd' – that is, closed or diverted. No public roads were, in fact, closed in Catton in this period, but it seems very likely that Repton and Ives originally planned a further diversion of the road created in 1778, running along the western edge of the park, along a route which would have passed still further to the west. This idea was eventually abandoned, perhaps in anticipation of opposition from the wealthy residents of Catton, perhaps on grounds of expense. Instead, the new area of parkland and plantations continued to be divided from the park by the public road, and the western belt was retained, but provided with gaps through which the new area of parkland could be viewed. A little later, and certainly by 1835, the pasture here was ploughed up and the area divided into fields, but glimpses were retained through the perimeter belt of the maturing plantations and tree-clumps beyond.

The Ordnance Survey drawings, and the 1819 estate map, both show the building now known as the 'Holiday House', but in the nineteenth century as the 'Gothic Cottage', which is located to the east of the hall, close to the northern boundary of the park. It is also visible on Repton's second painting of Catton Park, showing the prospect to the east, nestling in trees, with the new north-eastern approach to the hall in the foreground. This cottage ornée was clearly supposed to be seen from the house, and from various points within the park (Figure 31). Its designer is unknown, but this is probably where the reference in Repton's accounts to the day spent 'with Mr Ives and Wilkin' comes in. As noted, this has sometimes been interpreted as indicating that the architect William Wilkins designed Catton Hall but as we have seen, this cannot have been the case as the hall had been built a good decade earlier. Instead, it almost certainly refers to discussions regarding the design and placing of the Cottage.

William Wilkins Senior was born in Norwich in 1751 and is less well known than his son, the Greek Revival architect William Wilkins Junior (the designer of, among other things, Downing College in Cambridge and the National Gallery in Trafalgar Square), with whom Repton was also to

Figure 31. Early 20th Century postcard of the 'gothic cottage', now known as the Holiday House.

work, most notably at Haileybury in Hertfordshire.[96] Wilkins Senior may have known Repton through their shared membership of the Society of United Friars (sometimes known as the Society for the Participation of Useful Knowledge), a Norwich-based philosophical fraternity (see below, page 62). As John Chambers described in 1820:

> His education was limited, but his taste, his studies, and his manners, were greatly above his condition and he cultivated, with extraordinary diligence, pursuits which led to his after success. Among these were architecture, and his plans and drawings were peculiarly beautiful. In the course of his business he became acquainted with Mr Repton, the landscape gardener . . . and to that circumstance he is in a degree indebted for his elevation.[97]

Chambers adds that a key point in his career came when Repton recommended him to Lord Moira as the architect for a new mansion at Donnington Park in Leicestershire. It is noteworthy that Wilkins' design for that house (never executed) was in a simple gothic style, and he was something of a student of gothic architecture, preparing detailed drawings of mouldings and other medieval features in Norwich Cathedral and elevations and details of Bury Abbey gateway. In 1792 he revamped Stanfield Hall in Wymondham (Norfolk) in a medieval gothic style, complete with a staircase hall featuring fan vaulting. As we shall see, he also designed a small building called 'The Cottage' at Northrepps in Norfolk for Bartlett Gurney.[98] It seems almost certain, given the character of his style and interests, that Wilkins was the architect for the 'gothic cottage' at Catton, but that Repton decided – in consultation with Ives – its precise location within the park.

What else Repton may have contributed to the landscape at Catton remains uncertain. It is possible that he augmented the planting within the park; more probably, he may have made changes to the pleasure grounds, especially given that his new approach drive from the north-east ran through their western section. The sales particulars of 1835 describe them as 'tastefully laid out in a handsome lawn, with parterres of flowers and choice exotics, beautiful shrubberies and exotic evergreens, intersected with walks, with an aviary and an elegant greenhouse 50 feet long and 21 feet wide'.[99] Further on the particulars wax lyrical over 'the WALKS from the MANSION to the ivy-towered CHURCH, to the GOTHIC COTTAGE occupied by Mrs Hobart, and to the GREAT ROAD through the much-admired Pleasure Grounds, planted on each side at an enormous expense, with the choicest Flowers and Shrubs'.

All this sounds rather Reptonian, and may indeed have been designed by him, although much may have been added or altered in the intervening 47 years. The illustrations contained in the sales catalogue drawn up when the property was again placed on the market in 1852 similarly depict the kind of grounds we might have expected Repton to have designed (Figures 32, 33 and 34). But both sources also suggest that many of features for which Repton provided designs were never put in place. There is no evidence that his proposed ha-ha was ever constructed; the 'lawn' around the house always appears to have been separated from the wider parkland by an iron fence.

Repton's first commission may thus, in certain respects, have been misunderstood in the past by garden historians. He did not create a new park for a new house. A park of around 50 acres, bounded along much of its western, southern and eastern perimeter by a woodland belt, already existed at Catton when he was commissioned to make 'improvements'. Repton appears to have created a new entrance drive, leading off Church Street and approaching the house from the north-east; added the 'gothic cottage', almost certainly designed by William Wilkins, as an eye-catcher within the park; and designed two new areas of parkland, one to the east of the existing park (the 'Deer Park') and the other, much larger, to the south-west. The former was, almost certainly, always intended to be a detached area, separated from the park proper by a public road and forming a backdrop to the view; the latter, however, was probably originally envisaged as an actual extension of Catton Park, following the diversion of the road running along the existing park's western boundary. If so, this plan was abandoned at an early stage and this area likewise became a detached backdrop to the view.

Whatever the precise nature of Repton's contribution to the landscape of Catton, subsequent changes have served to modify it significantly. In 1835

Figure 32. View towards Catton Hall from the 1852 sales catalogue.

Catton Hall and its estate, now amounting to 630 acres (c.255 hectares), was sold by Frances Ives, Jeremiah's widow, to Captain G. Morse, on whose death in 1852 it was sold to the banker John Hudson Gurney.[100] A few years later the park was finally extended to the west, following the diversion of St Faith's Road along its present line in 1856.[101] The park was increased in area to around 75 acres (c.30 hectares), a rather smaller expansion than that apparently envisaged by Ives and Repton, and the three plantations which they had established remained outside the park, although the new belt planted along the western margins of the park probably incorporated some of the smaller clumps which they had planted here. This is the belt which survives to this day: a fine piece of planting, mainly composed of an understory of yew interspersed with cedars, both Atlantic and Lebanon. The original, late eighteenth-century belt was largely removed, but its line can still be picked out as a band of mature oaks running through the middle of the park. Around the same time another profound change was made. A new approach to the hall was created, running from south to north through

Figure 33. Catton Park looking towards the Cathedral, from 1852 Sales catalogue.

Figure 34. A meandering path through the trees to St Margaret's Church, Old Catton.

the entire length of the park from an entrance (provided with an elaborate wrought-iron gate designed by Barnard, Bishop and Barnard of Norwich, and flanked by a single-storey lodge in a simple classical style) on Oak Lane. In addition, in 1858 a footpath running through Till's Pasture to the west of the park was diverted by a road order.[102] It remains unclear whether it was J. H. Gurney, or his cousin Samuel to whom the estate passed in 1866,

who fenced the area and introduced deer there: this was the origin of the name 'The Deer Park' which has since been applied to the area, although deer do not appear to have been kept in this diminutive 'park' for very long. A little later a large camellia house was erected on the south side of the hall, and a new kitchen garden built some way to the north while the existing walled gardens were removed. A narrow belt of trees was planted along the

Figure 35. The view today, looking north towards Catton Hall.

northern edge of the park, and the parkland planting was much augmented, most notably with a number of Wellingtonias which have now become huge specimens. Whatever the legacy of Repton, in other words, much that we see at Catton Park today actually dates to this mid–late nineteenth-century period, and to the time of the two Gurneys.

Catton Hall was requisitioned by the army during the Second World War and much of its park's interior ploughed. In 1948 Catton Hall, and the northern section of the park, were sold by Desmond Buxton to Norfolk County Council and the building used as an old people's home. The park remained under arable cultivation and the surrounding land was steadily developed as housing. Scarecrow Plantation was destroyed completely to make way for the development associated with the road called Partridge Way. Night

Plantation and Fiddle Plantation have survived, although flanked on all sides by houses and gardens. Nevertheless, the perimeter belts of the park remain largely intact (except where Hall School was erected to the south-west of the hall, and on the northern side, where land was sold for housing), and some of the internal planting has survived, mainly old oaks, especially pollards, of little value to the timber merchants. Although the park remains today in divided ownership – and with Catton Hall itself forming a third property – it is now a public open space, restored with support from the Heritage Lottery Fund, which is administered by the Catton Park Trust. Some replanting has taken place and the interior has been returned entirely to pasture. A number of surfaced paths have been laid out and 'Hayman's Lodge', a public meeting room, has been constructed in the far south, close to the entrance on Oak Lane.

Hanworth

Figure 36. Hanworth in Peacock's Polite Repository, 1793.

Hanworth in north Norfolk was probably Repton's second commission after he became a professional landscape designer. His account book shows that he spent two days here, one in July 1789 and the second a year later.[103] He also prepared two watercolours, which survive in the Colman Collection in the Millennium Library in Norwich. One has Repton's characteristic lifting flap but does not appear to have come from a lost Red Book. An engraving of Hanworth also appeared in the *Polite Repository* for 1793 – all, perhaps, suggesting an extended involvement (Figure 36).

Unlike Catton, Hanworth was a long-established seat, built by the Doughty family, who had resided in the parish since at least the fourteenth century. Robert Doughty, who died in 1669, built up the family's property in Cork in Ireland as well as his business activities and property in Norwich, while his half-brother William spent eleven years travelling in and around Barbados, perhaps involved in the slave trade. On his death in 1673 the estate was inherited by his son Robert (c.1656–1742), who built the hall sometime around 1700, after a fire had destroyed a previous house. It is a fine two-storey building of nine bays, with a central three-bay pediment featuring a

circular window, and the doorway has Tuscan capitals and brick pilasters. As Haslam has observed, the design is strongly influenced by houses built a few decades earlier in the simple classical style practised by the Norfolk-based 'gentleman architect' Sir Roger Pratt, such as Coleshill in Berkshire or Horseheath in Cambridgeshire.[104] Later in the century the Norwich architect Matthew Brettingham, who had an important role at Holkham, worked on the interior of the hall, remodelling the drawing room in 1742–3, around the same time that he was employed at nearby Gunton.[105]

Robert Doughty had two sons, both called Robert, who died in infancy in 1683 and 1688, and his eldest son William died in 1698 at the age of 21. His fourth son, Guybon, survived but suffered from 'melancholia' (some form of depression) and so Robert passed the management of the estate to Guybon's son, another Robert (c.1717–1757), when he came of age in 1738.[106] His son, Robert Lee Doughty, inherited the estate at the age of eight in 1757 and in 1776 married Ann (or Anne) Powys, the daughter of Thomas Powys Esquire of Lilford, Northamptonshire. She came with a fortune of £30,000, giving him ample funds to make improvements.[107] It was this Robert who brought in Repton to advise on the grounds, although whether the activities

Figure 37. Illustration of Hanworth from Armstrong's History and Antiquities of the County of Norfolk (1781), based on a drawing by Humphry Repton.

45

Figure 38. Repton's pen and ink sketches – the view from Hanworth Hall, the top 'before' image with the flap down, the lower 'after' image with the flap up.

noted in the account book, and suggested by the watercolours, represent the totality of his involvement at Hanworth remains very uncertain. As noted earlier, Doughty had been Repton's friend and neighbour while the latter resided at Sustead (between 1778 and 1786) and may well have benefited from his advice then.

No maps or relevant documents relating to the estate survive from before the end of the eighteenth century, making it difficult to determine when the park at Hanworth was originally laid out, but it was evidently in existence by 1781, when Repton, writing in Volume III of Armstrong's *History*, described 'an elegant and convenient house pleasantly situated in a small park . . . the pleasure grounds about it are laid out with much taste.'[108] The accompanying engraving shows the hall set in parkland with a belt of trees to the west (Figure 37).

A Repton pen and ink sketch, with a lifting flap, shows how the view southeast from the hall could be enhanced by clearing away trees, in order to provide an unimpeded view of – and thus establish a 'connection' with – Hanworth parish church (Figure 38). Here generations of the Doughty family were interred, Doughty's tenants and dependents assembled each Sunday for worship, and the family had built their own private box pew in 1764. The other painting shows a view across the park, with the River Scarrow meandering in leisurely fashion and crossed by a bridge (Figure 39). As there is no lifting flap it is unclear what 'improvement' is being proposed, but the apparent width of the river, here little more than a stream in its natural state, may imply that it was to be dammed or otherwise broadened in some way. The account book entry notes that on 31 July 1789 Repton spent 'A day staking towards kitchen garden', and on 3 July 1790 'A day staking New approach'. Neither was charged for, a note in the first entry stating, 'I charge nothing – but he says he will call it a day'.[109] At the time, to judge from other account book entries, his daily rate was three guineas, but as we have seen, Doughty was a personal friend.

Figure 39. *Hanworth – view across the park with meanders in the River Scarrow, by Humphry Repton.*

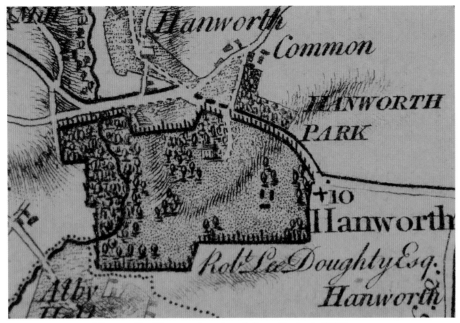

Figure 40. Hanworth – detail from Faden's 1797 map.

Figure 41. Hanworth – detail from the Ordnance Survey Drawing, Cromer Sheet 1816.

William Faden's map of 1797, the earliest cartographic evidence for the appearance of the local landscape, shows the house situated towards the north of the park, and approached along a drive leading in from a northern entrance near Hanworth village (Figure 40). This was presumably the approach laid out by Repton in 1790, given that Faden's map was surveyed in the early 1790s, although the situation is slightly confused by the fact that the 1816 Ordnance Survey drawings show two drives approaching from this direction, merging shortly before the house was reached (Figure 41). The same source also shows a park of typical eighteenth-century form, with a belt of trees to the west, screening plantations to the north and a scatter of trees and clumps. The view from the hall, to the church, was unobstructed, as Repton had advised. By the time the tithe map was surveyed in 1840, however, the church was partly screened by a belt of trees, as was Dairy Farm in the south-east of the park. The kitchen garden,

which lies some 300 metres to the north-west of the hall, was hidden by a more substantial block of woodland, called 'Icehouse Grove' on later maps (Figure 42). The walls of the kitchen garden still survive and may be contemporary with the hall. The account book reference to 'staking towards the kitchen garden' could refer to marking the positions of shrubs and trees, planted to obscure views of the walls, but may indicate that a new path was being made to the garden. Much money was certainly spent on the garden by Doughty, who regularly purchased fruit and vegetable plants from Mackie's nursery in Norwich. A bill from 1801 lists Red Roman Nectarines and Morello Cherries while another in 1803 shows purchases of vegetables including Early Scarlet Radish, Mustard, Deptford Onion, Strasburg Onion, Cauliflower and Early York Cabbage. Mackie was also paid for a number of conifers (300 Scotch fir, 150 Spruce fir and 30 Silver fir in the period 1801 to 1803), suggesting that further planting was going

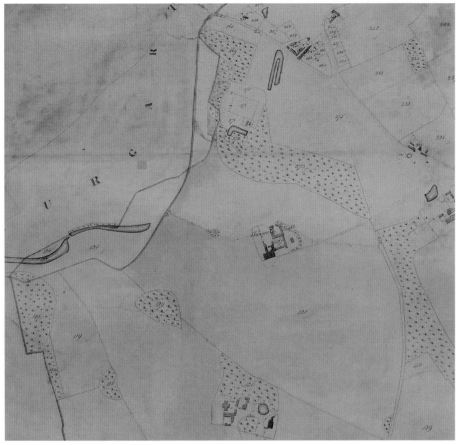

Figure 42. Hanworth Tithe Map, 1840.

adorned by stately Oak, Chestnut, and other Forest Trees, with groups of thriving plantations'. They also mention the 'Walled-in Garden well stocked with the choicest Fruit-trees & Bushes, Two Vineries, a Capital Ice-House, &c. &c.'[111] At the end of the nineteenth century Hanworth was sold to Joseph Gurney Barclay for his third son, Henry Barclay, the final sale completed in 1900. It is still owned by the Barclay family.

The work described in the account book, and illustrated in Repton's watercolour, was limited in nature. It seems to have involved the creation of a new entrance drive, and modifications to the planting to improve the view towards the parish church and, perhaps, to hide the kitchen garden walls. It remains possible, however, that a longer and more extensive involvement is obscured by an absence of evidence.

Figure 43. Hanworth Hall, from a drawing by J. S. Cotman, 1818/19.

on in the park at this time.[110] The tithe map shows that the river had been artificially widened, perhaps a belated attempt at implementing one of Repton's proposals.

Robert Lee Doughty had no children and on his death in 1819 the estate passed to his nephews, Philip Wynell-Mayow and Vice Admiral William F. Lukin. On the death of the former in 1845 the estate was bought by William Howe Windham of Felbrigg for £65,000. The auction particulars prepared at the time described the park as being 'in a Ring Fence, beautifully

Holkham

Holkham, where Repton was employed in 1789, was a more prestigious commission. The landscape here already had a long and complex history. Holkham Hall was built between 1734 and 1760 on a new site, a little to the north-east of a previous house, for Thomas Coke. A vast Palladian mansion, it was designed by a group of individuals: Coke himself, the architect Matthew Brettingham, Lord Burlington and William Kent.[112] The surrounding landscape went through a number of phases of development and when Thomas Coke died in 1759 the hall stood within a park of around 370 acres (c.150 hectares), containing a mixture of grand yet simple geometry, serpentine lines, and classical and Palladian structures, mainly designed by

Kent. Key features were Obelisk Wood, containing the temple and obelisk within it, on the rising ground to the south of the hall; the great southern avenue; lodges, designed by Kent, at the north and south entrances; and the lake, originally created between 1725 and 1731, but altered in the 1740s. A few changes were made to this landscape in the 1760s and 70s: Lady Margaret, Coke's widow, employed 'Capability' Brown (or possibly one of his 'assistants') in 1762 but his activities were restricted to the pleasure grounds in the immediate vicinity of the hall. When Thomas William Coke succeeded to the estate in 1776, much about the landscape was old-fashioned, and he immediately set about making improvements.[113]

The old kitchen garden, on the western side of the hall, was soon demolished

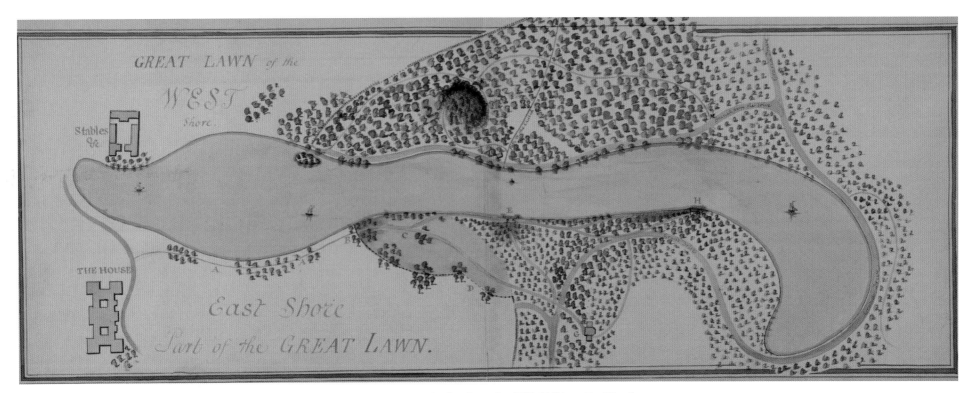

Figure 44. Repton's plan from the 1789 Holkham Red Book.

50

and a replacement, located 600 metres further to the west, was constructed, together with a new orangery, designed by the architect Samuel Wyatt. The lake, now considered too stiff and formal in shape, was given a serpentine 'twist' at its northern end by the designer William Emes in 1784–5 (and another at its southern end by his former pupil, John Webb, in 1801–3).[114] The most important change, however, was the expansion of the park, mainly to the south but to some extent in all directions. New lodges were built, again to designs by Wyatt, and well over two million trees were planted, in large clumps and in an unbroken perimeter belt which incorporated some existing areas of woodland. This enclosed an area of nearly 12 square kilometres. Much of this – almost all the southern section of the 'park', out of sight of the hall – in fact remained under arable cultivation, something which may, in part, reflect Thomas William Coke's great interest in agricultural improvement. It was here that the Great Barn was built in 1790, to designs by Wyatt, to serve as the venue for the 'sheep shearings' – an annual gathering of farmers and landowners at which the latest ideas in agriculture could be demonstrated.

The clumps and the perimeter belt, and probably other aspects of the new landscape, were designed by John Sandys, who seems to have come to Holkham with Emes in 1784 and who was appointed as head gardener there in 1786.[115] Repton, who was consulted while all this new work was underway, was asked to advise only on the creation of an extensive area of pleasure ground beside the lake, to the north-west of the hall. He appears to have become involved here through contacts originally forged in politics. In 1788 Windham, and Repton's friend Robert Marsham, had persuaded Thomas Coke to stand in the elections for one of the Norfolk parliamentary seats, and Repton worked for his campaign. His account book records how he functioned in effect as a political agent, and among other things prepared a map of the county, showing the main political influences operating in each of its constituent hundreds. This was clearly an undertaking that Repton felt to be arduous and time-consuming, noting in his account book that 'In my profession it is seldom necessary to give more than 5 hours attendance to the day – In this employment my time has generally been from daylight till 9 o'clock at night.'[116]

Figure 45. *Detail from Kent's view of the clumps of trees on the North Lawn and his proposed North Lodge, later occupied by the Mr Creak referred to in Repton's Red Book.*

In 1789, however, Repton recorded payments for very different work. In August: received nine guineas for three days in the pleasure grounds, in October: payments for preparing 'a map & 2 plans & 4 drawings for Mrs Coke', and in December: for '2 days staking'. The Red Book for Holkham, one of the earliest examples to survive, is dated August 1789 and is dedicated to Mrs Coke. Repton makes clear, at the start, the limited character of his interventions, stating that he had endeavoured 'to avoid any thing that may interfere with his [Coke's] more extensive plans'.

Some of Repton's proposals seem, from the standpoint of the twenty-first century, slightly odd. He suggested laying out a walk from the hall to the woods which had been planted a few decades earlier on the eastern side of the north end of the lake (Figure 44). When the path arrived at this area it was to divide in two. One branch was to lead to one of Kent's lodges, which had been left isolated by the park's recent northward expansion (its site is now occupied by the tall pillar erected in 1843 to Coke's memory). This he described as 'the building prepared for Mr Creak's dwelling', but it was also to contain 'a Room . . . reserved for a sea view' and was therefore to be renamed 'from its situation the Maritime Pavilion, or from its destination the Temple of Fidelity' (Figure 45).

Figure 46. *Repton's illustration of the proposed classical pavilion/fishing lodge/boathouse designed by Samuel Wyatt.*

52

Figure 47. *Repton's illustration for the Holkham Red Book of the proposed classical pavilion/fishing lodge/boathouse – from the side view.*

Figure 48. *Repton's view looking south-east from the west bank of the lake.*

Figure 49. *Repton's preparatory sketch for the above Red Book image.*

The other branch of the path would lead along the eastern shore of the lake, as far as 'the present boat house' at E on his plan. This was to be replaced by 'an elegant pavilion', a classical building, designed by Samuel Wyatt, which was illustrated in a drawing by the architect at the end of the Red Book (Figure 46). The lower floor, level with the water, was where the boats would be kept. The upper storey was to be 'a handsome room which looks on to the water and which will become a favourite retreat for fishing'. Repton provided views showing the side elevation of the building, with the mast of a boat in the background, and from across the lake (Figures 47 and 48). The Colman Collection in the Millennium Library contains a sketch by Repton on which this view is based (Figure 49). From the boathouse, a number of different paths would extend through the woods by the edge of the lake. One would run close to its shore, ending at H through an enclosed pergola/tunnel with a 'pebbled floor' (Figures 50 and 51). Another path, running roughly parallel and higher up the slope to the east, would provide a hidden route back to the house, Repton commenting that 'this sort of surprise, though easily practiced in hilly country, will appear a perfect wonder in Norfolk'.

Figure 50. The two openings at the end of the tunnels, terminating the upper and lower walkways on the Eastern Bank.

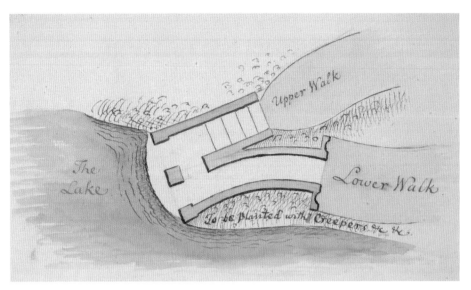

Figure 51. Repton's plan of the twin tunnel construction, which was to be covered in creepers to reveal a surprising view, south down the lake.

Repton found the western shore of the lake more attractive than the eastern. – it was 'the most beautiful ground in Holkham Park' – in part perhaps because of its more varied topography, but mainly because the woods here, planted by Thomas Coke in the 1730s and 40s, were now reaching maturity. Unfortunately, this area lay a good distance from the hall – a 'vast circuit had to be made by land around either end of the lake' to get there. The route needed to be shortened, and a direct connection made with the proposed pleasure ground on the eastern shore. This posed some problems, for as Repton wrote, 'a bridge, however elegant for the sake of magnificence, or however simple for the sake of convenience, would be intolerable, because it would destroy the effect of the lake, and make it a river'.

The opposing shores were instead to be connected by a 'ferry-boat of peculiar construction' (Figure 52). Repton illustrated a chain ferry (operated by a 'stout rope') which would run from Wyatt's fishing lodge/boathouse on the eastern side, to another new building on the opposing shore. The ferry was to be constructed in such a way that it could be used by 'any

lady with the greatest of ease without more trouble than turning a winch'. The building proposed for the western shore, Repton described as a 'snug thatched cottage . . . picturesquely embosomed in trees'. Its design would be based, rather bizarrely, on some fishermen's huts Repton had seen beside the River Severn in Gloucestershire (Figure 53). The building would form an interesting element in the view from the hall, especially as Repton suggested that a fire should be kept burning inside. He noted that chimney smoke 'is always a most interesting object when fleecy folds are revealed, as in the present instance, by a rich background of hanging woods'. It would also provide accommodation for a labourer charged with looking after the boats, fishing pavilion and woodland paths – 'a sort of aquatic game-keeper, and his house a kind of water-porter's lodge'.

The western shore of the lake was to be moderately wild in appearance – 'rural' but 'not neglected'. It would be crossed by paths, one leading back along the western side of the lake to the hall; one continuing on to Holkham parish church, located in the north-west corner of the park (there was already

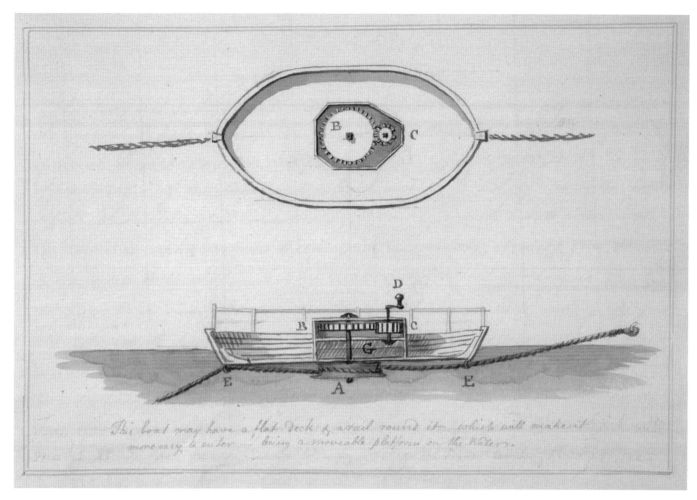

This boat may have a flat deck & a rail round it which will make it more easy to enter — being a moveable platform on the Water.

Figure 52. *Repton's construction plans for the Holkham ferry, designed to shorten the walk back to the house, from the western shore of the lake.*

a 'prospect-room' for views from the church tower) and another path to an old chalk pit (K), which still exists. This was to be modified, with a shallow cave excavated in one side in which visitors could sit on benches and enjoy 'this picturesque and awful spot'. On the final page of the Holkham Red Book, Repton cautions against the development of any further paths from the western shore garden to the house until 'the farmyard etc shall be displaced'. It would be hard to equal the beauty of the paths already described. He also states that it is essential to have a 'dry walk' to the church and the placing of 'a few evergreen trees . . . in and around the graves would give a proper character to the place'. He does not say if these should be traditional yews or another variety of evergreen tree, but he believes that the 'church would become, if possible, a more pleasing object when we see its tower "embosom'd high in tufted trees" '.

Figure 53. *Repton's snug, thatched cottage proposed for the western shore, with its fishermen's nets hung out to dry, a fishing rod propped up against the mounted bell and perpetual smoke.*

Holkham is interesting in that it is a typical example of how, even when commissioned to work at a major residence set in extensive grounds, Repton often designed only a small area – usually, as in this instance, a pleasure ground. But it is also important for what it tells us about the role of his Red Books. Few of the changes proposed in the Holkham Red Book appear to have been affected. There is no evidence that either the 'snug cottage' or the fishing pavilion were erected, that the church tower or the former lodge were altered in the manner he proposed, or that the cave was ever added to the old chalk pit. While an estate map of 1843 shows a pattern of paths which is vaguely similar to the arrangement proposed by Repton, the resemblance is not close (Figure 54).[117] Yet, as already noted, a few months after the Red Book was submitted, Repton spent 'two days staking' at Holkham, and in his book *Sketches and Hints on Landscape Gardening*, published in 1794, he described Holkham as one of the places where 'artificial pieces of water have been ornamented under my direction', and where 'the magnificent lake has been dressed by walks on its banks, and a peculiar ferry-boat invented to unite the opposite shores'.[118] The ferry boat was further discussed, and illustrated, in Repton's *Observations on the Theory and Practice of Landscape Architecture* of 1805, together with an extended extract from the Holkham Red Book.[119] These discrepancies suggest not simply that Repton's clients often implemented his suggestions only sparingly but also that these might have been quite extensively modified following the submission of his formal proposals. The Red Books may, as it were, have been the start of a conversation about improvement, rather than a blue-print, strictly and accurately followed.

Holkham park continued to change after Repton's time – the most radical alteration to the area with which he was involved was the demolition of Kent's old north lodge and its replacement by the great monument erected to the memory of Thomas William Coke in 1843. The shores of the lake, ornamented with mature woodland, are particularly attractive, but how much their present appearance owes to Repton's activities remains unclear.

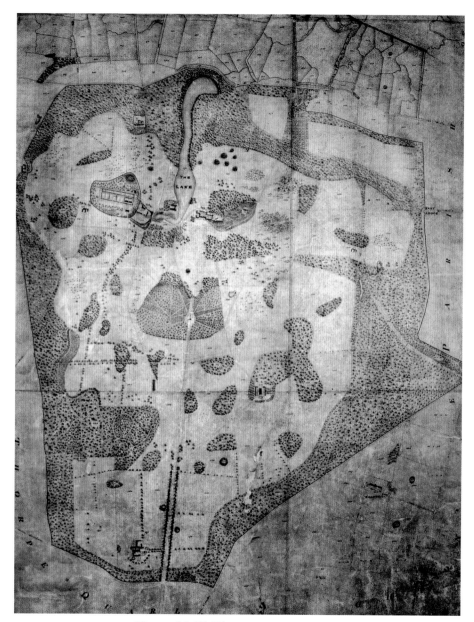

Figure 54. Holkham estate map, 1843.

57

'Baber', Buckenham Tofts and West Tofts

Three other Norfolk commissions are mentioned in Repton's account book, but very little is known about them. He was paid three guineas in December 1789 by John Patteson Esq. for 'one day at Baber'. John Patteson was, like Jeremiah Ives, a leading member of Norwich's mercantile elite. The Patteson family came to Norwich from Birmingham in the late seventeenth century. John Patteson's father died when he was a boy and he was brought up by his uncle John, a successful wool merchant. In 1774 he took over the business, but subsequently became a leading local brewer (his firm later became Stewart and Patteson, which survived into the twentieth century). Patteson prospered, becoming a city alderman in 1781, sheriff in 1785 and mayor in 1788.[120] By this time he was living at Surrey Street in Norwich, but he also appears to have rented, probably as a country retreat, Bawburgh Hall, to the west of the city. This was a manor house, built in the seventeenth century, which was owned at the time by the Norton family.[121] In 1791, however, Patteson purchased nearby Colney Hall, a more modern residence (built only a decade or so earlier) and a more imposing one than Bawburgh, set on a low hill within a park of around 125 acres (c.50 hectares).[122] Being just under a mile (1.6 kilometres) east of Bawburgh, it is not far away, and might conceivably have been thought of as lying within that parish. While it might seem more likely that Repton would have been commissioned to advise on this place, rather than on Bawburgh Hall – which was rented, and soon to be vacated, by Patteson – there is no doubt that the payments to Repton were made *before* Patteson acquired Colney. But not that long before – little more than a year – and it is possible that his advice was sought before the property was acquired. There is little evidence of anything obviously 'Reptonian' at either place. Bawburgh had some pleasure grounds by the end of the nineteenth century, but its date is unknown and nothing survives today – the hall was demolished in 1963 and the site built over in the 1970s. Colney Hall was largely rebuilt around 1840 and the gardens much altered in the course of the nineteenth century, but a sale catalogue of 1834 describes the grounds as 'tastefully disposed', with walks within the plantations beside the house that were 'skilfully varied', with fine views across the River Yare (Figure 55). The more distant prospects were 'enlivened by the picturesque view of the village of Bawburgh and the beautiful wooded demesne of the Rt. Hon.

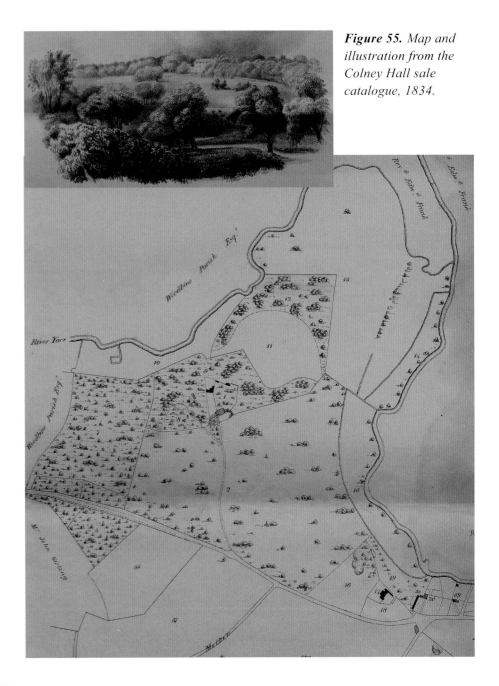

Figure 55. Map and illustration from the Colney Hall sale catalogue, 1834.

Lord Suffield' (Costessey Hall).[123] Whatever Repton did, and wherever he did it, the commission was a small one.

Repton's account book also includes rather more substantial payments received in 1789 and 1790 from Stephen Payne Gallwey of 'Tofts'. Gallwey, a member of the Society of Dilettanti, had purchased West Tofts Hall and its estate (which covered 2,792 acres, or c.1,130 hectares) from Mr George Nelson in 1780.[124] West Tofts was a depopulated parish in the heart of Breckland, containing only the hall, the nearby parish church, and a handful of other dwellings. Nelson had been responsible for creating the most striking feature of the local landscape, the great woodland belt, planted by the nurseryman Griffin of Mundford in the 1770s, which embraced more than 10 square kilometres of land.[125] Faden's county map of 1797 details most of the land lying within the belt as 'park' but the Ordnance Survey drawings of 1821 show a much smaller area of true parkland, around the house and church, the rest of the enclosed area comprising arable fields and heath (Figure 56).

West Tofts lay in close proximity to Buckenham Tofts, owned by Lord Petre, and the account book shows that Repton was also working here, at around the same time, receiving payments from Petre in 1789 and 1790. Over the years preceding Repton's involvement here, Payne Gallwey and Petre had worked together to improve the local landscape, expanding their parks and establishing plantations. Some of this activity had been directed by a Mr Lapidge, who is referred to in a letter of April 1788.[126] This was almost certainly Samuel Lapidge (1740–1806), one of the leading members of Capability Brown's team from 1767 until his death in 1783, when he was named in Brown's will as his successor in the business.[127] This raises the possibility that Brown had himself earlier made plans for 'improvements' here which Lapidge was now executing, and the extensive park at Buckenham Tofts in particular has a very 'Brownian' appearance – a perimeter belt, well-placed clumps and a fine serpentine lake.[128]

Repton's activities at Buckenham Tofts appear to have been relatively limited. He made one visit there – a 'morning walk at Buckenham House' – for which he received two guineas, but he also supplied two 'large drawings'

Figure 56. *Detail from the 1821 Ordnance Survey drawings, East Harling Sheet, showing West Tofts Hall and Buckenham (Tofts) Hall.*

Figure 57. Buckenham House illustration from Peacock's Polite Repository, 1792.

in frames, for which he charged 13 guineas. These, somewhat surprisingly, were executed not by Repton himself, but by the noted topographic artist George Samuel. The account was not continued into a later account book. Nevertheless, an engraving of Buckenham Tofts was published in Peacock's *Polite Repository* in 1792, possibly after a further, undocumented, commission there (Figure 57). The evidence of the account book suggests that his work at West Tofts was more substantial. While it details only three days of work which, with incidental expenses, amounted in all to £17 15s. 6d., it also shows that the account was still 'live' at this point and was carried over to the next ledger book. The earliest surviving large-scale map of the parish – the tithe map – was made much later, in 1845.[129] But the Ordnance Survey drawings of 1821, although drawn at too small a scale to provide much useful information, show a park covering around 100 acres (c.40 hectares. The hall and parish church stood close to its centre, belts ran along much of its eastern and part of its southern boundary and it contained a number of small clumps of trees (Figure 56). These were clustered in the area lying to the south of the hall, reflecting the fact that its main views were in this direction, and that the main approach drive ran through this area, entering the park at its south-eastern corner and approaching the mansion at an oblique angle. Much of this is vaguely Reptonian, but there is nothing which could with confidence be attributed to him. The estate passed to John

Moseley, who had married Payne Galwey's daughter Charlotte, around 1830 and was subsequently acquired by Sir Richard Sutton, 2nd Bt. (d.1855) of Lynford, and became incorporated into the Lynford estate. The hall became the rectory for West Tofts.[130] Together with neighbouring parishes, West Tofts and Buckenham Tofts were requisitioned to form part of the STANTA Battle Training Area in 1942, and the halls demolished soon afterwards. The remains of their parks survive in reasonable condition but there is little that could confidently be attributed to Repton.

Conclusion

Although the scale and nature of Repton's activities at 'Baber', West Tofts and Buckenham Tofts remain unclear, we know more about what he proposed at Hanworth, Catton and, in particular, Holkham. As with his other commissions undertaken in these years, elsewhere in England, these places already display some of the features which came to characterise Repton's style later in his career, especially a concern for entrances and approaches, a delight in whimsical ornamental buildings, and a particular interest in pleasure grounds. It is only during the 1790s, however, in Norfolk as elsewhere, that Repton's approach to landscape gardening really crystallised, and its underlying principles came to be clearly articulated.

Chapter 3

The Prophet in his own Country

Our knowledge of Repton's style as a landscape gardener, and of the ideas and concepts underpinning it, increases in the period after 1790. This is partly because of the large number of Red Books surviving from this period, and partly because of the publication in 1794 of his book *Sketches and Hints on Landscape Gardening,* followed in 1803 by *Observations on the Theory and Practice of Landscape Gardening.* These texts provide a clear statement of Repton's principles and ideas in what might be called his 'classic' phase of landscape design, after 1790 but before he began to work closely with his son, John Adey Repton, in the years following 1800. Key to Repton's approach was the concept of 'appropriation'. He was keen on developing ways in which the owners of estates could display to the full the extent of their property and their dominance of a locality.[131] This might take bizarre or extreme forms. In the Red Book for Tatton Park in Cheshire, for example, he argued that the coat of arms of the family should be displayed on milestones, or the parish church ornamented in a similar way to the country house. This would establish, in clear visual terms, a connection between landowner and place.[132] But it was usually carried out more subtly. 'Appropriation' was closely connected with another key concept, much discussed by Repton, that of 'character'. Repton was a social conservative, so that while he was happy to manipulate the landscape to exaggerate a client's social standing, he was nevertheless much concerned that the grounds attached to a residence should be of the appropriate size and degree of elaboration – proportionate to the site and perhaps also to the 'rank of its possessor'[133] Great palaces required vast gardens and parks but smaller manor houses or villas did not: magnificent houses in diminutive grounds were as unwelcome as homely ancestral mansions in wide, sweeping, empty parks. Repton, in short, saw a close connection between social status and landscape, but the connection might be complex and subtle.

The same year that Repton published *Sketches and Hints,* two works appeared which articulated a very different approach to the landscape, Richard Payne Knight's *The Landscape: a didactic poem* and Uvedale Price's *Essay on the Picturesque.*[134] These advocated a more romantic and picturesque style of design, both writers hammering home William Gilpin's earlier accusations that Brown's style was bland and repetitive. Price stated that 'monotony and baldness are the greatest defects of improved places'.[135] The two men wanted designs that, in their spatial composition, echoed the paintings of Lorraine and Poussin, and which were more rugged and, in particular, more *varied* in character.

> The stately arch, high rais'd with massive stone
>
> The ponderous flag, that forms a bridge alone;
>
> The prostrate tree, or rudely propt-up beam,
>
> That leads the path across the foaming stream;
>
> May each the scene with different beauty grace.[136]

Features like ruined buildings, exposures of rock strata, ancient trees and even old quarries provided not only interest and variety but also a sense of place. Within parkland, they believed, the planting should be made denser, more varied, and rougher, with scattered thorn bushes for example being used to break up the open expanses of smooth turf. Both men were fiercely critical of Repton, whom they accused of simply perpetuating the style of Brown. They ridiculed, in particular, the concept of 'appropriation', Price noting that 'There is no such enemy to the real improvement of the beauty of grounds as the foolish vanity of making a parade of their extent, and of various marks of the owner's property, under the title of 'Appropriation'. [137]

The first three Norfolk sites discussed in this chapter mainly date to the early and mid-1790s and show clearly the extent to which Repton's approach differed from that of Price and Knight. In part, we should note, this was because Repton had to make money from his profession, while Price and Knight were dilettantes, wealthy landowners who simply wrote about landscape and provided informal advice to friends and acquaintances. Repton also used features like gothic buildings, picturesque cottages and (as at Holkham) abandoned quarries as important elements in his designs. However, he was obliged to take a more practical approach, and one which (especially by indulging their desire for status) appealed to clients. It is not, perhaps, surprising that it was the style practised by Repton, rather than the kind of landscaping advocated by Knight and Price, which predominated in the last decade of the eighteenth century, and the first decade of the nineteenth century, in Norfolk as elsewhere in England.

By the time Repton started out as a professional landscape gardener he had been resident at Hare Street in Essex for several years, but it is clear that he maintained regular contacts with friends and relatives in Norfolk. Following his involvement in Thomas Coke's election campaign in 1788, he worked in a similar capacity for William Windham in 1790. He made regular visits to his sister in Aylsham, and to his younger brother John, who continued to farm at Oxnead. His son William (1783–1858) trained as a lawyer and joined the practice of his uncle, John Adey, in Aylsham and continued the practice after his uncle's death in 1809.[138] Repton also continued to attend the meetings of an organisation known as the Society of United Friars, to which he was proposed in March 1787 and, after a ballot at Carrow Abbey, was elected as a full member in April 1787, on account of his literary talents.[139] It was one of several societies, clubs and fraternities that emerged in late eighteenth-century Norwich. Founded in 1785, it was dedicated to the promotion of science and learning and held regular meetings, at which papers were read and discussed. It included amongst its members such local luminaries as John Sell Cotman and William Beechey (artists) and Hudson Gurney (banker), together with various members of the city elite and local gentry.[140] Other members included Mostyn John Armstrong who, as we have seen, had earlier employed Repton when preparing his *History*; and the architect William Wilkins (senior), who we have met working with Repton

at Catton in 1788. The Friars originally met in premises in Crown Court on Elm Hill, later moving to rooms in St Andrew's parish in 1791.[141] Members wore mock medieval costume and carried rosaries. The proceedings of the society were regularly published, and a library was developed, but the Friars also had philanthropic objectives, one example being the organisation of soup kitchens for the poor within the city, in 1793.[142]

Figure 58. *Nos. 22–26 Elm Hill, Norwich also known as Crown Court or Paston House, where the Society of United Friars met in the late eighteenth century.*

Northrepps

The first of Repton's Norfolk commissions which post-dates his account book was Northrepps near Cromer on the north-east coast. Northrepps Hall, built in the sixteenth and seventeenth centuries, was acquired by the banker Robert Barclay of Bury Hill in Surrey in 1790. He had married Rachel Gurney of Keswick in Norfolk, a member of a prominent Quaker family, with numerous branches in the county and many important banking connections.[143] Repton's Red Book does not, however, relate to this property, but to a different block of land in the parish, lying a little to the north-east, which was acquired in 1792 by Rachel's cousin, Bartlett Gurney (1756–1803) (Figure 59). He had long resided in Norwich but now planned to build a new house on the hill to the east of Northrepps Hall, to the south of Hill Lane. He commissioned William Wilkins to draw up plans, possibly because both men were acquainted through the Society of United Friars, through which Bartlett would also have known Repton, if they were not otherwise acquainted. Repton notes in the Red Book that he had 'long had the pleasure of being personally known to you'. In the event, although plans for a new mansion were drawn up and the Red Book prepared, nothing was ever done. Bartlett instead erected a much smaller building, now known as 'Northrepps Cottage', in a more dramatic location, a short distance to the north, in 1793. This too, was designed by William Wilkins.[144] It was apparently intended to function as a holiday retreat rather than a permanent residence, although it is noteworthy that it is shown on William Faden's county map of 1797 using the symbol which is employed for other gentlemen's residences and country houses. It is labelled as the home of B. (i.e. Bartlett) Gurney, as opposed to R. (Richard) Gurney, who is shown as the owner of Northrepps Hall to the east. The two properties became united following Bartlett Gurney's death in 1803, and after this the 'Cottage' served a variety of purposes, subordinate to the main hall: as a residence for unmarried sisters, young married heirs and invalid members of the family.[145]

Figure 59. *Portrait of Bartlett Gurney* by Frank Vandermine (anglicised spelling of Frans van der Mijn, 1719–1783).

The Red Book, which survives in private ownership, does not carry a date, but was almost certainly drawn up in 1792, soon after Gurney acquired the site for his intended house. It is a particularly interesting document. At most other places in Norfolk – indeed, at most places where he worked – Repton adapted and improved parks and gardens associated with existing mansions. Here in contrast, as at Bracondale (and at Sheringham, later in his career – below, page 144), he worked on a virgin site, and one largely devoid of features. In his own words, he was supplying a 'plan for <u>creating</u> rather

Figure 60. Northrepps Red Book – proposed site of the new house, with flap down.

Figure 61. The same view showing the new house, with the flap up.

than <u>improving</u> the scenery since the situation yields no actual materials of beauty', except 'the ground itself'. Repton begins, in his customary manner, by describing the 'Situation and Character' of the site, and by laying out some general rules for selecting the sites for houses. These, in line with his thinking at this time, are based on the size of the residence to be erected; its 'character', and whether, in particular, it is to be in constant occupation; its aspect, or orientation in terms of the compass points; the form of the raw topography near the house (which, as Repton notes, can be altered to an extent, but only at significant expense); and the views to be enjoyed from it. The last consideration, he notes, often takes precedence when sites for new houses are being chosen, but 'every day's experience convinces me that an extensive prospect is not a sufficient compensation for the many inconveniences to which lofty and exposed situations are generally liable'.

The spot chosen for Gurney's house, Repton explains on the following page, is in full accord with these rules. It was well suited to the architecture of the house designed by 'my ingenious friend, Mr Wilkins', which was 'elegant, simple and compact' – the Red Book illustration shows it as a

neat Neoclassical box (Figures 60 and 61). It was also appropriate to what Repton describes as a house of '*mixt character*', part permanent residence and part an intermittently occupied sporting seat or villa. Gurney – still only 38 years old and actively involved from 1777 in running the family's bank in Norwich – did not intend to spend all his time by the sea. The position chosen was also, Repton considered, the right one for a building facing south-east ('the best possible aspect in Norfolk'), and for the disposition of the ground, which fell away steadily from the main elevation towards the south, providing fine views from the principal rooms, across the proposed new park. This, to judge from the attached plan (Figure 62), would have covered around 220 acres (c.90 hectares), 'amply sufficient for the Character, Stile [*sic*], and magnitude, of the house proposed to be built'. It was a smaller landscape than he had originally proposed, in part because – with no raw materials to play with – all the planting would be new, and 'young plantations have no effect at a distance, altho' when placed in proper situations they will immediately give variety and shelter to a scene without appearing to give it an air of confinement'. He cautioned against establishing a continuous belt of trees around the perimeter of the park, on the grounds

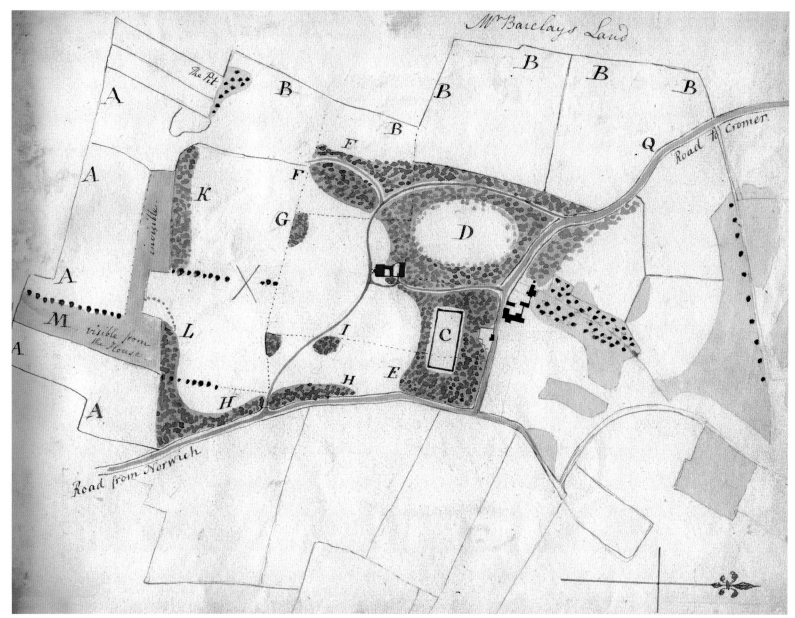

Figure 62. Repton's plan for the Northrepps Red Book.

Figure 63. *Northrepps Red Book – view to the sea 'before' image with the flap down.*

that the lie of the land would have made the separation between the park and the surrounding farmland highly visible and would thus have rendered it an 'offensive and tedious line of confinement'. It would have made only too clear the limited extent of Gurney's ownership, which did not extend much beyond the land acquired for the new house and its grounds. Repton further argued that narrow plantations would not grow well so close to the coast, and instead suggested that the 'whole country must be richly and amply cloathed', with the trees planted in substantial blocks – especially

Figure 64. Same view to the sea, 'after' image with flap up.

to the north and west of the house, to protect it from the winds. Here the woodland would have contained two clearings. One, which Repton thought might be dispensed with, was to be for growing 'corn for pheasants'. The other was to contain the kitchen garden, suitably located near the stables in order to facilitate movement of manure, and close to the house for convenient access, yet hidden from view by the trees.

Belts of woodland were also to be planted along the southern and eastern

Figure 65. Northrepps Red Book – view to south from the new house, 'before' image with both flaps down.

bounds of the park, and between these and the house there were to be a small number of tree clumps. The belt to the east was to be provided with a gap, to allow a framed prospect of the sea (Figures 63 and 64). More extensive sea views were to be avoided because, as Repton put it, they were 'precarious' – vulnerable to poor weather, sea mists and the like – and should therefore form a subordinate part of the prospect, even of a house intended as a coastal retreat. Some land beyond this gap, and beyond the public road, would need to be laid appearance of continued lawn', a typical

Figure 66. *Same view with left flap up.*

Reptonian illusion. Repton discussed at some length, and illustrated, the prospect south from the house, towards the churches of Northrepps and Southrepps (Figures 65, 66 and 67). The proposed park was to mainly extend downhill, away from the house, and was to be ornamented as far as possible with trees retained when the hedges surrounding the fields were removed. Indeed, because hedgerow trees were few in number, the more wind-deformed specimens being improved by judicious trimming. The house would be approached from two directions. From the north,

Figure 67. *The final reveal to show the view south from Bartlett Gurney's proposed new house, with both flaps up.*

travelling from Cromer, a drive would run through Repton's proposed block of woodland. From the direction of Norwich in the south, another drive would enter the park by 'a few trees now on the spot'. This approach would reach the house in such a way that it would not intrude on the views from the windows.

The Northrepps Red Book is interesting in showing how Repton approached the problem of creating an entirely new park in a particularly exposed and windswept situation; how he made a relatively small park (without an attendant landed estate of any size) appear larger and more important than it really was; and how he dealt more generally with the tricky question of 'character'. It also includes a number of passages which inform us about Repton's attitudes to landscape more generally. He thus describes, in one memorable section, how amongst the disadvantages which accrue from erecting houses in elevated positions, was the way in which it made a landscape less 'appropriated' to a mansion. In other words, the views would unavoidably include the properties of neighbouring owners. Elsewhere, he criticised the habit amongst Norfolk people of valuing a prospect simply by the number of church towers it embraced, asserting that 'it is the business of taste to shake off the fetters of local opinions and to value objects by their qualities or beauty, and not by their quantity'.

The view he drew of the prospect to the south of the new house might thus, he notes, have omitted a large number of distant church towers, but those at Northrepps and Southrepps (which he does include) were 'quite sufficient for the scene'. It was not the only time, as we shall see, that he was critical of local practice, or expressed a desire to bring the county more in line with national taste. Indeed, it is noteworthy that he hints that his work had so far been poorly received in Norfolk, stating that it would be particularly gratifying to have his proposals accepted in a county 'where I am less known professionally than in most other parts of the kingdom'.

In the event, as noted earlier, nothing came of Bartlett Gurney's plans for a new house, or for Repton's new park. Instead William Wilkins designed for him the much smaller Northrepps Cottage at a point some 300 metres to the north (Figure 68). This was placed in a dramatic valley, surrounded by steeply rising ground,

Figure 68. *Victorian engraving of Northrepps Cottage, which was built instead of the new house shown in the Red Book.*

Figure 69. *1921 photograph of Northrepps Cottage and the view down the tree-fringed valley to the sea.*

71

and enjoyed a well-framed view, northwards to the sea (Figure 69). There is a strong family tradition that Repton had a hand in designing the surrounding landscape and, while direct evidence is lacking, there are strong hints that this may be correct. If Repton supplied a design for one house by Wilkins, why should he not have done the same for another, especially since Bartlett Gurney was not simply a commercial client but an acquaintance of long standing? In this context, attention should be drawn to the final paragraph in the Red Book, which refers directly to the area in question – the dissected, dramatic landscape, the north of Hill Lane – in a manner which suggests Gurney had already shown interest in implementing some suitable 'landscaping' there.

> The romantic ground north of the road, with the variety of sea prospect is certainly capable of much improvement, but while there is so much necessary to be immediately done about the house, it would be useless to enter into a detail which cannot be executed till the house scenery has been rendered comfortable.

It is perhaps possible that Gurney's preference for the new 'Picturesque' ideas may have contributed to the change of plan, from classical villa on a commanding hilltop, to romantic cottage embosomed in wooded hills. Faden's county map of 1797 shows the 'cottage' at the south-east end of a block of well-timbered parkland which corresponds with the area of woodland later described as Cottage Wood. The 1840 Tithe Map shows that – a little to the north of the Cottage – this wood was crossed, south-east to north-west, by a broad serpentine drive, which is labelled as the 'Green Drive' on the Ordnance Survey 6-inch map of 1886 (Figure 70).[146] This feature appears to be shown, indistinctly, on the draft Ordnance Survey drawings of 1816.[147] The tithe map, and the Ordnance Survey 6-inch, also show a complex pattern of serpentine paths threading through the woods and clearings, and the latter map depicts two small buildings within the woods, one of which may be the 'reed house' which is pictured in a number of drawings still kept at Northrepps Hall, and which is again attributed by family tradition to Repton. Evidently, the rising ground to the west of the Cottage was some kind of designed landscape, perhaps broadly Picturesque in style to complement the romantic architecture of the cottage itself. There is a strong possibility that Repton had a hand in all this, but no hard evidence.

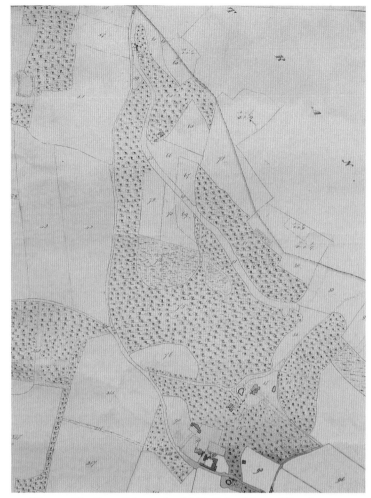

Figure 70. *Detail from the 1840 Tithe Map of Northrepps.*

The site proposed for the new house at Northrepps, and for Repton's park, remains an arable field. The 'Cottage' is now a restaurant, and while altered and extended since first built remains an important and interesting example of Wilkins' architecture. Cottage Wood is now in part a caravan park, but the Green Drive has recently been cleared and restored by the current owner of the Northrepps estate.

Honing

Around the time that he was working at Northrepps, Repton was asked to prepare proposals for Honing Hall, some 10 kilometres to the south-east, the property of Thomas Cubitt. The Cubitts were an old-established Norfolk family but the house was purchased as a home for Thomas' son, also called Thomas, a London lawyer who had recently married the daughter of a rich city merchant. The hall, a rather tall red-brick building, had been built for the Chambers family around 1748 and the Cubitts almost immediately called in the architect John Soane to make alterations. Between 1788 and 1792 he added a fashionable full-height bow window on the western side and made various alterations to the internal layout.[148] We do not know how Repton secured the commission. The proximity of Honing to Aylsham suggests a local family connection, or recommendation by one of Repton's wealthy friends, but we should also note that around the same time Soane and Repton were both working at Moggerhanger in Bedfordshire. Soane was designing a new hall (between 1791 and 1793) and Repton the grounds (this Red Book is dated 1792), so the work may have come by that route. Honing Hall already stood on the northern edge of a small park, covering some 18 hectares, probably created shortly after it had been built. An undated and rather schematic plan shows that this was only partly bounded to east and west by perimeter belts, and by a hedge line alone, containing scattered trees, to the south.[149] It occupied fairly level, uneventful ground. The walled kitchen garden lay, as it still does, less than a hundred metres to the south-west of the hall.

On the first page of the Honing Red Book Repton, echoing comments made in relation to Northrepps, stated that 'there is hardly any part of England in which I am less known professionally than in Norfolk (perhaps from its being 'The Prophet's own Country')'. He also states his desire to use the opportunity presented by the Red Book to set down some of his more general attitudes and principles towards landscaping: this was still three years before the publication of *Sketches and Hints* in 1794. Already, however, he seems to be anticipating some of the arguments made in defence of his position against the attacks of Uvedale Price and Richard Payne Knight. He comments in the introduction that any improvement needs to be 'convenient, simple, elegant and cheerful', and that 'picturesque effect is too dearly bought at the price of Comfort'.

Repton begins, in his usual fashion, by discussing the 'situation and character' of Honing, arguing that 'no improvement can be rationally conducted without proper attention to the character, stile [*sic*] and purpose of the house'. This he categorised as a respectable country seat, permanently occupied, rather than a 'shooting seat or a mere retreat from the capital'. He is aware that the distribution and extent of the property owned by Cubitt meant that the 'lawn' or parkland could quite easily be extended 'far beyond what its character would make advisable'. But he cautioned against this, and also warned against having the grass of the park and the adjacent 'corn lands' present in the same view. This he described as another distinctive 'fashion in Norfolk', and one he considered a 'false taste', because the two kinds of landscape were incompatible with each other, each having its own distinct 'character'. A mansion should look out across a park, and a farmhouse across its fields. Cornfields, and the pastures of a park, carried very different meanings, as he explained in a particularly memorable passage:

> Labour and hardship attend the operations of agriculture, whether cattle are tearing up the surface of the soil, or man reaping its produce; but a pasture shows us the same animals enjoying rest after fatigue, while others sporting with liberty and ease excite the pleasing idea of happiness and comfort annexed to a pastoral life. Consequently, such a scene must be more in harmony with the residence of elegance and comfort, and marks a degree of affluence, so decidedly that we never see a park ploughed up, but we always attribute it to poverty.

The park at Honing should thus be of an appropriate size for a modest mansion and should be enclosed in such a way that near views of the working countryside were excluded – with a belt of woodland, rather than a hedge or fence (Figure 71). Such an arrangement brought other advantages, he explained, explicitly quoting from an earlier Red Book drawn up for Hanslope in Buckinghamshire:

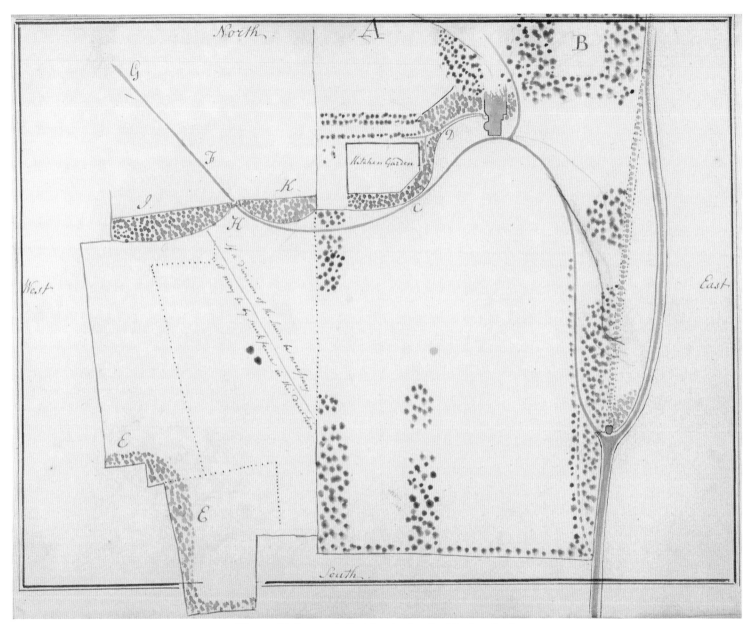

Figure 71. Repton's Red Book plan for Honing Park.

74

Figure 72.
Repton's 'before' (top – flap down) and 'after' (bottom – flap up) watercolour illustration of the view from Honing Hall, looking south.

If the park be divided from the <u>farm</u> only by a hedge, we know the breadth of a hedge, and its proximity is as offensive as if the pale made the line of separation; but if instead of a pale or hedge we substitute a wood of sufficient depth to act as a screen, the imagination gives still greater depth to that wood than it really has, & the park derives extent from what in fact is its boundary.

In order to explain the nature of the changes he proposed, Repton next describes how there are three key viewpoints from which a landscape around a mansion is experienced: from the rooms within it (the most important); from the approaches to the house (which should be relatively direct but also serve to display the beauties of the situation); and from the 'walks and drives about the place'. In terms of the first of these, Repton believed that the kitchen garden at Honing, which lay less than a hundred metres to the south-west of the hall, was poorly placed, in the sense that its walls were clearly visible from the windows. This may not have mattered much when the hall and the walled garden were first erected but was less acceptable by the 1790s, perhaps especially at Honing given that the construction of the bow window on the west side of the house in 1784 encouraged views in this direction. It is noteworthy that, sometime in the mid-1780s, the surveyor Thomas Woodward had been commissioned by the Cubitts to draw up a plan for a new kitchen garden, to be located on a site to the *north* of the hall, but this had not been implemented.[150] Rather than rebuild the walled garden on a new site, Repton – always sensibly economical – proposed reducing the length of the east wall and planting a screen of trees. This would also form a sheltered walk, ornamented with flowering shrubs, and would be extended north as far as the park boundary (Figure 72).

Next, Repton returned to the theme of the park – its proper extent, and the manner in which it should be bounded. He ruled against any expansion to the north or west but was keen to extend it onto the gently rising ground to the south – he meant the south-west – if the land there could be obtained from a neighbouring owner, Lord Orford. A keeper's lodge in the form of a tower might then be erected there. In terms of the approaches to the

house, Repton was critical of the main entrance drive because it led in at right angles off the ruler-straight public road which bounded the park to the east. This arrangement, he believed, gave the impression that the road continued 'to some object of greater importance beyond it'. Instead he suggested moving the public road slightly to the east and expanding the park by a small amount in this direction, so that the drive could be made to leave the road in a more gradual curve (Figure 73). He also proposed erecting a 'cottage' or lodge at the entrance. These were, once again, typical Reptonian touches. By carefully manipulating the landscape, the apparent importance of the mansion was increased, and by implication that of its owner. The view of the house from this eastern approach, moreover, would be improved by adding a string course to the hall, which would make it appear less tall (Figure 74). He also proposed adding a new entrance drive, entering the park from the north-west, skirting the new screen around the kitchen garden and approaching the house from the west. On his 'Conclusion' page, Repton writes that he wished the builder of the existing kitchen garden had had the foresight to place it somewhere else, and he goes on to say that if it were proposed to build a new version in the future, he would suggest siting it at A on his plan, north-west of the hall. Then, the belt of trees planted to mask the present kitchen garden could be converted into a number of clumps. He also says in his conclusion that when the proposed plantations have reached an age when they 'no longer need protection' that 'many beeches to be mixed in to the plantations' with their 'glossy stems' that could let in 'distant views of those particular objects whose exclusion may now for a while be regretted'. Repton rounds off the Honing Red Book with a watercolour of a couple of people battling the elements in a wintery landscape (Figure 75). He writes, 'in the meanwhile I shall conclude with a vignette of the kind of winter scene, which during one third of the year at least, will be hid by the plantations that I have dared to recommend'.

In spite of what some previous accounts have suggested, most of Repton's proposals for Honing appear to have been largely accepted and implemented.[151] The changes to the kitchen garden were certainly carried out. The eastern and western walls have clearly been reduced in length, and the south wall rebuilt to the north of its original line, as Repton suggested.

Figure 73. *The proposed view along the new curving drive to the house, from the Honing Red Book.*

Figure 74. Repton's proposed changes to the house – to make it appear less tall. (Top: 'before' image with flap down. Bottom: 'after' image with flap up.

The park was also extended to the south-west, following an exchange of lands with Lord Orford, which was carried out in 1793. The area of the park was thus increased from roughly 18 to 28 hectares.[152] The change had evidently been completed – and new perimeter belts put in place – by the time the Ordnance Survey drawings were prepared in 1816 (Figure 76).[153] The same source shows that Repton's proposed new approach from the north-west had been created, and that the sharp turn of the eastern entrance had been changed, although the park had not been expanded in this direction nor the proposed lodge erected. A third approach, entering the park in the far south-west and running its full length to terminate at the hall, was also in place by this time. The horizontal 'plat band' was added to the house, as Repton illustrated, and can still be seen today.

In addition, as is often the case with places where Repton worked, the landscape at Honing includes a feature which, while not mentioned in the Red Book, appears rather 'Reptonian' in character, and may well have been added after the proposals were drawn up, following consultations with the owner and his family. Hidden within the southern woodland belt is the 'reed house', with circular red-brick walls and conical reed-thatched roof. It may have been designed by Repton as an alternative to the castellated pavilion he originally suggested for the rising ground here. We have already noted that he may have constructed something similar at Northrepps. The brickwork certainly appears to be of the right period.

Relatively few changes were made to the Honing landscape in the course of the nineteenth and twentieth centuries although new gardens were laid out to the west of the hall, enclosed by shrubberies featuring rhododendron, Portugal laurel, beech, sweet chestnut and Wellingtonia. Both of the western drives have now disappeared – that from the north-west, suggested by Repton, had already gone by the time the tithe map was surveyed in 1841.[154] Despite this, James Grigor, visiting in 1841, would have seen a very Reptonian landscape perhaps reflected in his comment 'that a place possessing but few natural advantages, may, by the aid of well-disposed woods and plantations, assume a handsome and imposing character'.[155] The kitchen garden walls, as already noted, remain. The walls to the north, east and west are laid in Flemish bond and are probably coeval

Figure 75. Winter scene vignette which concludes Repton's Red Book for Honing.

Figure 76. Detail from 1816 Ordnance Survey drawing, Cromer sheet.

with the house itself. The southern wall is more recent, apparently erected following the garden's truncation on Repton's advice. Within the wider landscape the older free-standing trees are mainly oaks with some beeches, the oldest specimens probably dating from Repton's time. There has been some replanting over the last few decades, mainly of oaks but including some planes and a clump of walnuts. The tree belts are mainly of oak, with sweet chestnut and some beech. The park remains in excellent condition, one of the most attractive of the county's smaller, later eighteenth-century designed landscapes, and one of the best-preserved of Repton's creations (Figure 77).

Figure 77. *Honing Hall in its Repton park today.*

Bracondale

The well-preserved state of Honing is in marked contrast to the condition of Repton's landscape at Bracondale, just to the south of Norwich, which he designed around the same time, in 1793. Indeed, standing on Norwich's Martineau Lane – part of the city's outer ring road – the view is now dominated by Uren and Levy's huge County Hall, completed in 1968 – a building very different to the elegant, classical house, Bracondale Lodge, which was built here for Philip Meadows Martineau in the early nineteenth century. Martineau's house survived until demolition in 1966 (it would have stood in what is today the car park directly behind County Hall). Much of Martineau's parkland and gardens have disappeared under acres of tarmacadam, leaving only a few remnants of the planting – together with the intriguing remains of a former garden building.

Bracondale Lodge (Figure 78) stood centrally within its modest landscape park, a mile outside the walls of Norwich, on sloping land with far-reaching views across the Yare Valley towards Thorpe, Trowse and Whitlingham. The site was originally part of the lands of nearby Carrow Abbey, given in 1538 to Sir John Shelton by Henry VIII. Inherited by two subsequent generations of the Shelton family, the property passed through a number of owners before John Ridge sold it to the Norwich surgeon Philip Meadows Martineau in 1792 (Figure 79).[156] He was born in 1752 (the same year as Repton), the fourth generation of a family of surgeons descended from Gaston Martineau, a Huguenot who escaped persecution by moving from Dieppe to Norwich in 1685.[157] After schooling in Norwich, Warrington and Macclesfield, Philip Martineau returned to Norfolk as an apprentice to Mr William Donne, the city's leading surgeon at the time. On completion of his apprenticeship Donne sent Martineau to Edinburgh in order to continue his professional studies – it was a centre of learning much frequented by Nonconformists in this period – before undertaking a six-month tour, visiting London hospitals and giving professional lectures. He then returned to Norwich, to take up a position in Donne's practice and, aged 26, married Elizabeth Humphry, daughter of the Rector of Thorpe. They set up home on Gildengate (later known as St George's Street) in the parish of St George's Colegate, and Martineau's career blossomed. He eventually became a principal surgeon

Figure 78. Bracondale Lodge which stood on the site now occupied by County Hall.

Figure 79. Philip Meadows Martineau (1752–1829) by William Beechey.

specialising in lithotomy (the removal of bladder and kidney stones).[158] Like Bartlett Gurney, William Wilkins and Repton himself, Martineau was a member of the Society of United Friars. He was a keen Unitarian (his monument can still be seen in Octagon Chapel on Colegate) and an active philanthropist. His niece, the author Harriet Martineau, would become one of the leading advocates for social reform. He was involved in the founding of the city's first public library and the Triennial Music Festival, the proceeds from which went to support the newly founded Norfolk and Norwich Hospital.[159]

The year after acquiring the Bracondale property, in 1793, Martineau obtained a road order which diverted the lane that formed its eastern boundary, moving it further towards Trowse.[160] Around the same time Repton's friend William Wilkins was commissioned to design a new house. Unfortunately, its precise construction history remains unclear. In 1831 Simon Edwards described in his *Memoir* how Martineau had bought the property 'as a . . . retreat from the cares and anxieties of a profession which left him little time for relaxation', and how 'his love of the beauties of the natural scenery, led him to the purchase of an estate at Bracondale. Here he built a small house to which he frequently resorted with his friends, during the summer months, after the fatigues of the day.'[161] This must be the house designed by Wilkins, and for which Repton provided his Red Book, rather than the striking building of white brick, square in shape and with a semi-circular, two-storey central bay topped by a lead-covered dome, which survived until 1966. Edwards makes it clear that the latter was only erected following Martineau's second marriage, to Anne Clarke, and the birth of their daughter Dorothy in August 1812: 'with this addition to his domestic happiness, he was stimulated to erect a mansion suited to his improved fortunes and the rank in which he held in society; and in 1813 was laid the first stone of the present house at Bracondale'.[162]

It is just possible, given its rather 'Greek revival' appearance, that this second house was in fact designed by Wilkins' more famous architect son, William Wilkins the Younger, who had worked with his father on the restoration of Norwich Cathedral a few years earlier, and who was to work with him at nearby Keswick Hall four years later.[163] In one way, however, the character

of the house built in the 1790s is irrelevant, for the text of the Red Book makes it clear that when Repton was commissioned its construction had not yet begun.

In the Bracondale Lodge Red Book Repton yet again expresses a concern for the 'character' of the house to be erected, finishing with words which make clear its central role as a rural retreat from the bustle of city life:

> I must beg your acceptance of this volume as a tribute to the eminence you have acquired in your profession. That the improvement of this villa may tend to soften the anxieties of your profession and contribute to prolong a life on which the life, health and happiness of so many others depend, is the sincere wish of my dear Sir, H. Repton.

On page 4 Repton provides a plan of the site (Figure 80), which includes a diagram showing the quality of the 180° view from the front elevation of the proposed house. He describes how he is perfectly happy with the 30° sector of the view which looks eastwards, towards Thorpe and Whitlingham; and with the 80° sector looking towards Lakenham, which is 'Good, without requiring much improvement'. However, work was required to improve the 50° sector which faced industrial Trowse Millgate, and the village of Trowse, to the south-east.

The plan is annotated with letters K–V (U is missing), which relate to features referred to in the text. Boundaries of fields to be removed are shown in dotted lines, and several parcels of land have 'PM' written in pencil, indicating additional land owned by Martineau, or perhaps to be purchased in the future.

The course of the lane which Martineau had recently closed is shown by parallel dotted lines. Other interesting details include an area of trees, added in pencil, in Hill Field, south-west of the house. On page 14 Repton notes that 'the view south-east towards Lakenham Church may be very pleasing; and the form of the plantations Q and R must depend on the acquisition of the Hill Field.' When this acquisition had taken place somebody (possibly

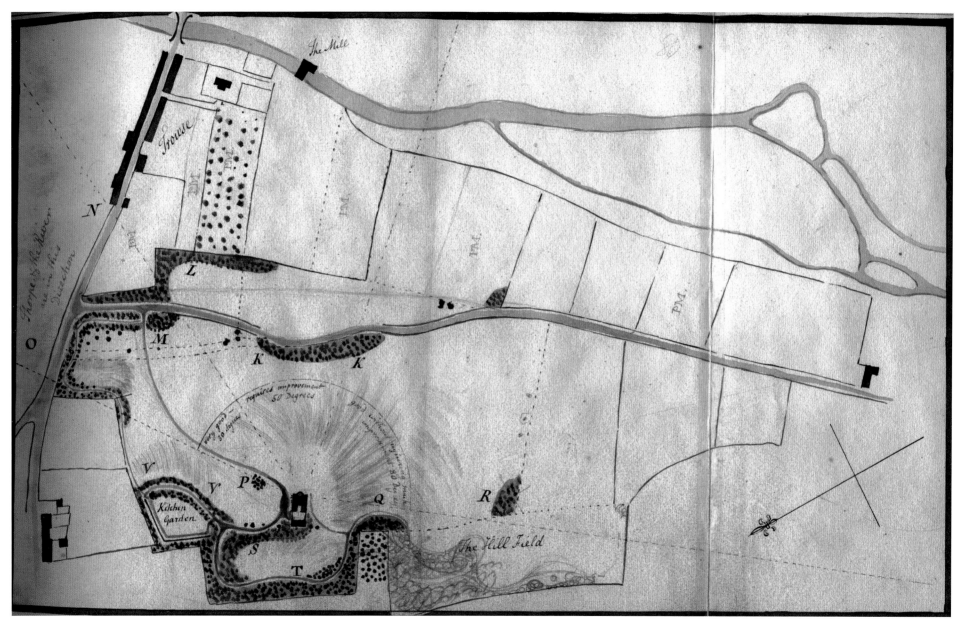

Figure 80. Repton's plan from the Red Book for Bracondale.

83

Repton himself) pencilled in the additional trees, together with the path running through them. This, interestingly, became the site of a garden building, the character of which is described below.

Before Repton begins to describe his specific proposals for Martineau's new grounds, he deals in general terms with the topic of views from windows, using rather mathematical terms and a diagram which may have been chosen to appeal to the scientific mind of his client (Figure 81). He explains that the site for a new villa must be selected with careful regard for the views available, and that owners are often disappointed by the way that important features of the surrounding landscape are invisible from inside the building – in contrast to the situation outside, where they are able to turn their heads a full 360°. Problems can arise from the size of the windows, the thickness of walls and the position of the viewer in relation to the apertures. The diagram explains how the angle of vision diminishes the further back a person stands from a window. Repton further suggests that the use of a bow window will remove any blind spots (between H and F on his diagram) and is 'peculiarly applicable to a villa altho' I must acknowledge that its external appearance is not always pleasing.'

The rest of the text is laid out in four sections, accompanied by several watercolours, some featuring his trademark flaps. The first section, *Views from the House*, describes the site for the proposed villa as a 'delightful bank' and again refers to the three sectors of the prospect, as shown on the plan. Repton confines most of his proposed changes to the 50° sector looking towards Trowse and Whitlingham, illustrating them with a watercolour view with a lifting flap (Figures 83 and 84). The 'before' view, looking towards Trowse village and St Andrew's Church, includes a windmill, the entrance to lime workings (Repton says 'the mouth of a cavern'), a quarry and a white house on the skyline with Whitlingham Lane running below. While none of this made for a highly offensive scene, Repton wanted to give Martineau the illusion of being in a completely rural setting, with no indication of the various industries nearby. He wrote:

> The village of Trowse tho' not very distant appears much nearer
> than it really is because the ground slopes towards it and is

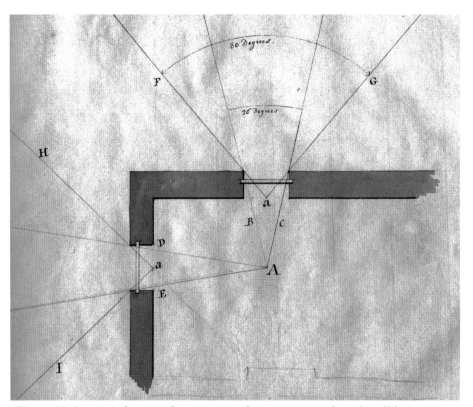

Figure 81. *Repton's diagram demonstrating how views seen from **A** will be narrower than those views seen at **a** and the blind spot which occurs between **H** and **F**.*

of course fore-shortened and the appearance of the population immediately under the windows counteracts the impression of retirement and seclusion from the bustle, which should be the leading character of a villa for altho' its views may be cheerful, extensive and abounding in variety of distant objects yet there should appear a certain distance betwixt the house and the habitation of other men.

When the flap is lifted, new tree belts are revealed, which serve to hide from view the cottages, lime-workings and quarry, leaving only the top of the church tower peeping up above the foliage. Typically, Repton cautioned against planting a continuous strip of plantation all along the side of the public road, recommending a subtler approach, with two separate blocks of trees – 'K' and 'L' – instead obscuring views of the busy highway.

> Together, these plantations will effectually screen all the houses and yet preserve that play of light shewn betwixt them . . . the road from points K to M must be effectually hid by a sunk fence on one side, and a rail or hurdle on the other . . . the southern end of plantation at K should be extended far enough to mask not only the mill but the part of the meadow intersected by ditches and occasionally subject to flooding.

In the second section of the Red Book, discussing the *Site of the House*, Repton emphasises that the best view in the area is to the east, towards Thorpe – between N and O on his plan (Figure 85). The only improvement he suggests for this prospect is the placing of a small clump of trees at the point marked 'P', something which would help frame the view across the Yare Valley as well as hide an unsightly barn ('O'). He then explains why the site chosen for the new house is the best available.

> It brings us rather nearer that part of ground where the lawn may be extended to the river . . . it shews more of the valley to the south and the turn of the ground towards R beyond it . . . it will widen the line of approach and remove the house a little farther into the country . . . there is only one objection: viz that it is a greater distance from the kitchen-garden: the difference is however only a few yards.

This last comment is rather odd, implying as it does that the site of the kitchen garden had already been chosen – or that it had already been created, in anticipation of the building of the house. Either way, Repton suggested placing a curving plantation ('V–V') to screen its walls from the approach drive and the house (Figure 82). Later in the Red Book he describes the convex shape of this plantation and the path within it, emphasising how it will 'hide the wall without excluding the sun'. The Red Book plan shows two walls running at an oblique angle to each other and facing south and south-east.

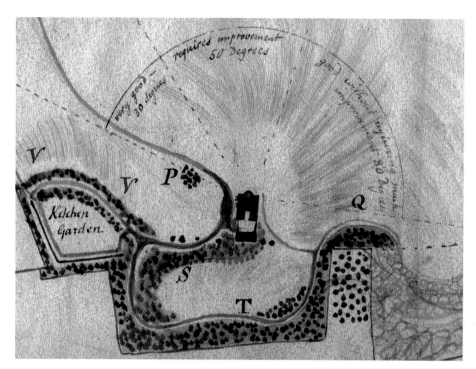

Figure 82. *Detail from the Bracondale Red Book Plan, showing the area immediately around the house and the kitchen garden.*

The third section of text, *Oblique Views*, discusses the advantages which would arise from the purchase of Hill Field, and especially the improvements which this would bring to the views from the house towards Lakenham. Without it, according to Repton, 'the shape of the ground will appear from the window hanging to the south without any check or counterbalance'. A footnote refers the reader to the discussion in an earlier Red Book, relating to Holwood near Bromley in Kent, the home of William Pitt the Younger, where Repton worked between 1790 and 1798. Repton then describes how

> It will not be difficult for the inventive genius of my friend Mr Wilkins, to depart from all quadrilangular ideas, bow windows and other hackneyed forms, and adapt a building to this situation, which should form only towards the most favourable

Figure 83. *Repton's 'before' view (flap down) from Bracondale Lodge to the east, showing the village of Trowse and the hill behind Whitlingham Lane.*

Figure 84. *Repton's 'after' view (flap up) from Bracondale Lodge to the east, showing plantations of trees masking the village of Trowse (the 'habitation of other men').*

Figure 85. *Repton's watercolour of the view looking down the Yare Valley, towards Thorpe, from his Red Book for Bracondale Lodge.*

Figure 86. Watercolour of Bracondale Lodge, circa 1820 and to attributed to David Hodgeson

points, excluding all that is defective, and yet be a beautiful example of correct architecture.

It would be interesting to know what Repton thought of Martineau's new house, built after 1813, with its striking quadrilangular form and prominent bay windows (Figure 86). He also made suggestions for placing of the stables, and for concealing them with planting, which appear to have been carried out.

The fourth part of the text, *Walks and Plantations*, discusses the hill rising above and behind (to the north-west of) the site proposed for the house. This had already been planted with new trees but more needed to be added in order to 'cover the hill and embosom the house'. Repton did not intend that this land should be entirely wooded, suggesting rather that by judiciously creating a 'tongue of plantation at "S"' the rear of the house and the kitchen garden could be hidden by trees. Through these, a sheltered path could lead up to the summit of the hill, and where this ran beside an area of open

pasture, at point 'T', there would be a view across the valley, one unspoilt by any glimpse of the house and stable block below – the reward, according to Repton, of undertaking the steep climb! The rest of the section describes the various paths to be laid out around the grounds, although Repton notes that he has not marked the line of any track to the river, as that was a matter for future consideration. This may imply that Martineau had imparted to Repton his intention to buy further parcels of land to the south-east, allowing his property to flow uninterrupted down to the banks of the Yare. From the viewpoint at 'T', Repton informs his client, the paths will continue under hedges and through narrow plantations until they reach

> a large pit which may be dressed by planting its banks, and round the edge of this pit the walk may be continued towards the orchard where some new points of view may be introduced. The approach will from thence be an easy return walk to the house.

– a suggestion which echoes his proposals for the old chalk pit on the western shores of the lake at Holkham, made a few years earlier (above, page 55).

The pit still survives in the woods behind County Hall and although no sign of ornamental planting now exists it contains the remains of two folly-like features – a standing arch, and the foundations of a stone and flint building (Figures 87, 88 and 89). These are not referred to in the Red Book but, as we have already observed, Repton often provided additional advice on how places might be improved, sometimes proffered over several years, and it is quite possible that he was involved in their design and siting. They are referred to by several nineteenth-century commentators, starting with John Chambers in 1829.

> The antiquarian taste of Mr Martineau has induced him to collect many remnants of Gothic architecture from the monks' dormitory, next the cathedral, pulled down in 1804, which were presented to this gentleman by the late dean of Norwich, and were highly appreciated by Mr Martineau, long before it became the fashion to preserve the ancient architecture of our

Figure 87. *The standing arch in the woods behind County Hall.*

Figure 88. Top: left-hand foundations and base of the moulded door opening on the Priory's front elevation. Bottom: foundations of the south-west corner buttress.

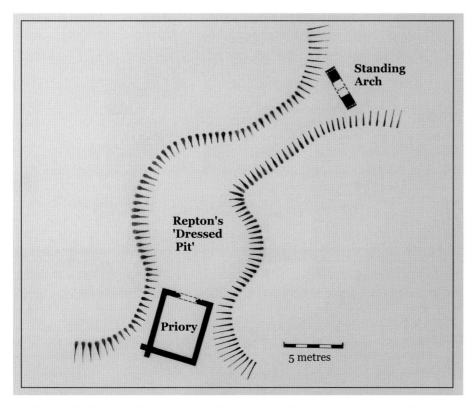

Figure 89. Survey of the remains of the garden buildings in the woods behind the Norfolk Archive Centre.

forefathers, and he has had the taste and ability to make them highly ornamental to his grounds. Part of these materials are worked into a pointed arch, with an open cinque-foil window, forming an entrance through a sequestered walk, to an excellent imitation of an ancient oratory or priory, at the entrance of which is a wooden door (probably Saxon).[164]

Over the doorway was an inscription in Latin, celebrating the sealing of the foundation deed for Norwich Cathedral in 1101, as well as the erection of this 'priory', and neighbouring arch, by Martineau in 1805. Chambers writes about the windows of the 'priory' being composed of ancient and modern

stained glass, and at the entrance a large gravestone bore the arms of the monastery of St Benet-in-the-Holme at Ludham, above an engraving of the robed figure of an abbot with the words 'Father Ricardus of South Walsham, Abbot of St Benet's, who died 1439'. This stone Martineau acquired from another source, as Blomefield's *Essay towards a Topological History of the County of Norfolk* describes the same memorial residing at Duke's Palace Yard in Norwich.[165] Chambers also notes how the approach to the 'priory' was decorated with various antiquarian features, and inside the building there was a visitor's book containing beautiful and original poems. One poem, written in middle English by F. Sayers M. D. in 1805, was painted onto a stained-glass panel. [166]

A number of other writers commented on what was clearly a notable feature of the local landscape. An early railway guide for the Cambridge to Norwich line, for example, describes how, on the outskirts of Norwich, passengers could glimpse a gothic priory, with windows of ancient stained glass.[167] But only one illustration of Martineau's 'priory', by J. B. Ladbrooke, appears to survive (Figure 90). This shows a building with a large gothic window, walls of reused stone, and a small tower, complete with two buttresses. A few later sources have queried whether some of the stone used in its construction came from Carrow Priory due to the unusual twelfth-century nicked bases of the standing arch. It is possible that Martineau used material from a number of sources.[168]

Passing through the gothic arch and travelling along the sunken pathway beyond, visitors would have discovered the dell, planted with shrubs and ornamented with fragments of medieval stonework, and within it the modest 'priory' with its stained glass and poetic inscriptions – all calculated, in Picturesque fashion, to inspire the creative muses. Such romantic gothic medievalism might seem at odds with Martineau's Nonconformist, and scientific, background, but were very much at the cutting edge of fashion.

The 1882 Ordnance Survey 25-inch map (Figure 91) describes the priory building as a *Memorial Chapel* and shows another building a little to the south-west of it, marked as 'Knucklebone Hall' – with the words 'summer house' in brackets beneath. No illustrations, or contemporary descriptions,

Figure 90. The Priory, an etching by J.B. Ladbrooke, 1820

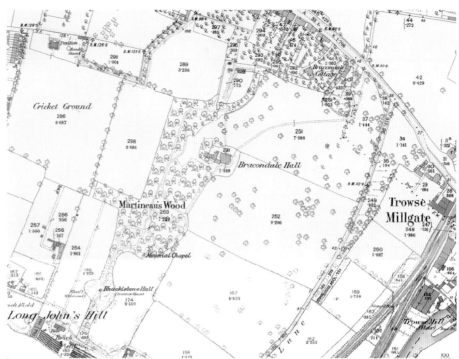

Figure 91. 1882 Ordnance Survey 25-inch map, showing Martineau's Wood, south-west of Bracondale Lodge (Bracondale Hall), with its Memorial Chapel and Knucklebone Hall marked.

of this structure have been traced, but Roger Lloyd (a current member of the Norfolk Gardens Trust) remembers seeing it, in a derelict condition, in 1962, its floor made of cow knuckle bones, placed vertically and tightly packed, forming a star-pattern. The date of the building – which stood at the southern end of Martineau's park, commanding fine views from the lower part of Long John Hill – is unknown, but it almost certainly post-dates Repton's involvement at Bracondale.

As well as showing the presence of these buildings, the 1882 Ordnance Survey shows the belt of trees proposed by Repton along the north-western margins of the park, now called Martineau's Woods, and other features of

the landscape, much as Repton proposed. It also shows a variety of later additions, including the early nineteenth-century lodge (now known as 'Bracondale Cottage' and much extended), built of gault brick under a slate roof. The west wall of the garden has a stone bearing the initials of PMM, for Philip Meadows Martineau, and a date of 1829, the year of his death.[169] As already noted, Martineau's house has now disappeared, and most of his diminutive park has been built over. Humphry Repton designed it, not as a true country house, but as a 'villa' – a rural retreat where his client could entertain his friends and colleagues. It is possible that the Norwich and Norfolk Public Library was conceived here, born out of meetings of the Unitarian discussion club which Martineau often hosted.[170] It is particularly appropriate that the much-acclaimed Norfolk Archive Centre has its home here today.

92

Blickling

Blickling is rather different from the three places just discussed. They were all specific, defined commissions, for which Red Books have survived. Repton's involvement at Blickling appears extended and intermittent, and its character is unclear but probably small in scale. Given both the importance of Blickling Hall, and its proximity to Aylsham, it is not surprising to find Repton engaged here at various times, in various roles. In the 1780s, probably before he embarked on his professional career as a landscape gardener, he prepared two illustrations of the 'Lady's Cottage', a small ornamental building which had been erected around 1781 in the Great Wood on the western side of the park for Lady Caroline, wife of the Second Duke of Buckinghamshire (Figures 92 and 93).[171] The Frenchman François de la Rochefoucauld, who visited in 1784, described how

> Leaving this edge of the park, you plunge into a wood of magnificent forest trees, in which someone has put together a cabin on the edge of quite a steep gully, with great trees growing upright and semi-prostrate and making the place picturesque. The cabin is built like a simple cottage, with straw seats, two prominent deal shelves all around the walls, furnished with all the pottery necessary for milk and tea and making a simple meal, but as plain and as unadorned as you could find in the homes of the people.[172]

There are shades here of Marie Antoinette playing the milkmaid at Hameau de la Reine. De la Rochefoucauld continues:

> In front of the cabin, in an open space, some ruins have been put together, statues and urns set up and spread very effectively over a slight natural elevation. At one side is an apparently modern urn containing the ashes of one of Lady Buckingham[shire]'s children, as you read on an inscription on the pedestal. One of the sides of the pedestal is inscribed with some perfectly chosen lines of Milton.[173]

Figure 92. Repton's watercolour of Lady's Cottage at Blickling.

Figure 93. Repton's monochrome painting of Lady's Cottage at Blickling.

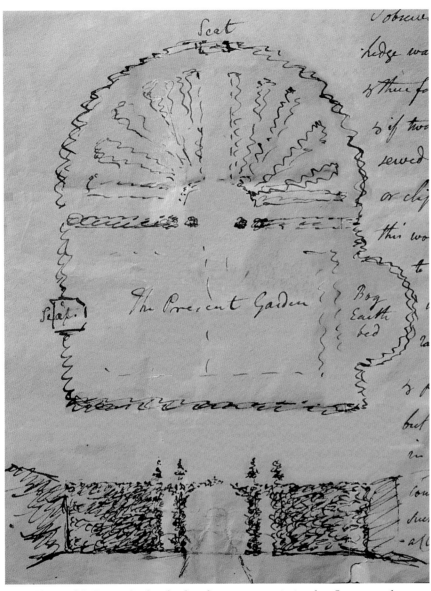

Figure 94. Repton's sketch plan for a new semi-circular flower garden next to Lady Suffield's existing flower garden and below, for the new entrance to it. From an undated letter he wrote to his sister Dorothy.

Repton's sketches show the cottage as a gothic summer house, apparently built of wood, enclosed by a wooden fence and with statuary and other features placed around it – including the great seventeenth-century fountain brought to Blickling from the Paston's mansion of Oxnead Hall, to the south-east of Aylsham, in 1732 (and which has since been relocated to the centre of the Parterre Garden below the east front of Blickling Hall).[174] The fact that the disposition of the statuary and masonry fragments is different in the two pictures suggests that Repton provided advice on how the setting of the 'cottage' might be improved. The building has disappeared, finally destroyed by a tree fall in 1973: only its foundations, and some box planting from the associated gardens, remain.

Repton made further suggestions for the grounds following the death of the Second Duke in 1793, when his daughter, Caroline, Lady Suffield inherited the estate. Something called 'Lady Buckinghamshire's Flower Garden' had existed since the 1760s in the area now occupied by the 'Secret Garden', in the ornamental woodlands to the east of the hall. In 1764 it was said to be planted with 'the greatest profusion of Mignonette Roses, myrtles and honeysuckles'.[175] Sometime after 1800, perhaps around 1811, Repton suggested improvements for this part of the grounds in a letter sent to his sister, Dorothy Adey (to whom he affectionately writes, 'Dear Dee'). These changes, he argued, she ought to 'explain to Lady Suffield as your own idea', on the grounds that he did not think she would take much notice of advice offered by a professional man that was not charged for.[176] The letter contains a sketch-plan which shows both the existing garden and Repton's proposed extension to it (Figure 94). From this, and from with comments in the letter itself, we learn that the garden was rectangular, bounded in part by a holly hedge (rather than the present beech hedge), and had a seat at one end and an apsidal projection containing a 'bog earth bed' at the other. Repton's plan was to add a large semi-circular flower garden to the eastern side which would be reached through a gap cut in the hedge. The hollies on either side of this were to be trained and clipped into an arch – 'this would become the Proscenium of a fine Amphitheatre'. He added that 'nothing could be more appropriate than such an amphitheatre surrounded by a clipped hedge over which the fine wood will appear like a scene in one of Wateau's paintings'.[177]

Figure 95. *Repton's sketch of the proposed trellised arch. From the same letter to Dorothy.*

Figure 96. *The covered seat in Blickling NT Secret Garden.*

Figure 97. *Victorian photograph of the covered seat.*

The flower beds within this new addition were to be arranged in a radiating fan pattern to either side of a central path leading to an alcove or seat, and the whole was to be surrounded by a new hedge. He includes another sketch (Figure 95), showing the proposed trellised arch in elevation, and explains that it should not be of such 'solid carpentry as French trellis . . . but using laths . . . and only playful twigs and tendrils should be permitted to stray on to the trellis'. He concludes the letter with the interesting comment that his sketch will 'serve as a hint for your new paper grapery and also for the trellis seat at Blickling which looks very bald without creepers – and which I understand Miller [the gardener?] had left unplanted lest the creepers should pull the trellis in pieces'. 'Paper grapery' is a rare reference to an inexpensive alternative to glass in the garden, employed before the abolition of glass excise tax. Thick paper (or calico) was stretched over a light wooden frame and brushed with boiled linseed oil to form cloches or larger structures which were used to protect vulnerable plants from frost and other vagaries of the weather.[178]

There is no evidence that any of these ideas were implemented, although the covered seat in Blickling's Secret Garden today (Figure 96) has trellised side-panels and a Victorian photograph (Figure 97) shows the original trellised parapet, with scalloped detailing on the top – both very reminiscent of Repton's sketches to his sister. Whilst the layout of features in the area of the Secret Garden shown on the First Edition 6-inch Ordnance survey map from the 1880s shows some similarities to the plan sketched by Repton, the 1840 tithe map shows a rather irregular arrangement which does not resemble it.[179] The garden was redesigned in the 1930s, along with other parts of the grounds, by Norah Lindsay.

There is little other evidence, other than architectural drawings of a Hot House and a Peach House (drawn in 1816 by his son John Adey but signed by them both[180]) that Repton himself suggested any other improvements at Blickling. The association with John Adey Repton, the architect, and Blickling was more extensive. It was he who later provided a design for

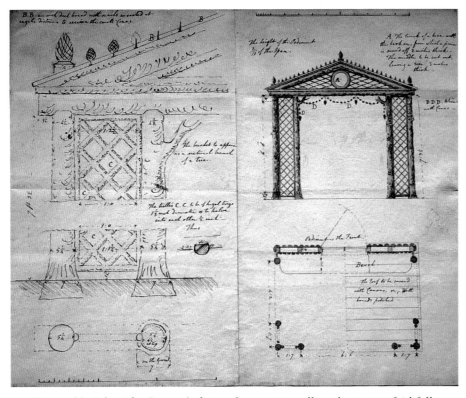

Figure 98. John Adey Repton's design for a rustic trellis arbour, now faithfully reproduced in Blickling NT's Dell Garden.

a trellis-backed tree-seat and for a rustic trellis arbour (Figure 98) for the gardens, and recent reconstructions of both can be seen in the Orangery and Dell Gardens today.[181] They were two of the many drawings he prepared for the owner Assheton Harbord and his wife, Lady Caroline, in the 1820s and 30s, in the years after his father's death. He was responsible for a number of changes and additions to the hall, including the central clock tower on the south front and the arcades which connect the main house to the east and west wings. He also prepared designs for rebuilding and altering a number of farms and cottages on the estate, as well as the Keeper's lodge.[182]

Figure 99. Repton's seal on his letter to his sister Dorothy.

Conclusion

Repton's work in Norfolk in the 1790s was typical of that carried out elsewhere in the country at this time. While he was happy to include in his designs features or structures not entirely dissimilar to those favoured by his Picturesque critics, he did so in a sensible and moderate way: he designed landscapes for practicality, for comfort, to be enjoyed in a low-key, domestic manner by his clients. His designs were characterised by a particular interest in 'appropriation' and in the use of subtle devices to enhance the apparent importance of a place and thus the status of its owner. But only within limits: for Repton was also much concerned to match the 'character' of a house, its size and function – whether it was a palace or a manor house, villa or a shooting lodge – to the extent of its grounds. In more general terms he was interested in the connections between a house and its grounds: by the end of the decade, however, his involvement in architecture was beginning to move to a new level.

Chapter 4

Working with John

The key change in Repton's activities after c.1800 was his growing involvement in architecture and, closely connected to this, his increasing close professional cooperation with his son, the architect John Adey Repton. As we have seen, from the start of his career Repton had worked with architects like William Wilkins Senior and Samuel Wyatt, and his Red Books often emphasised the close connections between the design of landscapes, and that of the houses which they complemented. From 1789 his trade card stated that, in addition to providing advice on landscape, he also provided 'designs for hot houses, stoves, ice-houses, and all other buildings which belong to Landscape-Gardening'. In his first major work, *Sketches and Hints on Landscape Gardening* published in 1794, Repton noted that the successful landscape gardener 'must possess a competent knowledge of surveying, mechanics, hydraulics, agriculture, botany and *the general principles of architecture*'.[183] Already in the early 1790s his Red Book for Honing included proposals for minor changes to the external appearance of the mansion, in effect, regarding it almost as a garden building. His Red Book for Bracondale shows an interest in how the internal layout of the house could be best arranged to obtain the best views across the surrounding landscape; Repton's interest in architecture was, therefore, a long-standing one. But after 1800 his published writings and Red Books show a much greater involvement, and he began to provide advice on such things as the internal planning of houses. His second great work, *Observations on the Theory and Practice of Landscape Gardening* of 1803, was actually subtitled 'with some remarks on Grecian and Gothic architecture'. In it he commented that he had

often witnessed the absurdity of designs for a house where the builder had never seen the situation; I have therefore, long been compelled to make architecture a branch of my own profession.[184]

In a footnote to this statement he added the crucial observation that 'Before I had the advantage of my eldest son's assistance in this department, I met with continual difficulties'.

Repton had obviously planned, from an early date, for John (who had been deaf from birth) to follow a career as an architect. In 1789, when he was just fourteen years old, he went to work in the office of Repton's old friend William Wilkins, subsequently producing with him detailed drawings of Norwich Cathedral. In 1796 he was formerly apprenticed to the architect John Nash, born the same year as Humphry and whose career was, at this time, just beginning to flourish again after something of a hiatus. Humphry Repton and John Nash had formed a formal partnership the previous year, with Nash providing plans for new houses and Repton the designs for their settings. The two men collaborated at Burley-on-the-Hill in Rutland (1795), Corsham Court in Wiltshire (1796–1800), Southgate Grove in London (1797), Attingham Park in Shropshire (1798) and Luscombe in Devon (1799), among other places. Unfortunately, in 1800 they fell out bitterly, in part because Repton accused Nash of stealing his son John's ideas without giving him full credit.[185] John then joined his father at Hare Street. Interestingly, despite the disagreement Repton's younger son, George Stanley, went on to train with Nash and continued to work with him until 1820, although he too often worked with his father in the later stages of Repton's career. In his *Memoir*, Repton noted that two objects he had hoped to achieve in his career were that he

might be consulted by my Sovereign and the other that I might succeed as an architect as well as a landscape gardener. The attention of two of my sons had been directed to architecture and with their assistance I felt myself competent to undertake plans of any magnitude.[186]

John Adey Repton continued to live in Aylsham, and it was in Norfolk that the two men worked most closely together.

Witton

Figure 100. Witton Hall, the seat of Hon. Col. Wodehouse.

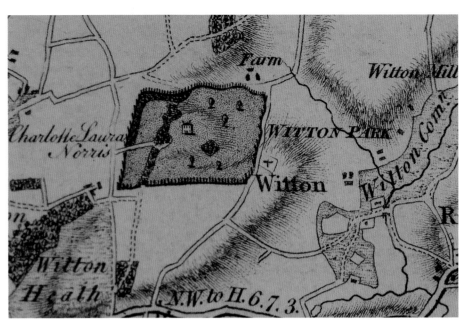

Figure 101. Witton Park, detail from Faden's Map of Norfolk, 1797.

Repton prepared a Red Book for Witton Hall in north-east Norfolk in 1801. The hall no longer exists, and the grounds are in a somewhat degraded state, but the Red Book survives in the library of the University of Florida and is of particular interest as it casts important light on the development of Repton's ideas in this crucial period of his career.[187] In addition, Repton offered further advice to the owner in a letter, dated 8 March 1802, and the house was illustrated in Peacock's *Polite Repository* for the following year (Figure 100).[188] Witton Hall was built around 1770 by John Norris (founder of the Norrissian Professorship at Cambridge University) on an elevated site which was probably previously unoccupied. It commanded fine prospects towards the sea, which lies about three kilometres to the east.[189] Faden's county map of 1797 shows that the hall was set within a large park which mainly extended to the east of the house, with the ground falling away in the direction of the coast: most of the area to the west of the hall comprised woodland, crossed by an entrance drive (Figure 101). When Norris died in 1777, the house was probably still uncompleted, and

the property passed to the Wodehouses of Kimberley through the marriage of Charlotte Norris to John Wodehouse, later Second Baronet, in 1796. She lived in the house alone before the marriage, being named as the occupier on Faden's map.

Repton begins the Red Book – which contains only three illustrations – by praising aspects of the existing setting of the house, most notably the manner in which 'the nakedness of this Spot has been cloathed by Plantations'. Some observers, he believed, might consider that these extended too close to the house but, in his opinion, they could have been brought even nearer, so as to prevent the sea being visible along the approach from the west – a circumstance which he evidently found distasteful, perhaps on the grounds suggested at Northrepps (above, page 68). Unfortunately, no detailed map survives which shows the landscape before Repton's visit, and his own plan of the grounds – apparently drawn from memory – does not indicate the earlier disposition of features very clearly (Figure 102). The wording of

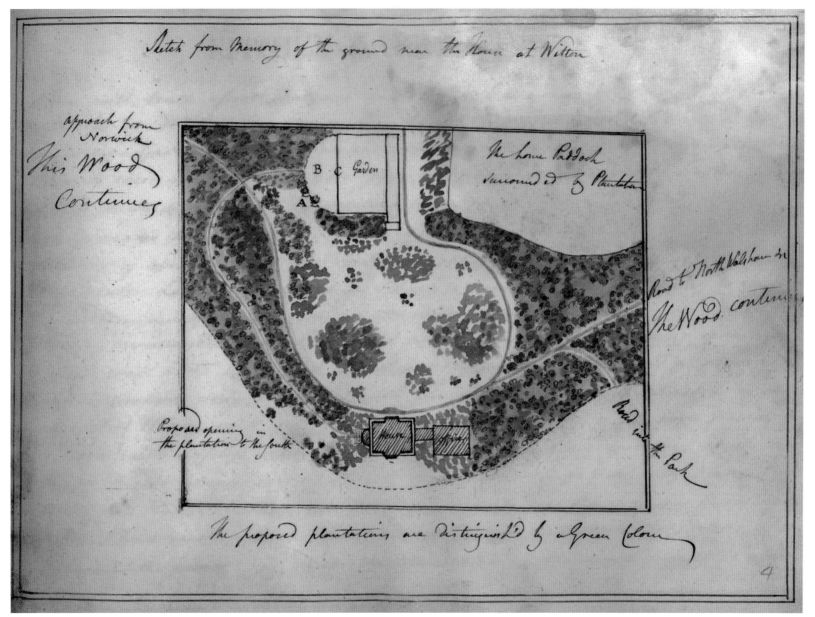

Sketch from Memory of the ground near the House at Witton.

approach from
Norwick

This Wood
Continues

B C Garden

A

The Home Paddock
surrounded by Plantation

Road to North Walsham &c

The Wood continues

Proposed opening in
the plantation to the south

House   offices

Road into the Park

The proposed plantations are distinguished by a Green Colour

4

Figure 102. *Repton's plan for the Witton Red Book.*

99

the Red Book does, however, makes it clear that there were originally two drives leading to the hall. One, which is shown on Faden's map, approached it fairly directly from the west, and passing close to the north wall of the kitchen garden. Another, which is not clearly shown by Faden, seems to have led to the house from the south-west. Repton suggested making new drives, which would approach the house obliquely, from the north-west (the direction of North Walsham) and the south-west (from Norwich and Worstead), the two joining below the west front. This arrangement, he thought, would have two advantages. Firstly, it would ensure that the sea would not be visible from the approach, but only after the hall had been entered. Secondly, it would mean that the main western elevation of the house would not be visible, front on, as the visitor approached it. Repton thought that this was important for two reasons: because at present the view from this direction 'looks as if some Wings had been intended and omitted'; and because Wodehouse intended to add a new range of offices on the northern side of the hall (which Repton included in his plan), and this would give the building a decidedly asymmetrical appearance when viewed in full elevation.

Repton describes how the area immediately to the west of the house comprised a wide circular lawn, flanked by plantations. This he wanted to break up by planting a number of small, irregularly shaped clumps (coloured green on Figure 102) on the grounds that

> However paradoxical it may appear, the present confined appearance of this lawn can only be done away by planting it boldly, since an Area however Large it may be, will always appear confined if it is surrounded by a visible boundary whether of Trees or Fences.

He also suggested that the proposed change in the line of the south approach (that coming 'from Worstead') would provide 'the opportunity of taking a part of the present beautiful drive into the pleasure ground, at the spot marked A'. This is a slightly obscure comment, given the absence of a map showing the appearance of the grounds before Repton's proposed changes. The other changes suggested to the grounds mainly relate to the kitchen garden. Here Repton, in a comment which displayed another change in attitude which occurred at this point in his career, criticised the approach of his predecessor, Capability Brown, noting that

> I may with truth assert that one half of my business in places which have been improved by Mr Brown, has arisen from the injudicious choice of a site for the kitchen garden.

He was referring to the fact that Brown (but more usually, in fact, his immediate predecessors and contemporaries) had sometimes placed kitchen gardens at an inconvenient distance from the house. Repton, in contrast – at least by the middle years of his career – was keen to have them more conveniently positioned and easily accessible, partly because of their recreational use. As he elsewhere described:

> There are many days in winter when a warm, dry but secluded walk, under the shelter of a north or east wall, would be preferred to the most beautiful but exposed landscape; and in the early spring . . . some early flowers and vegetables may cheer the sight.[190]

Although the kitchen garden at Witton did lie some way from the house, and unconnected with it, Repton did not propose that it should be re-located. Instead, its degree of separation from the house was to be reduced by extending the 'oval' of ground lying between them. This was to be achieved by cutting a 'deep bay' out of the plantations to the south of the walled enclosure, which would provide space for a new cross wall, with (presumably ornamental) hot houses set against it, and with a flower garden in front of it. Approached along the path leading from the hall, this area would provide a transitional space between the mansion and the walled garden. Repton made few other proposals for the grounds. He suggested that the areas immediately north and south of the hall should be planted with trees and shrubs, forming extensions to the existing blocks of woodland and preventing views of the sea from the lawn, and the approach drives, to the west. Otherwise, he made only the vague proposal that 'hardy shrubs and flowers' should be planted 'all round the house, to 'dress the base of the building'.

Figure 103. Repton's proposals for the front elevation of Witton Hall.

What is particularly interesting is that the rest of the Red Book – not far short of half the text – is entirely concerned with improvements to the house itself, which Repton illustrated in elevation (Figure 103). Here he notes, significantly, that he had 'availed myself of my Son's knowledge of Architecture' to deliver his opinions. The proposals are illustrated by a plan which Repton described as a 'rough sketch from memory' (Figure 104). He notes how the principal floor of Witton Hall contained not only a library, a drawing room and a dining room, but also bedrooms and dressing rooms, all set around a central oval stairwell. Repton suggested that this arrangement should be changed, partly because it served to separate 'rooms that should be together' (thus the dining room and drawing room

had a bedroom between them) and partly because the central stairway 'makes the house cold and noisy'. Repton recommended changing the rooms around, adding a new staircase and converting the central stairwell into a room, perhaps a library.

The following spring John Wodehouse wrote to Repton at Hare Street, requesting advice on how the proposed new drives were to relate to the range of offices which he intended building to the north of the hall. Repton replied by return of post, with a sketch showing how the entrance to the proposed new range might be arranged, and requesting more information about its character so that he would be able to provide a proper plan,

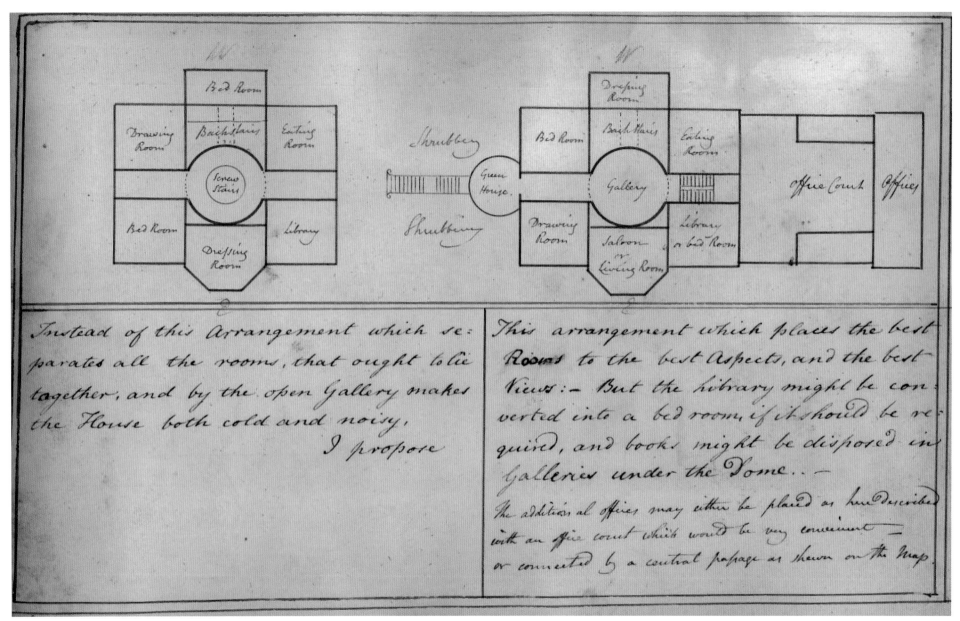

Labels in left floor plan: Bed Room · Drawing Room · Back Stairs · Eating Room · Screw Stairs · Bed Room · Library · Dressing Room

Labels in right floor plan: Dressing Room · Bed Room · Back Stairs · Eating Room · Shrubbery · Green House · Shrubbery · Gallery · Drawing Room · Saloon or Living Room · Library or bed Room · Office Court · Offices

Instead of this Arrangement which se:parates all the rooms, that ought to lie together, and by the open Gallery makes the House both cold and noisy,

I propose

This arrangement which places the best Rooms to the best Aspects, and the best Views:— But the Library might be converted into a bed room, if it should be required, and books might be disposed in Galleries under the Dome..—

The additional offices may either be placed as here described with an office court which would be very convenient — or connected by a central passage as shewn on the Map.

Figure 104. Repton's floor plans for the changes he proposed for the layout of Witton Hall.

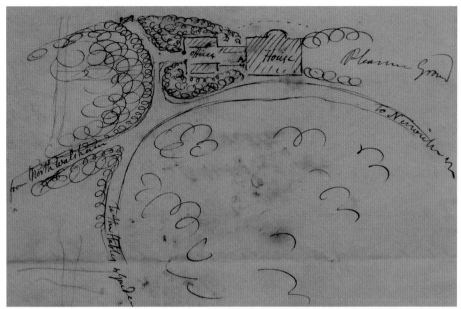

Figure 105. Repton's sketch map in a letter to John Wodehouse, 1802.

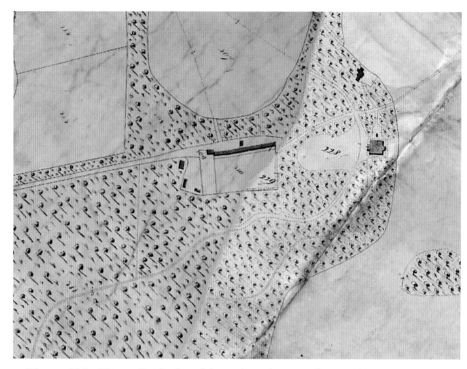

Figure 106. Witton Park, detail from the tithe award maps for Witton, 1842, and Edingthorpe, 1840.

based on his memories of the place, 'whether I visit Norfolk this year or not' (Figure 105).[191] The Red Book does not discuss the new north range, although some of Repton's recommendations are made in anticipation of its construction. Later maps make it clear that such a range was not in fact erected until the second half of the nineteenth century. No structure is shown here on the tithe award maps of 1842, but one is shown on the First Edition Ordnance Survey 6-inch map of 1884. (Figures 106 and 107), It is of some interest that Repton notes in the letter that 'in the architectural department of my profession I act under the firm of Mr John Adey Repton – and that we shall at all times be happy to be known in that capacity, particularly in Norfolk'.

How many of Repton's proposals for Witton were implemented by Wodehouse remains uncertain. This is in part because of a lack of any surviving large-scale map earlier than the tithe award map of 1842;[192] but also a consequence of the fact that the hall, having been retained by the Wodehouses as a secondary residence until the 1920s, was then sold to local

farmer Herbert C. Owles, who let it for a few years before demolishing it in 1927.[193] All that remains are the cellars, now 'landscaped' as a garden area for a small house erected within the former 'lawn' immediately to the west. The park has been ploughed and the woodland to the west of the hall has partly expanded over adjacent areas of the grounds. On balance, however, it appears that some at least of Repton's advice was implemented. In particular, the oblique approaches to the hall depicted in Repton's sketch plan are shown almost identically on the tithe award map of 1842 and, less certainly, on the Ordnance Survey drawings of 1816 (Figure 108).[194] The former source also shows that the immediate vicinity of the hall had been planted much as Repton suggested. There is, however, no obvious trace on these maps of the proposed clumps on the oval lawn, or of the suggested alterations to the kitchen garden. No plans or descriptions

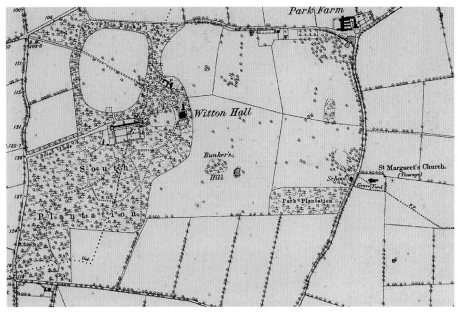

Figure 107. First Edition Ordnance Survey map, 1884.

Figure 108. Detail from the Ordnance Survey drawing, Cromer Sheet, 1816.

Figure 109. Looking east to the sea, from the site of Witton Hall, where Repton suggested the need to plant groups of trees to mask this view from the approach drives from the west and the lawn on the western side of the house.

of the house other than those provided by Repton appear to exist, and it is thus uncertain whether any of his proposed changes to the interior were implemented, although on balance it seems probable that they were not.

Much of the timber in the adjacent woodland was felled when the estate was sold in the 1920s, and although some beech and mature sycamore remain the woods are now mainly composed of relatively young specimens of the latter species. The walls of the kitchen garden, now partly ruinous, still remain: they are in part of eighteenth- and in part of nineteenth-century date. Some fragments of the pleasure ground planting in the immediate vicinity of the house – beech, horse chestnut, and yew – survive amongst the sycamores, but the striking collection of rhododendrons in the woods was established after the hall was demolished. Nothing now survives on the ground which might, with any real confidence, be attributed to Repton.

Wood Hall, Hilgay

A few years after he worked at Witton, Repton prepared a Red Book for Wood Hall in Hilgay, a few miles to the south of Downham Market. Wood Hall was an ancient mansion, built by Henry Hawe sometime around 1579 on land granted to his father by Henry VIII following the Dissolution. The property passed through a number of families – the Willoughbys, the Saundersons and the Wrays – before being purchased around 1755 by Captain George William Manby (celebrated as the inventor of a mortar designed to fire a rescue line to stricken vessels).[195] He in turn sold the property to William Jones, Repton's client, in 1797. The estate, although ancient, was modest in size and the hall stood at the southern end of an 'island' of raised ground on the eastern edge of the Fens (the village of Hilgay occupied a position at the northern end of the island, its name meaning 'island of Hydla's people').[196] To the south, east and west the prospects from the hall were over flat drained peat fen. To the north, the ground rose in a low hill above the level of the hall (Figure 111).

In 1806 the hall was damaged by fire: large sections needed to be rebuilt and many of the windows replaced. Repton visited in September of that year, making plans of the site and discussing possible changes with Jones. In February 1807 he presented the Red Book. Expressing what were now widely shared views about the picturesque qualities of old 'gothic' manor houses, he affirmed his satisfaction that 'it was proposed rather to restore than to destroy the original character' of the place. Following his familiar format, Repton began by discussing the *Situation*, making a clear reference to Faden's map of the county, published a few years earlier (Figure 110):

> In the Great Map of Norfolk, the parish of Hilgay is described as a hill surrounded by Fenland in every direction, & to those, who have only known it in former times, it may perhaps, appear in- capable of being made the pleasant, the healthy, and even the beautiful Situation which my promises hold forth…

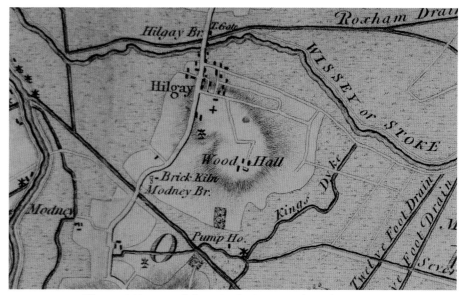

Figure 110. Detail from Faden's Map of Norfolk, 1797.

He acknowledged that, as a consequence of improved drainage over previous decades, the 'most desperate morasses' had been 'changed into sound land, yielding plenteous harvests'. But it was 'not sufficient that the bogs & fens should be turned into Corn fields & sound pasture, the <u>appearance</u> as well as the <u>reality</u> must be affected; and it is my peculiar province to produce <u>beauty</u> in addition to <u>profit</u>.'

But this, he acknowledged, was a challenge. The local fens might be better drained than before, but they were still level, bare and windswept.

> In a Country where the vastness of a flat horizon terminates the distant views it is necessary to hide the fore ground & divide the distances into smaller portions, since extent of prospect is seldom to be set in competition with the interest of home scenery, and especially where flat & level fens, take more the appearance of the Ocean than of Landscape. To counteract the general prevalence of Level or straight lines, it is requisite to shew every spot of ground that rises above the general plain, &

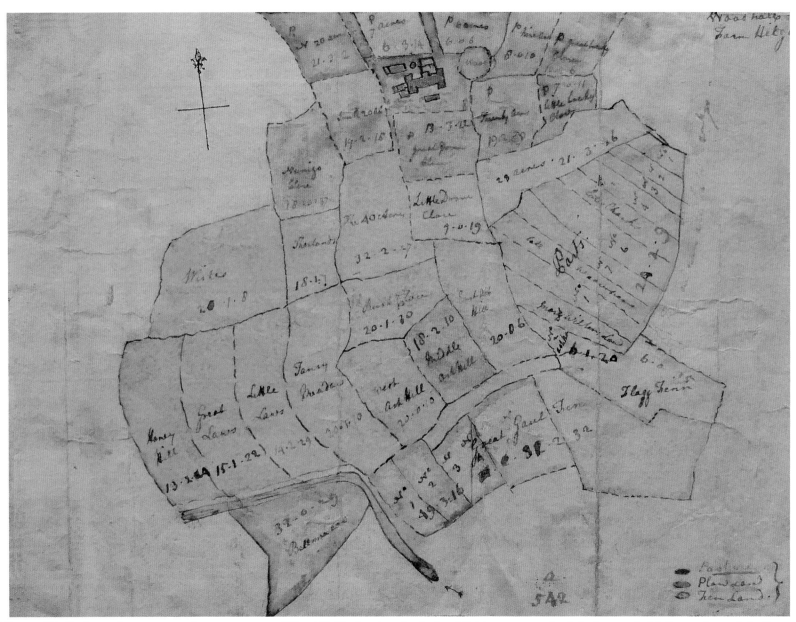

Figure 111. Eighteenth-century pocket estate map of Wood Hall, showing the fenland field system south of the house. (with Repton's north indicator)

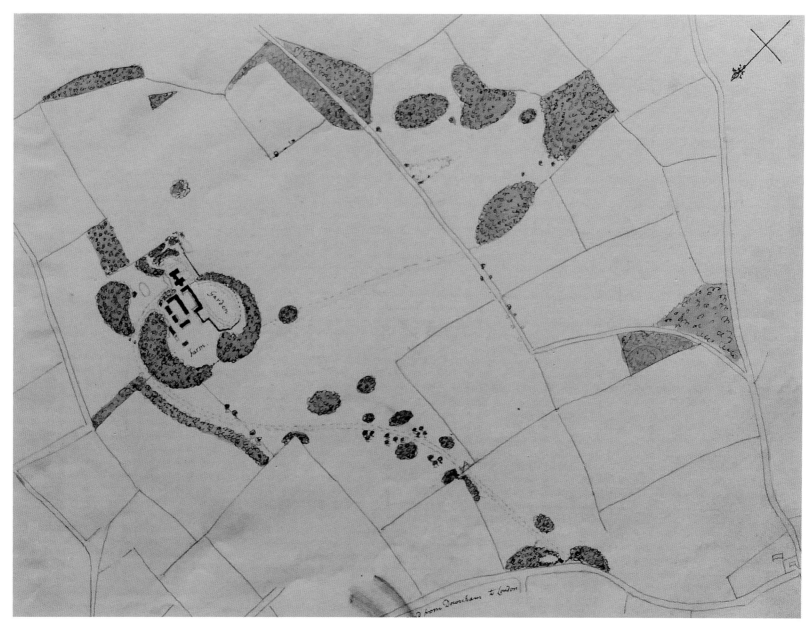

Figure 112. *Repton's plan from the Wood Hall Red Book.*

to disguise the flat land which may be mistaken for Fen, altho' it is actually reclaimed & perfectly sound, & this management will form the basis of all improvement at Woodhall.

Much of the Wood Hall Red Book is accordingly concerned with mitigating the dismal prospects across the level drained fenlands and providing more shelter for the rather exposed mansion (Figure 112).

On the north side of the hall the ground rose slightly, something which served to make the building appear to occupy an even lower spot than it really did, an effect intensified by the existence in this direction of two parallel fences which 'render more conspicuous, the horizontal lines of the distance'. Repton thus proposed planting a wood in this direction, in the middle distance, both to provide shelter and to give an impression of more varied topography (Figures 113 and 114). To the south of the hall the view extended across the flatness of the fens, but the immediate foreground was more varied topographically, providing possibilities for improvement – a fortunate circumstance given that the best rooms in the house were located on the south side. Repton suggested that the terrain could be made to

appear more undulating through careful planting of such slight rises in the ground as existed (Figure 115).

I much recommend thorns, or Maples or pollarded Trees in the low grounds where the hills are not more lofty than those at Woodhall, and where every expedient must be used to preserve as well as to increase their natural importance.

He emphasised the need to remove and replant, in the medium term, the faster growing trees on the damper, lower ground, to maintain the effectiveness of the proposed illusion.

On the eastern side of the house, where Repton proposed adding a new conservatory, there was a 'cabbage-garden bounded to the north by a screen of Orchard and Shrubbery, and open towards the East to the distant fen and flat country', as well as being exposed to the sharp east winds. Here he proposed planting a thick screen of shrubs, both to exclude the views in this direction and to 'form a shelter to the interior scenery of a flower garden [and] at the same time more freedom may be given, by opening

Figure 113. View from the house looking north, 'before' image – (flap down).

Figure 114. Same view from the house, 'after' image – (flap up).

Figure 115. *The view looking south from the house, with Repton's 'before' image (flap down) above and his proposed improved 'after' image (flap up) below.*

Figure 116. *Repton's view looking east, from the house, across the 'cabbage garden'. 'Before' image – flap down.*

Figure 117. *The same view, now showing a pleasure garden in Repton's 'after' image – with flap up.*

Figure 118. Repton's 'before' view, from the grounds, looking towards Methwold Church (flap down).

Figure 119. His improved 'after' image of the same view, on the edge of the proposed pleasure grounds (flap up).

a winding glade to some trees, now buried among the shrubs' (Figures 116 and 117). Nevertheless, the view would not be entirely enclosed, and Repton suggested planting trees in the foreground, as well as scattered plantations in the middle distance, so that

> A degree of intricacy is created, the prevailing horizontal lines are broken, & the sound ground is so blended with the fen land beyond, that the whole is in a manner melted in one general Mass, & as the plantations are nearest the eye & denote the improved soil, the fen is also supposed to be part of the same improved surface, and is thus conquered by Art in appearance, if not in reality.

He presented a 'before' and 'after' view, drawn from a position outside and beyond the shrubbery, to illustrate this suggestion (Figures 118 and 119).

To the west of the hall, however, the sheer extent of the level prospect across the drained fen defied improvement. This side of the house was therefore to be reserved for 'Offices, Gardens, Yards, and unsightly, but useful purposes', all surrounded by a curving screen of plantation. Lastly, and rather humorously, Repton proposed creating a new western entrance drive, running in from a picturesque lodge on the Ely Road (Figures 120 and 121), which would cross the pasture to the west of the house and then bend round to approach the north front, where the main entrance was located.

What is again striking about the Red Book proposals, however, is the extent to which they concern the architecture of the hall, rather than just the design of its grounds. The hall was still, following the fire, divided into two separate portions, but these were now to be reunited with the rebuilding of the two bays lying to the west of the entrance porch, in

Figure 120. *Travellers on the Ely Road, unaware of the estate by which they pass.*

Figure 121. *The picturesque lodge proposed by Repton, in his 'after' image (flap up)*

a simple but appropriate style (Figure 122). In addition, new windows were to be inserted in the main elevations, in a more robust gothic style (Figure 123). A gothic conservatory was to be constructed on the east side of the house, and two new bow windows were to be added to the southern elevation.

> These sketches are sufficient to show the external improvement of this once respectable mansion – but the internal arrangement, & the best manner of adapting the Comforts of Modern life to the old Character, without very expensive alteration; belongs to that branch of my Art, which I commit to the skill of my son as an Architect.

Many of Repton's proposals for Hilgay appear to have been implemented. Indeed, in the Red Book he notes on a number of occasions that the location of various features had already been staked out on the ground. The draft Ordnance Survey drawings of 1812 show the line of the new west drive much as he had proposed, and many of the woods and clumps, especially the outlying plantations to the south of the mansion and the curving screen to the kitchen garden and yards, appear similar to those shown in the Red Book plan (Figure 125).[197] Elsewhere, it is true, there are differences in detail, but it is possible (as was often the case) that Repton's proposals were modified following discussions with the owner. There is no evidence that the conservatory was built (although one was later added to the east side of the house). But the severed halves of the building were reunited, albeit with a rather plainer range than originally proposed, and one of the bow windows (that to the east side of the southern elevation) was built much as the Reptons had proposed (Figure 124 and 126). The kitchen garden to the south-west of the house, enclosed by walls of local gault brick within a curving belt of trees and shrubs (mirroring a similar

Figure 122. Above: The north front 'before' image showing the gap in the house, resulting from a fire in 1806 (flap down).
Below: The proposed new porch and infill section linking the two parts of the house, along with some alterations to the window openings (flap up).

Figure 123. *Above: Repton's 'before' image of the south-eastern corner of Wood Hall with the 'cabbage garden' to the east and a garden wall and cold frames to the west (flap down).*

Below: His 'after' view showing the design for a large gothic conservatory on the east gable. The parkland has been pushed back to the south, to allow a lawn with island flower beds, bordered by a new gravel path leading up to an arched, rose-covered screen (flap up).

Figure 124. *The Repton gothic window on the south front.*

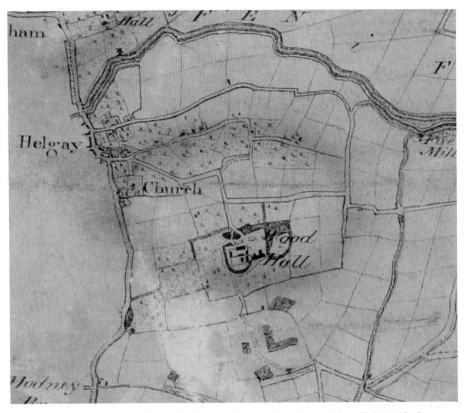

Figure 125. Detail from Ordnance Survey drawing, Feltwell St Nicholas sheet, 1812.

belt to the north, hiding the yards and offices from view), is not mentioned by Repton and was presumably already in existence. It has an unusual plan, superficially an oval, but in reality, comprising a dozen short stretches of straight wall.

In 1878 the Wood Hall estate was sold to Major Michael Stocks, subsequently passing to his son, who lived there until his death in 1957, and then to the latter's nephew, Eric Philip Stocks. He died in July 1974, when the present owner inherited the estate.[198] Over the last century Repton's landscape has undergone some modification. The west drive had already disappeared by the time the tithe award map was surveyed in 1839, although the point at

Figure 126. View of Wood Hall's parkland from Repton's gothic window.

which it met the public road is still marked today by 'Lodge Farm'.[199] The planting in the pleasure grounds in the area around the house includes a number of trees of possible Reptonian date, including beech, yew, holm oak, sweet chestnut and ash; but also much from later in the nineteenth century, including cedar, horse chestnut, Scots and Corsican pine, swamp cypress and Wellingtonia. Above all, the outlying plantations, especially those to the south of the hall, survive in good condition, and the hall itself is beautifully preserved. All in all, Repton would certainly recognise this landscape as close to that envisaged in his Red Book.

116

Barningham Hall

Although there is no Red Book for Barningham Hall, an important collection of plans and drawings by Humphry and John Adey Repton survive in private hands, while the changes made to the house and its setting were described by Repton in his final book, *Fragments on the Theory and Practice of Landscape Gardening*, published in 1816.[200] Like Wood Hall, Barningham was an ancient manor house. It was built in 1612 for Sir Edward Paston, and remained in that family's hands until 1756, when the estate was sold to William Russell, a whale bone merchant from London. He held the property for nineteen years before selling it to Thomas Lane, who in turn sold it in 1785 to Thomas Vertue Mott. He died in 1788 and the property passed to his son, John Thurston Mott, then aged only three.[201] As soon as John attained his majority in 1806 or 1807, and a year before his marriage, he asked the Reptons to submit proposals for improvement. Since then the property has remained in the same family.

A number of architectural drawings and plans by John Adey Repton survive (Appendix 2), together with a series of watercolours of the house in its grounds by Humphry.[202] Many of these illustrations seem to date from around 1807 but some may be later, suggesting involvement over an extended period of time. In particular, the collection includes a drawing for the north lodge, which does not appear to have been built until 1813. This may explain why Barningham figures prominently in Repton's *Fragments*, published as late as 1816, shortly before his death.

The watercolours, signed and dated by Repton, offer different options for improvements to the house and its immediate grounds. Perhaps not knowing exactly how much the young John Thurston Mott would be prepared to invest, Humphry Repton cannily presented him with two sets of illustrations, one showing 'the least alteration proposed' (presumably the cheapest), the other the 'utmost alterations proposed'. One such pair presented alternative treatments for the 'west and south fronts combined' (Figures 128 and 129). That depicting 'the least alterations proposed' shows the house as it stood in 1807, not much changed since its construction in 1612 and with the enclosed courts to north and south bounded by tall brick

Figure 127. Barningham Hall, near Holt, Norfolk

walls. There was a garden to the south and a stable yard to the north. A flap, when lifted, shows the garden wall to the south of the house removed and that surrounding the stable court lowered. A new drive is included, sweeping up to the west front of the house from north and south, the surrounding pasture grazed by deer. The windows of the stable block were to be changed, to make them resemble more closely those of the house itself. The 'alterations' to the south front, revealed when the flap was lifted, were more extensive. A new bay was to be added to the east of the building, carefully matching the style of the existing fabric, together with full-height bow windows; and a terrace was to be constructed immediately below the façade. This terrace is one of the earliest examples of what was to become a favourite Repton device (and one later designers, including William Andrews Nesfield, would embrace and further elaborate). The second watercolour, showing 'the utmost alterations proposed', does not

Figure 128. Repton's 'before' view of the south and west fronts for Barningham Hall.

Figure 129. *Repton's 'after' view, showing the removal of the wall, moderations to the stable court and a new extension to the house. The 'least alterations' option.*

Figure 130*. Repton's second watercolour of Barningham Hall (with no flap) which shows his 'utmost alterations' option, which includes the application of stucco to the whole building.*

have a lift-off flap, simply showing the result of the proposed changes to the south and west fronts (Figure 130). These are broadly similar to those in the first watercolour, except that the alterations to the south façade are more extensive – including the remodelling of all the windows on the ground and first floors in the form of crenelated bows – and the entire building is shown as rendered, in imitation of stone.

The 'least alterations' to the south front are shown rather differently on a third watercolour. This again has a flap which, when lifted, shows the old-fashioned garden wall removed, along with a greenhouse standing within the garden and an outbuilding beyond it, in order to open up views towards the lake, which lay to the east of the house (Figure 131). It shows both the proposed new terrace and the new bay added to the eastern side of the hall, although the latter lacks the bow windows proposed in the views just discussed. To the east of the terrace, extending down towards the lake, a pleasure ground with shrubs and flowers is shown, probably the area later described by James Grigor as 'Mrs Mott's flower-garden'.[203]

A fourth watercolour shows the north front of the hall, with the stable block (Figure 132). This again has no flap, the painting simply showing the proposed alterations, which included once again the extension of the hall to the east, with full-height bow windows on the new east front, and a single ground-floor bow on the north side, looking out across a fenced pleasure ground containing island beds planted with shrubs, and threaded with curving gravel paths.

Three of the four watercolours – those with lift-off flaps – are dated 1807 and signed by Humphry. Although they are similar to the illustrations included in his Red Books, they do not seem to have been intended for one. Very different from these are a collection of 'working plans' drawn up by John Adey Repton, also dated 1807 (Appendix 2), suggesting that there was a rapid move from initial proposal to detailed commission and execution. They are precise, architectural drawings – plans and elevations – which are signed by both the Reptons, and by Joseph Stannard and Joseph Stannard junior (local contractors and architects who had been brought in to oversee the work) and countersigned by John Thurston

Figure 131. *Above: Repton's 'before' watercolour of the south front (flap down) Below: His 'after' image, showing the proposed new bay, new porch and the removal of the low wall and early example of a greenhouse.*

Figure 132. *Repton's watercolour of the north front of Barningham Hall and the remodelled stable block and elegantly fenced north garden.*

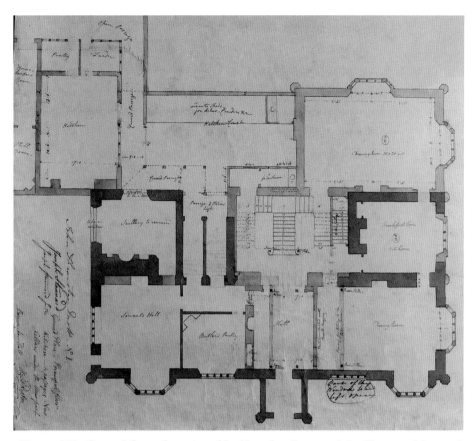

Figure 133. *Ground-floor plan, signed by Humphry Repton, John Thurston Mott and both Joseph Stannard senior and junior, 1807 (walls in yellow to be removed).*

Mott.[204] The drawings most closely resemble the 'utmost alterations' of Humphry Repton's watercolours and feature such things as the removal of pediments above existing first floor windows. They include specifications concerning materials and minor construction details: the ground floor bays were thus to be of brick and deal, with windows that should 'open on hinges', and have stone steps leading down to the terrace below. The floor plans show where existing partitions were to be removed and new walls built, to better align the entrance hall with the entrance porch and make the ground-floor rooms more symmetrical with the new addition

BARNINGHAM *NORFOLK*, J.T. MOTT, ESQ.ʳ

BARNINGHAM *NORFOLK*, J.T. MOTT, ESQ.ʳ

Figure 134. *The same view as Figures 128 and 130, as reproduced in Repton's book, Fragments on the Theory and Practice of Landscape Gardening, 1816.*

(Figure 133). It is noteworthy that the new ground-floor room is described as the 'Drawing Room', and that the anteroom between it and the 'Dining Room' in the old range is named 'Breakfast Room'. 'Drawing rooms' and 'breakfast rooms' were, at the time, closely associated with women, and this may reflect Mott's impending marriage and, perhaps, his future wife's involvement in developing the design.[205] All these plans appear to have been executed, and the house today – complete with terrace below the south front – is much as the Reptons planned, although the building was not, as one of the watercolours proposed, rendered to resemble stone. Indeed, of particular note is the way that the alterations, including much of the new eastern extension, were built with seventeenth-century bricks, recycled from the old east wall of the hall and the demolished garden walls. This ensured that the 'old' and 'new' work merge seamlessly.

As noted, the alterations at Barningham were also illustrated in Repton's *Fragments* of 1816. The improvements depicted in these engravings differ in a number of details from those shown in the watercolours. More attention is given to the south garden, with steps down from the terrace to the lawn and a low fence to exclude grazing livestock – but the hall itself is much as shown in the working plans and, indeed, much as it appears today (Figure 134). One minor difference is that the 'Drawing Room' of the architectural plans had become a 'Dining Room' on the published plan, perhaps because of the views it offered across the lawns and lake; while the original 'Dining Room' had become a 'Billiard Room' (Figure 135). Barningham was included in this, Repton's final book, ostensibly to illustrate his views on how to improve gothic windows while at the same time preserving their original Picturesque appeal, but he also took full opportunity to showcase the more general improvements to the hall made by himself and his son (Figures 136 and 137).

While the extent of the changes made by the Reptons to the hall and its immediate grounds is thus clear, their contribution to the wider landscape is less certain. Barningham was one of the places which Repton illustrated for Volume III of Armstrong's *History and Antiquities of the County of Norfolk* of 1781 (Figure 138) and his engraving shows the Jacobean house with its enclosed gardens to north and south and pasture to the west,

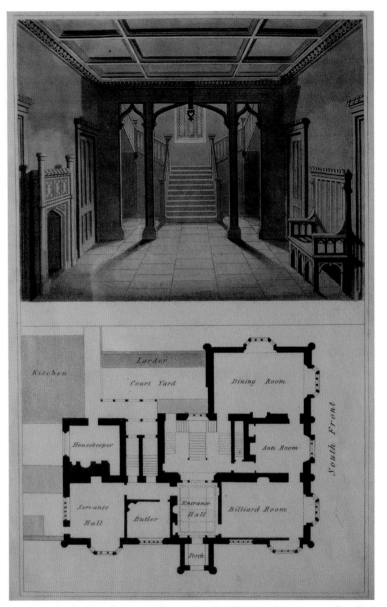

Figure 135. *The hall and ground floor plan for Barningham, printed in Repton's Fragments on the Theory and Practice of Landscape Gardening.*

124

Figures 136 (right) and 137 (far right). *The 'before' and 'after' illustrations of Repton's proposed changes to Barningham's gothic windows, to allow more extensive views of the landscape, whilst maintaining their Picturesque quality.*

Figure 138. Repton's Barningham illustration from Armstrong's History and Antiquities of the County of Norfolk, 1781.

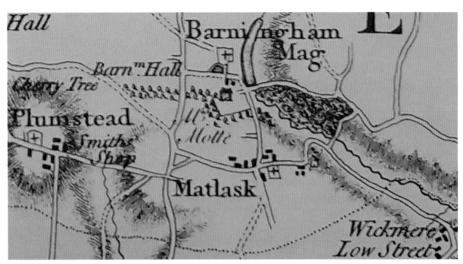

Figure 139. Barningham, detail from Faden's Map of Norfolk, 1797.

much as on his 'before' paintings of the south and west fronts.[206] It also corresponds with what is shown, somewhat schematically, on Faden's county map of 1797, except that this also indicates that an avenue of trees extended away from the western façade, and that a small lake of some kind – probably a large fish pond – already existed to the east of the house (Figure 139). No park is shown on the map, and public roads ran close to the hall to both north and east, and a little further away on the western side.

All these roads were closed by a Road Order made in 1815, and the Ordnance Survey drawings of 1816 show that a park had now been laid out, covering some 100 hectares (Figure 140).[207] To the west it was bounded by a narrow and discontinuous belt of trees; a larger, 50-hectare block of wood lay to the east of the hall, beyond the lake. The avenue still remained in place, but new drives ran through the park, approaching the hall from north and south. The creation of this new landscape may have begun well before the roads were officially closed, for a lodge built at the new south entrance carries the date 1807 above its door.

Figure 140. Barningham, detail from Ordnance Survey drawing, Cromer sheet, 1816.

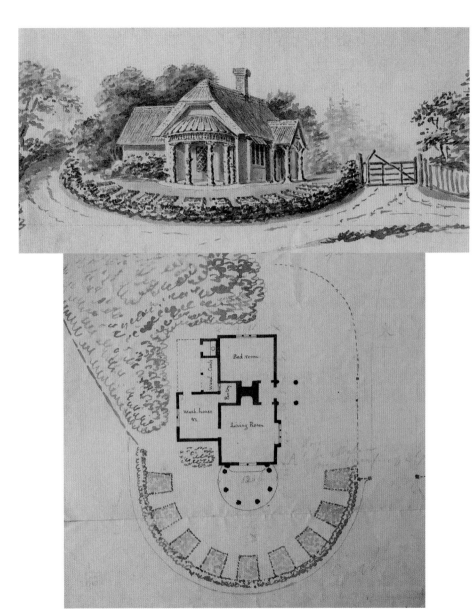

Figure 142. *Repton's design for the South Lodge at Barningham.*

Figure 141. *Repton's design and plan for the North Lodge, an apsidal, covered seating area on the south gable. The front garden's curved hedge line echoes this feature, with its radiating flower beds.*

Figure 143. *A third design for a possible lodge at Barningham.*

There is no real doubt that most, if not all, of these changes were made following Repton's advice. In addition to the watercolours showing the hall and its immediate surroundings, there are also sketches and plans for two lodges to be built at the south and north entrances (Figures 141, 142 and 143). Both, like most of the examples which Repton proposed elsewhere, were single-storey cottage-like buildings, rather different from the kind of paired gatehouses favoured by an earlier generation of 'improvers', and which Repton criticised in *Observations*, noting that a 'poor man's cottage, divided into what is called a pair of lodges, is a mistaken expedient to mark importance in the entrance to a park'.[208] The design for the south lodge is restrained, echoing in subdued form the 'gothic' style of the hall in its set of imposing chimneys, but that for the later north lodge (the plan is dated 1813) was more picturesque, with thatch, trelliswork, climbing plants and a covered porch. The southern lodge was built much as drawn; the northern to a different, but probably Reptonian, design (Figures 144, 145 and 146). If Repton designed the two lodges, it is very likely that he was also responsible for laying out the two drives. The north approach in particular has a very 'Reptonian' feel. It appears, visually, to continue the line of the public road (which veers to the west as a consequence of the diversion of 1815); it runs close to the picturesque ruins of the parish church, which is itself illustrated in an undated and annotated sketch (based on an earlier drawing) which Repton sent to Mott (Figure 147);[209] and it was so arranged that the hall was revealed to the traveller moving along it in a sudden and characteristically Reptonian 'burst'.

The wider parkland, as depicted on the Ordnance Survey drawings and on the tithe maps (for Matlaske, Plumstead and Town Barningham) of c.1840, has many classic Reptonian touches.[210] The parkland to the east of the hall contained scattered clumps, beyond which was a perimeter belt which was discontinuous in character. The old western avenue was allowed to remain, something which Repton advised on a number of occasions when dealing with old manor houses of sixteenth- or seventeenth-century date. Nevertheless, in detail his ideas for the grounds may have been compromised. Another of Repton's Norfolk clients, Abbot Upcher of Sheringham, visited Barningham in 1812 and reported: 'Repton hurt at seeing his oaks cut down in the park and his plans which he had given to Mott so entirely departed from.'[211]

Figure 144. *Victorian photograph of North Lodge, Barningham.*

Figure 145. *North Lodge, Barningham.*

128

Figure 146. *South Lodge, Barningham.*

Figure 147. *Repton's sketch of the remains of St Mary's Church in a letter he wrote to J.T. Mott. He writes underneath that it is based on a drawing he made in 1779 (See Appendix 1).*

By the time the nurseryman James Grigor visited Barningham shortly before 1841 the planting in the park was beginning to mature, and to display its 'mingled beauties' – comprising both newly established trees, and older ones retained from the farmland which the park replaced. Some of the woodland was being thinned to improve the view across the lake from the east.[212] Since then, remarkably few changes have been made to the landscape, or the hall. The lines of the two drives remains much as they were in 1816; a large amount of the original planting survives, as does the terrace placed below the south front.

Figure 148. *The section of St Mary's Church in use today in, Barningham Park.*

Worstead, Bracon Ash, Lyng and Hoveton House

Figure 149. Worstead House illustration from Peacock's Polite Repository,1803.

Figure 150. Worstead House engraving by Neale.

While the extent and character of the Reptons' work at Barningham, Wood Hall and Witton is reasonably well understood, their contribution at a number of other places in Norfolk in this period remains less clear. An illustration of Worstead House in north-east Norfolk, based on an engraving by Repton, was published in 1803 in *The Polite Repository*, presumably indicating that he had recently undertaken some work here (Figure 149). Unfortunately, the house was demolished in 1939, and its history remains poorly documented. Even its date of construction is uncertain. There is general agreement that it was designed by the noted architect James Wyatt for Sir Berney Brograve and erected between c.1791 and 1797. Neale in 1820 identified him as the architect, and this was repeated by numerous local sources in the nineteenth century, including White's 1845 *Directory of Norfolk* (Figure 150).[213] However, the historian Armstrong, as early as 1781, was able to describe how

> Berney Brograve Esq. of Waxham, has lately built a most beautiful seat in this parish, which he has very judiciously ornamented by a canal and plantations, office &c. It stands in a park, about three quarters of a mile south-east of the town,

and is esteemed by most travellers to be the neatest *box* in Norfolk.[214]

The hall is already shown, standing within its park, on William Faden's county map, surveyed in the early 1790s and published in 1797. It is possible that Wyatt modified a recently erected house, and that Repton made alterations to the grounds at the same time. But the situation is further complicated by the fact that a note, written in the eighteenth century and preserved in the Buckinghamshire Record Office, states that the architect of the house was not James Wyatt, but Samuel, his brother – with whom Repton worked closely at Holkham (Norfolk), Broke Hall in Nacton (Suffolk) and elsewhere.[215] The house certainly looks typical of Samuel's work, which featured many modest, rather simple classical houses with a central, domed bow flanked by over-arched tripartite windows.[216] The house was described by Neale in 1820 as standing in

> a most delightful Park of from three to four hundred acres in

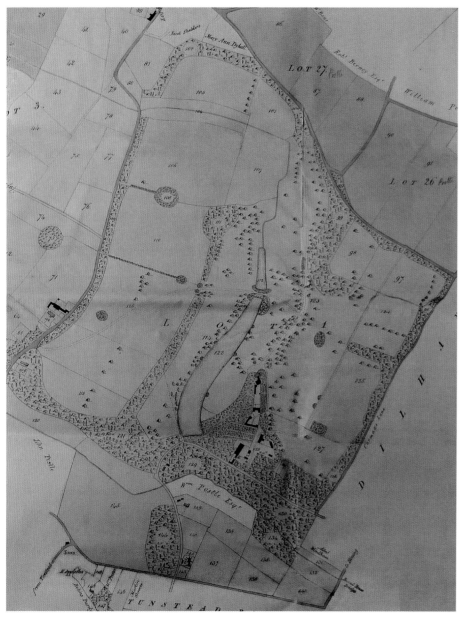

Figure 151. Worstead Park estate map from an 1828 sale catalogue.

Figure 152. Similar view to Neale's, from Marshall's Select Views, 1825.

extent: a fine canal running through it, considerably improves the home views, while every variety of prospect meets the eye in the distant landscape.[217]

The 'canal' was in fact a slightly serpentine lake, orientated roughly north-south, which lay to the west of the house. The tithe map of 1844 shows that there was a walled kitchen garden, offices and outbuildings extending to the south of the mansion.[218] The 1828 particulars also mention an orchard and 'pleasure grounds . . . intersected with walks, lawns and flower gardens', which sound rather Reptonian[219] (Figure 151). These, to judge from the tithe map, lay mainly to the south and south-west of the house. They are also shown, more schematically, on the draft Ordnance Survey drawings of 1816.[220] On the death of Sir George Berney Brograve in 1828 his heir, Henry John Conyers of Copped Hall in Essex, sold the estate to the Hon. Wm. Rufus Rous, in whose family it remained until sold and broken up in 1938.[221] The house was demolished the following year, although the stables and the walled kitchen garden remain, together with the park and lake, complete with much early planting.[222] So far the

131

Figure 153. Mrs Berney's House - Brecon (sic) in Peacock's Polite Repository, 1804.

only evidence of Repton's connection with Worstead remains the *Polite Repository* engraving: his involvement here (and perhaps that of his son John) is likely but its extent and character may never be known.

In 1804 the *Polite Repository* featured an engraving of a building named 'Brecon', described as the residence of 'Mrs Berney' (Figure 153). Given the importance of the Berney family in the Norfolk parish of Bracon Ash, south-west of Norwich, at this time, there seems little doubt that the caption has been misspelt. The building shown does not appear to be Bracon Ash Hall, however, but rather Mergate Hall, which lies just over half a mile to the south. Bracon Ash Hall, the main manor, is shown as the residence of John Berney Esquire on Faden's county map of 1797 (Figure 154), but it is very likely that the house had been demolished by this time, for Armstrong in 1781 described Bracon Ash Hall as 'the large building that was lately demolished', while sales particulars for the estate, drawn up in 1828, refer to 'the Site of Bracon Hall'.[223]

John Berney died in 1800 and left the estate to his grandson Thomas Trench Berney, aged 16: the executors of his will were his widow Margaret Berney and Elizabeth Berney, widow of his son Thomas, who died in 1786.[224] It is Elizabeth who is shown by Faden as the occupier of Mergate Hall, which she

Figure 154. Left: Mergate Hall is marked with Mrs Berney in the south of the parish; the Hall is marked but may not have been standing at this time. Faden's Map, 1797.

Figure 155. Right: Detail from the Ordnance Survey drawings, Norwich sheet, 1818. Mergate Hall and its small pleasure ground, next to the K of Kinningham (sic). The building shown on the Hall site is probably the 'coach house with stabling for 28 horses', mentioned in the 1828 sale catalogue.

acquired by lease in 1789;[225] and it was she who must be the 'Mrs Berney' who is given as the owner of the house in the *Polite Repository* illustration. Indeed, this building is immediately recognisable as Mergate Hall – a large seventeenth-century building with prominent gables and dormer windows (the engraving shows the western or entrance front). Quite what Repton may have done here is uncertain. The hall is shown standing in a small park on Faden's map, depicted with more accuracy as a large pleasure ground on the Ordnance Survey drawings of 1818[226] (Figure 155). Repton clearly did not create this setting, although he may have modified it. But once again, the commission may have been largely architectural in character, as the house was extensively modified in the early nineteenth century. A staircase block and a two-storey wing with an apsidal bow were added to the rear of the house, between the two existing wings; and the south front was remodelled, with sash windows and a new cornice.[227]

Figure 156. Lyng Rectory,
Peacock's Polite Repository, 1806.

Figure 157. J. A. Repton's sketch of Lyng, from a description given to him by his aunt, Mrs Adey.

The evidence connecting Repton with Lyng Rectory is a little stronger. In addition to an illustration published in the *Polite Repository* for July 1806 (Figure 156) there is also a watercolour painted by John Adey Repton, preserved in the Colman Collection in the Millennium Library at Norwich (Figure 157). The house, which is viewed from the south in the engraving and from the east in the watercolour, was occupied by the Rev. Charles Anson, one of Repton's personal friends. Here, almost certainly, John was *not* involved, for the sketch of the house carries the words: 'Lyng – a sketch by J.A. Repton of a spot he never saw – taken from a verbal description by Mrs Adey', apparently written in John's hand. The house is shown surrounded by shrubberies and lawns, with water in the foreground

– probably the River Wensum, which bounded the property to the north and east, although possibly the moat on which the house stood, and still partly stands (the eastern arm of the moat is now incorporated into the river, but the two are shown as still distinct on the tithe map of 1842).[228] The tower of the parish church can be seen in the near distance. If Repton's work was restricted to the grounds, it must have been on a limited scale for these, to judge from later maps, extended over less than 5 hectares, divided roughly evenly between shrubberies and lawns around the house and an area of park-like pasture to the south. Most of the features of the grounds today appear to be of later nineteenth-century or twentieth-century date, but several trees, including a fine London plane, may date back to Repton's time.

Rather more is known about Repton's work at Hoveton House, in Hoveton St John. The first Thomas Blofeld (1635–1708) had acquired Hoveton House as a villa from which he could retreat from his business and civic responsibilities, for on top of his activities as a textile merchant and manufacturer he was also a JP, MP and Mayor of Norwich.[229] The house stands around 400 metres to the north-east of the River Bure, on the opposite side of the water to Wroxham road. Blofeld and his wife

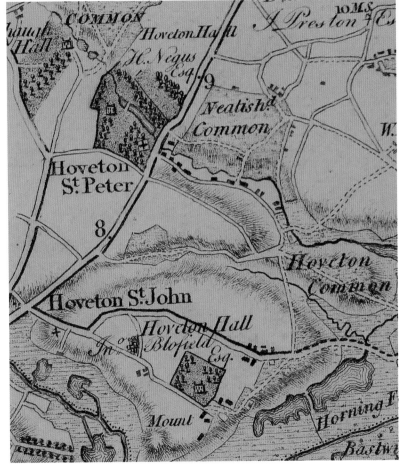

Figure 158. *Detail from Faden's Map of Norfolk, 1797, showing Hoveton Hall to the north and Hoveton House (here, shown as Hall) to the south.*

Figure 159. *Portrait of John Spencer Blofeld, as a young man.*

comprehensively rebuilt the property, which then passed to an infant great-nephew, Thomas Blofeld of Briston (1697–1766), who made further changes to the house. His only child Sarah (1734–1817) prudently married her cousin John Blofeld of Norwich and Gray's Inn (1725–1805), neatly keeping the Blofeld name and estate together.

When their son, Thomas Blofeld (1753–1817), inherited in 1805 the south façade of the house still faced directly onto an east–west public road, and Faden's county map shows that the small park, covering around 10 acres (c.4 hectares), lay only on its northern side (Figure 158). The road was a minor one, and a portrait of Thomas Blofeld's eldest son, John Spencer Blofeld, has as a backdrop a view towards a distant river which is surely based on the prospect from the hall towards the Bure, and which suggests that the area

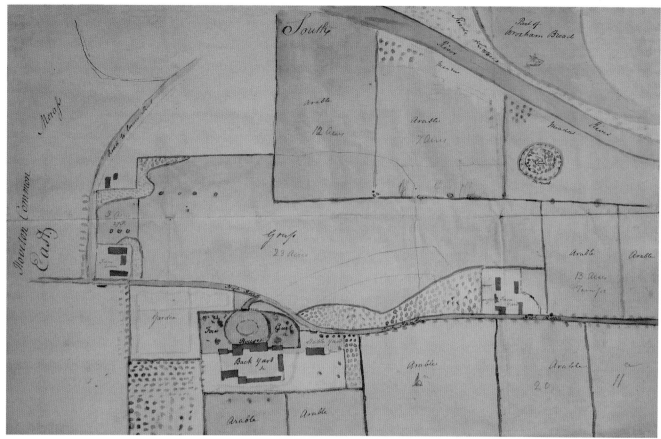

Figure 160. Hoveton House estate map, dated c.1770s–80s.

on this side of the house was already rather park-like in character (Figure 159).[230] An undated estate map, from the 1770s or 80s, shows a circular clump of trees occupying a natural knoll by the river to the south-west of the house and marks the site of a reed house at its centre (one still survives at this spot, although of more recent date) (Figure 160). The area to the south of the house was thus to an extent ornamental, but the lack of a true park and the proximity of even a minor public road were not, by this date, acceptable to a man of Blofeld's status.

When he inherited the estate in 1805 he swiftly put in hand a number of improvements. A mason's bill for work carried out between 1805 and 1806 includes the costs of making new marble fireplaces for the library (grey) and dining room (red-veined), and for repairs to other fireplaces, as well as for removing and refixing the external pilasters on the south front of the house.[231] Blofeld also arranged a survey relating to the closure of the road in front of the house, which was carried out by a Road Order on 20 February 1807.[232]

Figure 161. Repton's 'before' (above) and 'after' (below) watercolours of Hoveton House.

In early 1807 Humphry Repton was asked for his opinion, visited Hoveton and soon sent a letter detailing his proposals. This was accompanied by two small watercolours, 'before' and 'after' views of the south front, which he modestly suggested Mrs Blofeld might use to decorate a fire-screen (Figure 161).[233] The first of these, drawn from memory, shows the house (with the size of the pediment and the height of the roof rather exaggerated) with a carriage sweep around a circular lawn immediately in front of it, separated from the public road by white-painted wooden pales. The second shows Repton's proposals for a complete remodelling of the south front, intended to create a more stylish appearance. Here, as in some of his proposals for Barningham, the old brickwork was to be covered in a pale render, in imitation of stone; and the central gable was to be replaced with a pediment featuring scrolls, and with a larger window than the original. Wooden balustrading, for Repton 'the usual enrichment of mansard roofs', was to be substituted for the plain cornice, and a balcony supported on brackets added to the first-floor drawing room. Below it, three matching French windows were to replace the old-fashioned, ornate door surround and flanking sash windows. The equally old-fashioned stone corner pilasters could remain, he thought, as they 'will hardly be noticed when the house is brought to one colour'. Alternatively, he suggests, 'they may be cut out by a mason', and he provided a rough sketch of some corner quoins which might replace them, and which are also shown on the watercolour. Repton seems to have been unaware that Blofeld had only just settled a large bill for repairing them.

The painting also suggests that the entrance could be improved by cutting back some of the shrubs, and by reducing the gravel sweep to a simple turning circle, without a central lawn. Repton scribbled a quick plan in his letter showing how the sides of the house could be 'embosomed' by shrubs, where a cedar might be placed, and where a walk towards the pleasure ground to the east of the house might be made (Figure 162). The paling fence separating the house from the road was to be replaced by a ha-ha, which Repton wanted to appear as a long-established feature:

In making of the wall of the Ha!ha! use the old bricks of the most dingy colour with mortar mix'd with Blacksmith's cinder ashes instead of sand, and put some moss in the joints

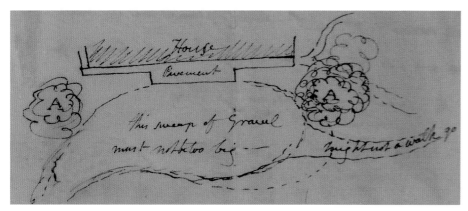

Figure 162. Repton's sketch plan in his letter to Thomas Blofeld, 1807.

to render it less offensive.

A wall was to be demolished somewhere on the property to make way for a proposed new carriage drive and – echoing again his activities at Barningham – he suggested that 'as the bricks are on the spot we might perhaps use some of them to advantage in building a wall and piers at this entrance . . . and perhaps with little trouble alter the old farmhouse into an Entrance Lodge'. [234]

Repton also asked Blofeld for accurate measurements of the house and windows in order that scale drawings could be made, presumably by John Repton, and these were duly sent. However, at the end of March, Repton wrote from Hare Street, making no attempt to conceal his exasperations at the details Blofeld had sent him.:

> From the very inaccurate drawing which your man serves to value, I doubt the brilliancy of his faculties. I have in vain tried to make a scale to his drawing that would correspond to his figures and therefore am convinced it is not drawn to any scale, so I have not ventur'd to figure my drawing, but the relative proportions must be observed. [235]

Following this exchange, a final undated note from Repton enclosed his account, addressed to the Blofelds' second son, another Thomas, indicating

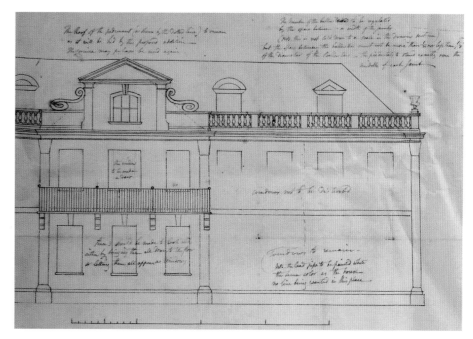

Figure 163. Repton's architectural drawing showing his proposals in detail for the south front of the house, drawn to scale probably by John Adey Repton. 1807.

that father and son were now working together on the project. Evidently, the Blofelds had decided not to pursue the proposals (Figure 163) or retain Repton to supervise any groundworks. But the families clearly remained on cordial terms, and Repton's note closed with a pressing invitation for the Rev. Thomas and his wife to come to dinner the next day. [236]

Repton's proposals for the exterior remodelling of the house, probably drawn up in association with John Adey Repton, were clearly too radical and possibly too expensive for the family and were not carried out. But following the closure of the road the ha-ha was built as he proposed, and the Ordnance Survey drawings of 1816, and Hoveton enclosure map of 1819 (Figures 164 and 165), show that field boundaries had been removed and a small (c.10 acres) area of parkland laid out on this side of the house, extending down to the old reed house clump, which formed its south-western corner. [237] Belts of woodland ran along the eastern boundary of the

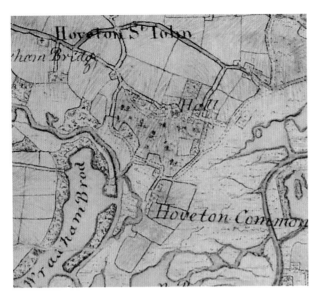

Figure 164. *Detail from the Ordnance Survey drawings, Yarmouth sheet, 1816.*

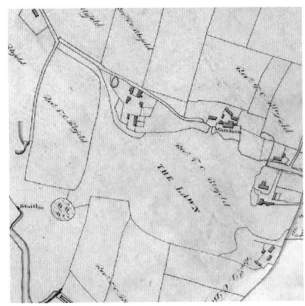

Figure 165. *Enclosure Map for Hoveton St John, 1819.*

Figure 166 *Watercolour, circa 1840, showing the parkland south of Hoveton House.*

park, and along the higher ground to the west of the western boundary. The 1819 map shows a new entrance drive which, in Reptonian style, took a sweeping bend to the south of the old road into the woodland surrounding Home Farm before arriving at the house at an oblique angle from the north-west. By the time of the 1840 Tithe Award map the open grass area (described as the 'Lawn') had been increased to 28 acres (11 hectares). A watercolour made at about the same time shows the house set in parkland, flanked by blocks of trees, with no sign of the surrounding arable land (Figure 166). How far all this was laid out following Repton's specific advice remains uncertain. There have been a number of changes to the landscape since the mid-nineteenth century, but the scene depicted is still recognisable today.

Chapter 5

Last Works

Hoveton Hall

The later years of Repton's career in Norfolk were characterised by a continuing involvement with his son John in projects that were as much to do with architecture as with landscape design. Indeed, whereas in the first years of their association their architectural work in the county involved making (or proposing) changes to houses already in existence, they now began to be commissioned to design entirely new mansions, on virgin sites. Elsewhere in England they had begun to do this from the start of their cooperation – Panshanger in Hertfordshire, for example, was commissioned in 1801. But in Norfolk the first of their country houses to be built from scratch was Hoveton Hall, the surviving plans for which are dated 1809.

The Hoveton estate in Hoveton St Peter and Neatishead had been owned by the Negus family throughout the eighteenth century, having been acquired by Henry Negus in 1667, two years after Thomas Blofeld purchased Hoveton House in Hoveton St John. The two men were partners in business, manufacturing worsted hosiery, and the families were to remain close, intermarrying on a number of occasions. The Negus family continued to own the estate throughout the eighteenth century and in 1789 Christobelle Negus, the only daughter of Henry Negus, married James Burkin Burroughes of Burlingham Hall. She was widowed at a relatively young age in 1803, and in 1807 inherited Hoveton Hall on her father's death. Aware that her eldest

Figure 167. *Detail from Ordnance Survey drawings, Norwich sheet, showing the old house south-west of the lake.*

son, also Henry, was to inherit Burlingham Hall at the age of twenty-one, she was determined to build a home for herself and the younger children back on her own land.[238]

William Faden's county map of 1797, surveyed in the early 1790s, exhibits some confusion in the names it gives to different country houses in the locality but clearly shows Hoveton Hall on a site some 300 metres to the west of the present hall, close to the kitchen gardens which still survive here, and at the northern end of an avenue. It stood within a park of some 168 acres (68 hectares), containing a long, narrow lake covering about 4 acres (1.6 hectares), created by damming the infant River Ash (see Figure 158): this formed the parish boundary between Hoveton St Peter and Neatishead. The whole landscape was partly surrounded by woodland belts. The hall was oddly located, lying to the west of the lake – and it is possible that Henry Negus had intended constructing a new house, better placed within the new park. The Ordnance Survey drawings (Figure 167) show a similar arrangement of features, but the Neatishead enclosure map

Figure 168. H. Repton and Sons, south elevation of a new house at Hoveton, 1809.

of 1813 shows that the present hall had been built by Christobelle, on a different site, some 300 metres to the east, and thus to the north of the lake, in Neatishead parish.[239] There is little doubt that it was designed by the Reptons. Two drawings, both bearing the text 'the new house at Hoveton in Norfolk according to the Plan B as proposed by H. Repton and sons 1809', survive in the Colman Collection in Norwich Millennium Library (Figures 168 and 169). Plan A seems to have been lost. The use of the word 'Sons' is noteworthy, suggesting as it does the involvement of George Repton as well as John Adey Repton.

One of the drawings shows the south elevation of the proposed house, the other both the south and the east elevations. It was to be a substantial Neoclassical construction with two projecting bays enclosing a large orangery, which would have provided fine views to the south, across the park and lake. The house as built bears little resemblance to the drawing, and presumably follows the proposals in the lost 'Plan A'. It is of gault brick, of two storeys under a hipped roof, with three bays on the north and east and nine bays on the south. It has a semicircular Ionic porch (on Doric columns), flanked by tripartite windows, on the eastern entrance front. It is fairly typical of Regency period houses in Norfolk but has some sophisticated features, such

Figure 169. H. Repton and Sons, south and east elevation of the new house, 1809.

as the two-storey three-bay bow on the south side, the single-storey bowed windows on the north and east, and the pedimented Wyatt windows with ashlar surrounds on the south and east fronts.

In 1812 Mrs Burroughes was billed for £147, indicating a considerable amount of time devoted to Hoveton.[240] Some of this may have been related to the glasshouse which still survives on the edge of the pleasure grounds to the north-west of the house, with which it is probably contemporary. While the idea for an integral conservatory included in Plan B may have been rejected, Mrs Burroughes appears to have been determined to have

something to contain the kind of exotic and tender plants which were now so fashionable. The glasshouse, extensively restored in 1988, measures 12.7 metres by 4.5 metres and has a substantial heated rear wall with boiler room, fuel store and potting sheds behind (Figure 170). There are chimneys at each end – one serves the boiler, the other is a dummy, to provide symmetry. There are doors with gothic arches, and the interior includes a heated bench under the front wall for very tender specimens, and two separate seating areas, surrounded by raised beds, for taller exotics, against the rear wall. The simplicity and elegance of the building is a consequence of the innovative use of wrought iron for the framework, sashes and stanchions. Detailed

Figure 170. The restored glasshouse at Hoveton Hall, probably designed by the Reptons.

examination prior to its restoration in the 1980s concluded that the glasshouse was a rare survivor which provided important insights into an early phase in the development of rolled wrought iron as a building material, prior to the development of the wrought-iron glazing bar patented by J.C. Loudon in 1818. In many ways the construction displays considerable ingenuity, evidence of a close association between architect and smith.[241] Repton's admiration for the possibilities of cast iron as a construction material had already been expressed in his *Observations on the Theory and Practice of Landscape Gardening* of 1803; he had suggested using cast-iron rafters and columns at Plas Newydd in 1799; and had proposed an orangery in the same material at the Brighton Pavilion in 1806. All this makes it very likely that the Reptons were responsible for the Hoveton design, especially given that wrought iron was also used in the construction of the cantilevered staircase inside the house, probably designed by John Adey Repton.[242] They may also have been responsible for the gault brick ice-house in Ice Well Wood which likewise appears to have been built at the same time as the house.

The surviving evidence, such as it is, indicates a purely architectural commission. Nevertheless, as at Barningham, there are signs that Repton contributed to the design of the grounds. As noted, a park already existed here before the hall was rebuilt on its new site, and many of the features of the present landscape – the fine lake, the woodland belts – appear to be shown on Faden's map. The main change, accompanying or more probably following the construction of the new house, was the addition of a new entrance drive, approaching the residence from the east. This still survives and leaves the Norwich Road in the kind of smooth, continuous line which Repton advocated at Honing and elsewhere. A lodge was erected, a single-storey, free-standing cottage of gault brick, in a rather plain but vaguely Picturesque style, similar to other buildings known to have been designed by John Repton.

The planting within the park features a number of ancient oaks – some with girths of 6.5 metres – inherited from the earlier agricultural landscape, as well as others – especially in the woodland belts and pleasure grounds to the north-west of the house – which were probably, to judge from their girths, planted in the late eighteenth century. But some of the planting, especially that visible from the new house and drive, may well have been Repton's work. The so-called 'Repton's Clump' in the south-east corner of the park includes five fine oaks with girths of between 3.2 and 3.8m, consistent with an early nineteenth-century planting date. It is not shown on the tithe award map of 1841 (perhaps because it was by then not fenced off from the surrounding landscape), but four others of similar size are depicted to the south of the lake, while another is shown in the north park, all possibly designed by Repton, or placed following his advice.

The 1841 tithe maps for Hoveton St Peter and Neatishead (Figure 171) show the now mature parkland in some detail, covering around 120 acres (c.50

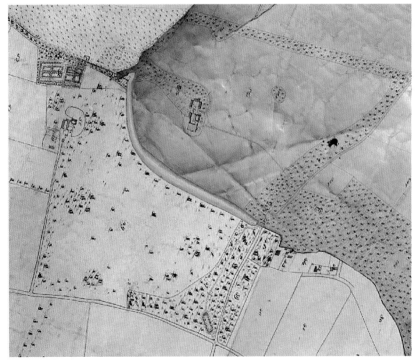

Figure 171. *The Hoveton Hall estate, combined Hoveton St Peter and Neatishead tithe maps, 1841.*

hectares) and with around 15 acres (c.6 hectares) devoted to the pleasure grounds. Interestingly, the avenue which had led to the old hall still survived, perhaps in part to act as a screen towards Hall Farm. James Grigor, writing a few years earlier, praised the 'elegant' flower garden with its old-fashioned flowers, such as sweet william, lychnis, carnation, primula, ranunculus and anemone, noting that 'the proprietor' clearly shared his admiration for traditional favourites. He was impressed by the parkland trees and called the avenue on the south-west side of the house a 'grand sight'.

> Whilst the flower-garden here is of such perfect character, the scenes of the shrubbery and pleasure-ground are of an equally interesting description. The shrubbery is a well-managed piece of work, successfully blended with the lawn of the pleasure-ground, and though modern, already contributing to the general beauty of the place. The most elegant part of the picture lies betwixt the hall and the kitchen-garden, a locality which art has rendered very ornamental, and where the shrubs are assuming a high degree of beauty. The whole place is so judiciously laid out that we hazard the opinion that it has been done by someone who has become eminent in his profession.[243]

Although Grigor appears to have been ignorant of the designer, much of this sounds very like something Repton might have designed.

Two years after Grigor's visit Mrs Burroughes died and her son Henry Negus Burroughes inherited the estate, but remained at Burlingham, allowing a younger brother to take up residence at Hoveton. The hall was subsequently sold to Sir Jacob Preston of nearby Beeston St Lawrence and was then leased to a succession of tenants. In 1909, the estate was bought by the Buxton family, previously residing at Catton Hall. During their time the wood and water garden was established in Ashmanhaugh Plantation, but the property was sold again twenty years later and after several short ownerships was acquired in 1946 by a cousin of the previous Buxtons. The park was largely ploughed up in the course of the twentieth century, but a programme of restoration began in the 1980s. Park, woodland and gardens are opened to the public on a regular basis.

Stradsett and Sheringham

In 1808, the year before the drawings for Hoveton Hall were prepared, Repton was asked to submit a design for the grounds of Stradsett Hall near Downham Market in west Norfolk. The hall had been built by the Pigot family in the sixteenth century and was acquired by Philip Case in 1747.[244] On his death in 1791 it passed to his son-in-law Thomas Bagge, member of a leading merchant family in King's Lynn, with interests in shipping and brewing. Thomas died in 1807 and the estate was inherited by his son Thomas Philip Bagge (1771–1827). It was he who decided to rebuild the hall and improve its grounds and for the latter approached three possible candidates. John Claudius Loudon was later to become a leading landscape designer and writer but in 1807 was still at an early stage of his career. John Haverfield (1744–1820) was in charge of Richmond Gardens in London from 1762 until 1795, when he embarked on a career as a landscape designer and architect: he was currently working on remodelling Walsingham Abbey in north Norfolk and redesigning the grounds there, which is probably how Bagge had heard of him.[245] The third, and by far the best known, was Repton. The estate accounts record a payment in October 1808 of £26 5s. 'To Repton for Plan of Stradsett', together with £7 15s. in expenses.[246] These are reasonably large sums, suggesting that he probably provided T. P. Bagge, if not with an actual Red Book, then with something very close to one: whatever their character, the proposals are lost.

In the end Bagge rejected Repton and chose instead the young and less experienced Loudon. Why he did so remains unclear. John Phibbs has suggested that it was because Repton had recently fallen out with his old friend William Windham, who was also a friend of Bagge.[247] More probably it was because Repton only prepared proposals for his clients and was unwilling to organise their implementation, whereas Loudon promised to be directly involved in the all stages of his scheme, a much more attractive arrangement from Bagge's point of view. Whatever the reason, it was Loudon whose plans were approved and who began work at Stradsett in 1810. Evidently, while Repton's career was still continuing, other new stars were on the rise; and it is noteworthy that within a few years the number of commissions he was given nationally fell back significantly, although this was in part because of Repton's declining health. In January 1811 Repton accompanied his daughters Mary and Elizabeth to a ball at Belhus in Essex, the home of Sir Thomas Lennard. On the return journey the carriage overturned in icy conditions and Repton sustained spinal injuries and was partially paralysed for several weeks. He never fully recovered, and continued to make visits, prepare reports and create Red Books only with the assistance of his two architect sons. In Norfolk he worked on only one further major commission: Sheringham.

This is perhaps one of Repton's best known and most frequently cited works, not least because the text of the Red Book was included, almost verbatim, in his last book, *Fragments on the Theory and Practice of Landscape Gardening*, published in 1816 [248] (Figure 172). Presented in 1812, it sets out Repton's vision and plans for the house and estate but also – to a greater extent than other examples – places these within a wider social and moral context. The commission, undertaken in close cooperation with John Adey Repton, involved both the design of a new house and improvements and enhancements to the surrounding landscape. Repton claimed that 'this may be considered as my most favourite work' and asserted that his task was to 'render Sheringham a place of Residence to its possessor and his family for all seasons and for future generations'. In fact, neither Repton nor his client – Abbot Upcher – were to see the commission completed, and Sheringham was to stand empty for more than twenty years after Repton's death before it was finally inhabited.

The three men must have made an odd trio, the disabled and ageing Repton, his deaf architect son and the nervous, devout Abbot Upcher, but they shared a love for Sheringham and its landscape, all seeing potential for making an idyllic family home. Repton's relationship with the young and passionate Upcher was both paternal and opportunistic, guiding his hand in the moral improvement of his estate while at the same time making a reasonable amount of money from him. The Reptons did not work on a completely blank slate. Before Upcher purchased the estate in 1811, it had been owned for several generations by the Flower family. Although there was no park here, nor a grand house, Mr Cook Flower II had made a number of improvements to the landscape including extensive tree planting. Repton

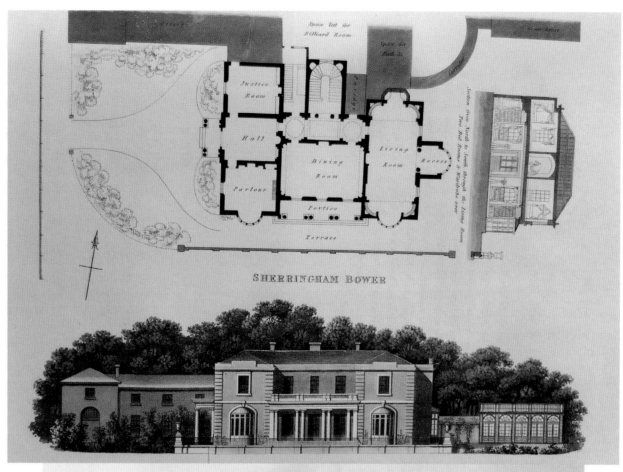

SHERRINGHAM BOWER

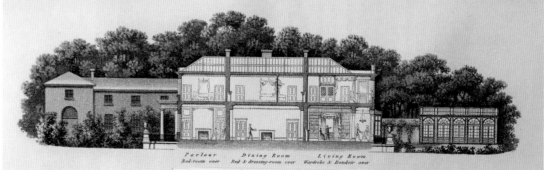

Figure 172.
The illustrations of Sherringham
Bower (Hall) from Repton's book:
Fragments on the Theory and
Practice of Landscape Gardening,
1816.
Above: Ground floor plan and front
elevation (flap up).
Below: Section through the house
(flap down).

himself, writing in 1781 in the third volume of Armstrong's *History and Antiquities of Norfolk*, described Upper Sheringham as 'beautifully adorned by the extensive woods of Mr. Cook Flower' and praised the way in which the young trees had been planted amongst the 'furze and ling' to afford them protection.[249] The new woods are shown clearly on a map surveyed in c.1805.[250] Following the death of Cook Flower II in 1782 the estate passed to his son Robert Flower who held it until his death in 1790, at which point it passed to his eldest son Cook Flower III. For some years he farmed 140 acres in hand, living in the old farmhouse whilst the rest of the land was tenanted out, but in 1808 he instructed his land agent to look for a purchaser for the estate, in the hope of a quick sale.[251] By a remarkable stroke of luck that agent was Repton's solicitor son in Aylsham, William Repton.

William alerted his father, who had been in correspondence with Charles Abbot, the Speaker of the House of Commons, about the potential purchase by Parliament of a country seat for Earl Nelson, in memory of his late brother Admiral Nelson.[252] Although Sheringham met the criteria of an 'elevated site overlooking the sea' it was ultimately rejected due to the value of the estate being too low, and having no grand mansion.[253] Despite some interest from other local landowners (including William Lukin, the heir of William Windham of Felbrigg Hall) the estate remained unsold, not least because it was felt to be overpriced, with much of the land tenanted on long leases.[254] It was three years before the purchase by Abbot Upcher was secured in 1811, during which time William Repton oversaw the enclosure of 102 acres of land later described in the sale particulars as 'part of the valuable Dole Land of Sheringham'.[255]

Abbot Upcher (Figure 173, left), born in Great Yarmouth in 1784, was the third son of Peter and Elizabeth Upcher and, following the unexpected deaths of his two older brothers, inherited his father's wealth in 1796. In 1809 he married Charlotte Wilson (Figure 173, right), the daughter of Reverend Henry Wilson of Kirby Cane in south Norfolk, and the couple leased a house at Thompson near Watton.[256]

Upcher's journals reveal him as a man of delicate health (afflicted by headaches and fevers) who shared with his wife a deep religious fervour;

Figure 173. Abbot Upcher and Charlotte Upcher, owners of Sheringham Hall.

and, as a family man, devoted to his wife and children (of which there would be six before his death). By 1811 Upcher already had two children and was becoming desperate to find a suitable and permanent family home. In May 1811 he offered £50,000 for the Wroxham Estate, but was declined; a few days later he 'offered for Lindford' (presumably Lynford in Breckland), likewise without success; and by June his interest in Mount Ida (Bagthorpe Hall in west Norfolk) was also thwarted when it was sold to another interested party. He recorded in his journal: 'it seems doomed that we never should be settled'.[257]

Perhaps in some desperation (and in a state of grief, having recently lost his grandmother) Upcher visited Sheringham at the end of June 1811, where he was 'cruelly disappointed in the house, it being only a better kind of farmhouse'.[258] But he was impressed by the 'beautiful and romantic grounds' and on 10 July, following a dinner with William and Humphry Repton, signed the purchase contract, agreeing to pay a sum of £52,500

Figure 174. *Repton's view of the proposed new house for Abbot and Charlotte Upcher, from the Red Book from Sheringham, 1813.*

Figure 175. *Sheringham Red Book 'before' illustration to show the industry needed to create a new entrance to the park (flap down).*

Figure 176. Sheringham Red Book 'after' illustration to show that the hard work would be worth it, to reveal the house in its setting (flap up).

with a view to taking possession at Michaelmas 1812. Although Upcher may have had 'some little fear whether I was doing right', any concerns were quelled when, on a further visit to Sheringham on 19 July, his wife was moved by the 'romantic scenery and bold swells crowned with woods'.[259] By June 1812 an agreement had clearly been made to commission the Reptons to make improvements, for they spent five days viewing the estate and deciding on a site for a new mansion. Cook Flower joined them on 10 June and showed them a road leading through the woods to the site of the proposed new house, which could be adapted as a new drive, a contribution for which Upcher was very grateful, noting that 'the discovery of that road through the woods I must ever regard as providential as by it I am saved such an enormous expense'.[260]

After that visit, Repton returned to Hare Street and produced a Red Book which, unlike most examples, is a large portrait volume.[261] The text echoes Upcher's own romantic approach to the landscape which, Repton asserted, 'possessed more natural beauty and local advantages, than any place I have ever seen'. Flower's woods already had paths running through them and Repton proposed only 'some trifling changes' to ensure that they displayed the beauties of the place more effectively. Having commented on the situation, the woods, plantations and sea view, he suggested further tree planting, the creation of drives and walks through the parkland, the construction of a garden terrace below the main façade of the new house and the erection of a Temple on the knoll to the south-east. Most of the Red Book, however, is devoted to the plans for the new house. Described as a 'gentleman-like residence', it was to be a modern villa in Italian style, complete with Doric portico and bay windows (Figure 174). The simplicity of the rooms was designed to meet all the family's needs 'without being extravagant in size or quantity'. Echoing attitudes which we have already seen expressed in the Red Books for Northrepps and Witton, the house did not look out directly onto the sea but was instead placed in a sheltered location to the south of a low hill, with the main prospects looking inland, across a new park to the south and over a pleasure garden to the east.

As in many of his designs Repton was particularly concerned about the layout of the approach drives, of which there were two. One (converted from an existing road) ran in from the east, from the direction of Sheringham. Another approached from the south, running for much of its way through woodland. Repton had particularly ambitious ideas for this second approach, which, as at many of the places at which he worked, was to be so arranged that the house appeared suddenly to the visitor: he proposed to 'cut boldly into the narrow ridge of hill' so that it would 'burst at us on the Sight like some enchanted Palace of a fairy Tale!' The accompanying illustrations in the Red Book depict both the extent of the work and labour required to achieve the desired effect and the rewarding outcome when completed. It shows a couple admiring the view, other visitors arriving by carriage and an artist (perhaps Repton himself) painting the scene (Figures 175 and 176). Repton as usual gave particular consideration to the entrance, which was provided with a lodge of rustic but stylised simplicity. This was also to serve as a 'look out both for Sea and Land, overlooking the covers for game' (presumably to keep watch for any poachers) but the illustration nevertheless presents a rural idyll, complete with a figure gazing out across the view to sea. The design of the lodge itself suggests both benevolence on the part of its owner and contentedness on the part of its occupier (Figure 178).

Indeed, in a number of ways the Sheringham Red Book marks a shift in Repton's ideas. Rather than, as at Honing for example, trying to restrict views from the park out into the working countryside, at Sheringham Repton rejected the modern taste for 'lawning an hundred good acres of wheat' in favour of keeping a view across 'cornfields and woods', on the grounds that it 'makes some variety in the colouring of the picture' (Figure 177). He also lamented the 'modern fashion of placing the house in the middle of a park, at a distance from all Mankind' which he contrasted with the more ancient practice of separating the 'country gentleman's seat' from 'neighbours and dependents by court-yards and garden walls'. The landscape was to be made less exclusive in other ways. He suggested that the 'Treasures of Sheringham' should be unlocked to strangers and that 'one day in the week permission should be given at the Lodge to admit all proper persons', and even allow them take refreshments at the Temple (Figure 179). More radical still was Repton's proposal to allow the poor into the woods around the hall one day a month to 'pick up dead sticks for firing', and his suggestion that the park might on occasions be used for coursing a 'social enjoyment' in which

This view is supposed to be taken from the dining room, but it includes more in length than the painters field of vision admits in one Picture & might more properly be divided into two distinct Landscapes.

VIEW
FROM THE HOUSE
LOOKING SOUTH.

It is rather to be considered as part of a panorama Sketch, than as a Landscape, notwithstanding a licence used in contracting the length of the hill betwixt the Temple & the road at the Scalp.

Figure 177. *Sheringham Red Book, fold-out watercolour of the view south, for the new house to be built at Sheringham.*

the local villagers might partake, 'thus promoting a mutual endearment betwixt the landlord, the tenant, and the labourer' (Figure 180). All this, it has been argued, expressed a growing paternalism on Repton's part, born of the social upheavals and increasing rural poverty which accompanied the long French wars, and the unsettling example set by revolutionary France. We might wonder, however, how far such sentiments – which are less apparent in other Red Books which Repton produced at this stage in his career – in large measure reflected the beliefs and attitudes of his client.

Figure 178. Repton's proposal for the thatched Heath Lodge.

Figure 179. Repton's view north across the park from a proposed temple.

Abbot Upcher's diaries and journal show him as an evangelical Christian of the new kind, a man whose keen interests in land improvement were underpinned by a religious and philanthropic fervour. Repton's tone in the Red Book is sentimental and even nostalgic, perhaps reflecting his declining health and old age, but the extent of his kindly attitudes to the poor should not be exaggerated. He was able to list, amongst the 'Local Advantages' of Sheringham, the fact that there were 'no manufactories near', which he described as the 'cradle of discontent and of Rebellious principles'.[262] The idea of genteel visitors flocking to the spot, moreover, was also doubtless intended in part to flatter Upcher.

This said, the Red Book for Sheringham is pervaded by a belief that landscapes should be humanised as well as animated.[263] They could and should be designed and used in ways which helped reinforce social order and good relations, whilst at the same time asserting both Upcher's benevolence, and his authority. Repton even provided a design for a new parish workhouse (the old one having been demolished by Upcher in 1813 to improve the view of the church) – one which was intended to look 'more like a hospital, or an asylum, and less like a prison', and which would thus be less of an 'object of terror to the poor'. It was never built. Indeed, several other aspects of Repton's proposals never came into being, including the proposed temple.

In spite of the 'intercourse of congenial minds' which underpinned the Red Book's proposals, the project did not get off to a good start. In October 1812, shortly after taking possession of Sheringham, Upcher fell ill with a 'violent nervous fever' and had to go to London for three months to convalesce.[264] However, *Sherringhamia*, Upcher's short account of the work undertaken following his receipt of the Red Book, shows that many of its proposals were nevertheless being implemented, and that new suggestions by the Reptons were made and adopted. On Tuesday, 12 January 1813 Upcher and his family 'returned to Sherringham to reside', in the old farmhouse, and some five months later (almost a year after their initial visit) the Reptons set out the site for the house and the terrace garden. Building work began on 2 July with Upcher's son, Henry Ramey Upcher, laying the first stone.[265]

Figure 180. Repton's image of public hare coursing on Sheringham beach.

Figure 181. Repton's design for Laundry (or Park) Lodge, Sheringham.

By November the foundations of the house and the wall of the upper terrace had been finished. Then, however, building work came to an end for two years. Whether the delays were due to costs, or to difficulties with the Clerk of Works, Mr Harrison, is uncertain but during the hiatus Upcher occupied himself with tree-planting, in part employing Fife's nursery of Thetford, following the advice of his friend John Thomas Mott, who had 'employ'd him to a very considerable extent' at Barningham. [266] In June 1814 Upcher spent £1,250 adding to his estate, buying an area of heathland from Mott at what he considered a good price of less than £20 an acre. Some of this was to be planted up as woodland, some brought into cultivation. From January to March 1815 Upcher records a frenzy of work in the landscape; the Heath Lodge (Figures 178 and 182) and the Lower (Laundry) Lodge (Figures 181 and 183) were built, farm buildings were repaired, the construction of the kitchen garden was begun, tree-planting continued and the approach road through the woods completed, together with the garden terrace – which Upcher described as the 'Greatest possible masterpiece of Repton's Art in Landscape Gardening'. [267]

In April 1815 Upcher appointed Thomas Bedford as a new Clerk of Works and construction on the house resumed, with Upcher recording how the two Reptons made a 'love-visit' (one for which they did not charge) in June 1816. Together they 'spent 3 days advising etc indefatigable in their exertion to improve our grounds, views from the Bower, and thousand other things'. [268] Throughout 1816 work continued on the house, and one of the last entries in *Sherringhamia*, dated 6 November, records that the workmen had 'finished slating the house'. [269] By the turn of 1817 the works were almost complete. Unfortunately, in March 1817 Upcher was once again taken ill, construction work was halted, and the family moved first to Kirby Cane and then to Brompton in Kent, so that Upcher could be cared for by one Doctor Heberden, who had previously done so much to nurse him back to good health. Despite rallying briefly, Upcher never returned to Sheringham and at the turn of 1819 his condition worsened, and he died in March of that year. Charlotte Upcher returned to Sheringham to live in the old farmhouse but could not bring herself to complete the works or live in 'Sheringham Bower' or 'Hall' as it would later become known. The house stood empty for some

Figure 182. *Photograph of Heath Lodge (now Ivy Lodge) before the 1905 fire.*

Figure 183. *Early postcard of Laundry (or Park) Lodge still looking Reptonian in style after being re-located, a little to the north, in the mid-1850s.*

twenty years and was only finally completed, and then occupied, in 1839, when the newly married Henry Ramey Upcher moved in with his new wife. On 25 September 1839 Charlotte Upcher, along with the new Master and Mistress of the Hall, servants, workmen, and employees gathered to hear Upcher's friend Mr Wilkinson consecrate the house to God's service. Alone at the old house Charlotte's diary entry of 12 October states simply: 'The new house is finished. Sheringham Hall is inhabited.'[270]

The Sheringham estate stayed in the Upcher family until 1986 when it was acquired by the National Trust. Most recently it was owned by Henry Thomas Simpson Upcher (1906–1985), who, with his partner Douglas Fitzpatrick, created an extensive collection of Regency furniture and art work, much of which was sold in an auction held by Christies in 1986. In the grounds

Upcher laid out a wild garden on the edge of Oak Wood, and expanded the rhododendron collection, whilst Douglas Fitzpatrick enlarged a pond to the east of the Hall. In addition, in 1975 Upcher erected a new temple, in part to realise Repton's original vision although the new temple was scaled down in size and located on a different site.[271]

Since its acquisition in 1986 the National Trust has been engaged in a programme of actively restoring and managing the park and has opened up a number of the original views while also improving and repairing the buildings across the estate.

Gunton

Figure 184. Gunton Church, Thompson's engraving based on a Repton drawing.

Sheringham may have been Repton's final full commission in Norfolk – the last entire landscape that he designed – but the more limited work undertaken with his son John at nearby Gunton is either contemporary or a little later. Gunton Hall, the seat of the Harbord family, lay only 3 miles (c.5 kilometres) south-east of Repton's old home at Sustead. The mansion, designed by Matthew Brettingham in the 1740s and remodelled by Samuel and James Wyatt in the 1770s, was set in extensive grounds partly laid out by Charles Bridgeman in the 1730s, and which featured the parish church rebuilt as a Greek temple by Robert Adam in the 1760s.[272] Repton appears to have been acquainted with Sir Harbord Harbord, 1st Baron Suffield, who inherited the estate in 1770, through Robert Lee Doughty of Hanworth Hall, and there is a caricature of him drawn by Repton in the Avery Library in New York. The direct evidence for Repton's involvement with the house and grounds comes from much later, however, in the form of a series of drawings which are now in the Blickling collection (on Harbord Harbord's death in 1810, William Assheton Harbord succeeded: he had married Caroline Hobart of Blickling and the archive at the latter place includes several items relating to Gunton).

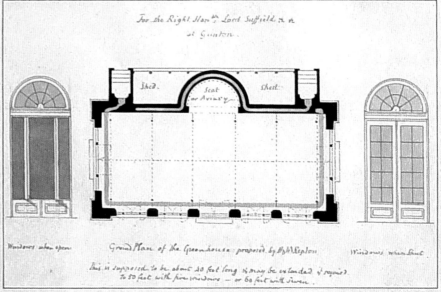

Figure 185. The Reptons' design for a greenhouse at Gunton, 1816.

Figure 186. Repton's sketch for a trellised seat and aviary for the Orangery. Below: a round, raised bed with niches for pot plants. 1816.

Figure 187. Proposed alterations to the entrance lodge at Gunton, H. and J. A. Repton.

Figure 188. Thorpe Lodge, Gunton, which could have been influenced by the Reptons along with the accompanying new drive.

There is a plan and watercolour elevation of a proposed greenhouse at Gunton, set in a formal flower garden and dated 1816; a plan for a trellised seat and aviary, for the orangery, also 1816; and a 'design for altering the lodge at the Entrance to Gunton park', again dated 1816 (Figures 185, 186 and 187). All are signed by both John Adey Repton and Humphry.[273] There is no evidence that any of these proposals were executed. Following his father's death John Adey Repton alone prepared a number of further plans and drawings which are now in the Blickling Collection, most of which seem to relate to Blickling but at least one, an architectural drawing for alterations to part of the hall, to Gunton.[274] The Gunton landscape was changing rapidly under William Assheton Harbord, with the erection of the rustic Saw Mill

Figure 189. J. B. Ladbrooke's lithograph of Gunton Park, 1823.

around 1800, the construction in 1812 of a new bridge across the canal linking the two lakes in the park, and most importantly the expansion of the park itself.[275] Some of the features established in this period have a vaguely Reptonian feel, including the rustic Thorpe Market Lodge (Figure 188) and its associated drive, and the large clump of trees in the south-west of the park, which is traditionally attributed to him.[276] It is perfectly possible that Repton provided further undocumented advice at various times, but there is no firm evidence. The present landscape anyway owes far more to the work of William Sawrey Gilpin in the 1830s and William Teulon in the 1840s, and more specifically to a formidable programme of restoration undertaken by the present owner following a period of twentieth-century decline and dereliction.[277]

157

Conclusion

The last few years of Humphry Repton's career, and especially the period after the carriage accident in 1811, saw him working so closely with his son John that it is sometimes hard to believe that he always remained the lead partner in their relationship. Certainly, while at both Hoveton Hall and Sheringham improvements to the landscape do appear to have been a major part of the work undertaken, the design of a new mansion, on a new site, was an equally if not more important aspect. Despite his mobility difficulties, resulting from his accident, Repton visited Norfolk regularly, particularly the Aylsham area where many of his family and friends were based. He continued to paint for pleasure, recording the Festival of Peace celebrations on 15 July 1814, where 1200 people dined at trestle tables in Aylsham Market Place, listening to a band of musicians on a raised platform above the barrels of ale (Figure 191).

Repton died suddenly on 24 March 1818 and was brought back to Aylsham to be buried in the parish church, where his father and mother, and his brother-in-law John Adey, were already interred. He was laid to rest in a small enclosure by the south chancel wall, beside a fine gothic memorial bearing an inscription which he himself composed (Figure 190). Several years later, in 1833, John Adey Repton designed a reredos for the church, erected at the expense of the vicar, Reverend Charles Norris, which was at the time classed as 'a masterpiece of neo-Gothic architecture'.[278] John's own career continued with reasonable success after his father's death. In 1822 he went abroad for a short period, and worked on a number of commissions in Germany, and his subsequent work in England included remodelling Earl De La Warr's seat of Buckhurst Park, near Tunbridge Wells. He also continued his antiquarian interests, publishing a number of articles and communications in the journal *Archaeologia*. He retired at a relatively young age, moving to Springfield in Essex where he designed a new church in 1843. He lived until November 1860, reaching the age of 86, and was buried in this same church. Of the other Repton children, George Stanley died two years earlier, after a less successful career as an architect, but a perhaps more dramatic life. In 1817 he eloped with Lady Elizabeth Scott, the daughter of Lord Chancellor Eldon, who promptly estranged her for marrying a 'a mere architectural assistant' (although they were reconciled in 1820 on the birth of her first

Figure 190. Humphry and Mary Repton's memorial stone against the south chancel wall of St Michael and All Angels Church, Aylsham. In front, is a small, garden, planted by the Norfolk Gardens Trust.

child). He is buried at Kensal Green, London. Mary Dorothy Repton (1786–1821), who had remained unmarried and living with her parents at Hare Street, subsequently went to live with brother John Adey Repton until her own death in 1821. She was buried with her brother Humphry junior at Hornchurch in Essex. William Repton remained in Aylsham, practising as a solicitor, and died in the town in 1858. He is interred, like his mother, father and grandparents before him, in the churchyard there.

Figure 191. *Humphry Repton's watercolour painting of 1200 residents celebrating the Festival of Peace, in Aylsham Market Square, July 1814.*

159

Chapter 6

Repton and his Contemporaries

Figure 192. *View across the River Bure at Oxnead, showing the church and the surviving wing of Oxnead Hall, Peacock's Polite Repository, 1807.*

Repton's Lost Commissions

As we have noted on a number of occasions, it is more than likely that Humphry Repton worked at other places in Norfolk for which we have, at present, no real evidence. Bolwick in Aylsham, for example, has often been suggested as one of his designs. Bolwick Hall stands near the centre of a park of around 55 acres (c.23 hectares) lying to the east of the Norwich Road and on the parish boundary with Marsham. The park is bounded by a plantation to the north and by narrower shelter belts to the west and south. There is now a diminutive lake to the east of the house, formed by damming the Mermaid Stream, which also served as the supply pond for the nearby watermill; but this appears, in its present form at least, to be a mid-nineteenth-century addition.[279] The house is approached by driveways that leave the public road at the north-western and south-western corners of the park. All this is typical of many small late eighteenth- or nineteenth-century Norfolk parks, and there is nothing which we might, on stylistic grounds, necessarily associate with Repton. But the park is in the right kind of place, and of the right period. No park appears to have existed here in the early 1790s, when William Faden's county map was surveyed; but one is shown on the Ordnance Survey drawings of 1816.[280] It appears to have been laid out soon after 1799, when the enclosure award for Marsham realigned the turnpike road to Norwich further to the west.[281] Before this the hall lay much closer to the road, the old path of which is preserved as lines of trees running

through the parkland. The hall itself was enlarged and refaced around 1800, by the Warne family.[282] It is quite possible that Repton had some input here. But hard evidence remains elusive.

Nearby Oxnead Hall, which lies 3 miles (5 kilometres) to the south-east of Aylsham, has also been suggested as a possible place where Repton worked. The vast sixteenth- and seventeenth-century mansion of the Paston family was ruinous by the eighteenth century and was largely demolished after it had been purchased by Admiral Anson in 1742, only the east wing remaining in use as a substantial farmhouse.[283] This was occupied for several years by John Repton, Humphry's father, and subsequently by Repton's brother John. The latter was a leading agricultural improver whose activities were praised on a number of occasions by Arthur Young in his *General View of the Agriculture of the County of Norfolk*.[284] The house was illustrated in Peacock's *Polite Repository* in 1807 (Figure 192) but this is perhaps a case where such an illustration does *not* show improvements by Repton. John was a farming tenant of the Ansons: any changes to the gardens (this was a working farm and did not have a park) would have been small-scale and ephemeral in nature, and certainly not visible in this distant view. This said, Oxnead may have a certain relevance to the Repton story. A watercolour, said to be by Humphry Repton, shows his idea of Oxnead Hall in its heyday

Figure 193. *Undated watercolour of Oxnead Hall and its formal, terraced gardens, attributed to Humphry Repton, from a scrapbook of his paintings in the Colman Collection. The hall was demolished in the eighteenth century.*

Figure 194. *Above: J. A. Repton's Oxnead Hall illustration, 1809, looking very similar to Figure 193.*

Below: J. A. Repton's illustration from the Gentleman's Magazine, Vol 21, January 1844.

(Figure 193). It seems to have inspired his son John Adey Repton (and John's nephew) to produce two 'reonstructions' of the hall and its grounds as they would have appeared in the seventeenth century, based on careful examination of the surviving remains. These drawings were engraved, and one of them published (together with a description of the house) in Volume II of John Britton's *Architectural Antiquities of Great Britain* in 1809, the year of John Repton's death (Figure 194).[285] They represent one of the first examples of country house and garden archaeology ever attempted in England and are yet another manifestation of John Adey Repton's wide antiquarian interests. The published engraving shows the gardens below the south front of the hall, with their prominent terraces, loosely modelled on those found in the grounds of Italian Renaissance villas, which provided fine views southwards across the River Bure. The sketch on which this engraving was based had probably been made several years before 1809, and thus around the time that the Reptons were beginning to provide terraces for some of their clients, placed between the house and its pleasure grounds – the start of their shared interest in creating more formal, structured and geometric gardens. Although this development had many influences, it is possible that John's close study of Oxnead was one of them.

Another attribution, occasionally repeated, is 'The Orchards', a house in vaguely Tudor style which stands beside the old Norwich road to the south of Aylsham town centre.[286] It was built for William Repton, Humphry's solicitor son, and it has been suggested that it was designed by John Adey Repton and even, perhaps, that Humphry laid out the grounds. For many years William owned and occupied 'Bank House', which stands about 180 metres to the north, on Aylsham market place. By 1830 he had acquired the plot on which The Orchards stands, but no house was built there until the 1840s. His account book records payments of over £850 made between 1848 and 1849 to the builder William Bartram, almost certainly for building the house, although this is not explicitly stated.[287] By this time John Adey Repton was 73 and had been living for many years at Springfield in Essex; Humphry was long dead.[288] While it is possible that John provided a design for his brother as a special favour, the Orchards never seems to have been William's own home. It was built for his son-in-law, William Henry Scott (1818–1882), and his daughter, Helen, who were living there at the time of the 1851 census. William Repton was still residing at Bank House, where he died in 1858. The Orchards has a brick terrace running east–west below its south front, which still survives. Below is a rectangular sunken area which in the 1880s contained a simple arrangement of flower beds, and beyond this an area of lawn, screened from the Norwich Road by shrubberies.[289] The west of the property contained a grid of straight paths each bounded by yew and box hedges, to judge from the surviving remains: those running north–south, directly to the west of the house, are still flanked by slightly raised banks, apparently to conceal them from view. While some of these features, such as the terrace, are vaguely characteristic of John and Humphry Repton's later work, by the 1840s and 50s they had become standard in smaller villa gardens. Some of the more distinctive aspects of the grounds

in fact have their closest parallels in the work of mid-century designers like Edward Kemp, who for example advised that garden paths should be invisible from the house, hidden if necessary by low banks of earth of the kind evident here.[290] In short, there is no real evidence that the house was designed by John Adey Repton, and Humphry cannot possibly have had any direct influence on the layout of its grounds.

Another place which Humphry Repton may have 'improved' is Stratton Strawless, the home of his friend Robert Marsham, who died in 1797. But again, there is no firm evidence and Repton, who was a great admirer of Marsham's tree-planting activities, gives the impression that he required no help or advice.

Stanfield Hall in Wymondham (later the scene of a famous murder) is also a possibility. The hall was built in the sixteenth century but was extensively altered in 1792 in an innovative gothic style by Repton's friend the architect William Wilkins (although it was further altered in the 1830s).[291] It does not appear to have had a park before Wilkins' interventions (none is shown on Faden's county map) but a small one was in place by the time the Ordnance Survey drawings were made in 1816. The hall was approached by three long drives, running in from the north-east, north and south: the former, which lay closest to Norwich, was the main approach. It ran through farmland but was flanked by ribbons of woodland and had a lodge at the entrance, which still survives.[292] There were no belts, but small blocks of woodland existed on the northern side. The park survives, although much reduced in size. In its current state it displays no obviously Reptonian features (the rather dense planting, and unobstructed views across the surrounding farmland, appear decidedly unlike anything he might have recommended) but it is just the kind of place, given Wilkins' involvement, where he might have worked.

Repton's hand might be suspected at a number of other places where new houses were built (or old ones altered), and the surrounding landscape created or transformed, in the 1790s or early 1800s. But without supporting evidence (ideally in the form of a Red Book!) firm attributions are impossible. Stylistic similarities may be suggestive, but hardly conclusive, given that Repton's ideas on design were widely disseminated in his published works, and thus

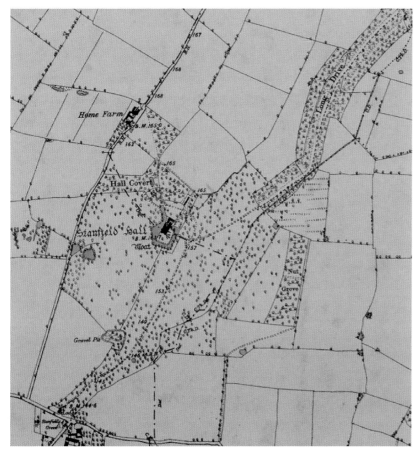

Figure 195. Stanfield Hall from 1884 Ordnance Survey map.

presumably widely emulated. But there is an additional difficulty. We do not really know how far the particular stylistic traits we now associate with Repton were, in reality, more widely shared by contemporary designers. He was not the only landscape gardener working in England, or indeed in Norfolk, in this period. As we have already seen, designers of Brown's generation, such as Richard Woods, Thomas White and in particular William Emes, continued to work well into the 1790s. Perhaps more importantly, the early nineteenth century saw the rise of new players, keen to practise their skills in landscape design.

Haverfield and Loudon: Walsingham, Stradsett and Gillingham

One example of an elaborate garden laid out in the county during Repton's lifetime, but not designed by Repton himself, is Abbey House at Little Walsingham. The ruins of the medieval Priory of Our Lady at Walsingham became a subject of antiquarian interest in the eighteenth century and in 1720 the Society of Antiquaries published an engraving of the ruins.[293] In the same year Abbey House was built for Henry Lee Warner into what remained of the eastern dormitory range of the abbey, and a sketch of 1736, and an engraving made two years later by Samuel and Nathaniel Buck, show that the ruins of the priory church, and in particular the great eastern arch, were incorporated as Picturesque features within an impressive formal garden.[294] This still survived in the 1790s, when the diarist Silas Neville described it as having 'clipped hedges and ponds of water' and as being 'quite in the monkish style'.[295] In 1804, however, the estate was inherited by Daniel Henry Lee-Warner and between 1806 and 1816 the house was remodelled to designs by John Haverfield (1744–1820). He was an architect, but also a garden designer and Keeper of the Royal Gardens at Kew and Richmond. He worked closely with Sir John Soane, as at Tyringham House in Buckinghamshire.[296] As well as remodelling Abbey House, he also transformed its setting. A large area of parkland was laid out to the south of the house, with a small serpentine lake (Figure 196); and surviving formal features of the grounds were removed, although the huge east window of the priory church was retained as a central feature in the pleasure grounds. New 'gothic' features were also added. They included the 'Packhorse Bridge' across the River Stiffkey, which incorporates genuine medieval masonry from the site (Figure 197); the flint-lined 'Dell Gate', a gothic tunnel running beneath Sunk Lane, with buttresses and gothic tracery; and the 'Knight's Gate' in the north wall of the property.[297] Haverfield also laid out paths connecting these features, one of which led to the Dell Garden, a woodland garden created out of an old extraction pit. Much of this landscape survives, maintained in beautiful condition and open to the public on a regular basis, although Haverfield's lake has disappeared. Many of its features would not be out of place in one of Repton's designs.

Figure 196. J. B. Cotman's illustration of the parkland south of Abbey House, 1819.

Figure 197. The packhorse bridge built across the River Stiffkey, Walsingham Abbey.

As we have seen, Haverfield also – together with Repton and John Claudius Loudon – submitted proposals for the grounds of Stradsett Hall, as well as a plan for rebuilding the hall itself. Haverfield's plan and an architectural drawing survive (Figures 198 and 199).[298] The rather flat landscape of the area mainly comprised, to judge from an estate map of 1791, agricultural land with little in the way of woodland.[299] Haverfield proposed creating an extensive park, mainly located to the north of the hall. The brook running east–west through this area was to be widened to create a narrow lake, new entrance was to be made in the north-west corner of the park, and walks were to wind through a series of clumps in its northern section. Here a large five-sided walled garden, presumably a kitchen garden, was to be placed. Further trees, planted in clumps and singly, were to be established along the park's perimeter, and a more continuous screen planted against the Lynn Road to the west. There is no sign on the plan that there was, as yet, any intention to build a hall on a new site: the mansion designed by Haverfield was presumably to replace the existing mansion *in situ*.

In the event Haverfield's plans were, like those of Repton, rejected in favour of those proposed by John Claudius Loudon. Loudon was born in Lanarkshire in Scotland in 1783 and studied biology, botany and agriculture at the University of Edinburgh, before moving to London in 1803. In the same years he published an article, 'Observations on Laying out the Public Spaces in London'; in 1806 his first book, *A Treatise on Forming, Improving and Managing Country Residences* appeared;[300] and from 1808 he was employed by George Stratton to landscape and manage the estate of Tew Park. As many readers will be aware, Loudon, assisted by his wife the garden writer Jane Webb Loudon, became one of the most significant figures in the nineteenth-century gardening world. His most well-known books include *An Encyclopaedia of Gardening* (1822) and *Arboretum et Fruiticetum Britannicum* (1838); he established *The Gardener's Magazine*; and his designs included Birmingham Botanic Gardens (1831) and Derby Arboretum (1839). He was originally critical of Repton, following instead the ideas and principles of the Picturesque, as promoted by Payne-Knight and Price. In *A Treatise on Forming, Improving and Managing Country Residences*, published in 1806, he mentions the proposed ferry boat at Holkham, which Repton suggested might have a deck covered with cement

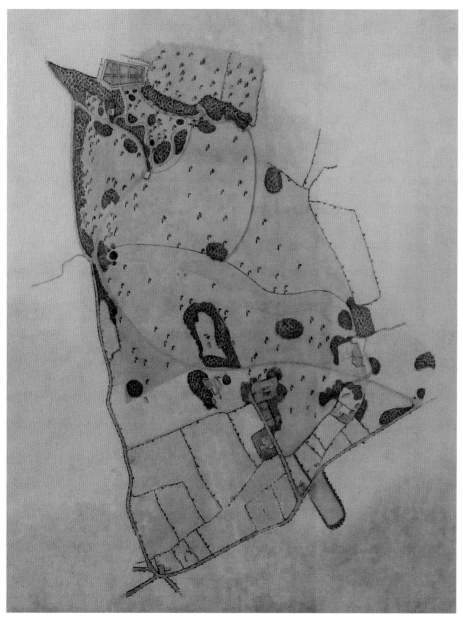

Figure 198. Haverfield's plan for the park at Stradsett.

Figure 199. Haverfield's design for a new hall at Stradsett.

and gravel, so making it a part of the gravel walk. This Loudon believed served to destroy any contrast between walking and sailing, of the kind that were an important part of Picturesque scenery, and he ends his discussion of the topic with the dismissive comment: 'It is of a piece with the rest of Mr. Repton's improvements, they tend to prettiness which, like *puns* in conversation, may produce momentary amusement.'[301] But he later modified his views, and in *The Landscape Gardening and Landscape Architecture of the late H. Repton, being his entire works on these subjects* in 1840, he described him as 'a man not less eminent for his artistical genius and taste, than for his goodness of heart, and amiability of character'.[302] In 1808 Loudon had a great future ahead of him, but was still only twenty-five years old and relatively unknown.

Loudon's design for the new landscape at Stradsett no longer exists but an estate plan of 1816 (Figure 200) shows it soon after completion.[303] Loudon's scheme was more sophisticated than Haverfield's and included the creation of a much larger (22-acre, c.9-hectare) lake with islands, a large bridge and four smaller bridges, the whole embellished with picturesque planting including an extensive pleasure ground around the eastern shore. A new entrance drive would lead in from an entrance in the north-western corner of the park, equipped with a lodge, to a new house on a new site, more centrally positioned within the park, to the north of the lake. A large walled kitchen garden would be built, also to the north of the lake, between the house and the pleasure ground.[304]

Surviving accounts and correspondence provide a vivid picture of the

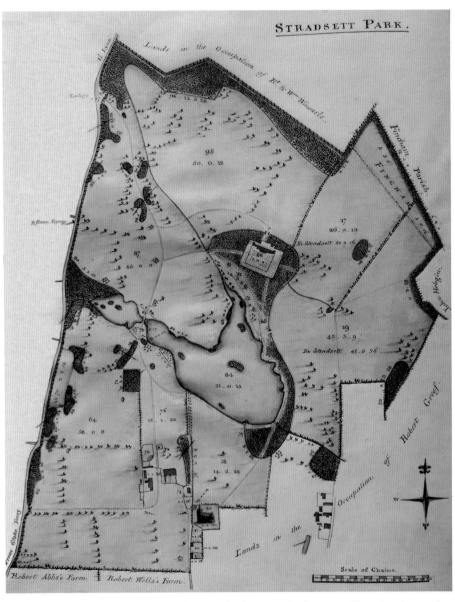

Figure 200. 1816 plan of Stradsett Park showing the house still on its site to the south of the lake and the new walled kitchen garden to the north.

work, and the problems, involved in implementing the design. Although all three men had been approached by Thomas Philip Bagge in 1808 it was not until early in 1810 that Loudon was asked to proceed. Work began soon afterwards and, as the year went on, he provided plans and designs for various parts of the grounds. In a letter dated 18 May he described how he had sent a plan for 'a Garden Melon ground Peach Grape & pine Stove & pine pits', enclosing a bill for ten guineas for the three drawings, as well as one for a further three guineas for the designs for two lodges which he had supplied in April.[305] By July he was able to write that 'It gives me great satisfaction that my sketches have met the approbation both of yourself and Mrs Bagge'. However, the question of costs, which was to prove so contentious later in the commission, had clearly not been settled, for in the same letter Loudon stated that he would do all the work needed to complete the plan submitted for £200, plus expenses, which should not exceed £180. Alternatively, he was prepared to charge for his time at a daily rate of five guineas, 'always excluding the House which you do not speak of'.[306] It appears that, at this time, Bagge had not yet decided to relocate his mansion. In July Loudon, apparently responding to Bagge's concerns about costs, suggested that he could do the work for £100 plus expenses, if Bagge decided not to create a lake.[307] The latter was the focal point of the design and its omission would have seriously compromised the aesthetic effect: fortunately, Bagge decided to continue with it as planned, but did not build a new house (Figure 201).

Loudon's scheme for Stradsett involved a huge amount of work which was carried out by estate workers, local builders and contractors. As he was only on site for a few days at a time, it is perhaps not surprising that work did not always run smoothly. In October 1810 he had discussions at Stradsett with Thomas Bagge and his adviser, Colonel Sir George Preston, which Loudon later described as covering the placing of the plantations, the situation of the proposed house and the removal of the existing lodge.[308] The new lodge had already been built but was 'placed totally different from the direction he intended to give it'.[309] Again there were problems over costs and fees. Loudon initially stated he thought it impossible to say how much it would cost to construct the lake but, when pressed, suggested that the new garden would cost £1,500 and the lake somewhere between £1,200 and

Figure 201. *Stradsett Hall, which escaped demolition to make way for a new house on the knoll north of the lake.*

Figure 202. *One of the four smaller bridges designed by Loudon. Stradsett Park.*

£2,000, concluding the 'he should imagine the whole expense of everything intended to be done without building a house would not exceed £4,000'.[310] At this point it was decided that someone was needed to guide the works on a day-to-day basis and a foreman, Alexander McLeish, was appointed. He began at Stradsett in November 1810 and remained there until 1813, keeping detailed records of progress in a series of diaries. He dealt with all the contractors and suppliers, including the nurseries supplying the plants for the park and pleasure grounds.

Work began on the lake in 1810 and the soil excavated was used to build up the 'knoll' to the north, the intended site of the new hall. A series of islands were formed in the lake and one large bridge and four smaller bridges, designed by Loudon, were constructed to cross it at various points (Figure 202). Loudon had set out his thoughts on lakes in his book *A Treatise on Forming, Improving and Managing Country Residences*, stating that they 'should be of irregular shape, more or less wooded and never entirely naked; always disguised by prominences and masses; and as often as occasion serves further varied by islands similarly managed'.[311] These principles he followed closely when forming the lake at Stradsett, and when viewed from the north it was so contrived that it seemed to appear and disappear behind the trees, almost like a meandering river. We can form a clearer impression of the effect Loudon was trying to achieve, both with the lake and the wider landscape, from oil paintings commissioned in 1811 from the Italian artist Agostino Aglio (Figures 203 and 204). Aglio had worked with the architect William Wilkins junior (son of Repton's friend), who employed him as draughtsman on his travels in Greece, Egypt and Italy from 1799 to 1802.

Figure 203 and Figure 204. *Above: the view south across Stradsett's new lake, with one of Loudon's bridges far right.*
Below: clumps of trees framing views inside the park and out across the wider countryside. Agostino Aglio.

Aglio came to England in 1803 and worked on the painting and decorating of theatres, churches and country houses: in 1808 he painted the ceiling of the Thornery at Woburn Abbey, which had been designed by Repton. His paintings of Stradsett show the landscape as it was intended to look after a few years, when the planting had begun to mature, and clearly illustrate the romantic, Picturesque effect Loudon was aiming at.

Loudon visited Stradsett in March 1811 and made sketches showing 'the effect of the water', and these may have been used by Aglio as the basis for his paintings.[312] Loudon, as his career developed, followed a different practice to Repton in that he presented drawings which only illustrated the effect of proposed improvements, and was critical of Repton's use of watercolours with slides which provided both 'before' and 'after' views. The purpose of these, he believed, was to 'save the expense or trouble of making two landscapes where it is thought one and a half, or less, may suffice'.[313] More importantly, he argued that the use of a flap made it impossible to make a fair comparison of the 'before' and 'after' views, as they could not be viewed at the same time.

Loudon provided further drawings for Stradsett, as well as instructions, as the scheme progressed. In May 1811 he supplied 'A whole sheet sketch for planting the islands promontories and margins of the lake' for which he charged three guineas.[314] This again has not survived but some hints of his planting style are provided by the minutes of a meeting held at Stradsett in October 1810. In these he expressed strong opposition to placing tall trees beside the new drive leading from the north-west entrance towards the lake, preferring instead the use of plants 'only of low growth, such as Box, Holly & Thorne, thereby forming a rest for the Eye to give an appearance of greater expanse to the water'.[315] Like Repton, he was clearly aware of how planting could be used to create an illusion of space. Early in the work Loudon ordered trees from the London nursery of Gray & Co., but local nurseries were also used, the main one being John Griffin of Mundford, who had already been supplying Stradsett before Loudon started there. From early 1811 to March 1813 the Mundford Nursery provided around 92,000 deciduous trees and almost 39,000 conifers for the new park. These included 19,800 alder, 17,600 beech, 12,600 birch, 22,800 spruce fir and 10,750 larch. Smaller numbers of chestnut, ash, elm, hazel, oak, poplar and weeping willow, among others, were also bought. Fruit trees, including apples, cherries, pears and pomegranates, were purchased, together with a range of shrubs such as barberries, broad-leaved laurels, Portugal laurels, holly, lavender, variegated box, syringa and pyracantha. The nursery continued to supply trees and shrubs for the design after Loudon's involvement at Stradsett had ended, delivering in late 1813 and early 1814 a rather wider variety of shrubs, including Euonymus, broom, lilac, rhododendron, guelder rose, potentilla and sweet briar, all probably intended for the pleasure ground.[316]

Another feature of Loudon's design was the large walled kitchen garden with its extensive range of glasshouses. Plans, elevations and specifications of the garden walls, towers, sheds, melon pit and hothouses were prepared by Loudon in January 1812, and a copy of the specifications for the hothouses sent to the firm of Jordans in Birmingham. They supplied the materials for the centre house and peach houses, and even sent a workman for fifty-one days to fit them up. The total cost for the hothouses alone was £940 15s., giving some idea of the overall sums involved and the huge scale of the work.[317]

Most of the work was complete, except for the construction of the planned new hall, by 1813 when a dispute arose over the 5% commission that Loudon wanted to charge on the materials and work. Loudon proposed arbitration but Bagge refused and the case was referred to the King's Bench, although it never came to court. By this time costs had soared from Loudon's estimated £4,000 to more than £7,000. In March 1813 Loudon left for an extended trip to Russia and northern Europe, only returning to England in September 1814. In his many writings he does not appear ever to mention Stradsett, despite the fact that it was such a large project and exemplified many of his ideas on Picturesque design. Almost certainly, this was because of the acrimonious way that it ended. Nevertheless, Stradsett remains a largely intact example of a Picturesque landscape and a reflection of the ideas and fashions of the time, as well as a fascinating illustration of John Claudius Loudon's early work. The new hall was never built, however, and as a result the landscape we see today is, in one important sense, the reverse of what was intended. In particular, the lake lies to the north of the house rather than to the south, as planned, and was thus never seen from the windows of the house with the sunlight playing on the surface of the water.

In spite of the escalating problems he was experiencing at Stradsett, in 1812 he supplied proposals for another Norfolk country house, Gillingham, in the south-east of the county. Gillingham Hall had been built by Sir Nicholas Bacon in the early seventeenth century. It was altered and extended by Sir Edmund Bacon, who inherited it in 1721. More changes were made following the marriage in 1755 of Susan Bacon and Francis Schutz (sometimes spelt Schultz), when the windows of the entrance front were replaced with sashes, and a new drawing room and bay window were built at the south end of the house.[318] At the end of the eighteenth century there was only a small (c.20 hectare) park here, hemmed in to west and north by public roads, to judge from Faden's county map of 1797, and the two parish churches (St Mary and All Saints – the latter already ruined) lay outside it. It seems likely that the hall had originally been provided with elaborate formal gardens, of which only a rectangular canal, to its south, survived by this time. Following the death of Francis Schutz in 1779, his son John Bacon Schutz inherited Gillingham Hall, but he died aged just thirty-four years in 1790, leaving a widow, Elizabeth (1761–1817) and two daughters, Susan Elizabeth (1783–1853) and Harriet (1787–1861).

A road closure order was passed in 1811, terminating the public highways lying north and west of the park, and the following year the young Loudon was commissioned to suggest improvements.[319] He produced a handwritten volume of proposals, accompanied by four maps, which was addressed to 'Miss Schutz'. While this suggests that he was employed by the unmarried daughter Susan Elizabeth, in all probability it was actually her mother, Elizabeth, who commissioned him, and who annotated his proposals with a number of pithy marginal comments. Following soon after his disastrous commission at Stradsett, Loudon may have hoped that his work at Gillingham would be less problematic and would give him an opportunity to put some of his Picturesque ideas into practice.[320] In his opening remarks he described how

At Gillingham, which may be truly called a fine old place, every important feature of a country residence already exists.

A venerable mansion, in the ancient English style – old woods – considerable extent of Park, – and well cloathed distant scenery – the house and Park centrically situated, with respect to the valuable and highly improveable property to which they belong.[321]

He praised other local features of the landscape which chimed with his Picturesque sensibilities, including the parish church of St Mary and the 'detached ivied tower and Churchyard' of the ruined All Saints.[322] However, he was not confident enough to set out a single Picturesque vision, and instead offered Miss Schutz two sets of plans, both of which primarily addressed the need to extend the park. In what he described as the 'modern' design he proposed a small landscape park, relatively enclosed and self-contained in character, reflecting normal current practice. But the park in his 'ancient' design was bounded by sunk fences, providing wide views over the surrounding countryside, which would be embellished with tree-planting, including a 'strip of planting or even a row of hedgerow trees along the

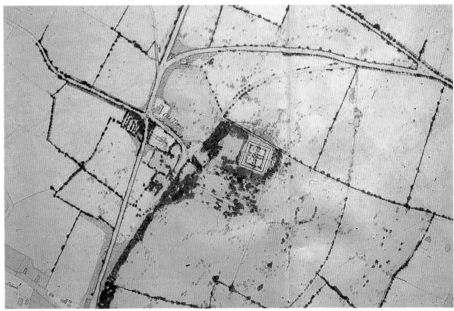

Figures 205. One of Loudon's plans for Gillingham, near Beccles.

170

Figures 206 and 207. Two more of Loudon's plans for Miss Schutz at Gillingham.

fences' (Figures 205, 206 and 207). There was also to be an avenue of trees focused on the house.

Miss Schutz, seemingly ever conscious of cost, responded to his suggestions with the remark, 'Will not this plan of sinking fences be very expensive?'[323] Loudon offered different approaches to the hall, designed with the intention of 'shewing to a stranger the chief beauties of the place before he enters the mansion', as well as advice on tree-planting and woodland management. Miss Schutz seems to have agreed with many of his proposals regarding the thinning and pruning of existing woodland, and she commented that 'the necessity of all this I have seen for years but had not judgement to direct it'. His plans for planting further woods, with oak, ash, elm and Spanish chestnut 'as permanent trees'; holly, box and thorn – together with oak coppice – as undergrowth; and Scotch larch, spruce and poplars for 'immediate effect and early profit in 15–20 years' – also seem to have been acceptable. However, his proposal for removing some existing trees met with the sceptical comment that 'local attachment almost prevents the possibility of this' while his plans for planting individual trees, whilst aesthetically pleasing to Miss Schutz, provoked the frustrated comment that 'Beech grows very slowly at G', suggesting that Loudon had not fully appreciated the landscape which he had been asked to consider for improvement.

Loudon also put forward plans for concealing the marshes beside the River Waveney – which flanked the parkland to the south, for improving the stables and constructing a coach house. Many of his suggestions are minor aesthetic improvements or practical alterations and seemingly not that original, with Miss Schutz commenting wearily 'I have had many consultations as to making a coach house of the small stable'. Only in relation to the existing canal, which he advocated retaining, does a nod to modern planting tastes creep in to his proposals, with Loudon suggesting the use of 'American shrubs here and there on its margins and aquatics such as water lilies', but even then, he remains firmly focused on his Picturesque vision, suggesting it could still 'harmonize with the ancient character of the place'.[324]

Loudon's advice on extending the pleasure ground was fairly simple, proposing that it be enlarged to include the existing flower garden and orchard, with the whole enclosed using sunken fences or hurdles. He did not suggest additional planting but recommended that the area should be grazed by sheep. In addition, he argued that

> Some more walks may be desirable; as from the pleasure ground at the stables winding through both churchyards – across the park and round the outside of the garden, to join the present walk at the flower garden.[325]

Perhaps conscious of the difficulties with payments he had encountered at Stradsett and wary of Miss Schutz's reluctance to invest too heavily in the improvements, he stated that 'every alteration proposed on the grounds according to either design' could be achieved for two thousand pounds, including all the 'alteration on the stables, tower and the erection of fences, and one cottage at the pound'. However, his suggestion that the sum could be reduced through selling the trees felled as part of the proposed changes met with the sharp response: 'I doubt Mr Loudon does not know how low Timber sells in this part of the World.'[326]

Other than the annotated comments on Loudon's proposal there is no record of how his plans were received, but an estate map of 1818 suggests that in the end elements of both the 'ancient' and 'modern' designs were implemented.[327] A new approach was created, the park was expanded to take in the two churches, shelter belts were established and an extensive lawn created below the main façade of the house. The canal was extended and considerable tree-planting took place. James Grigor included an account of Gillingham Hall in his *Eastern Arboretum* of 1841, which was reproduced in the *Gardeners Magazine* the same year, edited by Loudon. He was enthusiastic not only about the Picturesque ruined church tower 'mantled in ivy', but also about the many and varied trees found in the park.[328] Whilst many of the larger specimens clearly pre-dated Loudon's work here, others were probably established on his advice. Grigor thus praised the groups of trees that had been planted across the park, including the beeches, which 'have here free scope, the spray falling and feathering downwards on all sides, and blending happily with the silver fir and larch'. He noted, however, that they were 'not of great size': Loudon may have succeeded in persuading Miss Schutz to plant this species, but her prophetic warnings, written in the margins of his plan, appear to have come true!

Loudon's designs for Gillingham were, as at Stradsett, largely influenced by his desire to fulfil Picturesque principles, based on the ideas of William Gilpin.[329] But his proposals in fact share many similarities with the ideas of Repton, in their emphasis on the approach to the house, in the use of 'borrowed' views (as at Sheringham), in the introduction of walks to connect the varied parts of the landscape. Even the desire to incorporate the ruins of the church into the design, although Picturesque in inspiration, was also classically Reptonian, as we have seen in the design for Barningham.[330]

The Kennedys at Stow Hall

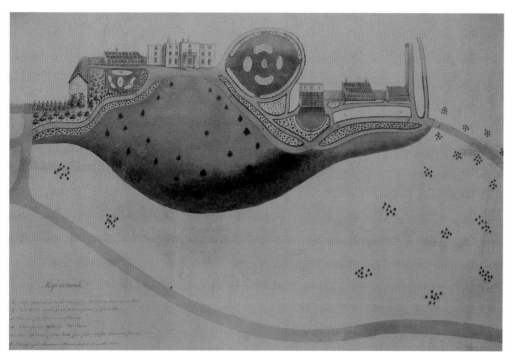
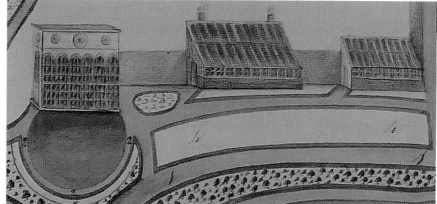

Figure 208. Left: the Kennedys' 1802 plan for Stow Hall. Right: details of the glasshouses, conservatory and the hall itself.

Another interesting and well-documented example of an elaborate garden laid out in this period, but not by Repton, was that at Stow Hall, situated in Stow Bardolph, around 2 miles (3.5 km) north-east of Downham Market. The house and its grounds had had a long and complex history since first acquired by Sir Nicholas Hare in 1553. Relics of the seventeenth-century landscape still remain today and include the east wall of the present kitchen garden, evidently a survivor from the enclosed gardens near the old hall; and a mile-long avenue of trees extending north from the house, known as The Chase. James Grigor, writing around 1840, describes the 'magnificent avenue of oaks and elms'.[331] No elms survive today and the oldest trees remaining are oaks and sweet chestnuts.[332] The estate was inherited in

1791 by Thomas Leigh (c.1749–1834) when his uncle, Sir George Hare, died without an heir. Thomas changed his name by Act of Parliament to Hare and in 1818 was made the 1st Baronet of the new creation. His first wife was Mary, daughter of Admiral Sir Francis Geary, and, after her death in 1801, he was married for a second time, in 1803, to Anne Elizabeth Graves, daughter of Admiral Graves. In 1796 Thomas replaced the old Elizabethan hall with a new house and set about enhancing it with a suitably fashionable garden. He turned, not to Repton, but to the landscape designers and nurserymen John Kennedy (1759–1842) and his son, Lewis (1789–1877). They supplied plans for improving parks and gardens through their nursery business, Lee and Kennedy, based in Hammersmith near London. Horticultural experts at the centre of the burgeoning trade in exotic plants, they were well placed both to provide plants to their clients and to design the settings in which they would be placed, something which marked them out strongly from Repton.

A plan dated 1802 is a proposal for the grounds of the newly completed house (Figure 208).[333] It was probably drawn by John Kennedy: it has been suggested that it might be the work of a very young Lewis, but he would only have been around 13 years old at the time.[334] A conservatory is shown, adjoining the west side of the house, in front of which are 'Clumps for American plants' and a 'New Border of Peat Earth Four feet wide for American Plants'. A large circular lawn to the east of the house is edged with borders and has lozenge-shaped beds cut into it. South of the kitchen garden a greenhouse, hothouse and a third smaller glasshouse are shown. In front of the greenhouse, a circular lawn is edged with a border for 'Roses and Flowers'. The plan, which may have been only gradually executed, focuses on the area around the mansion but in 1809 the Kennedys together produced a signed design for a new approach to the hall, running in from a new entrance at the junction of the Lynn Road and Stradsett Road (Figure 217).

In 1812 Lewis Kennedy presented Hare and his wife Anne Elizabeth with a bound volume, containing a series of sketches of Stow Hall, all beautifully drawn and similar to one of Repton's Red Books, but more 'portrait' in shape and with a green cover.[335] He had begun to present his proposals in this way a few years earlier. Some of the views show work already completed or underway, others proposed changes, which are explained and justified in the accom panying text. Kennedy states in his introduction that, on a previous visit to Stow, Mrs Hare had expressed 'A wish that some drawings may be done in the way here attempted',[336] while in 1820 John Wiggins, the agent for the estate, praised the activities at Stow of 'Mr Kennedy' but also emphasised how 'the embellishment of the elegant Mansion and Grounds of Stow Hall . . . are much indebted to the taste of the Hon[ble] Lady Hare for many of their present useful and decorative features'. All this indicates, perhaps, that she played a major role in the development of the grounds.[337]

Figure 209. *Originally from a bound book presented to Thomas and Anne Hare, the Kennedy's design for the new entrance to Stow Park. 1812.*

Figure 210. *The Kennedys' view from the south of Stow Park.*

Figure 211. *The second view towards Stow Hall from the south, but a little further to the east than Figure 210.*

The first view shows the entrance gates with a lodge to the right and almshouses to the left (Figure 209).[338] Like Repton, Kennedy clearly considered the first impressions of the hall and its grounds to be of prime importance, and thought that the entrance drive at Stow required improvement (as had his father 'ever since his first visit to Stow'). He described, in terms very reminiscent of Repton, how 'the Approach to the House should correspond with it in consequence, & the entrance to a Gentleman's residence should point out such character'. But both were here marred by the presence of buildings or structures which were purely functional, unattractive, or both. The 'wretched smith's shop, almshouses, &c.', which could be picturesque enough in the right place, 'were here perfect nuisances, as were the whole contents of the Coach Yard on the left, viz. the pig yard, horse pond, &c. &c.' He proposed creating a new farmyard and stables to the left of the drive, screened with plantations. On the right-hand side would be a pheasantry and pleasure ground, and the new drive would join the old road to the hall just beyond the end of the conservatory. This was the new approach shown on the plan drawn up in 1809: Kennedy's comment in the 1812 book of proposals, that it 'has now received your sanctions', makes clear that it was about to be put in place.

The next two sketches show the hall viewed from the south, each from a slightly different angle (Figures 210 and 211). This Kennedy considered to be the best view of the mansion and its gardens, and it certainly presents a most picturesque scene. The house is seen across a lawn and the 'noble Greenhouse' can be glimpsed, surrounded by shrubberies, Kennedy describing the 'varied tints produced by a fine inter-mixture of the most beautiful & ornamental hardy exotics'. This view shows a landscape which had 'nearly attained to a state of perfection': only the area of planting screening the big barn and conservatory was still to mature. The second view, from the south-west side, shows a similar scene, but includes a glimpse of the conservatory to the west of the hall.

The third, fourth and fifth views all show the hall from the north and, as well as showing works already carried out, or in progress, include a number of options for further improvements. These mainly concern a small pond in the park, dismissed by Kennedy as 'the unsightly bit of

Figure 212. One of the three views from the north; the pond is hidden by trees.

water'. One shows how the pond could be partially hidden by placing posts and chains and some bushy shrubs around its margins, but this is hardly a great improvement (unfortunately, this painting has been removed from the album and is badly damaged, so cannot be reproduced). The next view shows how the pond could be totally hidden by a mass of shrubbery and trees (Figure 212). But the best option Kennedy leaves until last: the enlargement of the pond into a lake, extending out into the park. Kennedy acknowledged that this would be a costlier option, but emphasised that there is 'no doubt, it will be consider'd as amply repaid in the sequent consequence and beauty it will add to STOW HALL' (Figure 213). Thomas Hare was not convinced, or perhaps he felt that he had, by this time, spent enough on the grounds. Either way, the lake was never constructed. One of these views also shows the entrance to what Kennedy describes as 'the most beautifull (*sic*) COVERED WALK in the Kingdom'. Just discernible in the painting are two figures about to enter the walk, which appears to have extended along the outside of the west wall of the kitchen garden. It consisted of wrought-iron arches over which climbing plants were grown, a feature Kennedy was to use elsewhere, as in the trellis-work entrance

Figure 213. *The Kennedys' most ambitious suggestion, converting the pond into a lake.*

to the flower gardens at Oddington, Gloucestershire, or the tunnel arbour at Chiswick.[339] The arches remained beside the kitchen garden wall long after the structure had collapsed or been taken down (they were still there in 1993) and some have been reused over recent decades elsewhere in the grounds.

Later in 1812, after he had presented his book of sketches and proposals to the Hares, Kennedy prepared a design for a flower garden to be placed in front of the Greenhouse (Figure 214).[340] It was to be elliptical in shape, surrounded by a gravel walk, and with flower beds edged with grass, those nearest the Green House having quite elaborate shapes. At the centre was

Figure 214. Plan for the flower garden in front of the greenhouse at Stow Hall.

Figure 215. The ornamental aviary designed for Stow Hall, probably by the Kennedys.

a small oval pond for goldfish. Lewis Kennedy was later to become known as a designer of flower gardens, at Chiswick House and Wanstead amongst other places, but Stow may have been his first foray in this direction.

Illustrations survive for a number of buildings which were planned for the gardens around this time. A drawing of an aviary in Chinese style may be by the Kennedys (it is unsigned: Figure 215);[341] while William Newham, a King's Lynn architect, supplied ideas ranging from a triumphal arch and a domed temple to a rustic shelter (Figure 216). The rustic shelter carries a note stating that this was the design chosen by the Hares, implying that the grandiose and inappropriate arch had been wisely rejected.[342] These drawings are dated 1809 and may have been commissioned by the Kennedys around the time they were considering their design for the new approach to the hall.

Glasshouses were a key feature of the Stow gardens and allowed the Hares to display a wide range of exotic plants, many introduced quite recently from America, Australia and South Africa. There were three in all: the conservatory which adjoined the mansion; the Great Greenhouse; and the Great Pine Stove. The conservatory was the first to be built and appears on both the 1809 plans for the approach and on an estate map surveyed in 1812 (Figures 217 and 218).[343] The Greenhouse and Pine Stove do not appear on the latter, and were thus presumably erected later, although the Greenhouse appears in Lewis Kennedy's sketches of 1812 and the text implies that it was in existence by this time, so it may have been built in that year. All three glasshouses are mentioned in particulars of the estate prepared in 1829 when Sir Thomas was hoping to lease the property.[344] A list of plants in the glasshouses was prepared by Lee and Kennedy (probably by Lewis, judging by the handwriting) which vividly demonstrates the variety and sheer scale of the collection, including numerous members of the genera

Figure 216. *Newham's designs for (clockwise from top left) a rustic shelter, a triumphal arch, a domed temple and summerhouse, dated 1809.*

Figure 217. John Kennedy's 1809 Stow plan for a new entrance, showing the hall (far right) next to it the conservatory with an ornamental flower garden in front. The stable complex is top left and the square in the middle is marked 'pheasants'.

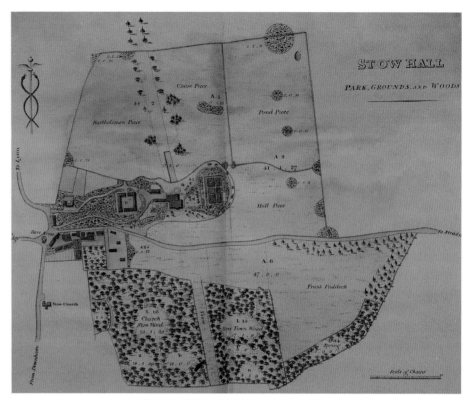

Figure 218. 1812 Stow estate plan.

Protea, Geranium, Camellia, Hypericum, Solanum, Mimosa, Amaryllis, Hibiscus and *Jasmin*; rare specimens like *Yucca filamentosa* and *Strelitzia reginae*; and more than 230 varieties of *Erica*. There was also a Rosary in the gardens, and the catalogue lists the 280 varieties of rose to be found there. A sale of furniture and effects from Stow Hall held in 1831 included plants to be sold from all three glasshouses.[345] Neither the greenhouse nor the pine stove appear on an estate plan of 1840, so they had presumably been removed by then.

Some idea of the gardens at their height is provided by particulars prepared by Wiggins in 1829 when Sir Thomas was hoping to lease the property. The Pleasure Grounds were:

> Very tastefully disposed in the modern style with agreeable Walks Shrubberies and Lawn, covered walks, flower gardens, American Plants, Rustic Seats, Arbours, Rockwork and Rosaries, forming altogether a unique specimen of the modern taste in Gardening and a most delightful retreat.[346]

Wiggins also describes how the gardens have 'under the professional

Figure 219. The Kennedys' Frontispiece from their book of illustrations created for their clients at Stow Hall. The military and naval themes were chosen to appeal to Sir Thomas, the soldier, and Lady Anne, the daughter of an admiral.

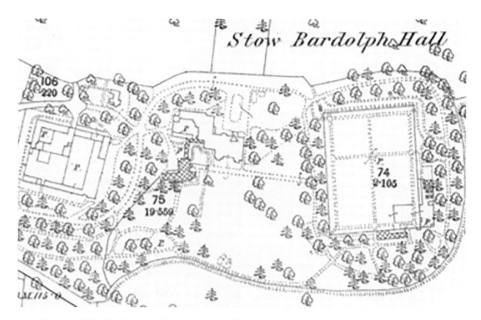

Figure 220. Ordnance Survey First Edition 25-inch map, surveyed in 1885 and published 1886. The map shows the hall with its impressive conservatory, the stables and other offices, and the kitchen garden with a glasshouse along its south wall.

direction of Mr. Kennedy become a most complete and costly example of ornamental gardening and few places can exhibit a collection of rare and valuable Exotic's and of the more beautiful Shrubs and Flowers'.

The Kennedys' association with Stow lasted for many years and the landscape they helped to create was at the cutting edge of fashion. In its emphasis on pleasure grounds, formal flower gardens, and entrances it invites comparison with Repton's designs – especially those made in his later years. The emphasis given in their plans to the choice and availability of plants also shows a burgeoning interest in plant collection and plant breeding which, by the middle decades of the nineteenth century, had come to dominate the design of elite gardens. Lewis Kennedy went on to have a short but influential career as a garden designer, but Stow was his first major project, and it exhibited many of the features and elements that

he would go on to use elsewhere. After Sir Thomas's Hare's death in 1834, the estate passed to his son, also Thomas, 2nd Baronet (1807–1880). It was he who, in 1873, demolished the Georgian house and had it rebuilt in neo-Tudor style to a design by David Brandon.[347] During the Second World War the house later became a hospital but, after its closure in 1980, fell into disrepair and was finally demolished in 1994. The Hares converted the stables into a residence and have continued to develop the gardens in new ways, partly around the few standing remains of the hall.

Conclusion: Repton and his Contemporaries

The places described above are notable as the work of men who were, or were becoming, garden designers of national importance. But the late eighteenth and early nineteenth centuries saw many landowners make alterations to their grounds along similar lines, often as their homes were rebuilt or modernised: in June 1819 Edward Everett, a successful King's Lynn brewer and merchant who had acquired Middleton Hall, typically described how he had 'commanded considerable alterations and improvements in and about my mansion house'.[348] Many parks were – as at Sheringham – provided with glimpses out into the wider estate land, forging a measure of 'connection' in the way that Repton often advocated; the sales particulars for the Wallington estate in west Norfolk boasted in 1828 that the mansion 'although secluded, commands interesting views'.[349] New and more direct entrance drives were laid out, with ornamental lodges at the entrance; and larger and more elaborate pleasure grounds were frequently created. At Earsham Hall, for example – a mansion built in the early eighteenth century by John Buxton, and which was acquired by the Windham family in 1721[350] – the immediate grounds of the house were progressively elaborated. William Windham commissioned the architect John Soane to convert an existing orangery into a new 'Music Room' between 1784 and 1786,[351] and the old wilderness (or woodland garden) beside it, and the pleasure grounds more generally, were developed by Windham's successors, Joseph Windham and William Windham Dalling. Accounts from 1797 show that four regular gardeners were employed, and extra labour was brought in for activities such as 'digging clumps'. Nursery bills from the period between 1816 and 1823 record the purchase of oak, ash, sycamore and other trees probably destined for the many new plantations established by Dalling, but the privet, laurels, double-blossom cherry, Balm of Gilead and probably the black Italian poplars and redwoods, were presumably for the 'wilderness' and pleasure grounds.[352]

A few years after Repton's death, probably in 1823, Seaman Holmes rebuilt Brooke Hall, a few miles to the south-east of Norwich, on a virgin site, some way to the south of the old hall, to designs by William Wilkins Junior (Figures 221 and 222). The project was completed, following Holmes' death

Figure 221. Watercolour of Brooke Hall, now hanging in Thetford Ancient House Museum.

Figure 222. Brooke Hall from 1912 sale catalogue.

182

Figure 223. Tudor-style North Lodge, Brooke Hall.

in 1826, by his brother the Rev. Thomas Holmes and his son John. A friend recorded in 1828 how he saw trees being transplanted in the new park using 'Sir H. Steuart's system', and how in 1831 John Holmes 'shows us his new trees he has transplanted and the new road and explains his plan for a piece of water'.[353] The tithe map of 1840s shows the new house overlooking a lake to the south, in a park of c.40 hectares, containing scattered clumps and only partially surrounded by belts of trees.[354] In the manner of Repton, the house was hidden from view of the approach drive until revealed in a classic 'burst': James Grigor described how the trees 'screen and partially hide what would have presented a full and staring front of the entire residence, at the same time occupying an otherwise bleak outline'.[355]There were two lodges: one, North Lodge, in Tudor style with a porch; the other in *Cottage Orné* style (Figure 223).[356]

While echoes of Repton's approach to the laying out of country-house landscapes can be found throughout Norfolk and continued (as at Brooke) for some decades after his death, what is less clear is the extent to which this was a simple consequence of his influence and example. His treatment of entrances is a case in point. As early as 1794 Repton advocated the creation of entrance drives which began close to houses and cottages, or within a village owned by the estate in question. At Houghton, several years before 1800, a new approach to the hall was laid out which began at the end of the 'model' village of New Houghton, the houses of which thereby came to cluster deferentially at the entrance: 'the rich man at his castle, the poor man at his gate'. Similar arrangements were put in place at Stow Bardolph by the Kennedys in 1809; at Holkham a few years later and at North Elmham in the 1830s, among other places.[357] While some of these examples may well reflect the direct influence of Repton's writings, the change made at Houghton, at least, seems too early. Whether motivated by a desire to 'appropriate' the local landscape, or to express a paternalistic concern for the local community, the development probably reflects complex changes in the relationship between landowners and their tenants, rather than the simple 'influence' of one gifted designer. Much the same can be said about the proliferations of entrance lodges in this period. Before the 1790s only a small number of country houses, mainly the larger examples, possessed lodges. By the 1840s around two-thirds of those in Norfolk were provided with them. Most examples were in Tudor, gothic or 'rustic' style, like most of those designed by Repton himself. Typical was that erected in 1837 at the entrance to Middleton Hall, of carstone rubble with brick dressings, elaborate bargeboards, pendants and finials and octagonal brick chimneys (Figure 224).[358] That at the entrance to Ryston in west Norfolk displayed such 'rustic' ingredients as a thatched roof and circular plan (Figure 225). But the explosion in their numbers seems to have begun before Repton's writings can have had much of an impact and, once again, their popularity must reflect shifts in social attitudes. They manifest a desire both to monitor arrivals at the residence, and to advertise its presence to passing travellers. They also express, in their design, an idealised and somewhat romanticised view of rural life. The enthusiasm for lodges, in other words, was not simply a 'fashion' arising from the influence and publications of one man.

Figure 224. *The Old Lodge built in 1837, Middleton Hall.*

Figure 225. *A rustic lodge known as The Round House, at Ryston Park.*

The wide adoption of many elements of Repton's design palette probably arose from the fact that the late eighteenth and early nineteenth centuries saw a massive expansion in the number of parks but, in Norfolk as elsewhere in the country, mainly in the numbers of small and medium-sized ones. Few really large parks were created, either from scratch or by expanding existing examples, after c.1790: Stradsett and Ryston are among the few exceptions in Norfolk.[359] The paucity of lakes in these new landscapes, and the small size of those which were constructed, is striking: almost all the true lakes (water bodies covering more than 2 hectares) to be found in Norfolk parks, date to the period before c.1790 and the exceptions, including Stradsett and Brooke, were not large by comparison with earlier examples, covering 7 and 3 hectares respectively, compared with the 13 hectares of the lake at Holkham or the 10 hectares of that at Kimberley. This is unlikely to be related to the fact that Repton himself designed few examples, compared to his predecessor Brown. Rather, it is simply because smaller parks, created by men with limited means, were less likely to contain expensive and extensive bodies of water than the great aristocratic landscapes of the previous period. An increasing focus by professional designers on villas and smaller manor houses, rather than large mansions, also partly explains the attention now paid to pleasure grounds and gardens, although this undoubtedly also had other causes – changes in styles of country-house architecture, the ever-rising numbers of exotic plants available from commercial nurseries, and the need to develop appropriate areas for their display. Again, Repton was at the cutting edge of fashion but other designers were probably level with him: the Kennedys' geometric flower garden at Stow Hall, laid out in 1812, was probably earlier than anything designed on similar lines by Repton.

This is not to suggest that all the landscape gardeners in this period – professional or amateur, national or local – were creating parks and gardens which were stylistically indistinguishable. Loudon, for example, designed at Stradsett a park more densely and lushly planted than anything created by Repton, in a style which looked back to the ideas of Payne Knight and Price and forward to landscape gardeners of the 1830s and 40s, such as William Sawrey Gilpin. Nor is it to deny that Repton, through his books as much as through his actual works, was the most influential and the most well known of landscape designers in the years around 1800. It is Repton, after all, who is referred to in Jane Austen's *Mansfield Park* of 1814, clearly by then a household name. But Repton was a man of his times, designing for a market, and other people were doing the same, and were thus working in a broadly similar style.

We might, however, note a suspicion that in the period after 1800, and certainly in the last years of his career, many of 'Repton's' commissions may have owed as much the ideas and artistry of his architect son John; and that over time his own interests shifted decisively in the direction of architecture in its widest sense – to the design of houses, garden buildings,

and the structured, built elements of gardens, such as terraces. It was perhaps his particular concern for such matters that really distinguishes Repton from his contemporaries, and also explains much of his success. An obituary published in 1818 perhaps summarises his career and his contribution as well as any modern observers.

> Mr Repton was an artist of elegant attainments and good taste, more calculated to follow than to lead, and more attached to the beautiful and pretty than to the grand style of art. He was evidently more at home in Gothic Architecture than Landscape Gardening.[360]

185

Appendix 1

Book of Humphry Repton's drawings

A book of Humphry Repton's black and white, pen and ink drawings in the Norwich Castle Museum and Art Gallery, was acquired from a private collection in 1985. These drawings are dated 1779 to 1880 and have been pasted into a tan-coloured, leather-bound book with a simple, gold floral border on the front cover (similar to some of the Repton Red Books) and gold floral decoration on the spin, with the title: *Drawings by H Repton*. Inside the front cover is a pencil inscription telling us: 'this book of drawings by my father, was given to me by my older brother John Adey Repton' and it is thought by the Museum to have belonged to George Stanley Repton. The title page (right) tells us they were drawn while he was living at Sustead and are of 'Noblemen and Gentlemen's Seats and other Striking Views in the County of Norfolk'. Many of the small drawings have been copied faithfully and reproduced as engravings within Mostyn Armstrong's *The History and Antiquities of the County of Norfolk*, 1781. Stuck in, next to several of these drawings, is an example of the engraving they inspired. The drawings in this Appendix, marked with a red dot, indicate that they appear as Armstrong engravings shown earlier in this book.

The Norfolk Gardens Trust was delighted that in March 2018, they were able to fund the photography of these images, in order that they may be available to the public to view on the Norfolk Museums Collections website. http://norfolkmuseumscollections.org/collections/. Sadly, this took place too late to include them in this book's main text, but they have been included below for the record, and the readers' enjoyment!

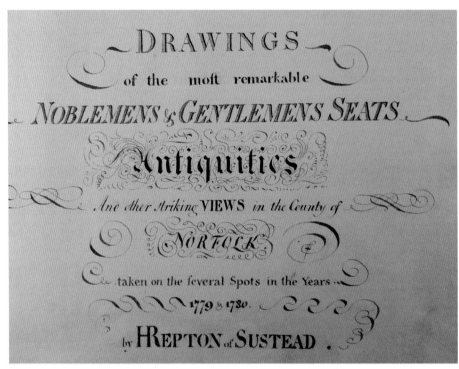

Title page from the book of Humphry Repton's drawings

1. View in Sustead – Grazing Lands.

2. Town Barningham Church in Norfolk.

3. Bayfield – from a spot near the road from Holt to Langham.

4. Beeston Priory - from the South West in Mr Woodrow's Yard.

5. Wolterton, from the Pleasure Ground facing the Library.

6. Heydon, from the South West.

7. Blickling, from the Aylsham Road.

8. Sall, from the Great Road betwixt Cawston and Reepham.

9. Hanworth, from the Lawn very near the House.

10. Sall Church, from the N.E.

11. Gunton Church.

12. Walsingham Abbey, in the garden.

189

13. Witton – this image is very close to the Peacock's image in Figure 100.

14. Warham, from the Danish Camp.

15. S.W. view of Cromer in Norfolk, near the road to Runcton.

16. Irmingland Hall in Norfolk, from the road to Corpusty, from Heydon.

17. Barningham, at the Entrance of the Avenue.

18. Spixworth, from the Norwich Road which leads to ye Church.

19. Easton Lodge.

20. Felbrigg, 'NB the stables and barns now standing, are here supposed removed'. (A tree has been placed over this area in Armstrong).

21. Irmingland Hall.

22. Wood Dalling.

23. Stifkey *als* Stukey Hall.

24. South West view of the Convent of Grey-Friers at Walsingham.

25. A View from Sherringham Heath (*sic*).

26. Engraving of Baconsthorpe, pencilled note reads 'N.B. The original drawing of this was given to the Rev'd Mr Hewitt of Baconsthorpe'.

27. Westwick.

28. Kimberley.

29. The only image sketched directly onto the book's page – rather than pasted in like all the others – there's no title but it could be Aylsham Church.

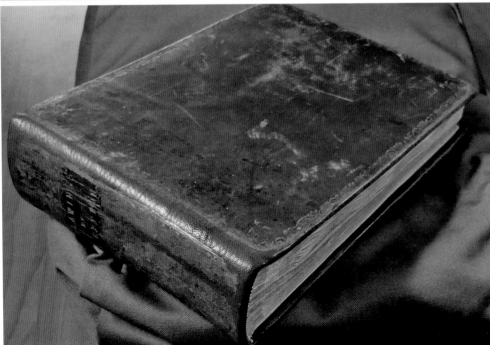

The leather-bound book of Humphry Repton's drawings, now kept at Norwich Castle Museum.

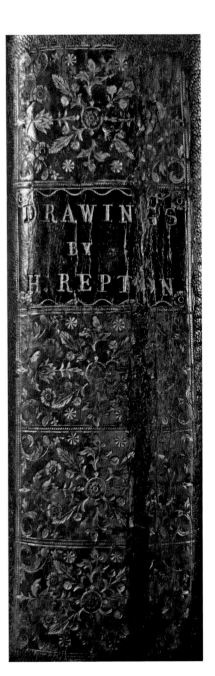

Appendix 2. Architectural Drawings for Barningham

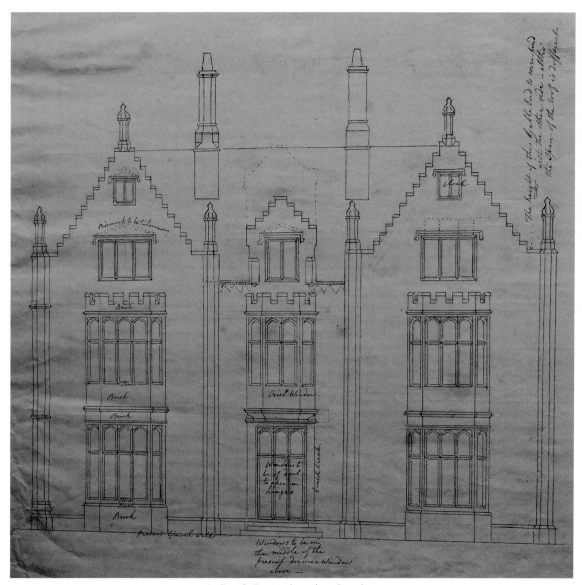

1. South Front elevation drawing.

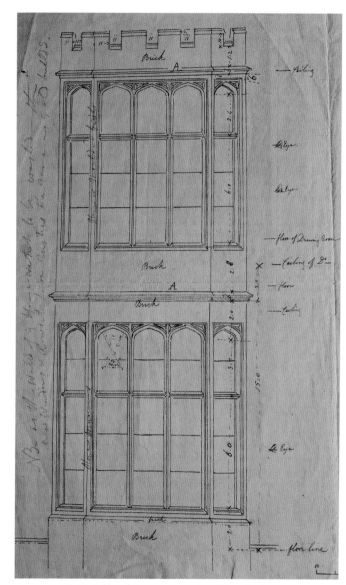

2. Details of the proposed gothic windows.

195

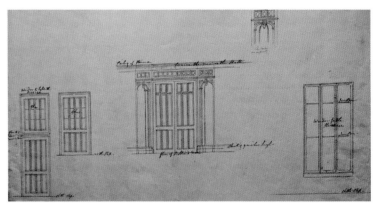

1. Window and door details

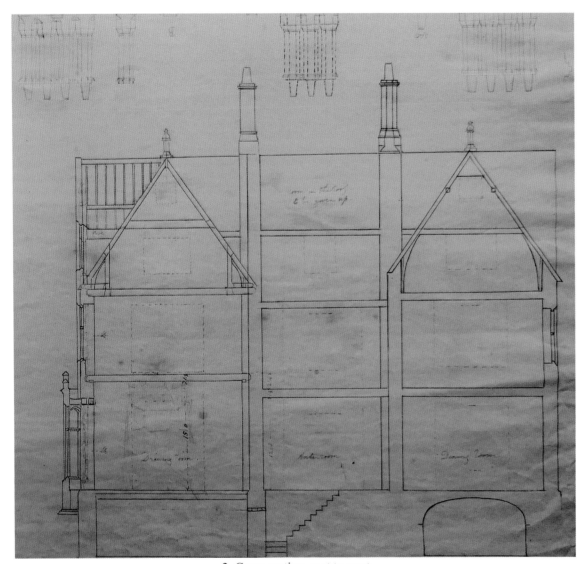

2. Cross section, east to west

3. Design for 2 chimney pieces in the Billiards Room

196

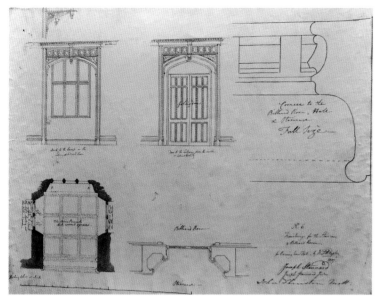

4. Finishings for the Staircase and Billiards Room

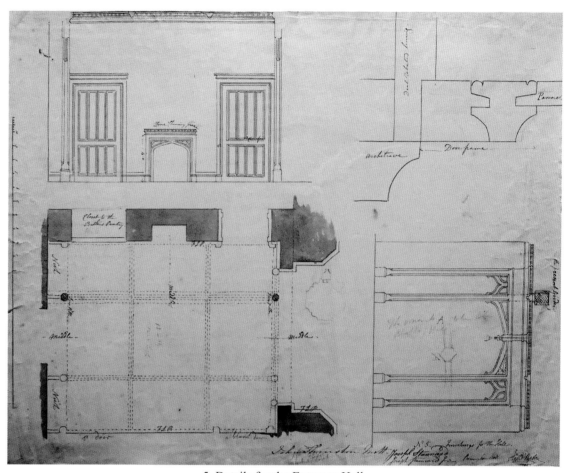

5. Details for the Entrance Hall

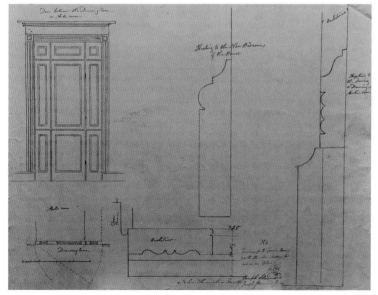

6. Drawing Room door, architraves and skirting

197

The Norwich Mail Coach withstanding an attempted highway robbery!

List of Illustrations and Credits

References

Chapter One

1 T. Turner, *English Garden Design: history and style since 1660* (Woodbridge, 1986); D. Jacques, *Gardens of Court and Country: English design 1630–1730* (London, 2017). For Norfolk, see A. Taigel and T. Williamson, 'Some early geometric gardens in Norfolk', published as *Journal of Garden History*, 11/1–2 [special issue] (1991), pp. 1–122.

2 P. Willis, *Charles Bridgeman and the English Landscape Garden* (2nd edn, London, 2002); A. Rowe and T. Williamson, 'New light on Gobions', *Garden History* 40 (2012), pp. 82–97.

3 T. Mowl, *An Insular Rococo: Architecture, Politics and Society in Ireland and England, 1710–70* (London, 1999), pp. 73–87.

4 T. Williamson, *Polite Landscapes: gardens and society in eighteenth-century England* (Stroud, 1995), pp. 68–71.

5 For Brown and his works, see: D. Stroud, *Capability Brown* (London, 1975); E. Hyams, *Capability Brown and Humphry Repton* (London, 1971); T. Hinde, *Capability Brown: the story of a master gardener* (London, 1986);
J. Brown, *The Omnipotent Magician: Lancelot 'Capability' Brown* (London, 2011); L. Mayer, *Capability Brown and the English Landscape Garden* (Princes Risborough, 2011); and D. Brown and T. Williamson, *Lancelot Brown and the Capability Men: landscape revolution in eighteenth-century England* (London, 2016).

6 *Public Advertiser*, 9 September 1772.

7 S. Bate (ed.), *Capability Brown in Norfolk* (Aylsham, 2016).

8 A. D. M. Macnair and T. Williamson, *William Faden and Norfolk's Eighteenth-Century Landscape* (Oxford, 2010), pp. 129–39.

9 Brown and Williamson, *Capability Men*, pp. 141–54.

10 J. Craddock, *Village Memoirs, in a series of letters between a Clergyman and his family in the Country, and his son in Town* (London, 1765), pp. 119–20.

11 W. Chambers, *A Dissertation on Oriental Gardening* (London, 1772), p. vii.

12 *Morning Post*, 30 March 1784.

13 Brown and Williamson, *Capability Men*, p. 221.

14 J. Loudon (ed.), *The Landscape Gardening and Landscape Architecture of the Late Humphry Repton Esq.* (London, 1840), p. 3.

15 A. Moore, *The Norwich School* (Norwich, 1985).

16 H. van der Eijk, 'Repton, Woudrichen and Rotterdam': accessed online at http://www.historicalgardensblog.com/ 4 January 2017.

17 Loudon, *Humphry Repton*, p. 6.

18 *Ibid.*, p. 8.

19 *Ibid.*, p. 9.

20 NRO PD 102.

21 Loudon, *Humphry Repton*, p. 6.

22 A. Young, *General View of the Agriculture of the County of Norfolk* (London, 1813), p. 375.

23 Aylsham Manor Court Books, NRO, no catalogue number.

24 Mrs Priscilla McDougall, personal communication.

25 Letter to Edward Chamberlayne in J. C. Loudon, *Humphry Repton*, p. 11.

26 R. W Ketton-Kremer, *A Norfolk Gallery* (London, 1948), p. 190.

27 G. Carter, P. Goode and K. Laurie, *Humphry Repton Landscape Gardener 1752–1818* (Norwich, 1982), p. 8.

28 H. Repton, *Observations on the Theory and Practice of Landscape Gardening* (London, 1803), p. 148.

29 NRO WKC 7/85/15.

30 NRO WKC 7/85/14.

31 NRO WKC 7/85/13.

32 Colman Collection, Millennium Library, Norwich.

33 Private collection.

34 R. W. Ketton-Cremer, *Country Neighbourhood* (London, 1951), p. 224.

35 M. J. Armstrong, *History and Antiquities of the County of Norfolk* (London, 1781), Vol. III, p. 109.

36 Private collection. Although now a monochrome painting, on close inspection traces of colour can be seen, and so it is likely that it was originally coloured perhaps in a manner similar to Figures 9 and 10)

37 Another Tudor feature which survives is an impressive drain, 0.7m in height, 0.5m in width, with flint walls and barrel-vaulted brick roof. This runs from the back of the house across the garden eastwards before veering off toward the property's boundary wall and possibly the site of the pitch-roofed building with the domed cupola and weather-vane, seen in the background of Figures 10 and 11.

38 Photograph, c.1886–7, Private Collection.

39 Armstrong, *History and Antiquities*, Vol. III.

40 Loudon, *Humphry Repton*, p. 13.

41 D. Stroud, *Humphry Repton* (London, 1962), p. 131.

42 H. Repton, *The Bee: a critique on the exhibition at Somerset House* (London, 1788).

43 Bristol University, 180/1.

44 J. Phibbs, 'A reconsideration of Repton's contribution to the improvements at Felbrigg, Norfolk, 1778–84', *Garden History* 13,1 (1985), pp. 33–44.

45 R. W Ketton-Kremer, *Norfolk Assembly* (London, 1957), p. 189.

46 Armstrong, *History and Antiquities*, Vol. III, p. 52.

47 NRO WRC 7/143.404 x 7.

48 N. Kent, *Hints to Gentlemen of Landed Property* (London, 1775), p. 202.

49 NRO WKC 5/229; 5/226.

50 NRO WCK 5/229.

51 *Ibid.*

52 J. Maddison, *Felbrigg Hall* (London, 1995), p. 90.

53 Armstrong, *History and Antiquities,* Vol. III, p. 54; Norwich Castle Museum, Todd Collection, 122.

54 Humphry Repton *Observations*, p. 49; J. Mitford (ed.), *The Correspondence of Thomas Gray and the Rev. Norton Nicholls; with other pieces hitherto unpublished* (London, 1843); J. Mitford (ed.), *The Works of Thomas Gray*, Vol. V, *The Correspondence* (London, 1858), pp. 8–10.

55 Armstrong, *History and Antiquities*, Vol. II, p. 3.

56 Bristol University 180/1.

57 G. Whately, *Observations on Modern Gardening* (London, 1770): W. Mason, *The English Garden*, 3 Vols. (London, 1772).

58 R. de Girardin, *De la Composition des Paysages: ou, des moyens d'embellir la nature autour des habitations, en joignant l'agréable à l'utile* (Paris, 1777).

59 M. Calder, 'Promenade in Ermenonville', in M. Calder (ed.) *Experiencing the Garden in the Eighteenth Century* (Bern, 2006), pp. 109–43; at p. 130.

60 W. Gilpin, *An Essay on Prints: containing remarks upon the principles of picturesque beauty; the different kinds of prints; and the characters of the most noted masters* (London, 1768); W. Gilpin, *Observations on the River Wye, and Several Parts of South Wales, etc. Relative chiefly to picturesque beauty; made in the summer of the year 1770* (London, 1782).

61 W. Gilpin, *Three Essays on Picturesque Beauty* (London, 1792), p. 57.

62 NRO MS 10, fol. 4.

63 F. Cowell, *Richard Woods (1715–1793): master of the pleasure garden* (Woodbridge, 2009).

64 The best general accounts of Repton's art and career are: G. Carter, P. Goode and K. Laurie (eds), *Humphry Repton, Landscape Gardener* (Norwich, 1982); S. Daniels, *Humphry Repton: landscape gardening and the geography of Georgian England* (London, 1999); Stroud, *Humphry Repton*; L. Mayer, *Humphry Repton* (Princes Risborough, 2014).

65 R. Payne Knight, *The Landscape: a didactic poem* (London, 1794), p. 99.

66 SRO, Ipswich, HA93.

67 P. Goode, 'The Picturesque controversy', in G. Carter, P. Goode and K. Laurie (eds), *Humphry Repton, Landscape Gardener 1752–1818*, (Norwich, 1982), pp. 33–9, at p. 34.

68 H. Repton, *Fragments on the Theory and Practice of Landscape Gardening* (London, 1816), p. 69.

69 *Ibid.*

70 Brown and Williamson, *Capability Men*, pp. 172–88.

71 *Ibid.*, pp. 135–8.

72 A. Rogger, *Landscapes of Taste: the art of Humphry Repton's Red Books* (London, 2007), pp. 199–210.

73 Repton, *Sketches and Hints*, p. 6.

74 *Ibid.*, p. 6.

75 William Mason to William Gilpin, 26 December 1794: Bodleian Library Ms Eng. Misc d. 571. f. 224.

76 NRO MS10.

77 N. Temple, 'Humphry Repton, illustrator, and William Peacock's "Polite Repository"1790–1811', *Garden History* 16 (2) (1988), pp. 161–73.

78 Colman Collection, Millennium Library, Norwich.

79 The figures are from Daniels, *Humphry Repton*, pp. 255–70.

80 Red Book for Sheringham.

Chapter Two

81 NRO MS10.

82 G. K. Blyth, *The Norwich Guide* (Norwich 1842), p. 231.

83 Information from R. Jones, Archivist to the Old Catton Society, from a conversation with C. Pond in March 2000.

84 D. Stroud, *Humphry Repton* (London, 1962); S. Daniels, *Humphry Repton*, pp. 79–80; *English Heritage Register of Parks and Gardens*.

85 NRO C/Sce1 Road Order Box 1, 25.

86 NRO Church Commissioners' Map 11911.

87 G. Matchett, *Norfolk and Norwich Remembrancer and Vade-mecum* (Norwich, 1822), pp. 220–3.

88 NRO BR 269/153.

89 *Ibid.*

90 Armstrong, *History and Antiquities of the County of Norfolk* (London, 1781), Vol. III, p. 15.

91 NRO TNA/PRO PROB 11/11/1151/222; NRO BR 269/153.

92 NRO MS 10.

93 NRO MC 958/1.

94 H. Repton, *Observations on the Theory and Practice of Landscape Gardening* (London, 1803), p. 143.

95 NRO MS 10.

96 R. G. Desmond, 'A Repton garden at Haileybury', *Garden History* 6 (1978), pp. 16–19.

97 J. Chambers, *A General History of the County of Norfolk, intended to convey all the information of a Norfolk Tour* (London, 1820), p. 1160.

98 N. Pevsner and B. Wilson, *The Buildings of England: Norfolk* (London, 2002), Vol. I, pp. 621–2; Vol. II, p. 806.

99 NRO MC 958/1.

100 NRO MC 958/2.

101 NRO C/Sce 1, 20, 3.

102 NRO C/Sce 2/10/3.

103 NRO MS10.

104 R. Haslam, 'Hanworth Hall, Norfolk', *Country Life*, 15 January 1987, p.153.

105 *Ibid.*

106 *Ibid.*; R. W. Ketton-Cremer, *Country Neighbourhood* (London, 1951), pp.170–1 and p. 180.

107 *Norfolk Chronicle*, 30 March 1776.

108 Armstrong, *History and Antiquities*, Vol. III, p. 72.

109 NRO MF/RO 432/9, p. 13.

110 NRO AYL 29.

111 NRO WKC 5/424, 464X6.

112 C. Hiskey, *Holkham: The Social, Architectural and Landscape History of a Great English Country House* (London, 2016); L. Schmidt, C. Keller, P. Feversham, *Holkham* (London, 2005).

113 T. Williamson, *The Archaeology of the Landscape Park: Garden Design in Norfolk, England, c. 1680–1840* (Oxford, 1998) pp. 100-4.

114 Holkham Hall archives, A/46 and A/47.

115 Holkham Hall archive, John Sandys' planting book.

116 NRO MS10.

117 Holkham archives, no catalogue number.

118 Repton, *Sketches and Hints on Landscape Gardening* (London, 1794), p.29.

119 Repton, *Observations,* p. 43.

120 http://www.historyofparliamentonline.org/volume/1790-1820/member/patteson-john-1755-1833, accessed 4 January 2018.

121 D. Clarke, *Country Houses of Norfolk: the lost houses* (Wymondham, 2008), p. 8; Staffordshire Record Office D641/3/F/1.

122 G. Kelly, 'A History of Colney Hall', unpublished typescript, Millennium Library, Norwich (1986); Williamson, *Archaeology of the Landscape Park*, pp. 226–7.

123 NRO MC30 476X9.

124 NRO MC 77/1, 521x7.

125 N. Kent, *General View of the Agriculture of the County of Norfolk* (London, 1796), p. 92.

126 NRO PTR 3/47 1.

127 Brown and Williamson, *Capability Men*, pp. 141–2. 128 S. Bate (ed.), *Capability Brown in Norfolk*, pp. 152–6. 129 NRO DN/TA 866.

130 NRO MC 77/1/521 X 7; NRO DN/TA 866; White's *Directory*, 1836 and 1845; D. Yaxley, *Portrait of Norfolk* (London, 1977), p. 203; T. Williamson, I. Ringwood and S. Spooner, *Lost Country Houses of Norfolk: history, archaeology and myth* (Woodbridge, 2015), p. 264.

Chapter Three

131 P. Goode, 'The Picturesque Controversy', in G. Carter, P. Goode and K. Laurie (eds), *Humphry Repton, Landscape Gardener* (Norwich, 1982), pp. 33–9, at p. 34.

132 National Trust, Tatton Park.

133 H. Repton, *Sketches and Hints on Landscape Gardening* (London, 1794), p. 7.

134 R. Payne Knight, *The Landscape: a didactic poem in three books, addressed to Uvedale Price Esq.* (London, 1794); U. Price, *An Essay on the Picturesque, as Compared with the Sublime and the Beautiful* (London, 1794).

135 *Ibid.*, p. 27.

136 Knight, *The Landscape*, p. 51.

137 Price, *Essay on the Picturesque*, p. 298.

138 He was joined in partnership by Henry William Scott in 1840 who carried on the business after William's death. Both William Repton and Henry William Scott are remembered on the memorial tablet in Aylsham churchyard and are buried in the same enclosure. The Adey/Repton/ Scott practice continued during the 20th century under various solicitors and eventually became part of Hansells who still have a presence in the town of Aylsham.

139 NRO COL/9/1. Transactions of the Society of United Friars, Nov. 1785–Nov. 1794.

140 NRO COL 9/193/1.

141 In C. Rawcliffe and R. Wilson (eds), *Norwich Since 1500* (London, 2004), p. 197.

142 NRO COL 9/1.

143 R. H. J. Gurney, 'A Hundred Years at Northrepps Hall', unpublished ms, private collection, 1895; V. Anderson, *The Northrepps Grandchildren* (London, 1968).

144 N. Pevsner and B. Wilson, *Norfolk*, Vol. I, pp. 621–2.

145 Gurney, 'Hundred Years at Northrepps Hall'; Anderson, *Northrepps Grandchildren*.

146 NRO DN/TA 516.

147 OSD sheet 243, British Library.

148 N. Wright, 'The Gentry and their Houses in Norfolk and Suffolk, 1550–1850', unpublished PhD thesis, University of East Anglia, 1990, pp. 297–303.

149 Private collection.

150 Private collection.

151 See S. Daniels, *Humphry Repton: landscape gardening and the geography of Georgian England* (London 1998), p. 86; T. Williamson, *Archaeology of the Landscape Park* (Oxford, 1998), pp. 247–8.

152 NRO WLP 1/29, 1042X5.

153 OSD sheet 243, British Library.

154 NRO DN/TA 842.

155 J. Grigor, *The Eastern Arboretum* (Norwich, 1841), p. 229.

156 G. Kelly, 'Bracondale Woods', Norwich Heritage Centre N/728/8/BRA pp.4–5.

157 J. Drummond and C. B. Upton, *Life and Letters of James Martineau* (London, 1902), p. 12.

158 S. Hankinson, 'Philip Meadows Martineau, Humphry Repton and Bracondale Lodge', *Norfolk Archaeological and Historical Research Group Annual Bulletin* 9 (2000), pp. 27–9.

159 *Ibid.*, p. 27; S. Edwards, *Memoir of Philip Meadows Martineau* (Norwich 1831), pp. 11–12.

160 Road order, formerly in the NRO, BR61/3/145/3 1–2, but now with Colman Papers in the Unilever Archive in Port Sunlight.

161 Edwards, *Memoir of Philip Meadows Martineau,* p. 10.

162 *Ibid.*, pp. 10–11.

163 N. Pevsner and B. Wilson, *Norfolk*, Vol. II, pp. 452–3.

164 J. Chambers, *A General History of the County of Norfolk*, Vol. I (Norwich, 1829), p. 1311.

165 F. Blomefield, *Essay towards a Topological History of the County of Norfolk*, Vol. IX (Norwich, 1810): this volume was published over fifty years after Blomefield's death by Charles Parkin, the information about the whereabouts of the gravestone may have been out of date by this time.

166 Chambers, *General History*, p. 1312.

167 Stevenson and Matchett, *A Guide to the Eastern Counties Railway – Cambridge Line* (London, 1847), pp. 76–7.

168 S. Heywood, quoted in Hankinson, 'Philip Meadows Martineau', p. 31.

169 Historic England List Entry Summary, ref no. 1051346, Bracondale Cottage, 80, Bracondale, Norwich.

170 E. Murphy, *The Moated Grange* (Hove, 2015), p. 203.

171 Blickling Hall architectural drawings, D33.

172 N. Scarfe (ed.), *A Frenchman's Year in Suffolk: French impressions of Suffolk life in 1788* (Woodbridge, 1988), pp. 202–3.

173 *Ibid.*, p. 202. The urn was probably to her second son; another, commemorating her first, John, appear to have been placed in the garden near the hall.

174 Blickling Hall architectural drawings nos. 45 and 46.

175 NRO MC3/284 467.

176 NRO MC3/100/3 466 X 4.

177 *Ibid.*

178 T. Abercrombie and J. Mawe, *Gardeners Kalender* (London, 1799), G. White, Kalender 1757, 14 February.

179 NRO DN/TA 447.

180 Blickling Hall architectural drawings, nos. 353754 and 353755.

181 Blickling Hall architectural drawings, no. 353752.

182 Blickling Hall architectural drawings nos. 353680-1, 353715.

Chapter Four

183 H. Repton, *Sketches and Hints* (London, 1794), p. xiv.

184 H. Repton, *Observations on the Theory and Practice of Landscape Gardening* (London, 1803), p. 268.

185 S. Daniels, *Humphry Repton* (London, 1999), pp. 93, 134–5, 184.

186 A. Gore and G. Carter (eds), *Humphry Repton's Memoirs* (London, 2005), p. 145.

187 University of Florida, SB471. R427 Oversize: online image available via the library catalogue.

188 NRO KIM 14/5/3.

189 White's *Directory*, 1845; D. Clarke, *Country Houses of Norfolk: the lost houses* (Wymondham, 2008), p. 105; T. Williamson, I. Ringwood and S. Spooner, *Lost Country Houses of Norfolk* (Woodbridge, 2015), pp. 268–9.

190 H. Repton, *Fragments on the Theory and Practice of Landscape Gardening* (London, 1816), p. 167.

191 NRO KIM 14/5/3.

192 NRO DN/TA 544.

193 Clarke, *Lost Houses*, p. 105.

194 OSD sheet 243, British Library.

195 Anon., 'Obituary – Captain Manby FRS', *Gentleman's Magazine* 197–8 (1855), pp. 208–20.

196 D. Mills, *A Dictionary of British Place-Names* (Oxford, 2011), p. 239.

197 OSD sheet 238, British Library.

198 J. Kenworthy-Browne, P. Reid, M. Sayer and D. Watkin, *Burke's & Savills's Guide to Country Houses*, Vol. III, *East Anglia* (London, 1981), p. 208.

199 NRO DE/TA 39.

200 Repton, *Fragments*, pp. 29–32.

201 M. J. Armstrong, *History and Antiquities* (London, 1781), Vol. III, pp. 21–26.

202 Private collection.

203 James Grigor, *The Eastern Arboretum of Register of Remarkable Trees* (Norwich, 1841), p. 116.

[204] N. Pevsner and B. Wilson, *Norfolk,* Vol. I, p. 157.

[205] M. Girouard, *Life in the English Country House* (London, 1978) p. 233.

[206] Armstrong, *History and Antiquities*, Vol. III, p. 24. [207] NRO C/Sce 2/5/8; OSD sheet 243, British Library. [208] Repton, *Observations*, p. 13

[209] Private collection.

[210] NRO DN/TA 680, DN/TA 496, DN/TA 345; OSD sheet 243, British Library.

[211] E. Pigott, *Memoir of the Honourable Mrs Upcher of Sheringham* (London, n.d. c.1860), p. 45.

[212] Grigor, *Eastern Arboretum*, pp. 120–1; T. Williamson, *Archaeology of the Landscape Park* (Oxford, 1998), pp. 217–18.

[213] N. Pevsner and B. Wilson, *Norfolk*, Vol. I, p. 737; J. P. Neale, *Views of the Seats of noblemen and gentlemen, in England, Wales, Scotland, and Ireland*, Vol. III, no. 21 (London, 1824).

[214] Armstrong, *History and Antiquities*, Vol. IX, p. 116.

[215] Suffolk Record Office, Ipswich Branch, P617/1.

[216] J. Robinson, 'Samuel Wyatt, Architect'. Unpublished DPhil thesis, University of Oxford, 1974.

[217] Neale, *Views of Seats*, Vol. III, no. 21.

[218] NRO DN/TA 775.

[219] NRO MS 18622/244, 477X2.

[220] OSD sheet 243, British Library.

[221] NRO MS 18622/244, 477X2; NRO BR 143/274.

[222] Williamson, Ringwood and Spooner, *Lost Country Houses of Norfolk*, pp.279–81.

[223] Armstrong, *History and Antiquities*, Vol. VII, p. 5; NRO DUN (C)/53, 499X5.

[224] NRO BER 263, 689X5.

[225] NRO BER 13, 684X9.

[226] OSD sheet 240, British Library.

[227] English Heritage Listing number 226582.

[228] NRO DN/TA 570.

[229] http://historyofparliamentonline.org/volume/16901715/member /blofeld-thomas [accessed 2 May 2017]

[230] F. Duleep Singh, *Portraits in Norfolk Houses* (Norwich, 1928), picture 7, p. 302.

[231] Bill from Thomas Ivory of King Street, Norwich, for works done for Thomas Blofeld between 5 September 1805 and 28 January 1806, for £28.

[232] NRO C/Sce 1, Road Order Book 9, pp. 154–5.

[233] Private collection.

[234] Letter from Humphry Repton to Thomas Blofeld, 9 February 1807 (private collection).

[235] Letter from Humphry Repton to Thomas Blofeld, 29 March 1807 (private collection).

[236] Undated letter from Humphry Repton to Thomas Blofeld, April/May 1807 (private collection). Thomas Calthorpe's address is to the Lubbocks of Lammas Hall, probably for his wife's confinement; their first child Thomas John Blofeld was born on 22 February 1807.

[237] OSD sheet 242, British Library; NRO C/Sca 2/172.

Chapter Five

[238] NRO MC 166/260 633 X 1; Cozens-Hardy, 'Some Norfolk Halls', *Norfolk Archaeology*, 32, p. 187: N. Wright, *The Gentry and their houses in Norfolk and Suffolk, 1550–1850*, unpublished PhD thesis, University of East Anglia, 1990, pp. 303–7.

[239] OSD sheet 242, British Library; NRO MC 36/161.

[240] Huntington Library, California, USA.

[241] E. Diestelkamp, 'The greenhouse, Hoveton Hall, Norfolk', unpublished report, 22 August 1999, p. 1, mentions the pinery at Downton Castle, Herefordshire (1820), the camellia house at Wollaton Hall, and the conservatory at Grove House on Regent's Park (c.1823). Although other glasshouses are known to have been built between 1807 and 1818 by Thomas Hopper, J. C. Loudon and John Nash, they no longer exist.

[242] Diestelkamp, 'The greenhouse', p. 2. In 2000 the greenhouse was upgraded to a II* listing by English Heritage.

[243] J. Grigor, *The Eastern Arboretum* (Norwich, 1841), pp. 162–3.

[244] Kenworthy-Brown *et al.*, *Burkes and Savills' Guide to Country Houses*, Vol. III, East Anglia (London, 1981), pp. 192–3.

[245] R. Desmond, *Kew, The History of the Royal Botanic Gardens* (London, 1995), p. 34.

246 NRO BL/BG 5/1/6/1–5.

247 J. L. Phibbs, 'Stradsett Park, Norfolk, A Survey of the Landscape' (unpublished report, 1988).

248 H. Repton, *Fragments on the Theory and Practice of Landscape Gardening* (London, 1816), pp. 195–212.

249 Armstrong, *History and Antiquities*, Vol. III, p. 101.

250 NRO NRS 4172.

251 J. Musson and C. Beresford, 'Sheringham Hall, Norfolk, Conservation Management Plan' (unpublished report for the National Trust, 2017), pp. 3–4.

252 Horatio, 1st Viscount Nelson died in battle on 21 October 1805 without a legitimate heir. His closest relative was his elder brother, the Reverend William Nelson, who lobbied Parliament for a title and an estate in honour of the late war hero. The Reverend Nelson was made Rector of Brandon Parva in 1786 and then of Hilborough in 1797, he was created 1st Earl Nelson in November 1805, a month after the Battle of Trafalgar. An Act of Parliament set aside a grant of £90,000 (over £100 million at modern property values) to buy a mansion and estate for the new earl and his successors. Eventually Stanlynch Park in Wiltshire was chosen for purchase in 1814 and renamed Trafalgar Park. Tom Pocock *Dictionary of National Biography* Vol 40. 2004 https://doi.org/10.1093/ref:odnb/19888

253 S. Daniels, *Humphry Repton: landscape gardening and the geography of Georgian England* (London, 1999), p. 91.

254 NRO WKC 7/91/1-13, letter from Windham concerning Sheringham.

255 NRO UPC57 640X8.

256 S. Yaxley *Sherringhamia, The Journal of Abbot Upcher 1813–1816* (Stibbard, Norfolk, 1986), p. 1.

257 E. Pigott, *Memoir of the Honourable Mrs Upcher* (London, n.d. c.1860), pp. 30, 34.

258 *Ibid.*, p. 35.

259 *Ibid.*, p. 36.

260 *Ibid.*, p. 45.

261 Red Book held by the National Trust.

262 Red Book, p. 18.

263 Red Book, p. 9.

264 Pigott, *Memoir* p. 48.

265 Yaxley, *Sherringhamia*, p. 6.

266 *Ibid.*, p. 11.

267 *Ibid.*, p. 17.

268 *Ibid.*, p. 27.

269 *Ibid.*, p. 35.

270 Piggott, *Memoir* p. 268.

271 Musson and Beresford, 'Sheringham Hall', pp. 5–6.

272 G. Carter, *Gunton Park 1670–1987* (Norwich, 1988); T. Williamson, *Archaeology of the Landscape Park* (Oxford, 1998), pp. 237–9; N. Pevsner and B. Wilson, *The Buildings of England: Norfolk*, Vol I (London, 2002), pp. 534–6.

273 Blickling Hall nos.354066 and 354067; 353760; and 354068.

274 Blickling Hall no. 353647.

275 Carter, *Gunton Park*; T. Williamson, *The Archaeology of the Landscape Park* (Oxford, 1998), pp. 208–9.

276 Carter, *Gunton Park*, p.13.

277 S. Piebenga, 'William Sawrey Gilpin (c.1762–1843), picturesque improver', *Garden History* 22, 1 (1994), pp. 188–9.

278 In 1913 a copper plate was discovered at the back of the reredos with an inscription: 'The thanks of the discerning individuals of this parish are due to John Adey Repton Esq. of Hare Street in the county of Essex, architect, for the masterly manner and correct taste displayed by him in disposing of the remaining parts of the fine old screen presented in the year 1508 by Wymer's order of Aylsham, of which this piece is composed'.

Chapter Six

279 P. Dallas, R. Last and T. Williamson, *Norfolk Gardens and Designed Landscapes* (Oxford, 2013), p. 274.

280 OSD sheet 243, British Library.

281 NRO C/Sca 2/149.

282 N. Pevsner and B. Wilson, *The Buildings of England: Norfolk*, Vol. I (London, 2002), p. 607.

283 A. Taigel and T. Williamson, 'Some early geometric gardens', *Journal of Garden History*, 11, 1 and 2 (1991), pp. 82–3.

284 A. Young, *General View of the Agriculture of the County of Norfolk* (London, 1813), pp. 34, 200, 226, 244, 250, 252, 276, 318, 375 and 427.

285 J. Britton, *Architectural Antiquities of Great Britain*, Vol. II (London, 1809), pp. 98–9. The originals are in the National Trust collection at the NRO.

286 See, for example, the list of commissions recently circulated by the Gardens Trust: thegardenstrust.org/wp-content/.../Phibbs-Repton-sites-attributions-July-2017.xlsx

287 Norfolk Records Office MC269 X 693.

288 K. Laurie, 'John Adey Repton, 1775–1860'. In G. Carter, P. Goode, and K. Laurie (eds), *Humphry Repton, Landscape Gardener* (Norwich, 1982), pp. 129–34.

289 Ordnance Survey 25-inch map, 1886.

290 Edward Kemp, *How to Lay Out a Small Garden* (London, 1850), pp. 55–6.

291 Pevsner and Wilson, *Norfolk*, Vol. II, p. 806.

292 OSD sheet 240, British Library.

293 *Vetusta Monumenta* (London, 1720), Vol I, Plate vi.

294 S. and N. Buck, *A Collection of Engravings of Castles, and Abbeys in England*, 2 Vols (London, 1726–39), Vol. II, n.p.

295 B. Cozens Hardy (ed.), *The Diary of Silas Neville, 1767–1788* (Oxford, 1950), p. 329.

296 John Soane Museum Collection, SM (163) 64/6/2.

297 Most of the relevant papers and drawings are in a private collection. See Dallas *et al. Norfolk Gardens,* pp. 263–7.

298 Private collection.

299 Private collection.

300 J. C. Loudon, *A Treatise on Forming, Improving and Managing Country Residences*, 2 Vols (London, 1806).

301 *Ibid.,* p. 714.

302 *Ibid.*, p. xii.

303 Private collection.

304 John Phibbs identified Stradsett as an important early landscape by J. C. Loudon in the late 1980s. This account draws on the report he prepared for the Bagge family and on a subsequent study of the development of the landscape by Marjorie Greville: J. L. Phibbs, 'Stradsett Park, Norfolk: A Survey of the Landscape', private collection, 1988, and M. D. Greville, 'Stradsett: Creation of a Picturesque Landscape' (Architectural Association, London, unpublished dissertation, Conservation of Historic Landscapes, Parks and Gardens Course, 1989).

305 NRO BL/BG 9/2/1: Loudon to Bagge, 18 May 1810. 306 NRO BL/BG 9/2/1: Loudon to Bagge, 10 July 1810. 307 NRO BL/BG 9/2/1: Loudon to Bagge, 22 July 1810.

308 NRO BL/BG 9/2/1: bill from Loudon to Bagge, 2 March 1813.

309 NRO BL/BG 9/2/1: minutes of meeting.

310 NRO BL/BG 9/2/1: minutes.

311 Loudon, *Country Residences*, p. 386.

312 Greville, 'Stradsett', p. 18.

313 Loudon, *Country Residences*, pp. 705–8.

314 NRO BL/BG 9/2/1, bill from Loudon to Bagge, 2 March 1813.

315 NRO BL/BG 9/2/1: minutes.

316 Greville, 'Stradsett', Appendix A.

317 NRO BL/BG 5/1/6/6–9.

318 S. Heywood *Impact Assessment of Proposed alterations at Gillingham* Hall (unpublished report, July 2008).

319 NRO C/Sce 2/3/30.

320 John Claudius Loudon, *Observations on the Formation and Management of Useful and Ornamental Plantations* (Edinburgh, 1804), p. 215.

321 NRO MF336/8.

322 *Ibid.*, p. 4.

323 *Ibid.*, p. 5.

324 *Ibid.*

325 *Ibid.*, p. 16.

326 *Ibid.,* p. 17.

327 NRO NRS 4092 CJ.

328 . Grigor, *Eastern Arboretum of Register of Remarkable Trees* (Norwich 1841), p. 259; *Gardeners Magazine* 17 (1841), pp. 273–74.

329 J. C. Loudon, *Observations on the Formation and Management of Useful and Ornamental Plantations* (Edinburgh, 1804), pp. 213–15.

330 T. Williamson, *Archaeology of the Landscape Park* (Oxford, 1998), p. 199.

331 Grigor, *Eastern Arboretum*, p. 347.

332 Williamson, *Archaeology of the Landscape Park,* p. 279.

333 NRO 5525 231 X 3.

334 J. Woudstra, 'Lewis Kennedy, landscape gardener and his work at Buckhurst Park', *Apollo* 135, April 1992, p. 220.

335 Lewis Kennedy, 'Sketches of Stow Hall Norfolk', private collection.

336 *Ibid.*

337 NRO HARE 5411, 222X2.

338 This lodge was demolished and replaced later in the nineteenth century with a new one, standing to the left of the entrance, designed in a gothic style in keeping with the hall, which was itself rebuilt (on a slightly different site) by David Brandon in the 1870s.

339 C. J. Bradney, 'The Italian garden in England 1787–1863' (University of Bristol, unpublished PhD thesis, 2008), p. 128.

340 NRO HARE 5525/231.

341 NRO HARE 5524/231.

342 NRO HARE 6819/1–2.

343 NRO HARE 6962.

344 Private collection.

345 NRO HARE 5562, 223X6.

346 NRO HARE 5440, 222X3.

347 J. Kenworthy-Browne, P. Reid, M. Sayer and D. Watkin, *Burke's & Savills' Guide to Country Houses*, Vol. III, *East Anglia* (London, 1981), p. 192.

348 The note appeared in a codicil to his will: NRO BL/EV 3/13.

349 NRO MC 111/74 581 x9.

350 Pevsner and Wilson, *Norfolk*, Vol, II, pp. 315–16; NRO MEA 1/43 676x5.

351 NRO MEA 3/653–653a 659 X5,

352 NRO MEA3/655, 659X5.

353 This refers to Sir Henry Steuart, author of *Planter's Guide* (1828).

354 Brooke tithe map, *c.*1840: NRO PD599/32.

355 Grigor, *Eastern Arboretum*, p. 243.

356 Almost all the documentary research for this summary has been carried out by Marion Folkes and Dorothy Warman and they have very generously agreed to its use here. *Brooke*. Marion Folkes and Daphne Warman. 2015.

357 Williamson, *The Archaeology of the Landscape Park*, p. 210.

358 NHER 44663.

359 T. Williamson, 'Parks in the 18th and 19th centuries', in T. Ashwin and A. Davison (eds), *An Historical Atlas of Norfolk* (Chichester, 2005), pp. 122–3.

360 *Gentleman's Magazine* 88 (1818), p. 648.

Bibliography

Published books and articles

Anderson, V., *The Northrepps Grandchildren* (London, 1968).

Anon., 'Obituary – Captain Manby FRS', *Gentleman's Magazine* 197–8 (1855), pp. 208–20.

Armstrong, M. J., *History and Antiquities of Norfolk*, 10 Vols (London, 1781).

Bate, S. (ed.), *Capability Brown in Norfolk* (Aylsham, 2016).

Blomefield, F., *Essay towards a Topological History of the County of Norfolk*, 11 Vols (Norwich, 1805).

Blyth, G. K., *The Norwich Guide* (Norwich, 1842).

Britton, J., *Architectural Antiquities of Great Britain*, Vol. II (London, 1809).

Brown, D., and Williamson, T., *Lancelot Brown and the Capability Men: landscape revolution in eighteenth-century England* (London, 2016).

Brown, J., *The Omnipotent Magician: Lancelot 'Capability' Brown* (London, 2011).

Buck, S. and N., *A Collection of Engravings of Castles, and Abbeys in England*, 2 Vols (London, 1726–39).

Calder, M., 'Promenade in Ermenonville', in M. Calder (ed.), *Experiencing the Garden in the Eighteenth Century* (Bern, 2006), pp. 109–43.

Carter, G., *Gunton Park 1670–1987* (Norwich, 1988).

——, Goode, P., and Laurie, K., *Humphry Repton Landscape Gardener 1752–1818* (Norwich, 1982).

Chambers, J., *A General History of the County of Norfolk, intended to convey all the information of a Norfolk Tour* (London, 1820).

Chambers, W., *A Dissertation on Oriental Gardening* (London, 1772).

Clarke, D., *Country Houses of Norfolk: the lost houses* (Wymondham, 2008).

Cowell, F., *Richard Woods (1715–1793): master of the pleasure garden* (Woodbridge, 2009).

Cozens-Hardy, B., 'Some Norfolk Halls', *Norfolk Archaeology* 32 (1968), pp. 163–208.

—— (ed.), *The Diary of Silas Neville, 1767–1788* (Oxford, 1950).

Craddock, J., *Village Memoirs, in a series of letters between a Clergyman and his family in the Country, and his son in Town* (London, 1765).

Dallas, P., Last, R., and Williamson, T., *Norfolk Gardens and Designed Landscapes* (Oxford, 2013).

Daniels, S., *Humphry Repton: landscape gardening and the geography of Georgian England* (London, 1999).

Desmond, R. G., 'A Repton garden at Haileybury', *Garden History* 6 (1978), pp. 16–19.

Drummond, J., and Upton, C. B., *Life and Letters of James Martineau* (London, 1902).

Duleep Singh, F., *Portraits in Norfolk Houses* (Norwich, 1928).

Edwards, S., *Memoir of Philip Meadows Martineau* (Norwich, 1831).

Folkes, M., and Warman, D., *Brooke: an handsome village with some neat houses* (Brooke, 2015).

Gilpin, W., *An Essay on Prints: containing remarks upon the principles of picturesque beauty; the different kinds of prints; and the characters of the most noted masters* (London, 1768).

——, *Observations on the River Wye, and Several Parts of South Wales, etc. Relative chiefly to picturesque beauty; made in the summer of the year 1770* (London, 1782).

——, *Three Essays on Picturesque Beauty* (London, 1792).

Girardin, R. de, *De la Composition des Paysages: ou, des moyens d'embellir la nature autour des habitations, en joignant l'agréable à l'utile* (Paris, 1777).

Girouard, M., *Life in the English Country House* (London, 1978).

Goode, P., 'The Picturesque controversy', in G. Carter, P. Goode and K. Laurie (eds), *Humphry Repton, Landscape Gardener* (Norwich, 1982), pp. 33–9.

Gore, A., and Carter, G. (eds), *Humphry Repton's Memoirs* (London, 2005).

Grigor, J., *The Eastern Arboretum of Register of Remarkable Trees* (Norwich, 1841).

Hankinson, S., 'Philip Meadows Martineau, Humphry Repton and Bracondale Lodge', *Norfolk Archaeological and Historical Research Group Annual Bulletin* 9 (2000), pp. 27–9.

Hinde, T., *Capability Brown: the story of a master gardener* (London, 1986).

Haslam, R., 'Hanworth Hall, Norfolk', *Country Life* 181 (15 January 1987).

Hiskey, C., *Holkham: the social, architectural and landscape history of a great English country house* (London, 2016).

Hyams, E., *Capability Brown and Humphry Repton* (London, 1971).

Jacques, D., *Gardens of Court and Country: English design 1630–1730* (London, 2017).

Kemp, E., *How to Lay Out a Small Garden* (London, 1850).

Kent, N., *Hints to Gentlemen of Landed Property* (London, 1775).

——, *General View of the Agriculture of the County of Norfolk* (London, 1796).

Kenworthy-Browne, J., Reid, P., Sayer, M., and Watkin, D., *Burke's & Savills Guide to Country Houses*, Vol. III, *East Anglia* (London, 1981).

Ketton-Kremer, R. W., *A Norfolk Gallery* (London, 1948).

——, *Country Neighbourhood* (London, 1951).

——, R. W., *Norfolk Assembly* (London, 1957).

Laurie, K., 'John Adey Repton, 1775–1860', in G. Carter, P. Goode, and K. Laurie (eds), *Humphry Repton, Landscape Gardener* (Norwich 1983), pp. 129–34.

Loudon, J. C., *Observations on the Formation and Management of Useful and Ornamental Plantations* (Edinburgh, 1804).

——, *A Treatise on Forming, Improving and Managing Country Residences* (London, 1806).

—— (ed.), *The Landscape Gardening and Landscape Architecture of the Late Humphry Repton Esq.* (London, 1840).

Macnair, A. D. M., and Williamson, T., *William Faden and Norfolk's Eighteenth-Century Landscape* (Oxford, 2010).

Maddison, J., *Felbrigg Hall* (London, 1995).

Mason, W., *The English Garden* (London, 1772).

Matchett, G., *Norfolk and Norwich Remembrancer and Vade-mecum* (Norwich, 1822).

Mayer, L., *Capability Brown and the English Landscape Garden* (Princes Risborough, 2011).

——, *Humphry Repton* (Princes Risborough, 2014).

Mills, D., *A Dictionary of British Place-Names* (Oxford, 2011).

Mitford, J. (ed.), *The Correspondence of Thomas Gray and the Rev. Norton Nicholls; with other pieces hitherto unpublished* (London, 1843).

—— (ed.) *The Works of Thomas Gray*, Vol. V, *The Correspondence* (London, 1858).

Moore, A., *The Norwich School* (Norwich, 1985).

Mowl, T., *An Insular Rococo: architecture, politics and society in Ireland and England, 1710–70* (London, 1999).

Murphy, E., *The Moated Grange* (Hove, 2015).

Neale, J. P., *Views of the seats of noblemen and gentlemen, in England, Wales, Scotland, and Ireland*, Vol. III (London, 1824).

Payne Knight, R., *The Landscape: a didactic poem in three books, addressed to Uvedale Price Esq.* (London, 1794).

Pevsner, N., and Wilson, B., *The Buildings of England: Norfolk*, 2 Vols (London, 2002).

Phibbs, J., 'A reconsideration of Repton's contribution to the improvements at Felbrigg, Norfolk, 1778–84', *Garden History* 13, 1 (1985), pp. 33–44.

Piebenga, S., 'William Sawrey Gilpin (c.1762–1843), picturesque improver', *Garden History* 22, 1 (1994), pp. 188–9.

Pigott, E, *Memoir of the Honourable Mrs Upcher of Sheringham* (London, n.d. c.1860).

Price, U., *An Essay on the Picturesque, as Compared with the Sublime and the Beautiful* (London, 1794).

Rawcliffe, C., and Wilson, R. (eds), *Norwich Since 1500* (London, 2004).

Repton, H., *The Bee: a critique on the exhibition at Somerset House* (London, 1788).

——, *Sketches and Hints on Landscape Gardening* (London, 1794).

——, *Observations on the Theory and Practice of Landscape Gardening* (London, 1803).

——, *An Inquiry into the Changes in Taste in Landscape Gardening* (London, 1806).

——, *Fragments on the Theory and Practice of Landscape Gardening* (London, 1816).

Rogger, A., *Landscapes of Taste: the art of Humphry Repton's Red Books* (London, 2007).

Rowe, A., and Williamson, T., 'New light on Gobions', *Garden History* 40 (2012), pp. 82–97.

Scarfe, N. (ed.), *A Frenchman's Year in Suffolk: French impressions of Suffolk life in 1788* (Woodbridge, 1988).

Schmidt, L. Keller, C., Feversham, P., *Holkham* (London, 2005).

Stevenson and Matchett. *A Guide to the Eastern Counties Railway – Cambridge Line* (London, 1847).

Stroud, D., *Capability Brown* (London, 1975).

——, *Humphry Repton* (London, 1962).

Taigel, A., and Williamson, T., 'Some early geometric gardens in Norfolk', published as *Journal of Garden History* 11, 1 and 2 (1991).

Temple, N., 'Humphry Repton, illustrator, and William Peacock's "Polite Repository" 1790–1811', *Garden History* 16 (2) (1988), pp. 161–73.

Turner, T., *English Garden Design: history and style since 1660* (Woodbridge, 1986).

Whately, G., *Observations on Modern Gardening* (London, 1770).

Williamson, T., *Polite Landscapes: gardens and society in eighteenth-century England* (Stroud, 1995).

——, 'Parks in the 18th and 19th centuries', in T. Ashwin and A. Davison (eds), *An Historical Atlas of Norfolk* (Chichester, 2005), pp. 122–3.

——, *The Archaeology of the Landscape Park: garden design in Norfolk, England, c.1680–1840* (BAR British series 268, Oxford, 1998).

——, Ringwood, I., and Spooner, S., *Lost Country Houses of Norfolk: history, archaeology and myth* (Woodbridge, 2015).

Willis, P., *Charles Bridgeman and the English Landscape Garden*, 2nd edn (London, 2002).

Woudstra, J., 'Lewis Kennedy, landscape gardener and his work at Buckhurst Park', *Apollo* 135 (April 1992), pp. 215–21.

Yaxley, D., *Portrait of Norfolk* (London, 1977).

Yaxley, S., *Sherringhamia, The Journal of Abbot Upcher 1813–1816* (Stibbard, Norfolk, 1986).

Young, A., *General View of the Agriculture of the County of Norfolk* (London, 1813).

Unpublished theses and reports

Bradney, C. J., 'The Italian garden in England 1787–1863', unpublished PhD thesis, University of Bristol, 2008.

Diestelkamp, E., 'The greenhouse, Hoveton Hall, Norfolk', unpublished report, private collection, 22 August 1999.

Greville, M. D., 'Stradsett: creation of a picturesque landscape', unpublished dissertation, Architectural Association, London, 1989.

Gurney, R. H. J., 'A hundred years at Northrepps Hall', unpublished ms, private collection, 1895.

Heywood, S., 'Impact assessment of proposed alterations at Gillingham Hall', unpublished report, private collection, July 2008.

Kelly, G., 'A history of Colney Hall', unpublished typescript, Millennium Library, Norwich, 1996.

——, 'Bracondale Woods', unpublished report, Norwich Heritage Centre N/728/8/BRA, n.d.

Musson, J., and Beresford, C., 'Sheringham Hall, Norfolk, Conservation Management Plan', unpublished report for the National Trust, 2017.

Phibbs, J. L., 'Stradsett Park, Norfolk, a survey of the landscape', unpublished report, private collection, 1988.

Robinson, J., 'Samuel Wyatt, architect', unpublished DPhil thesis, University of Oxford, 1974.

Wright, N., 'The gentry and their houses in Norfolk and Suffolk, 1550–1850', unpublished PhD thesis, University of East Anglia, 1990.

Online Sources

H. van der Eijk, 'Repton, Woudrichen and Rotterdam': accessed online at http://www.historicalgardensblog.com/ accessed 4 January 2017.

History of parliament: http://historyofparliamentonline.org/volume/16901715/ member /blofield-thomas [accessed 2 May 2017]

Time discovering Truth.

216

Index

Page numbers in **bold** refer to the Figures

A view north towards Cromer Church, Humphry Repton.

Watts' engraving of Wolterton Hall from a drawing by Humphry Repton.

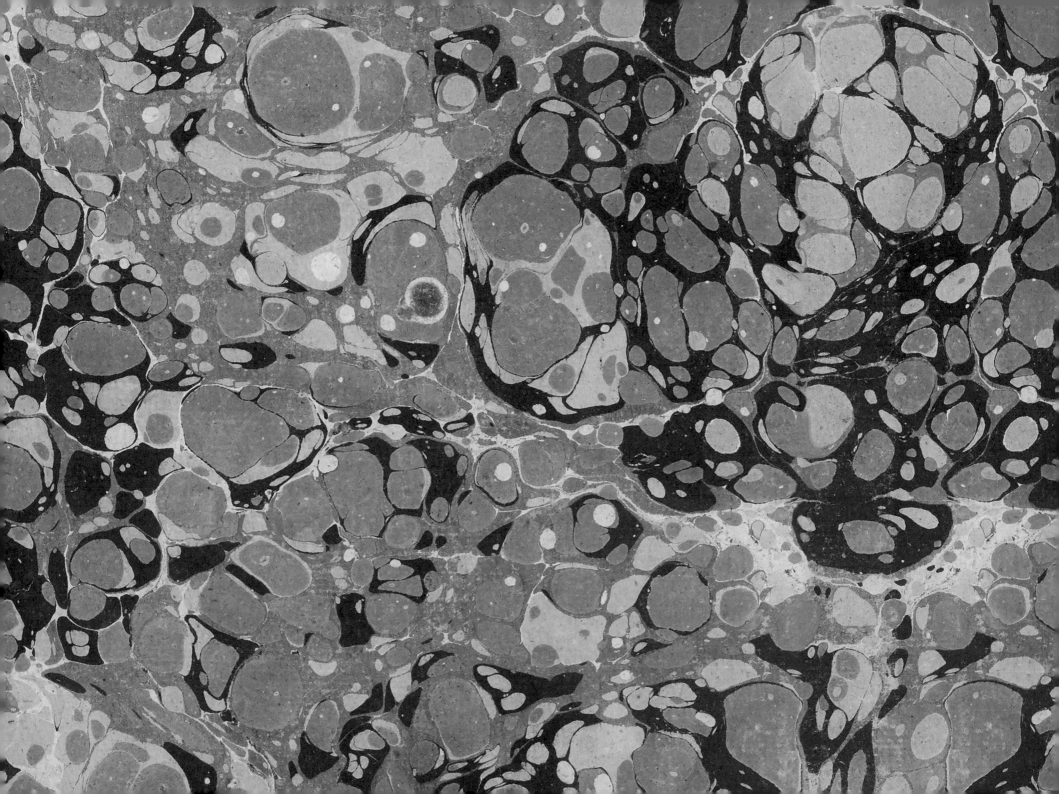

FAKING IT

how to cook delicious food without really trying

delicious.

For Phil, Toby and Henry, who have been with me through
every breakfast, lunch and dinner (the good, the bad and
the ugly) and never complained... I love you all.

FAKING IT

how to cook delicious food without really trying

VALLI LITTLE

Photography by Brett Stevens

CONTENTS

LE CHEF !
A TOUJOURS
RAISON

Welcome to my world... It's a pretty hectic one where, like most of you, I spend a great deal of time juggling all the elements that make life fulfilling and fun – home and work, family and friends.

Although cooking is my passion, finding time for it isn't always easy. I think the idea for this book first came to me one evening while I was on the phone to a publisher, clearing the debris our new puppy had created around the house, and running late to pick up my son from rugby training. Oh, and I was trying to wrap a beef fillet in pastry, as we were having friends around for dinner.

So I started thinking about ways to make the kind of food I love, but keep it simple. Don't get me wrong – 'faking it' doesn't mean you can't stay true to the way you like to cook and entertain, it's just about taking a few clever shortcuts.

Delis, gourmet food shops and many supermarkets stock an ever-increasing range of helpful items, such as quality pasta sauces, curry pastes and roasted or chargrilled vegetables. Together with a little planning and a few fresh ingredients, these products make it easy to create impressive dishes.

These days, I save restaurant-style, four-course dinners for when I go out. When cooking for family or friends at home, I opt for delicious, easy-to-prepare dinners that still call in the compliments.

My food is the product of many influences. My childhood in England encouraged my love of fresh, seasonal produce (nothing could compare with Dad's first crop of Jersey Royal potatoes or summer raspberries). Then there was the explosion of Thai flavours when I first tasted a betel leaf at Sydney's Longrain. And I always gather inspiration on my travels, whether it's a simple lemon pasta in Italy or an exquisite degustation at Joël Robuchon in Paris.

The recipes in this book reflect all these experiences, and the wonderful chefs and cooks I've worked with for *delicious.* magazine. I wanted to share dishes suited to our busy lives, but which keep the element of fun and excitement that we should all get from cooking.

Turning a few ingredients into a beautiful meal doesn't have to be difficult, but it is an act of love. So there's nothing wrong with using a few shortcuts and *Faking It* sometimes, as long as you always cook with passion!

Valli

vodka salmon with mini rosti

Serves 4 (makes 8-12 rosti)

This is great as a weekend brunch dish served with iced vodka, but works just as well as a midweek dinner.

3 desiree or pontiac potatoes (600g total), peeled
200g smoked salmon slices
2 tbs vodka
2 tbs finely chopped dill, plus sprigs to garnish
2 tsp wholegrain mustard
1/2 cup (120g) creme fraiche or sour cream
2 eggs, beaten
2 tbs rice flour
2 tbs olive oil
Lemon wedges, to serve

Simmer the potatoes in a pan of boiling water for 10 minutes to par-cook. Drain and chill for 30 minutes.

Place the smoked salmon in a shallow dish. Combine the vodka with 1 tablespoon of the chopped dill, then pour over the salmon. Cover and refrigerate until ready to serve.

Combine the mustard and creme fraiche with the remaining chopped dill in a bowl. Refrigerate until needed.

Coarsely grate the cooled potatoes into a bowl. Stir in the egg and rice flour, then season and stir to combine.

Heat the oil in a non-stick frypan over medium heat. Working in batches of 3-4 rosti, add 1 tablespoon of the mixture to the pan for each rosti and flatten slightly. Cook for 2 minutes each side until crisp and brown, then remove and keep warm in a low oven while you cook the remaining rosti.

Place 2-3 rosti on each plate, top with salmon and drizzle with the creme fraiche mixture. Garnish with extra dill sprigs and serve with lemon wedges.

breakfast cranachan

Serves 4

Cranachan is a Scottish dessert made with oats, whisky, berries and honey. It's a great breakfast, too, with or without the whisky.

300g thick Greek-style yoghurt
150ml evaporated milk
Finely grated zest and juice of 1 lemon
250g fresh or frozen (thawed) mixed berries
2 tbs honey, plus extra to drizzle
2 tbs whisky (optional)
3/4 cup (95g) toasted muesli

Place the yoghurt, evaporated milk, lemon zest and juice in a bowl and gently whisk to combine.

In a separate bowl, lightly crush the berries with a fork. Stir in the honey and whisky, if using.

When ready to serve, spoon alternating layers of fruit, muesli and yoghurt into 4 tall glasses. Serve drizzled with extra honey.

toffee-apple pancakes

Serves 4

20g unsalted butter
3 small Granny Smith apples, peeled,
    cored, cut into 2cm pieces
$\frac{1}{2}$ firmly packed cup (100g) brown sugar
$\frac{1}{4}$ cup (60ml) Calvados* or brandy
$\frac{1}{2}$ cup (125ml) thickened cream, plus extra to serve
400g packet frozen French-style crepes* (8 crepes total)
Icing sugar, to dust

Melt the butter in a frypan over medium heat. Add apple and brown sugar and cook, stirring occasionally, for 5-6 minutes until the sugar dissolves and apple softens slightly. Stir in the Calvados and cream. Cook, stirring occasionally, for 1-2 minutes until the sauce has thickened and the apple is tender.

Meanwhile, warm the crepes according to packet instructions.

Arrange 2 crepes on each serving plate, then spoon over the apples and toffee sauce. Drizzle with extra cream, then serve dusted with icing sugar.

* Calvados is an apple brandy from selected bottle shops. Frozen crepes are available from selected supermarkets (see Glossary).

"round the house" breakfast slice

Serves 4

My husband, Phil, was a Qantas flight steward when we met.
One of the highlights of his London trips was breakfast
at The Mayfair hotel, where they served "round the house"
– a cooked breakfast that included absolutely everything.
This is our homestyle version.

2 tbs olive oil
1 onion, thinly sliced
4 bacon rashers, cut into batons
150g button mushrooms, sliced
500g parboiled or precooked chat potatoes*, quartered
8 cherry tomatoes, halved
1 tbs chopped flat-leaf parsley
8 eggs, beaten
¼ cup (60ml) pure (thin) cream
Tomato sauce (ketchup), to serve

Preheat the oven to 190ºC. Grease a 1.25-litre baking dish.
   Heat the oil in a large frypan over medium heat. Add the
onion and bacon and cook, stirring occasionally, for 2-3 minutes
until onion softens and bacon starts to crisp. Add the mushroom
and potato and cook, stirring occasionally, for 2 minutes or
until the mushroom starts to soften.
   Tip the mixture into the baking dish, then scatter over the
tomatoes and parsley. Beat the eggs and cream together,
season with sea salt and freshly ground black pepper, then
pour into the dish. Bake for 15 minutes or until the egg has
set, then slice and serve with tomato sauce.
* Precooked potatoes are available from selected supermarkets.

summer fruit salad with pikelets

Serves 4

In a perfect world, we'd make our own pikelets, but this is a great way to turn ready-made ones into something special.

2 oranges
2 mangoes
2 bananas, peeled, sliced
250g punnet strawberries, hulled, quartered
1 tbs shredded mint leaves
2 x 200g packets pikelets
Honey or maple syrup, to serve
Icing sugar (optional), to dust

Zest both oranges using a zester, then place the zest in a large bowl. Remove the pith from 1 orange and segment the flesh into the bowl. Thinly slice the flesh of 1 mango and add to the bowl with the banana, strawberries and mint.

Juice the remaining orange, chop the flesh of the remaining mango, then puree both in a blender until smooth. Stir half the puree into the salad, reserving the rest to serve.

Heat the pikelets according to packet instructions, then divide among serving plates. Drizzle with honey or syrup, dust with icing sugar, and serve with the fruit salad and remaining mango puree to drizzle.

"espresso" scrambled eggs

Serves 1-2

Renowned New Zealand caterer Ruth Pretty told me about this clever recipe when I visited her beautiful home and cooking school just outside Wellington. Australia is such a coffee-loving society that many of us own an espresso machine, and now it has a second use. A Bloody Mary makes it extra special.

2 free-range eggs
2 tbs pure (thin) cream
1 tbs finely chopped chives or flat-leaf parsley,
   plus extra to serve
20g unsalted butter, softened
Hot buttered toast, to serve

Place the eggs and cream in the milk-frothing jug of an espresso machine and beat with a fork to combine. Season, then stir in the chives or parsley and butter.

Heat the espresso machine's steam jet according to instructions. Give the espresso machine's steam jet a blast, then place the jug under the jet and cook the egg mixture, swirling the jug, for 2-3 minutes until the eggs are just set (the mixture should be soft and light). Serve the scrambled eggs on hot buttered toast, garnished with extra chives.

deep-fried eggs
with asparagus

Serves 4

6 free-range eggs
2 tbs plain flour
1 cup panko breadcrumbs*
Sunflower oil, to deep-fry
2-3 bunches thin asparagus, woody ends trimmed,
    blanched for 3 minutes until tender
2 tbs extra virgin olive oil
1 tbs balsamic vinegar

Place 4 eggs in a pan of cold water, bring to the boil, then
cook for 3 minutes to soft-boil. Remove from heat and plunge
the eggs into a bowl of iced water.

Beat remaining 2 eggs in a bowl. Place flour and breadcrumbs
in 2 separate bowls. Peel the soft-boiled eggs very carefully and
gently pat dry with paper towel. Roll the eggs first in the flour,
then in the beaten egg and then in the breadcrumbs. Set aside.

Half-fill a deep-fryer or large heavy-based saucepan with
sunflower oil and heat to 190°C. (If you don't have a deep-fryer
thermometer, test a cube of bread – it will turn golden in
30 seconds when the oil is hot enough.) Fry the eggs in the oil
for 1 minute or until golden brown, then drain on paper towel.

Divide the asparagus spears among plates, place a fried egg
on each, drizzle with olive oil and vinegar, season, then serve.
* Panko are coarse, light Japanese breadcrumbs from selected
supermarkets and Asian food shops.

parmesan custards

Serves 4

When I worked in the food department of the famous London store, Harrods, many years ago, the gentry would buy beautiful little jars of Gentleman's Relish. It's a salty anchovy paste that goes well with eggs and, of course, toast. It's hard to find in Australia, but Vegemite works nearly as well.

300ml pure (thin) cream
300ml milk
1¼ cups (100g) finely grated parmesan
4 egg yolks
Freshly ground white pepper
Toast soldiers sandwiched with Gentleman's Relish*
   or Vegemite, to serve

Combine the cream, milk and parmesan in a saucepan. Stir over low heat until the cheese melts. Leave to cool completely.
   Preheat the oven to 150°C.
   Gently whisk the egg yolks into the cream mixture, then season with salt and white pepper. Strain the mixture through a sieve into a jug, pushing down on any solids. Divide among four 200ml ovenproof ramekins or ceramic bowls.
   Place the ramekins in a roasting pan, then pour enough boiling water into the pan to come halfway up the sides of the dishes. Place in the oven and bake for 15-20 minutes until the custards are pale golden and just set, but still with a slight wobble. Serve warm with the toast soldiers.
* From selected gourmet food shops.

quail egg & pancetta tart

Serves 6

375g block puff pastry
100ml creme fraiche or sour cream
2 tbs grated parmesan
150g thinly sliced pancetta
8 quail eggs* or 5 small eggs
Chervil sprigs* or flat-leaf parsley leaves, to garnish

Preheat oven to 180ºC. Line a baking tray with baking paper.

Roll out the pastry on a lightly floured surface to form a 16cm x 30cm rectangle. Place the pastry on the prepared baking tray. Use a knife to lightly score a 1cm border around the edge of the pastry, taking care not to cut all the way through. Prick the area inside the border with a fork.

Mix creme fraiche and parmesan in a bowl and season with salt and pepper. Spread the mixture over the pastry inside the border. Lay pancetta over the tart base, then bake for 12 minutes or until the pancetta is crisp and the pastry is puffed and golden.

Lightly beat 1 egg. Remove the pastry from the oven and brush the border with the beaten egg. Break the remaining eggs, one at a time, into a cup and pour over the pancetta. Season with salt and pepper, then return to the oven for a further 3 minutes or until the eggwhites are set but yolks are still runny. Scatter with chervil or parsley, then slice and serve.
* Quail eggs are available from selected poultry suppliers and Asian food shops. Chervil is from selected greengrocers.

spanish eggs

Serves 4

This makes a very special breakfast dish but also doubles
as a great midweek dinner. Jars of chargrilled or roasted red
capsicum are available in most supermarkets these days, and
are an easy shortcut if you don't have time to roast your own.

500g pontiac or desiree potatoes, peeled,
   cut into 2cm cubes
$2^{1}/_{2}$ tbs olive oil
1 red onion, thinly sliced
2 garlic cloves, finely chopped
1 chorizo sausage, cut into 2cm pieces
$1^{1}/_{2}$ tsp smoked paprika* (pimenton)
$^{1}/_{2}$ tsp ground cumin
280g jar chargrilled or roasted red capsicum*,
   drained, chopped
4 free-range eggs
1 tbs finely chopped flat-leaf parsley

Cook the potato in a pan of boiling salted water for 2-3 minutes
until just tender, then drain and set aside.

Heat 2 tablespoons oil in a large frypan over medium heat.
Add the onion and cook, stirring, for 2-3 minutes until just soft.
Add the garlic, chorizo, potato, paprika and cumin and cook,
stirring, for a further 2-3 minutes until the chorizo and potato
start to crisp. Add the chargrilled capsicum, season well,
then cook over low heat until heated through.

Meanwhile, brush a non-stick frypan with the remaining
2 teaspoons oil and place over medium heat. Break the eggs,
one at a time, into the pan. Cover with a lid and cook for 2 minutes
until the eggwhites are cooked but the yolks are still soft.

Divide the potato mixture among warm plates, top with an egg,
sprinkle with parsley, season with salt and pepper, then serve.
* Smoked paprika is from gourmet shops and selected delis.
Chargrilled capsicum is from supermarkets (see Glossary).

cheat's blinis with jamon and figs

Makes 32

Pedro Ximénez is a rich, sticky sweet sherry – it's not cheap, but if you keep a bottle on hand you can use it to add a special touch to desserts as well as this elegant canapé.

16 dried dessert figs, halved
¼ cup (60ml) Pedro Ximénez sherry or other sweet sherry
2 x 140g packets pikelet bites*
250g mascarpone cheese
100g sliced jamon serrano* or prosciutto, cut into strips
Olive oil, to drizzle
Chervil* or flat-leaf parsley sprigs, to garnish

Soak the figs in the sherry for 2 hours or until they have absorbed all the liquid.

Place the pikelets on a platter and spread each with a little mascarpone. Add a small scroll of jamon and a piece of fig. Sprinkle with sea salt and freshly ground black pepper, drizzle over oil and garnish with chervil or parsley.
* Pikelet bites are from supermarkets (see Glossary). Jamon serrano is Spanish cured ham from supermarkets and delis. Chervil is from selected greengrocers.

french goat's cheese dip

Serves 4-6

I'm a fan of goat's cheese but if you're not, cream cheese works equally well in this recipe. This dip can be used as a stuffing for roast chicken, too. Simply create a pocket between the skin and the breast, then carefully place the cheese mixture under the skin.

300g soft goat's cheese
1 tbs white wine vinegar
1 tbs dry white wine
2 tbs extra virgin olive oil
2 garlic cloves, crushed
2 tbs finely chopped flat-leaf parsley
2 tbs chopped chives
Baby (Dutch) carrots, celery sticks, radishes
   and crusty bread, to serve

Place the goat's cheese, vinegar, wine, oil, garlic, parsley and chives in a bowl with some sea salt and freshly ground black pepper. Beat well with a fork (or process in a food processor) until smooth, then serve with vegetables to dip and crusty bread.

quail eggs with walnut hummus and dukkah

Serves 4 as a snack

I love to make this dish as a simple starter or light lunch.

$^1/_2$ cup (60g) chopped toasted walnuts
250g tub hummus
2 tbs sour cream
1 tbs chopped flat-leaf parsley
12 quail eggs*
Roasted cherry truss tomatoes
   and warm pita bread, to serve
Walnut oil* or olive oil, to drizzle
$^1/_2$ cup dukkah*
Mint leaves, to garnish

Place the walnuts in a food processor and pulse to form fine crumbs. Add the hummus, sour cream and parsley, then pulse to combine.

   Place the eggs in a saucepan of cold water and bring to the boil, then boil for 4 minutes. Peel the eggs under cold running water while still warm.

   Place the hummus mixture and eggs on a serving plate with the cherry tomatoes. Drizzle with oil and sprinkle with the dukkah. Garnish with mint and serve with warm pita.
* Quail eggs are from selected poultry shops and delis. Dukkah (a spice, nut and seed blend) and walnut oil are from delis and gourmet shops.

chicken liver paté with rustic croutons

Serves 4-6

Chef Sean Moran of Sean's Panaroma, Bondi, serves these rustic croutons with patés and terrines – such a great idea!

400g unsalted butter
500g chicken livers, trimmed
2 eschalots, finely chopped
2 tbs each brandy and thickened cream
2 tbs black peppercorns
2 gold-strength gelatine leaves*
1/2 cup (125ml) chicken stock
1 loaf woodfired bread, crusts removed, torn into large chunks
2 tbs extra virgin olive oil
Onion marmalade*, to serve

Melt 100g butter in a pan over medium-high heat. Add the livers and cook for 2-3 minutes, turning once, until browned but still pink in the centre (be careful as it may spit). Transfer livers to a processor with tongs, then return frypan and butter to medium heat. Add eschalot and cook, stirring, for 2 minutes, then transfer to the processor. Add the brandy to the frypan and cook for 1 minute, scraping the pan to deglaze. Add to the processor with the cream and process to a rough paste.

Chop remaining 300g butter. With motor running, add 1 piece at a time until a smooth paste. Season, then push through a sieve into 2 ramekins or 1 larger terrine. Scatter with peppercorns. Chill while you make topping. Soften gelatine in cold water for 5 minutes. Warm stock over low heat. Squeeze excess water from gelatine, then add to stock and stir to dissolve. Cool. Pour over paté, cover and chill for at least 4 hours, or overnight, to set.

For the croutons, preheat the oven to 200°C and toss bread with olive oil on a baking tray. Toast for 10 minutes until crisp.

Serve the paté with the croutons and onion marmalade.
* From gourmet shops. Check gelatine pack for setting directions.

SMALL TASTES

posh popcorn

Makes 6 cups

If I'm feeling really posh, I use French butter from
the deli, which adds a special flavour to the corn.

80g unsalted butter, chopped
3 garlic cloves, bruised
¼ cup (60ml) light olive oil
1 cup (230g) popcorn kernels
2 tbs herbes de Provence*
2 tsp celery salt

Melt the butter in a pan over low heat. Add the garlic and
remove from heat. Set aside for 15 minutes to infuse.

Heat the oil in a large saucepan over high heat. Add the
popcorn and toss to coat. Cover and shake the pan over
the heat for 2-3 minutes until all the corn has popped.

Remove the garlic from the butter, then pour the butter
over the popcorn. Add the herbs de Provence and celery
salt, season with salt and pepper and toss to coat.

* Herbes de Provence is a dried herb mixture (including celery
seed, parsley, thyme, tarragon, marjoram, bay and lavender
flowers) from selected supermarkets and delis (see Glossary).

tuna sashimi with wasabi bean salad

Serves 4

Pick up some plastic soy sauce 'fish' at your local sushi bar
– it's fun to give each guest one to drizzle over their plate.

1-2 tsp wasabi paste (to taste), plus extra to serve
1 tbs red wine vinegar
2 tsp lemon juice
2$^1/_2$ tbs olive oil
350g thin green beans
1 small red onion, thinly sliced
Handful flat-leaf parsley leaves, torn
225g sashimi-grade tuna*, thinly sliced
Black* or regular sesame seeds, to sprinkle
Soy sauce, to serve

Combine the wasabi, vinegar and lemon juice in a bowl.
Gradually whisk in the oil until well combined.
   Slice the beans using an old-fashioned beaner (from
kitchenware shops) or slice on an angle. Blanch in a pan
of boiling salted water for 1 minute until just tender,
then drain, refresh in cold water and drain again.
   Toss the beans, onion and parsley in a bowl with the wasabi
dressing. Divide the beans among small bowls, then place on
serving plates with the tuna. Sprinkle with sesame seeds,
then serve with soy sauce and a dab of extra wasabi.
* Sashimi-grade tuna is from fishmongers. Black sesame seeds
are from Asian food shops.

beetroot & goat's cheese stacks

Serves 4

425g can sliced beetroot, drained
¼ cup (60ml) olive oil
¼ cup (60ml) balsamic vinegar
3 tsp chopped chives
2 tbs milk
120g soft goat's cheese
Micro salad and herb leaves* or regular mixed
    baby salad leaves, to garnish
2 tbs toasted chopped walnuts

Choose 12 even-sized slices of beetroot, pat dry with paper towel, then lay in a shallow dish. Cover with the oil and balsamic, then set aside at room temperature for 1 hour.

Place the chives, milk and goat's cheese in a bowl. Season with salt and pepper, then mash with a fork until smooth.

Just before serving, drain beetroot (reserving dressing) and pat slices dry with paper towel. Place 1 slice of beetroot on a serving plate. Spoon the cheese mixture into a piping bag and pipe some onto the beetroot (alternatively, spread about 1 tablespoon of the mixture over the beetroot with the back of a spoon). Repeat with more beetroot and cheese, then finish with a final beetroot slice. Repeat to make 4 stacks.

Garnish each stack with a few leaves, sprinkle some walnuts around each plate, then drizzle with the reserved dressing. Serve immediately.

* Available from selected greengrocers and growers' markets.

deep-fried brie with sweet chilli sauce

Serves 4

Back in the '70s, everyone served deep-fried brie as a starter. Extra crunchy panko breadcrumbs and sweet chilli sauce add a new dimension to this classic.

2 cups panko breadcrumbs* or coarse fresh breadcrumbs
Finely grated zest of 1 lemon
2 tbs chopped flat-leaf parsley
2 tbs plain flour
1 egg, beaten
2 tbs milk
350g piece brie or camembert, cut into 4 wedges
Sunflower oil, to deep-fry
Sweet chilli sauce and wild rocket leaves, to serve

Place the breadcrumbs in a food processor with the lemon zest and parsley, then pulse to fine crumbs. Place the crumb mixture in a shallow bowl, place the flour in a separate bowl, and gently whisk the egg and milk in a third bowl
   Toss the wedges of cheese first in the flour, shaking off excess, then in the egg mixture, then in the breadcrumbs. Place on a plate and chill for at least 30 minutes (or up to 4 hours ahead).
   Half-fill a deep-fryer or large heavy-based saucepan with oil and heat to 190°C. (If you don't have a deep-fryer thermometer, test a cube of bread – it'll turn golden in 30 seconds when the oil is hot enough.) Deep-fry the cheese for 1 minute or until golden all over, then drain briefly on paper towel.
Serve immediately with sweet chilli sauce and rocket.
* Coarse, light Japanese breadcrumbs from Asian food shops.

salmon & prawn timbales with chilli cucumber

Serves 4

16 slices smoked salmon
16 cooked prawns, peeled, deveined, chopped
1 cup (250g) sour cream or creme fraiche
2 tbs chopped coriander
1 tbs finely grated lemon zest
1 Lebanese cucumber
1 long red chilli, seeds removed, finely chopped
¼ cup (60ml) peanut oil
2 tsp soy sauce
1 tsp white wine vinegar
1 tsp caster sugar

Line four ½ cup (125ml) ramekins or coffee cups with plastic wrap, leaving some overhanging. Line each with 4 salmon slices, leaving enough overhanging to enclose.

Place the prawns, sour cream, coriander and lemon zest in a food processor, season with salt and pepper and pulse to combine. Fill the ramekins with the prawn mixture, cover with the overhanging salmon and enclose with the wrap. Chill for 4 hours until firm.

Meanwhile, use a peeler to shave long strips from the cucumber, turning as you go. Discard the seeds in the centre. Place the chilli and oil in a small saucepan over low heat. Add the soy, vinegar and sugar and stir to dissolve the sugar. Season, cool slightly, then add cucumber to the chilli dressing. Cover and chill for 30 minutes to marinate.

Unmould the timbales onto serving plates, top with chilli cucumber and drizzle with any remaining dressing.

roasted cherry tomato tarte tatins

Serves 4

4 x 190g jars roasted cherry tomatoes in oil*,
    drained, oil reserved
4 frozen puff pastry sheets, thawed
100g Persian feta*, crumbled
2 tbs small basil leaves, to garnish
Balsamic vinegar, to drizzle

Preheat the oven to 180°C. Lightly grease four 12cm blini pans
or small non-stick pie dishes with some of the reserved oil.

Arrange cherry tomatoes in a single layer over the base of
each pan, packing in close together, to completely cover.

Cut 4 circles from the pastry, slightly larger than the base
of the pans. Place pastry over the tomatoes, tucking in the
edges. Place on a tray and bake for 20 minutes or until the
pastry is puffed and golden.

Remove the tarts from the oven and stand for 10 minutes,
then turn out onto serving plates. Scatter with the feta and
garnish with basil. Serve drizzled with balsamic and a little
more of the reserved oil.

* Roasted cherry tomatoes in oil (see Glossary) are from
supermarkets and delis. Persian feta is available from
delis and gourmet shops.

hummus soup

Serves 4-6

I love hummus, so why not make it a soup?
This makes a lovely starter for a Moroccan meal.

1L (4 cups) chicken stock
3 garlic cloves, finely chopped
Grated zest and juice of 1 small lemon,
    plus wedges to serve
2 x 400g cans chickpeas, rinsed, drained
1 tbs chopped mint leaves
1 tbs chopped flat-leaf parsley leaves
Natural yoghurt, to drizzle
Extra virgin olive oil, to drizzle
2 tbs dukkah*
Flatbread, to serve

Place the stock in a saucepan with the garlic, lemon zest and
chickpeas and bring to the boil over medium-high heat. Reduce
heat to medium-low and simmer for 5 minutes. Cool slightly,
then add the mint, parsley and lemon juice and puree using a
stick blender (or puree in batches in a blender) until smooth.
   Season to taste with salt and pepper, then reheat over low heat.
Ladle soup into serving bowls, drizzle over yoghurt and oil and
sprinkle with dukkah. Serve with lemon wedges and flatbread.
* Dukkah is a spice, nut and seed blend from delis and
Middle Eastern food shops.

chilled cucumber soup with smoked trout tartines

Serves 4-6

30g unsalted butter, plus extra softened butter to spread
1 onion, chopped
4 telegraph cucumbers, peeled, seeds removed, chopped
200g pontiac or desiree potatoes, peeled, chopped
3 cups (750ml) chicken stock
3 dill sprigs, roughly chopped
200g creme fraiche
2 ficelle* loaves (or 1 baguette)
500g smoked trout, flaked
Mustard cress or rocket leaves, to garnish

Melt the butter in a saucepan over medium-low heat. Add the onion and cook, stirring, for 3-4 minutes until softened but not coloured. Add the cucumber, potato and stock, then season with salt and pepper. Bring to the boil, then simmer over medium-low heat for 20 minutes or until the potato is tender.

Cool slightly, then add the dill. Puree using a stick blender (or puree in batches in a blender) until smooth. Whisk in the creme fraiche and allow to cool. Cover and refrigerate for at least 4 hours until well chilled.

Just before serving, split the ficelle lengthways and spread with the softened butter. Fill with the smoked trout and season, then garnish with cress or rocket. Slice into 2-3 pieces each. Serve the chilled soup in bowls with trout tartines on the side.
* A ficelle is a thin half-baguette available from selected bakeries.

spiced carrot & lentil soup

Serves 4-6

2 tsp cumin seeds
Pinch of dried chilli flakes
2 tbs olive oil
1 onion, chopped
5 carrots (600g total), roughly chopped
3/4 cup (150g) red lentils
1L (4 cups) chicken stock
150ml pure (thin) cream, plus extra to serve

Heat a large saucepan over low heat. Add the cumin and chilli flakes and cook, stirring, for 1 minute until fragrant. Remove half the spice mixture and set aside to garnish.

Increase heat to medium and add the oil to the pan. Cook the onion, stirring, for 3-4 minutes until the onion starts to soften. Add the carrot, lentils and stock and bring to the boil. Reduce heat to medium-low and simmer for 15-20 minutes until carrot is tender. Cool slightly, then puree using a stick blender (or puree in batches in a blender) until smooth.

Return to the pan and season with salt and pepper. Stir in the cream and reheat gently over low heat. Serve drizzled with extra cream, scattered with the reserved spices.

bean, coconut & lime soup

Serves 4-6

1 tbs sunflower oil
1 onion, chopped
1-2 tsp Thai green curry paste or jungle curry paste
2 x 400g cans cannellini beans, rinsed, drained
350ml chicken stock
2 kaffir lime leaves*
Zest and juice of 1 lime
400ml coconut milk
2 tsp fish sauce
Sliced red chilli, coriander leaves and
   chopped peanuts, to serve

Heat the oil in a saucepan over medium heat. Add the onion and cook, stirring occasionally, for 1-2 minutes until soft. Add the curry paste and cook, stirring, for 1 minute or until fragrant. Add the beans, stock, lime leaves, zest and juice. Increase the heat to medium-high and bring to the boil, then reduce the heat to low and simmer for 10 minutes.

   Cool slightly, then remove and discard the lime leaves. Puree using a stick blender (or puree in batches in a blender) until smooth, then stir in the coconut milk and fish sauce. Reheat gently over low heat. Ladle into serving bowls and sprinkle with chilli, coriander and peanuts.
* From greengrocers and Asian food shops.

pea soup with croque monsieur

Serves 4-6

A toasted croque monsieur sandwich filled with ham, mustard and gruyere turns this soup into a great midweek dinner. Or, for a dinner party, cut smaller circles from the sandwiches and serve as a crouton in the soup.

1 tbs olive oil
20g unsalted butter
1 onion, chopped
2 celery stalks, chopped
1 leek (pale part only), thinly sliced
1 potato, peeled, chopped
1 bouquet garni*
2 cups (500ml) chicken stock
2 cups (240g) frozen peas (not baby)
½ cup (125ml) pure (thin) cream
½ cup mint leaves, chopped
Snow pea sprouts, to garnish
Toasted croque monsier sandwiches or croutons, to serve

Heat oil and butter in a pan over medium heat. Add onion, celery and leek and cook, stirring, for 5 minutes or until vegetables are soft but not browned. Add potato, bouquet garni and stock and simmer for 5 minutes until potato is soft. Add peas and cream and simmer for a further minute, then remove 2-3 tablespoons peas with a slotted spoon and set aside.

Puree using a stick blender (or puree in batches in a blender) until smooth. Return the reserved peas to the pan and reheat soup gently over low heat. Serve soup in bowls with a croque monsieur in the centre, if desired, garnished with snow pea sprouts.
* Bouquet garni is a bunch of herbs (usually parsley, thyme and bay leaves) tied with string and used to flavour soups and stews. Make your own fresh, or buy ready-made dried bouquet garni from delis and selected supermarkets (see Glossary).

SOUPS

the chicken that thought it was christmas

Serves 4

I love the flavours of Christmas and make any excuse throughout the year to cook up a mini festive roast.

8 slices pancetta
  or bacon
4 spatchcocks*, trussed
  with kitchen string
1 tbs olive oil
150ml dry red wine
150ml chicken stock
4 tbs redcurrant jelly
Fresh breadcrumbs fried in
  butter, to serve (optional)

Bread sauce
30g unsalted butter
1 large onion, finely chopped
100ml pure (thin) cream
1 bay leaf
5 cloves
1 1/2 cups (100g) fresh
  white breadcrumbs
300ml milk
Pinch of nutmeg

Preheat the oven to 180°C. Cross 2 pancetta slices over each spatchcock, season and drizzle with oil. Roast for 40 minutes or until the juices run clear when the thigh is pierced.

While spatchcocks are roasting, make sauce. Melt butter in a pan over low heat. Add onion and cook for 5 minutes or until softened. Add cream, bay and cloves and stir for 2-3 minutes. Remove from heat and stand for 20 minutes to infuse. Discard bay and cloves, then puree in a food processor and set aside. Simmer crumbs and milk in a pan on low heat for 5-6 minutes, stirring, until smooth. Add onion puree and nutmeg, then season. Cover surface of the sauce with baking paper.

Remove birds from pan and leave to rest while you make a gravy. Place roasting pan on the stove over medium heat. Add wine, stock and jelly, then simmer, stirring and scraping pan, for 5-6 minutes until gravy thickens. Serve spatchcocks with gravy and bread sauce, topped with extra crumbs if desired.
* From poultry shops and selected supermarkets.

easy coq au vin

Serves 4

Using flavoursome thigh fillet instead of whole chicken pieces is a great way to speed up a classic coq au vin.

8 eschalots, peeled
1 tbs olive oil
60g sliced pancetta, cut into strips
8 chicken thigh fillets, cut into 3cm pieces
2 tbs plain flour
3 garlic cloves, finely chopped
150g button mushrooms, quartered
2 tbs tomato paste
1 cup (250ml) good-quality chicken stock
　or chicken consommé
1 cup (250ml) dry red wine
1 tbs chopped fresh thyme leaves
2 bay leaves
Chopped flat-leaf parsley and toasted baguette, to serve

Par-cook the eschalots in boiling water for 5 minutes, then drain and set aside.

Heat the oil in a large deep frypan or casserole pan over medium heat. Add pancetta and cook, stirring, for 2-3 minutes until starting to crisp. Season chicken, then add to the pan and cook for 5-6 minutes until lightly browned. Add flour and stir to coat chicken, then stir in the garlic, mushrooms and tomato paste.

Once everything is well combined, add the stock, wine, thyme, bay leaves and eschalots. Season well, bring to the boil, then reduce heat to medium-low and simmer for 20 minutes or until the chicken is cooked through and the sauce has thickened.

Serve the coq au vin in deep bowls with parsley and toasted baguette to mop up the lovely sauce.

oregano chicken on bean & olive salad

Serves 4

I like to use the branches of dried oregano found in Greek delis and Middle Eastern food shops, as the flavour is so much better than regular dried oregano.

2 tbs dried oregano leaves
1 tsp dried red chilli flakes
Zest and juice of 1 lemon, plus lemon to serve
1/2 cup (125ml) extra virgin olive oil
4 corn-fed chicken breasts with skin*
  (wingbone attached, optional)
450g waxy potatoes (such as Anya or kipfler)
300g thin green beans, topped
1 small red onion, thinly sliced
2 tbs chopped flat-leaf parsley
100g pitted kalamata olives, crushed
2 tsp red wine vinegar

Mix the oregano, chilli, lemon zest and juice and 1/3 cup (80ml) of the oil in a bowl with salt and pepper. Make a few slashes in the chicken skin, then place chicken in a shallow dish and rub in the marinade, making sure it's well coated. Cover and marinate in the fridge for 1-2 hours.

Meanwhile, make the salad. Boil the potatoes in a pan of salted water for 8-10 minutes until just tender. Drain, return to the pan and lightly crush. Blanch the beans in boiling salted water for 2 minutes, then drain. Place in a large bowl with the crushed potatoes, remaining oil, onion, parsley, olives and vinegar. Season well, then set aside while you cook the chicken.

Meanwhile, preheat a chargrill pan or barbecue on medium-high. Grill the chicken for 5-6 minutes each side until cooked through (if browning too quickly, finish cooking in the oven).

Serve the chicken on the salad, with extra lemon to squeeze.

* Available from poultry shops and butchers.

chicken, leek & bacon pot pies

Serves 4

40g unsalted butter
1 tbs olive oil
3 leeks (pale part only), thinly sliced
4 bacon rashers, rind removed, chopped
800g chicken thigh fillets, cut into 2cm pieces
1 tbs plain flour
Pinch of nutmeg
200ml chicken stock
300ml light sour cream or creme fraiche
2 tbs chopped flat-leaf parsley
2 tbs lemon juice
4 sheets frozen puff pastry
1 egg, lightly beaten

Heat the butter and oil in a pan over low heat. Add the leek, bacon and chicken and cook, stirring, for 6-8 minutes until the leek is soft and chicken is almost cooked. Stir in the flour and nutmeg and cook for 1-2 minutes until the chicken is cooked through. Stir in the stock, increase heat to medium and bring to the boil. Season, then remove from the heat and stir in the sour cream, parsley and lemon juice. Cool completely.

Preheat the oven to 200°C.

Cut two 1cm strips from the sides of each pastry sheet. Set aside. Cut pie lids from the remaining pastry, 1cm wider than the top of four 300ml pie dishes or ramekins. Divide chicken mixture among dishes. Press pastry strips around the rim of each dish to make a 'collar' and brush with some of the egg. Carefully top with pie lids, press firmly into the collar to seal, then trim edges if necessary. Make 2 cuts in each pie top, then brush with remaining egg. Bake the pies for 20 minutes or until puffed and golden.

chicken with chilli chocolate

Serves 4

This easy version of the classic Mexican mole stew uses good-quality chilli chocolate to add depth and spice to the sauce.

1 tbs olive oil
20g unsalted butter
4 chicken breast fillets
100g pancetta, cut into strips
2 celery stalks, chopped
1 onion, sliced
2 garlic cloves, finely chopped
150ml dry red wine
400ml chicken stock
400g can chopped tomatoes
50g chilli chocolate*, broken into small pieces
300g can red kidney beans, rinsed, drained
Steamed rice, sliced red chilli, coriander leaves (optional),
    corn chips and avocado wedges, to serve

Preheat the oven to 180°C.

Heat the oil and butter in a casserole pan over medium heat. Add the chicken and cook for 2-3 minutes each side until golden, then remove and set aside. Add the pancetta, celery and onion and cook, stirring, for 5 minutes until vegetables soften. Add the garlic and wine and simmer for 2-3 minutes. Stir in the stock, tomato and chocolate, then return chicken to the pan. Cover and transfer to the oven for 25 minutes or until the chicken is cooked through.

Remove chicken from the pan, cover loosely with foil and set aside in a warm place. Return the pan to the stove over medium-high heat, add the beans and simmer for 4-5 minutes until thickened. Slice the chicken and serve on steamed rice, with the sauce, chilli, and coriander if desired. Serve with corn chips and avocado.

* Available from supermarkets (see Glossary).

rosemary lamb kebabs with lemon & olive relish

Serves 4

If you have a rosemary bush, strip most of the leaves from 4 long, thin branches to use as skewers.

2 garlic cloves, finely chopped
2 tbs olive oil
1 tbs chopped rosemary leaves
1 tbs paprika, plus extra to dust
1 tbs lemon juice
500g lamb fillet, cut into 2cm cubes
4 vine-ripened tomatoes, seeds removed, chopped
1 tbs chopped preserved lemon rind*
   (white pith and flesh discarded)
2 tbs chopped pitted kalamata olives
2 tbs chopped flat-leaf parsley
Thick Greek-style yoghurt, to serve

Soak 4 rosemary branches or bamboo skewers in cold water for 30 minutes to prevent them from burning.

Combine the garlic, oil, rosemary, paprika and lemon juice in a glass or ceramic dish. Season well, then add the lamb, tossing to coat well. Cover and marinate in the fridge for 1-2 hours.

Meanwhile, combine the tomato, preserved lemon rind, olives and parsley in a bowl. Season to taste (it will already be quite salty from the lemon), then set the relish aside.

Thread the lamb onto the branches or skewers. Heat a chargrill pan or barbecue on medium-high heat. Cook the lamb, turning occasionally, for 6-8 minutes until browned all over but still juicy in the centre. Serve the skewers with the relish and yoghurt, dusted with a little extra paprika.

* Available from gourmet food shops and delis.

porcini-dusted lamb with cheat's mushroom "risotto"

Serves 4

I often substitute risoni pasta for arborio rice when I am short on time – it's quicker to cook and there's no need to stir.

5 tbs (30g) porcini powder*
4 x 200g lamb backstraps, well-trimmed
2 tbs olive oil, plus extra to brush
300g Swiss brown mushrooms
1 tsp rosemary leaves
2 garlic cloves, crushed
$^1/_2$ cup (125ml) dry white wine
1 cup (220g) risoni pasta (orzo)
2 cups (500ml) chicken stock
$^3/_4$ cup (60g) grated parmesan
Rocket leaves, to serve

Spread 4 tablespoons of the porcini powder in a shallow dish. Brush lamb with extra oil, then season and roll in the powder. Heat 1 tablespoon oil in a deep frypan over medium-high heat. Cook the lamb, turning, for 3 minutes each side for medium-rare (or until done to your liking). Remove from the pan, cover loosely with foil, and keep warm in a low oven while you make the risotto.

Heat remaining oil in a large non-stick frypan over medium heat. Add mushrooms, rosemary and garlic and cook, stirring, for 3-4 minutes until mushrooms are just tender. Add the wine, risoni and stock, then bring to the boil. Reduce heat to low and simmer for 8-10 minutes until all stock is absorbed and risoni is al dente. Stir in the parmesan and remaining porcini powder and season. Thickly slice the lamb and serve on the risoni with rocket.
* Porcini powder is from gourmet food shops (see Glossary). If you can't find it, grind dried porcini mushrooms in a coffee grinder.

dukkah-crusted lamb with radish tzatziki

Serves 4

1 tbs pomegranate molasses*, plus extra to drizzle
1 tbs honey, warmed
1 cup dukkah*
12 French-trimmed lamb cutlets
1 tbs olive oil
6 radishes, trimmed
1 telegraph cucumber
250g thick Greek-style yoghurt
2 garlic cloves, crushed
2 tbs chopped mint, plus leaves to garnish
Fresh pomegranate seeds* (optional), to garnish

Preheat the oven to 180°C.

Combine molasses and honey in a bowl, and spread the dukkah in a separate shallow bowl.

Season cutlets with salt and pepper. Heat the oil in a frypan over medium-high heat and cook the cutlets, in 2 batches, for 1 minute each side until sealed. Brush the cutlets with the molasses mixture, then dip in the dukkah to coat. Place on a lined baking tray and cook in the oven for a further 5 minutes until cooked but still pink in the centre.

Meanwhile, coarsely grate the radishes and cucumber. Transfer to a sieve and squeeze out excess moisture. Combine with yoghurt, garlic and mint, then season with salt and pepper.

Drizzle the extra pomegranate molasses over the cutlets and garnish with pomegranate seeds. Serve with the tzatziki, garnished with extra mint leaves.

* Pomegranate molasses (see Glossary) and dukkah (a spice, nut and seed blend) are from Middle Eastern shops and delis. Pomegranates are available from greengrocers in season.

oven-baked lamb curry

Serves 4

I like to serve this with crispy pappadams or naan bread.

600g lamb fillets, cut into 2cm cubes
2 tbs olive oil
1 onion, thinly sliced
2 tbs mild curry paste (such as korma)
600ml chicken or vegetable stock
400g can chopped tomatoes
2 cinnamon quills
2 garlic cloves, finely chopped
12 fresh curry leaves*
1¹/₃ cups (300g) medium-grain rice
Natural yoghurt, to serve

Preheat the oven to 180°C.

Season the lamb. Heat half the oil in a frypan over medium-high heat. Brown the lamb, in batches, for 2-3 minutes, then remove and set aside.

Return the pan to medium heat with the remaining oil. Add the onion and cook, stirring, for 5 minutes until golden. Add the curry paste and stir for a few seconds until fragrant, then transfer to a 2.5-litre baking dish. Add the lamb, stock, tomato, cinnamon, garlic and curry leaves. Season with salt and pepper, stir well to combine, then cover with foil and bake for 20 minutes.

Stir the rice into the curry, then return to the oven, uncovered, for 10 minutes or until the lamb is tender and the rice is cooked. Serve the curry topped with yoghurt.

* Available from selected greengrocers and Asian food shops.

gnocchi-topped cottage pies

Serves 6

Update the classic cottage pie by swapping mashed potato
for a golden gnocchi topping.

2 tbs olive oil, plus extra to toss
100g sliced pancetta or bacon, chopped
1 large onion, chopped
2 small carrots, chopped
1 tbs plain flour
4 garlic cloves, chopped
1 tbs tomato paste
1kg lamb mince
300ml dry red wine
2 cups (500ml) beef stock
2 bay leaves
2 tsp chopped thyme
2 x 500g packets potato gnocchi
40g unsalted butter, melted
2 tbs grated parmesan

Heat the oil in a large frypan over medium heat. Add the pancetta,
onion and carrot and cook, stirring, for 5 minutes or until the
onion has softened. Add the flour, garlic and paste and cook,
stirring, for a further minute. Add the mince and cook for
5-6 minutes until well browned. Add the wine, stock, bay leaves
and thyme, season, then bring to the boil. Reduce the heat to
low and simmer for 1 hour or until sauce has thickened. Cool.

Preheat the oven to 190°C.

Cook the gnocchi according to packet instructions. Drain,
then toss in a little olive oil.

Divide the lamb mixture among six 400ml ovenproof dishes
and cover the top of each with gnocchi. Brush the tops with
the melted butter, then sprinkle with parmesan. Bake the
pies for 20 minutes or until golden.

new beef stroganoff

Serves 4

4 x 180g beef fillet steaks
¼ cup (60ml) olive oil, plus extra to brush
2 tbs mixed dried peppercorns, crushed
250g Swiss brown mushrooms, sliced
2 tbs brandy
1¼ cups (310ml) beef stock
1 tbs Dijon mustard
¼ cup chopped flat-leaf parsley,
    plus extra to serve
½ cup (125ml) thickened cream
400g pappardelle or fettuccine

Brush the steaks with a little oil, then season with salt. Sprinkle all over with the crushed peppercorns, gently pressing into the steaks. Heat 1 tablespoon oil in a frypan over medium-high heat. Add the steaks and cook for 2-3 minutes each side until well-seared but still rare in the centre (or until cooked to your liking). Set aside and cover loosely with foil to keep warm.

Add the remaining oil to the steak pan. Add mushrooms and cook, stirring, for 3 minutes until they start to soften. Add the brandy and stock, then bring to the boil. Decrease the heat to medium-low and simmer for 5 minutes or until reduced by half. Stir in the mustard, parsley and cream. Cook for a further minute, stirring, until heated through.

Meanwhile, cook the pasta in a saucepan of boiling salted water according to packet instructions. Drain, then add to the pan with the sauce and toss to combine.

Slice the steak 1cm-thick on an angle, then divide among plates with the pasta. Drizzle with any sauce left in the pan, then serve garnished with parsley.

my pho

Serves 4

My version of the Vietnamese noodle soup, pho, is quick and easy
– I just pick up some rare roast beef from the deli and lovely
aromatic herbs from the greengrocer on my way home. Serve
topped with chilli jam for a little extra heat.

200g flat rice-stick noodles
1 tbs sunflower oil
6 spring onions, sliced on an angle
2cm piece ginger, very thinly sliced
1 small red chilli, seeds removed, finely chopped
3 cups (750ml) beef consommé*
¼ cup (60ml) fish sauce
¼ cup (60ml) lime juice
100g bean sprouts, ends trimmed
¼ cup coriander leaves, plus extra to serve
¼ cup Thai basil leaves*, plus extra to serve
¼ cup mint leaves, plus extra to serve
400g thinly sliced rare roast beef

Soften the noodles in a bowl of boiling water according to
packet instructions.

   Meanwhile, heat the oil in a saucepan over medium heat.
Add the spring onion, ginger and chilli and cook, stirring, for
2-3 minutes until onion is soft. Add the consommé and 1 cup
(250ml) water, then bring to the boil. Decrease the heat to low
and simmer for 10 minutes. Stir in the fish sauce and lime juice.

   Divide the noodles, bean sprouts and herbs among soup
bowls, then ladle over the broth. Serve topped with beef
slices and extra herbs.

* Beef consommé is available in cans and tetra packs from
supermarkets. Thai basil is available from greengrocers
and Asian food shops; substitute regular basil.

thai-style braised beef cheeks

Serves 6

Don't be put off by the long list of ingredients – everything goes into the one pan so you can leave it in a slow-cooker or in the oven.

6 beef cheeks*
1/3 cup (50g) plain flour, seasoned
2 tbs sunflower oil
3 onions, sliced
4cm piece galangal*, sliced
1 lemongrass stem (pale part only), sliced
4cm piece fresh ginger, sliced into thin matchsticks
1/2 cup (135g) grated palm sugar* (or use brown sugar)
3 garlic cloves, sliced
3 kaffir lime leaves*

3 long red chillies, seeds removed, thinly sliced
1/3 cup tamarind puree*
2 cups (500ml) beef stock
1/2 cup (125ml) fish sauce
Steamed rice, to serve

Herb salad
2 cups mixed Asian herbs (such as coriander, Thai basil* and Vietnamese mint*)
6 spring onions, sliced into very thin strips
2 tbs olive oil
1 tbs lime juice

Coat the beef in flour, shaking off excess. Heat the oil in a large pan over medium-high heat. In 2 batches, brown the beef for 1-2 minutes each side. Transfer to a slow-cooker or flameproof casserole. Add 1 litre (4 cups) water and all the remaining ingredients, reserving 1 sliced chilli for the salad. Stir to combine, then cover and cook on low heat for 7 hours (or overnight) in a slow-cooker, or in the oven at 170°C for 3 hours 30 minutes until the beef is very tender. Remove the beef and set aside. Reduce liquid over medium-high heat until you have a thick sauce.

Just before serving, place the herb salad ingredients in a bowl with the remaining chilli, season with salt and toss to combine. Serve the beef on rice, topped with sauce and the herb salad.
* Order beef cheeks from your butcher. Substitute large pieces of chuck steak. All other ingredients are from Asian food shops.

steak with simple bearnaise

Serves 4

Use your blender to create this easy bearnaise sauce, instead of using the traditional double-boiler method. You can make the sauce up to 2 hours in advance and keep it warm in a thermos flask. Give it a good shake before pouring.

2 tbs tarragon vinegar*
1 eschalot, finely chopped
6 black peppercorns
2 tbs chopped tarragon leaves*
4 rib-eye steaks
2 tbs olive oil, to brush
3 egg yolks
140g unsalted butter
Watercress or rocket leaves, to serve
Shoestring fries, to serve

Place the vinegar, eschalot, peppercorns, half the tarragon leaves and 2 tablespoons water in a pan over medium heat and simmer for 1 minute until reduced to about 1 tablespoon of liquid. Strain through a fine sieve, pressing down on solids.

Brush the steaks with oil and season with salt and pepper. Heat a chargrill pan over high heat and cook the steaks for 3-4 minutes each side for medium-rare (or until cooked to your liking). Rest in a warm place, loosely covered with foil, for 5 minutes.

Meanwhile, place egg yolks and tarragon reduction in a blender and whiz to combine. Melt butter in a pan over medium-low heat. With the motor running, very slowly and carefully pour the butter through the feed tube of the blender while it's still hot and bubbling, to form a thick sauce. Stir in remaining tarragon. Drizzle sauce over steak, season and serve with watercress and fries.
* Tarragon vinegar is from delis and gourmet food shops.
Fresh tarragon is from selected greengrocers.

special steak tartare

Serves 4

For an extra treat, serve this dish with creme fraiche mixed with truffle oil (from gourmet food shops) and chopped chives.

400g good-quality beef eye fillet
2 eschalots, finely chopped
4 cornichons (small pickled cucumbers), finely chopped
2 anchovy fillets, finely chopped
1 tbs baby capers, rinsed, drained,
    finely chopped
1 tsp Dijon mustard
4 quail eggs*
4 green salad leaves
Olive oil, to drizzle
Good-quality potato crisps, to serve
Creme fraiche or truffled creme fraiche (optional), to serve

Cut the beef into wafer-thin slices. Place 3-4 pieces on top of each other and cut into strips, then very finely chop. Place in a bowl with the eschalot, cornichon, anchovy, caper and mustard. Separate the quail egg yolks from the whites. Stir 2 eggwhites into the beef mixture. Discard remaining eggwhites.

   Place the leaves on a serving platter, then place a metal egg ring over each leaf and gently press the beef into the mould. Make a small indent in the centre of each and slide in an egg yolk. Sprinkle with pepper and drizzle with oil. Serve with the potato chips and creme fraiche, if desired.
* Available from selected poultry shops and Asian food shops.

quick italian-style roast pork

Serves 4

600g desiree potatoes, peeled, cut into 3cm chunks
2 tbs olive oil
1 rosemary sprig, leaves finely chopped
2 garlic cloves, finely chopped
2 pork fillets (about 500g each), halved
8 thin slices flat pancetta*
250g cherry truss tomatoes, separated into sprigs
Good-quality basil pesto, to serve

Preheat the oven to 200°C and grease a large baking tray.
   Blanch the potato for 5 minutes in boiling salted water,
then drain well. Spread on the tray, toss with 1 tablespoon
of oil, then season and roast for 20 minutes.
   Meanwhile, mix together the rosemary, garlic and remaining
tablespoon of oil. Coat the pork in the mixture, then wrap
2 slices of pancetta around each fillet and secure with kitchen
string or toothpicks. Season with salt and pepper. Add the pork
to the tray with the potatoes and roast for a further 15 minutes.
Add the tomatoes to the tray, then season and return to the
oven for a further 5 minutes until the potato is golden, the
pork is cooked and the tomatoes are just starting to soften.
   Serve the roast pork and vegetables with pesto to drizzle.
* Flat pancetta is from selected delis and butchers.

sticky honey, soy & ginger pork ribs

Serves 3-4

5cm piece fresh ginger, grated
6 garlic cloves, finely chopped
½ cup (125ml) light soy sauce
½ cup (175g) honey
½ cup (125ml) Chinese rice wine (shaohsing)*
1 tbs sweet chilli sauce
1.4kg pork ribs, cut into individual ribs
Coriander, lime wedges and steamed rice, to serve

Combine the ginger, garlic, soy, honey, rice wine and
sweet chilli sauce in a large zip-lock bag. Add the ribs,
close the bag and shake to coat the pork thoroughly.
Marinate in the fridge for at least 1 hour or overnight.

Preheat the oven to 180°C.

Remove the ribs from the bag, reserving the marinade,
and place on a rack over a roasting pan filled with 1cm water.
Roast for 35-40 minutes until sticky and golden. Remove the
pork from the rack and set aside, loosely covered with foil,
while you make the glaze.

For the glaze, place the marinade in a small saucepan
over medium-high heat with any juices from the roasting
pan. Bring to the boil, then allow to bubble for 4-5 minutes
until the mixture is sticky, watching carefully to ensure it
doesn't burn. Brush over the ribs.

Place the glazed ribs on a serving platter with coriander
and lime wedges, then serve with steamed rice.

* From Asian food shops; substitute dry sherry.

stir-fried pork wraps

Serves 4

Small flour tortillas make a perfect wrap for this quick
pork stir-fry – a favourite TV dinner in my home.

8 dried shiitake mushrooms*
1 tbs sesame oil
2 tbs peanut oil
300g pork mince
1/4 cup (60ml) light soy sauce
2 tbs Chinese rice wine (shaohsing)* or dry sherry
2 tsp caster sugar
2 tbs grated fresh ginger
1 small red onion, thinly sliced
1/4 savoy cabbage, very thinly sliced
2 tbs plum sauce, plus extra to serve
1 tbs chopped mint leaves, plus extra leaves to serve
2 carrots, thinly sliced into matchsticks
1 Lebanese cucumber, thinly sliced into matchsticks
8 small flour tortillas, warmed according to packet instructions

Soak the dried mushrooms in 1/4 cup (60ml) boiling water
for 10 minutes, then slice. Reserve the soaking liquid.
   Heat the oils in a wok over medium-high heat. Add the pork
and stir-fry, breaking up with a spoon, for 3-4 minutes until
lightly browned. Add the soy sauce, rice wine, sugar, ginger,
onion, cabbage, plum sauce, chopped mint and shiitakes
and stir-fry for a further 2-3 minutes until cabbage wilts.
   Serve the pork, vegetables, warm tortillas and extra mint and
plum sauce separately, for people to make their own wraps.
* From Asian food shops and selected supermarkets.

spanish pork with orange & poppyseed salad

Serves 4

1 tsp cumin
1 tbs smoked paprika* (pimenton)
Zest and juice of 1 orange
1/3 cup (80ml) tomato sauce (ketchup)
1/3 cup (80ml) maple syrup
2 pork fillets (about 500g each), trimmed, halved

Orange & poppyseed salad

2 oranges
3 Lebanese cucumbers, halved lengthways,
   seeds removed, sliced
1/4 cup coriander leaves
2 long red chillies, seeds removed, finely chopped
1/3 cup (80ml) white wine vinegar
1/2 cup (125ml) olive oil
2 tbs caster sugar
2 tbs poppyseeds

Combine all the ingredients in a zip-lock bag and shake well to coat pork. Marinate in the fridge for at least 1 hour or overnight.

For the salad, zest the rind of 1 orange and set aside in a small bowl. Peel both oranges, then halve and slice the flesh. Place in a large bowl with the cucumber, coriander and chilli. Add the vinegar, oil, sugar and poppyseeds to the zest bowl, season well and whisk to combine. Set salad and dressing aside.

Preheat a chargrill pan or barbecue on medium-high heat. Cook the pork, turning, for 5-6 minutes until blackened on the outside and cooked through. Set aside loosely covered with foil for 5 minutes to rest, then slice. Divide the salad mixture among 4 plates, top with the sliced pork, then drizzle with dressing.
* From gourmet food shops and selected delis.

crispy herbed pork cutlets

Serves 4

3 cups panko breadcrumbs*
$^1/_2$ cup (75g) plain flour, seasoned
1 tbs fresh lemon thyme (or regular thyme) leaves
$^3/_4$ cup (60g) grated parmesan
3 eggs, beaten
4 pork cutlets
$^1/_4$ cup (60ml) olive oil
30g unsalted butter
8 sage sprigs
Lemon wedges, to serve

Whiz the breadcrumbs in a food processor with the flour, thyme and parmesan to fine crumbs. Season with salt and pepper, then transfer to a shallow bowl. Place egg in a separate bowl.

Use a meat mallet to lightly pound the eye fillet of each pork cutlet to an even thickness. Dip the pork in the egg, then press into the crumb mixture to coat well all over.

Heat the oil in a large non-stick frypan over medium heat. Add the pork and fry for 2-3 minutes each side until golden and cooked through. Remove from the pan and set aside.

Add the butter and sage sprigs to the pan. When the butter begins to foam, return the pork to the pan and turn to coat in the buttery juices. Serve immediately with lemon wedges.
* Panko are light, crunchy Japanese breadcrumbs, available from Asian food shops and selected supermarkets.

fettuccine with sausage and peas

Serves 4

This is my version of chef Andy Bunn's recipe from Cafe Sopra in Sydney. I love it because it has two of my favourite ingredients, sausages and peas!

400g pork and herb sausages, casing removed
2 tbs chopped mint, plus extra leaves to garnish
2 cups (240g) frozen peas
250g mascarpone cheese
Juice of 1 lemon
2 tbs olive oil
500g fettuccine
$^2/_3$ cup (50g) grated parmesan

Combine the sausage meat and mint in a bowl. Roll into about 24 small (3cm) meatballs and chill until needed.

Cook the peas in a pan of boiling salted water for 1-2 minutes until tender. Drain, then return to the pan and crush with a fork. Stir in mascarpone and lemon juice, then season and set aside.

Heat the olive oil in a frypan over medium heat. Add the meatballs in batches if necessary, and cook, turning, for 3-4 minutes until browned all over and cooked through.

Meanwhile, cook the pasta according to packet instructions. Drain, reserving 1 cup (250ml) of the cooking water. Add the pasta and pea mixture to the meatball pan with enough of the reserved water to form a sauce, then toss briefly to combine and heat through. Stir in half the parmesan. Divide among bowls, then serve topped with extra mint and remaining parmesan.

sausages with home-style baked beans

Serves 4

1 cup (250ml) dry white wine
2 cups (500ml) tomato puree
1 cup (250ml) good-quality barbecue sauce*
2 tbs brown sugar
1 tbs molasses
1 tbs Dijon mustard
2 x 400g cans cannellini beans, rinsed, drained
1 Toulouse sausage* or 12 thin pork sausages
Rocket leaves, to serve

Combine the wine, tomato puree, barbecue sauce, sugar, molasses and mustard in a saucepan over medium-low heat and simmer, stirring occasionally, for 6-8 minutes until reduced by half. Add the beans to the sauce and cook for a further 10 minutes until the mixture thickens.

Meanwhile, heat a lightly oiled chargrill pan, frypan or barbecue on medium heat and cook the Toulouse sausage for 5-6 minutes each side until cooked through. (Or cook the thin pork sausages, in batches, for 8-10 minutes until browned and cooked through.)

Cut the Toulouse sausage into 4 pieces, then serve with the baked beans and rocket leaves.

* Good-quality barbecue sauce is from gourmet food shops and delis. Toulouse sausage is a long, coiled French pork sausage, available from selected butchers.

vineyard sausages

Serves 4

1 tbs extra virgin olive oil, plus extra to drizzle
12 pork chipolatas (or use 4 chicken or pork sausages)
1 eschalot, finely chopped
2 cups (350g) mixed seedless grapes
1/2 cup (125ml) dry white wine
2 tsp chopped rosemary leaves
2 tsp honey
Grilled bread and chopped chives, to serve

Heat the olive oil in a frypan over medium-high heat. Add the sausages and cook, turning, for 8-10 minutes until cooked through and golden. Remove the sausages to a plate, cover with foil and keep warm.

Drain any excess fat from the frypan, then return the pan to medium heat. Add the eschalot and grapes and cook, stirring, for 3-4 minutes until the grapes start to soften and begin to lose their juice. Add the wine, rosemary and honey, then stir for a further minute until heated through. Serve the sausages and grape mixture over grilled bread, drizzled with extra oil and sprinkled with chives.

tomato soup with spaghetti and chicken meatballs

Serves 4-6

1 tbs olive oil
1 onion, thinly sliced
2 garlic cloves, finely chopped
1 tbs tomato paste
2 x 400g cans chopped tomatoes
1.25L (5 cups) chicken stock
500g thin chicken sausages
100g spaghetti, broken into 5cm lengths
Chopped basil, grated parmesan and crusty bread, to serve

Heat the oil in a large saucepan over medium heat. Add the onion and cook for 2-3 minutes, stirring, until softened. Add the garlic and tomato paste and cook, stirring, for a further 1 minute. Add the tomatoes and $2^1/_2$ cups (625ml) of the chicken stock. Bring to the boil, then reduce the heat to low and simmer for 20 minutes while you make the meatballs.

For the meatballs, place the remaining $2^1/_2$ cups (625ml) chicken stock in a saucepan and bring to the boil. Squeeze the sausage meat from the casings and form into about 30 small (3cm) meatballs. Add meatballs to the stock and simmer for 10 minutes until cooked through. Remove meatballs to a plate with a slotted spoon, then return stock to the boil. Add the spaghetti and cook until al dente. Drain, discarding the stock.

Use a stick blender to blend the soup until smooth (or blend in batches in a blender, then return to the pan). Add the cooked spaghetti and meatballs to the soup and warm through gently for 5 minutes over low heat. Ladle the soup into bowls, garnish with basil and parmesan, then serve with bread.

frankfurts with stir-fried red cabbage

Serves 4

8 good-quality Continental frankfurts
1 tbs sunflower oil
30g unsalted butter
1 red onion, thinly sliced
1 green apple, peeled, sliced
1 garlic clove, chopped
400g red cabbage, thinly sliced
2 tbs red wine vinegar
2 tbs apple and sage jelly* or redcurrant jelly
1 tbs chopped flat-leaf parsley
Rye bread (optional), to serve

Heat a chargrill pan or frypan over medium heat and cook
frankfurts for 2-3 minutes, turning, until heated through.
(Or simmer in a saucepan of boiling water for 3-4 minutes.)
   Heat oil and butter in a wok or deep frypan over medium heat.
Add onion, apple and garlic and stir-fry for 2-3 minutes until
onion just softens. Add the cabbage and stir-fry for 2-3 minutes
until wilted. Stir in the vinegar, jelly and parsley, then season
and heat through. Transfer to a platter or large serving dish
and toss with the frankfurts. Serve with rye bread, if desired.
* Sage and apple jelly is from gourmet food shops (see Glossary).

pepper steak burger

Serves 4

800g beef mince
1 onion, finely chopped
1 egg, lightly beaten
¼ cup chopped flat-leaf parsley leaves
1 tbs olive oil
2 tbs green peppercorns in brine, drained,
  lightly crushed with a fork
2 tbs brandy
1 tsp Dijon mustard
150ml thickened cream
4 slices sourdough, chargrilled,
  rubbed with a halved garlic clove

Preheat the oven to 170ºC.

Place beef, onion, egg and 2 tablespoons parsley in a bowl, season, then mix well with your hands. Using damp hands, form into 4 thick patties. Cover and chill for 10 minutes.

Heat the oil in a frypan over medium heat. Cook the patties for 2 minutes each side until sealed. Transfer to a baking tray, then bake for 5 minutes or until cooked through.

Meanwhile, drain the excess fat from the pan. Add the peppercorns, brandy, mustard and cream to the pan, then simmer over medium-low heat, stirring, for 2-3 minutes until slightly thickened. Season with sea salt, then stir in the remaining tablespoon chopped parsley.

Place a piece of grilled sourdough on each plate, top with burger patties, drizzle with the pepper sauce and serve.

prawn burgers

Serves 4

$1/2$ cup (150g) whole-egg mayonnaise
1 tbs capers, rinsed, drained
2 tsp wholegrain mustard
1 tbs chopped dill, plus extra to garnish
4 panini or hamburger buns, split
Butter lettuce leaves and
   thinly sliced red onion, to serve
1 avocado, sliced
16 cooked prawns (about 500g),
   peeled, deveined

Combine the mayonnaise, capers, mustard and dill in
a bowl, then season with salt and pepper and set aside.
   Grill or toast the buns. Spread both sides with the caper
mayonnaise, then fill with lettuce leaves, sliced avocado,
prawns, onion and extra dill.

smoked trout burgers with asparagus tzatziki

Serves 4

1 bunch asparagus, woody ends trimmed
1 egg
2 x 170g skinless hot-smoked ocean trout portions*
1¼ cups (85g) fresh wholemeal breadcrumbs
Grated zest and juice of 1 lemon
2 tbs chopped mint leaves
200g thick Greek-style yoghurt
2 garlic cloves, crushed
2 tbs olive oil
4 wholemeal rolls or hamburger buns, split, toasted
Watercress sprigs and lemon wedges, to serve

Cook asparagus in boiling salted water for 2 minutes, then drain and refresh in cold water. Remove and reserve the tips. Chop the stalks, then place in a food processor with the egg. Blend until well combined. Add trout, breadcrumbs, lemon zest and juice, and half the mint and pulse to combine. Season to taste with salt and pepper. Using damp hands, form the mixture into 4 patties. Cover and chill for 30 minutes.

Shred the asparagus tips using a sharp knife, then fold into the yoghurt with the garlic and remaining mint. Season well, then cover and chill the asparagus tzatziki until required.

Heat the oil in a frypan over medium-high heat. Cook the trout patties for 2 minutes each side or until golden brown. Fill the toasted buns with tzatziki, patties and watercress, then serve with lemon wedges.

* Available from supermarkets and delis.

pork, sage & onion burgers

Serves 4

450g pork sausages
1/2 packet (100g) sage and onion stuffing mix*
1 egg
Olive oil, to brush
4 Turkish rolls or panini, split, toasted
Baby spinach or rocket leaves, cranberry
   sauce and sour cream, to serve

Remove the sausage casings, then place the sausage meat
in a bowl with the stuffing and egg, season, then mix well with
your hands. Using damp hands, form the mixture into 4 patties.
Cover and chill for 30 minutes.
   Preheat the oven to 170°C. Brush a frypan or chargrill pan
with oil and heat over medium-high heat. Cook the patties for
2-3 minutes each side until golden. Transfer to a tray, then bake
for 5-6 minutes until cooked through. Fill toasted rolls with
spinach, patties, cranberry sauce and sour cream.
* Stuffing mix is available from supermarkets (see Glossary).

meatball sliders

Serves 4-6 (makes 12)

'Sliders', or mini burgers, are very popular in the US. This Italian meatball version is so good, you won't be able to stop at one.

200g each beef, pork and veal mince
1/2 cup (35g) fresh breadcrumbs
2/3 cup (50g) grated pecorino cheese
   or parmesan, plus extra to serve
1 egg, plus 1 extra yolk
2 tbs chopped flat-leaf parsley leaves
2 tbs olive oil
700ml jar tomato passata (sugo)*
12 small bread rolls, split
2 cups wild rocket leaves

Use your hands to mix the beef, pork and veal mince, breadcrumbs, cheese, egg, egg yolk and parsley together in a bowl, then season with salt and pepper. Using damp hands, form heaped tablespoons of the mixture into 12 large meatballs. Cover and chill for 20 minutes.

Heat the oil in a large ovenproof frypan over medium-high heat. Fry the meatballs, in batches, for 3-4 minutes, turning, until golden all over. Remove meatballs and set aside.

Carefully drain excess oil from the pan. Add the passata to the pan, then simmer over low heat for 5 minutes. Return the meatballs to the pan and simmer for a further 5-6 minutes until cooked through and the sauce thickens slightly.

Fill each roll with rocket, a meatball, sauce and extra cheese.
* Sieved tomatoes, from supermarkets and greengrocers.

asian-marinated baked salmon

Serves 4-6

This recipe comes from my dear friend Karen Thomas. She serves up this beautiful dish with big bowls of thick handcut chips – a little "out there" with an Asian-inspired dish, but that's Karen!

2 lemongrass stems (pale part only), chopped
1/2 cup (125ml) dark soy sauce
1/2 bunch coriander, leaves thinly sliced, stalks finely chopped
2cm piece ginger, finely grated
4 garlic cloves, finely grated
1kg piece skinless salmon fillet, pin-boned
   (ask your fishmonger for a whole fillet)
1/3 cup (115g) honey, warmed
4 spring onions, finely shredded
2 limes, halved
Mixed pea salad (we used fresh peas, snow peas
   and pea shoots), to serve

Bash lemongrass in a mortar with a pestle until fragrant. Stir in the soy sauce, coriander stalks, ginger and garlic. Place the salmon in a glass dish, then spread all over with the marinade. Cover and marinate in the fridge for 1 hour.

Preheat the oven to 200°C and line a large tray with baking paper. Place the salmon on the tray, then brush with the honey. Bake for 10 minutes or until the fish is just cooked but still a little pink in the centre.

Carefully transfer the fish to a board or serving platter, sprinkle with spring onion and coriander leaves, then serve warm or at room temperature with lime to squeeze and salad.

green curry with smoked salmon

Serves 4

3 kaffir lime leaves*
1 pontiac potato (about 300g), peeled,
   cut into 2cm cubes
3 tbs Thai green curry paste
300ml coconut milk
150g thin green beans, trimmed,
   cut into 4cm lengths
1 tbs fish sauce
1 tbs light soy sauce
Juice of 1 lime
2 tsp grated palm sugar* or brown sugar
4 x 175g hot-smoked salmon portions*,
   broken into large chunks
Jasmine rice, to serve

Finely shred 1 kaffir lime leaf and set aside to garnish. Par-cook the potato in boiling salted water for 5 minutes. Drain.

Heat a wok or deep frypan over medium heat. Add the curry paste and stir-fry for 1 minute until fragrant. Add the coconut milk and remaining 2 lime leaves, then bring to the boil. Add the potato, turn the heat to low, then simmer for 5 minutes. Add beans and cook for a further 2 minutes, then stir in the fish sauce, soy, lime juice and sugar, adjusting to taste. Gently stir in the salmon, then cook for a further 1-2 minutes until the vegetables are tender and salmon is heated through. Garnish with the shredded lime leaf, then serve with rice.
* Kaffir lime leaves and palm sugar are from Asian food shops. Hot-smoked salmon portions are from supermarkets.

tea 'smoked' salmon

Serves 4

Smoking fish is quite a performance, and the strong smell
can hang around in the kitchen for days. This cheat's version
uses smoky black lapsang souchong tea from China for a
similar flavour without the fuss.

2 lapsang souchong teabags*
1 garlic clove, finely chopped
5cm piece ginger, grated
1/3 cup (80ml) kecap manis (Indonesian sweet soy sauce)*
1 tbs honey
1 tbs sesame oil
4 salmon fillets with skin
1 tbs olive oil
Jasmine rice and steamed Asian greens, to serve

Place the teabags in a jug, pour over 200ml boiling water, and
leave for 5 minutes to infuse. Press the teabags against the
side of the jug to extract maximum flavour, then discard. Add
the garlic, ginger, kecap manis, honey and half the sesame oil
and stir until combined, then allow to cool. Place the salmon in
a glass or ceramic dish and pour over the marinade, then cover
and marinate in the fridge for at least 4 hours or overnight.

Remove the salmon from the marinade, reserving 1/2 cup
(125ml), and pat dry with paper towel. Heat the remaining
sesame oil and olive oil in a frypan over medium-high heat
and cook the salmon, skin-side down for 2 minutes, then
turn and cook for 2 minutes (or until done to your liking).

Meanwhile, bring the reserved marinade to a gentle simmer
over medium-low heat (don't allow to boil). Serve the salmon
on rice with Asian greens, drizzled with the sauce.
* Lapsang souchong teabags are from selected supermarkets.
Kecap manis is from Asian food shops.

salmon poached in olive oil and vanilla

Serves 4

It's a little extravagant to use a litre of olive oil for poaching, but a well-priced supermarket oil will do, and you'll be rewarded with amazing flavour thanks to the fragrant vanilla bean. You need a kitchen thermometer for this recipe.

1L (4 cups) extra virgin olive oil
1 vanilla bean, split lengthways, seeds scraped
1-2 tarragon sprigs*
2 eschalots, sliced
4 x 120g skinless salmon fillets, pinboned
Cauliflower puree or mashed potato, lemon wedges
  and baby spinach leaves, to serve

Place the olive oil, vanilla pod and seeds, tarragon and eschalot in a flameproof casserole or deep frypan (big enough to fit the salmon in a single layer) and warm gently over low heat for 3-4 minutes. Remove from the heat, then cover and stand for at least 4 hours, or overnight, for the flavours to infuse.

Season the salmon and place in the oil mixture, ensuring the fish is completely covered. Place the pan over very low heat, bring the temperature to 100°C (use a kitchen thermometer – there should be only the slightest ripple in the oil), then poach for 15 minutes. Remove the salmon from the oil with a fish slice – it will still be very pink inside but gently cooked.

Serve the salmon on cauliflower puree or mash with lemon wedges and spinach, drizzled with a little of the poaching oil.
* Fresh tarragon is available from selected greengrocers.

sesame salmon roulades with green papaya salad

Serves 4

250g green papaya* or green mango*
1/3 cup (80ml) lime juice
2 tbs fish sauce
2 tbs grated palm sugar*
2 small red chillies, seeds removed, finely chopped
4 x 150g skinless salmon fillets, pin-boned
1/4 cup (35g) sesame seeds
1 tbs sunflower oil, plus extra to drizzle
2 tbs chopped coriander, plus extra leaves to garnish
2 tbs chopped mint leaves, plus extra leaves to garnish
2 tbs chopped toasted peanuts, plus extra to garnish

Preheat the oven to 170°C.

Cut the papaya or mango flesh into thin matchsticks using a mandoline or coarsely grate. Place in a large bowl. Shake the lime juice, fish sauce, sugar and chilli in a screw-top jar, then toss with the papaya or mango. Set aside.

Slice each salmon fillet horizontally through the centre, leaving 1 end intact, then open out into a long strip. Turn each fillet over and season, then tightly roll and secure each one on a skewer. Place the sesame seeds in a dish, dip in the roulades to coat on both sides, then drizzle with extra oil.

Heat the oil in a non-stick ovenproof frypan over medium heat and sear the roulades for 1 minute each side to lightly toast the seeds. Transfer the pan to the oven for 5 minutes until the fish is just cooked.

Meanwhile, toss the herbs and nuts with the salad. Serve the salmon on the salad, garnished with extra herbs and peanuts.
* Available from Asian food shops and selected greengrocers.

cajun fish with corn & avocado salsa

Serves 4

2 tbs brown sugar
1/2 tsp each of chilli powder, ground cumin,
    paprika and mustard powder
4 skinless thick white fish fillets
    (such as blue-eye or coral trout)
1 tbs olive oil, plus extra to brush
Light sour cream, loosened with enough warm water
    to form a pouring consistency, to serve

Corn & avocado salsa
1 avocado, finely chopped
400g can corn kernels, drained
250g tomatoes, seeds removed, finely chopped
1 red onion, finely chopped
1 tsp sesame oil
2 tbs olive oil
1 cup chopped coriander leaves
Juice of 1 lime

Preheat the oven to 180°C.
   Combine the sugar, chilli, cumin, paprika, mustard powder,
1 teaspoon pepper and ½ teaspoon salt in a shallow bowl. Brush
the fish with extra olive oil, then coat well in the spice mixture.
   Heat the oil in a large ovenproof frypan over medium heat.
Add the fish and cook for 2-3 minutes each side until golden.
Transfer to the oven for 5 minutes or until just cooked.
   Meanwhile, for the salsa, combine all the ingredients in
a bowl and season to taste. Serve the fish topped with the
salsa and drizzled with the sour cream.

whole fish with roast capsicum & chilli butter

Serves 4

4 small (about 350g each) whole fish
   (such as lemon sole or small snapper)
2 tbs olive oil, plus extra to brush
1 roasted red capsicum
   (or a 280g jar chargrilled capsicum*, drained)
100g unsalted butter
Finely grated zest of 1 lemon, plus 1 tbs lemon juice
2 tbs finely chopped coriander leaves
1 small red chilli, seeds removed, finely chopped
1 garlic clove, finely chopped

Preheat the oven to 200°C. Lightly grease 2 baking trays.
   Cut 3 slashes in the thickest part of each fish on one side. Place 2 fish, cut-side up, on each tray, then brush with the extra oil and season with salt and pepper. Bake for 10-12 minutes until the fish is cooked (it will flake easily away from the bone).
   Meanwhile, very finely chop the capsicum, then place in a small saucepan with the olive oil, butter, lemon zest and juice, coriander, chilli and garlic. Season. Stir over low heat until butter is melted and well combined. Keep warm.
   Serve the fish drizzled with the capsicum & chilli butter.
* Available from supermarkets and delis (see Glossary).

pan-fried fish with malt-vinegar tartare

Serves 4

Fish and chips with malt vinegar was a regular Friday-night dinner when I was growing up in England. I love its rich caramel flavour, but if you prefer you can use white wine vinegar instead.

2 tbs olive oil
8 boneless white fish fillets with skin (such as coral trout)
1/2 cup (150g) whole-egg mayonnaise
3 tbs thickened cream
1/3 cup (80ml) malt vinegar, plus extra to serve
1 tbs finely chopped cornichons (small pickled cucumbers)
1 tbs chopped fresh tarragon leaves*
1 tbs finely chopped flat-leaf parsley,
    plus extra to garnish
Oven-baked chips, to serve

Heat the oil in a large non-stick frypan over medium heat. Season the fish, add to the pan and cook for 2 minutes each side or until the skin is crispy and fish is cooked through. Set aside in a warm place while you make the sauce.

Drain most of the oil from the pan. Add the mayonnaise, cream, vinegar and cornichon, and stir for 1-2 minutes to warm through. Remove from the heat, then stir in the tarragon and parsley.

Divide the fish and chips among plates, then drizzle with the tartare sauce. Season with salt and pepper, garnish with parsley, and serve with extra malt vinegar for the chips.
* Fresh tarragon is from selected greengrocers.

tandoori swordfish with lemon achar

Serves 4

3 tbs (75g) tandoori paste
3 tbs (70g) thick Greek-style yoghurt
4 x 180g swordfish steaks
1 tbs vegetable oil
2 tsp black mustard seeds
3 preserved lemon quarters*, white pith
   and flesh removed, rind thinly sliced
1 long red chilli, seeds removed, thinly sliced
1 tsp ground turmeric
12 fresh curry leaves*
1 tbs white wine vinegar
2 tsp caster sugar
2 tomatoes, seeds removed, sliced
Fried pappadams and steamed basmati rice, to serve

Combine the tandoori paste and yoghurt in a shallow dish.
Add the swordfish steaks and turn to coat in the mixture,
then cover and marinate in the fridge for 1 hour.

Meanwhile, for the lemon achar, heat the oil in a frypan over
medium heat. Add mustard seeds and cook for 1 minute or
until they start to pop. Add the preserved lemon, chilli, turmeric
and curry leaves and cook, stirring, for 3 minutes. Combine the
vinegar and sugar in a small bowl, stirring to dissolve the sugar,
then add to the pan with the tomato. Stir to combine, then
remove from the heat and set aside to cool.

Preheat a chargrill pan or barbecue on medium-high,
then cook the fish for 2 minutes each side or until cooked
but still moist in the centre. Serve the swordfish with the
achar, pappadams and rice.

* Preserved lemons are from gourmet shops and delis. Fresh
curry leaves are from selected greengrocers and Asian shops.

fish tagine

Serves 4

Meat-based tagines are all about long, slow cooking, but this seafood version is the fast route to Moroccan flavours. To make it even quicker, use a good marinara mix from your fishmonger.

2 tbs olive oil
1 large red onion, thinly sliced
2 tbs chermoula paste*
400g can chopped tomatoes
1 cinnamon quill
600g mixed fish and seafood (we used red mullet fillets, ling pieces and prawns)
1/2 cup green olives
1 tbs chopped coriander
Couscous and flatbread, to serve

Heat the oil in a large heavy-based saucepan over medium heat. Add the onion and cook for 2 minutes until softened. Add the chermoula and stir for a few seconds until fragrant, then add the tomato, cinnamon and 350ml water. Bring to the boil, then reduce heat to medium-low and simmer for 10 minutes until thickened. Add the seafood and simmer for a further 8-10 minutes until just cooked. Remove from the heat, stir in the olives and sprinkle with coriander. Serve with couscous and flatbread.
* Chermoula is a North African herb and spice paste, from Middle Eastern and gourmet shops (see Glossary).

spicy garlic prawns cooked in beer

Serves 4

This would have to be every man's died-and-gone-to-heaven dish. The idea is to suck the sweet meat from the prawn shell, then wash it all down with plenty more cold beer.

1kg green king prawns
80g unsalted butter
1/2 tsp smoked paprika* (pimenton)
4 garlic cloves, finely chopped
Pinch of peri peri spice mix* or 1/2 tsp Tabasco (to taste)
3/4 cup (185ml) lager
2 tbs chopped flat-leaf parsley
Shoestring fries, to serve

Halve prawns by splitting lengthways through the middle with a sharp knife. Remove vein, rinse, then pat dry with paper towel.

Melt 40g butter in a large frypan over medium-high heat. When sizzling, cook the prawns, in 2 batches, for 1 minute each side, then remove from the pan and set aside.

Melt the remaining 40g butter in the pan with the paprika, garlic and peri peri or Tabasco. Cook, stirring, for 1 minute until fragrant. Add the beer, increase the heat to high and cook for 2-3 minutes until the sauce thickens slightly. Remove from the heat, add the prawns and parsley and toss to combine. Serve the prawns with shoestring fries and cold beer.
* Smoked paprika and peri peri spice mix (see Glossary) are available from gourmet food shops and delis.

prawn, chilli & pesto pizza

Makes 2 pizzas

10 green prawns, peeled, deveined, chopped
2 tbs olive oil
2 garlic cloves, crushed
1/4 tsp dried chilli flakes
2 woodfired pizza bases*
1/3 cup good-quality tomato pasta sauce
   or tomato passata (sugo)*
100g shredded mozzarella or pizza cheese*
10 cherry tomatoes, halved
2 tbs basil pesto, to serve

Place the prawn meat in a bowl with the olive oil, garlic and chilli. Toss to combine, then set aside.

Preheat the oven to 220°C (or heat a pizza maker on 2^{1}/$_{2}$). Spread the bases with the pizza sauce and scatter with cheese. Arrange the tomato, cut-side up, over the base, then scatter over the prawn mixture, including the oil.

Cook the pizzas for 6 minutes or until the prawns are just cooked, the cheese is bubbling and the bases are crisp. Serve drizzled with pesto.

* Available from supermarkets and delis.

149

scallops with peperonata and aioli

Serves 4

290g jar peperonata*
2 tbs tomato passata (sugo)*
20 scallops without roe
2 tbs olive oil
50g mixed baby salad leaves (mesclun)
200g jar aioli (garlic mayonnaise)*
Extra virgin olive oil, to drizzle

Warm the peperonata and passata in a saucepan over low heat for 2-3 minutes until heated through. Season with salt and pepper.

Brush both sides of the scallops with the oil, then season. Heat a large frypan over high heat and cook the scallops, in batches, for 30 seconds each side until golden brown but still translucent in the centre.

Divide the peperonata mixture, scallops and salad leaves among serving plates. Season with salt and pepper, drizzle the plate with extra virgin olive oil, then serve with aioli.

* Peperonata (see Glossary), passata and aioli are available from supermarkets and delis.

prawn cocktails

Serves 4

Mascarpone cheese adds a perfect richness to this classic Marie Rose cocktail sauce.

2 tbs tomato sauce (ketchup)
$2/3$ cup (200g) mayonnaise
3 tbs (65g) mascarpone cheese
Lemon juice and Tabasco, to taste
400g cooked prawns, peeled,
   deveined, cut into chunks
$1/2$ telegraph cucumber,
   thinly sliced on an angle
$1/4$ iceberg lettuce, cut into thin wedges
Paprika, to dust

Combine the tomato sauce, mayonnaise and mascarpone in a bowl. Add lemon juice and Tabasco to taste, then season with salt and pepper. Add the prawn meat and stir to coat in the mayonnaise mixture.

   Arrange the cucumber slices and lettuce wedges in 4 martini glasses or glass serving bowls. Pile the prawn mixture on top of the lettuce, then serve sprinkled with a little paprika.

spanish mussels with chorizo

Serves 4

This is a one-pot-wonder that you can just pop on the table and serve with lots of crusty bread to mop up the sauce.

2 tbs olive oil
1 onion, sliced
1 chorizo sausage, peeled, chopped
1 tsp smoked paprika* (pimenton)
3 garlic cloves, finely chopped
1/4 tsp saffron threads
400g can chopped tomatoes
3/4 cup (185ml) dry sherry
2kg (about 36) black mussels, scrubbed, debearded
1/4 cup flat-leaf parsley leaves, torn
Crusty bread, to serve

Heat the oil in a large flameproof casserole or lidded deep frypan over medium-high heat. Add the onion, chorizo and 1 teaspoon salt and cook, stirring, for 2-3 minutes until onion is soft. Add the paprika, garlic and saffron and stir to combine. Add tomato and sherry and simmer for 3 minutes. Add the mussels, cover and cook for 3 minutes, shaking the pan from time to time, until the mussels open (discard any mussels that haven't opened after this time). Scatter with the parsley and serve with bread to dip into the sauce.
* From gourmet food shops and delis.

goat's cheese, roast capsicum & spinach lasagne

Serves 4-6

400g baby spinach leaves
200ml creme fraiche or light sour cream
100ml pure (thin) cream
2 eggs, beaten
$^1/_2$ cup (40g) grated parmesan
750g roast capsicum pieces*
250g soft goat's cheese
375g fresh lasagne sheets
Green salad, to serve

Preheat the oven to 190°C. Blanch the spinach for 1 minute in boiling water until wilted. Drain in a sieve, pressing down to remove excess liquid. Cool.

Combine creme fraiche, cream, eggs and half the parmesan in a bowl. Season with salt and pepper.

Pat the roast capsicum with paper towel to remove excess oil. Spread a third of the cream mixture over the base of a 20cm x 26cm (1.5-litre) baking dish, cover with half the capsicum, crumble over half the goat's cheese, then layer with half the spinach. Cover with pasta sheets, cutting to fit. Repeat the layers, then finish with a final layer of cream mixture. Sprinkle with remaining parmesan, then cover with baking paper and foil.

Bake for 30 minutes, then remove the paper and foil and bake for a further 10-15 minutes until the top is golden and bubbling. Stand for 5 minutes, then slice and serve with a green salad.

* Available from supermarkets and delis.

moroccan carrot & chickpea stew

Serves 4

2 tbs olive oil
1 onion, thinly sliced
3 garlic cloves, finely chopped
$^1/_2$ tsp each ground coriander, cumin,
   turmeric, ginger, cayenne and paprika
2 bunches baby (Dutch) carrots, peeled,
   ends trimmed with some stem left intact
1 parsnip, peeled, cut into batons
400g can chopped tomatoes
2 tbs lemon juice
1 cup (250ml) vegetable stock or water
400g can chickpeas, drained, rinsed
$^1/_3$ cup chopped coriander leaves
2 tsp chopped mint leaves
Couscous, to serve

Heat the oil in a large saucepan over medium heat. Add the
onion and cook, stirring, for 2 minutes or until starting to soften.
Add the garlic and spices and stir for a few seconds until
fragrant, then add the carrots and parsnip and stir to coat in the
spices. Stir in the tomato, lemon juice and stock or water, then
cover and simmer for about 20 minutes or until the vegetables
are tender. Add the chickpeas and heat through for 2-3 minutes.
Remove from the heat, then stir through the coriander and mint.
Serve with couscous.

vegetable terrine with tarragon and basil

Serves 6-8

1 carrot, cut into 1cm cubes
1 potato, peeled, cut into 1cm cubes
100g fresh or frozen broad beans
100g thin green beans, cut into 1cm lengths
100g fresh or frozen baby peas
6 eggs, lightly beaten
300ml thickened cream
1 tbs each chopped fresh tarragon* and basil leaves
Tomato chutney and salad leaves, to serve

Preheat oven to 180°C. Lightly grease a 1-litre terrine or loaf pan.

Cook the carrot and potato in a pan of boiling salted water for 2-3 minutes until just tender. Remove to a bowl with a slotted spoon. Return water to the boil, then add broad and green beans. Blanch for 1-2 minutes until thin beans are bright green. Drain, then slip the broad beans out of their tough skins and toss all the vegetables together in the bowl. Allow to cool.

Whisk the eggs and cream together in a separate bowl.

Pack a layer of vegetables in the terrine, then sprinkle with some of the herbs and season well. Carefully pour over enough egg mixture to cover, then repeat the process with remaining vegetables, herbs and egg mixture (this will help ensure the vegetables are evenly distributed). Cover with a sheet of baking paper cut to fit, then cover tightly with foil. Place the terrine in a roasting pan and fill with enough boiling water to come halfway up the sides of the terrine. Bake for 50 minutes or until a skewer inserted in the centre comes out clean. Remove the terrine from the water bath and cool completely. Chill for 1 hour to firm up, then bring back to room temperature before serving. Turn out and cut into 2cm-thick slices, then serve with chutney and salad.

* Fresh tarragon is available from selected greengrocers.

stuffed field mushrooms with pesto

Serves 4

6 slices sourdough bread, crusts removed
$2/3$ cup (180g) basil pesto
8 field mushrooms or large Swiss brown mushrooms,
    stalks trimmed
$1/3$ cup (80ml) olive oil
4 sprigs cherry truss tomatoes
2 tbs vino cotto* or balsamic vinegar

Preheat the oven to 180°C. Grease a large baking tray.
  Place the bread in a food processor and process until you
have fine breadcrumbs. Add the pesto, season with salt and
pepper, then process to combine.
  Place the mushrooms, cap-side down, on the tray and brush
with half the olive oil. Season, then fill each mushroom with
some of the breadcrumb mixture. Arrange the tomatoes around
the mushrooms, drizzle with the remaining olive oil, then
season with salt and pepper.
  Bake for 8-10 minutes until the tomatoes start to collapse and
the mushrooms are tender. Drizzle with the vino cotto, then swirl
the pan around to combine the vino cotto with any pan juices.
Serve the mushrooms and tomatoes drizzled with the juices.
* Vino cotto (also known as saba) is available from Italian delis
and gourmet food shops.

pumpkin, goat's cheese & onion marmalade jalousie

Serves 4-6

700g pumpkin, peeled, cut into 2cm pieces
1 tbs olive oil
1 tbs chopped rosemary leaves
2 x 375g blocks frozen puff pastry, thawed
375g jar onion marmalade*
150g soft goat's cheese
1 egg, beaten

Preheat the oven to 200°C.

Spread the pumpkin on a lined baking tray and toss with the olive oil, salt and pepper. Sprinkle with rosemary and roast for 30 minutes or until tender. Cool.

Reduce the oven to 180°C. Roll out 1 block of pastry on a lightly floured surface to form a 20cm x 30cm rectangle. Place on a lined tray and prick the base in several places with a fork, leaving a 2cm border. Spread the base inside the border with two-thirds of the onion marmalade, then top with the pumpkin and goat's cheese. Season with salt and pepper. Brush the pastry border with egg.

Roll out the second block of pastry slightly larger than the first. Fold the pastry in half lengthways and use a sharp knife to make cuts in the folded side, about 1cm apart and leaving a 2cm border on the unfolded side. Carefully open the pastry back out and place over the filling, pressing to seal the edges – the cuts in the pastry should separate slightly to reveal some of the filling. Trim the edges if necessary, then brush all over with beaten egg. Bake for 30 minutes or until puffed and golden, then serve with the remaining onion marmalade.

* Available from delis and gourmet food shops.

roast pumpkin & white bean salad

Serves 4

This salad is perfect as a vegetarian main course
or served with grilled meat, especially lamb.

1kg butternut pumpkin, peeled, cut into 2cm cubes
100ml olive oil, plus extra to drizzle
1 tbs soy sauce
1 long red chilli, seeds removed, chopped
2 tsp honey
1 garlic clove, finely chopped
400g can cannellini beans, rinsed, drained
2 cups wild rocket
1 cup coriander leaves

Preheat the oven to 180°C. Line a baking tray with baking paper.
  Place the pumpkin on the baking tray, drizzle with a little extra
olive oil and season with sea salt and freshly ground black pepper.
Roast, turning once or twice, for 25 minutes or until pumpkin is
golden and tender. Allow to cool slightly.
  Whisk the 100ml olive oil, soy sauce, chilli, honey and garlic
together in a large bowl. Add the beans, rocket, coriander and
pumpkin. Toss well to coat in the dressing, then serve.

mulled-wine pear & goat's cheese salad

Serves 4

2 cups (500ml) dry red wine
1/2 cup (110g) caster sugar
1 cinnamon quill
2 star anise
4 small sensation or corella pears, peeled, halved, cored
Bunch of watercress, sprigs picked
1/3 cup (50g) hazelnuts, toasted, roughly chopped
1 cup croutons
1/4 cup (60ml) olive oil
1 tbs red wine vinegar
2 x 150g ash-covered goat's cheese logs*, sliced into rounds

Place the red wine, sugar, cinnamon and star anise in a saucepan over low heat. Stir to dissolve the sugar, then add the pears and poach gently over low heat for 8-10 minutes until tender (this will depend on the ripeness of the pears). Leave to cool completely in the liquid.

Combine the watercress, hazelnuts and croutons in a large bowl. In a separate bowl, whisk the olive oil and red wine vinegar together with 1 tablespoon of the poaching liquid. Season well with salt and pepper. Divide the salad among 4 serving plates, top each with 2 pear halves and some goat's cheese slices, then serve drizzled with the dressing.
* From delis and selected supermarkets.

prawn, risoni & feta salad

Serves 6-8

1¹/₃ cups (300g) risoni pasta (orzo)
1 telegraph cucumber, peeled, seeds removed, chopped
1 bunch watercress, leaves picked
1 cup roughly chopped flat-leaf parsley
1 fennel bulb, halved, very thinly sliced
   (a mandoline is ideal for this)
800g cooked prawns, peeled (tails intact)
1 preserved lemon quarter*, white pith and flesh discarded,
   rind finely chopped, plus 1 tbs preserving liquid
1 cup (120g) pitted green olives, sliced
150g feta cheese
2 tbs lemon juice
¼ cup (60ml) extra virgin olive oil

Cook the pasta in boiling salted water according to packet
instructions. Rinse in cold water and drain, then place in a large
bowl with the cucumber, watercress, parsley, fennel, prawns,
lemon rind and olives. Crumble in the feta.
   Whisk the preserved lemon liquid with the lemon juice and
oil, then season to taste with salt and pepper. Add to the salad
and toss gently to combine, then serve.
* Preserved lemon is from delis and Middle Eastern shops.

the best green salad with white wine dressing

Serves 4-6

It makes me laugh when I order a green salad in a restaurant and it comes with tomato, onions and olives! This is the definitive green salad, and a dressing with a twist.

1 small frisee lettuce (curly endive)
2 baby cos lettuces
2 cups wild rocket leaves
1 handful chervil sprigs*
2 handfuls baby green beans, blanched for
   1-2 minutes in boiling water
Bunch of chives
1/3 cup (80ml) white wine
1/4 cup (60ml) lemon juice
1 tsp honey
3/4 cup (185ml) extra virgin olive oil

Remove the outer leaves from the frisee and cos. Wash the inner leaves with the rocket, then spin in a salad spinner or pat dry with paper towel. Pick the chervil leaves and place in a serving bowl with the lettuce and beans. Hold the bunch of chives over the bowl and use kitchen scissors to finely snip half the bunch into the bowl.

  In a separate bowl, whisk the wine, lemon juice and honey and season with salt and pepper. Slowly whisk in the oil until you have an emulsified dressing. Toss the salad and dressing together, then garnish with remaining chives and serve.
* Chervil is available from selected greengrocers.

heirloom tomato salad with cheat's burrata

Serves 6

Burrata is an Italian fresh mozzarella filled with cream, which oozes out onto the plate when you tear it open. It's hard to find here in Australia, but this makes a great alternative.

3 buffalo mozzarella balls* (about 750g total), drained
2 garlic cloves, finely chopped
200ml creme fraiche
200ml thickened cream
1.2kg assorted heirloom tomatoes* (such as Black Russian and Tigerella), or use vine-ripened tomatoes
2 loosely packed cups basil leaves
Extra virgin olive oil, to drizzle

Tear the mozzarella into large pieces. Toss in a bowl with the garlic, creme fraiche and cream, then season with sea salt and freshly ground black pepper. Set aside.

Slice the tomatoes and arrange on a platter or in a shallow serving bowl. Season and scatter with the basil leaves. Dot the mozzarella mixture over the salad and serve drizzled with extra virgin olive oil.

* Buffalo mozzarella is available from delis and gourmet food shops. Heirloom tomatoes are available from selected greengrocers and growers' markets.

SALADS

spaghetti carbonara

Serves 4

For a super-creamy sauce, sit an extra egg yolk in its shell on each dish, for your guests to stir through the pasta at the table.

1 tbs olive oil
20g unsalted butter
100g sliced pancetta, cut into thin strips
2 garlic cloves, finely chopped
400g spaghetti
3 eggs
150ml pure (thin) cream
$^2/_3$ cup (50g) grated parmesan
$^2/_3$ cup (50g) grated pecorino cheese
2 tbs chopped flat-leaf parsley

Heat the oil and butter in a frypan over medium-high heat. Add the pancetta and cook, stirring, for 3-4 minutes until starting to crisp. Stir in garlic, then remove from the heat and set aside.

Cook the pasta in a large saucepan of boiling salted water according to packet instructions. Meanwhile, beat the eggs and cream together in a bowl, then season with salt and pepper.

Drain the pasta, reserving ¹/₂ cup (125ml) of the cooking water, then return to the saucepan off the heat. Quickly add the egg and pancetta mixtures and toss to coat the pasta. Add half each of the parmesan, pecorino and parsley, then toss to combine (the residual heat from the pasta will cook the egg.)

Divide the pasta among warm bowls, then serve topped with the remaining cheese and parsley.

mushroom & taleggio ravioli

Serves 4 (makes 20)

Wonton wrappers are the perfect cheat's solution for fresh pasta dishes. They're available from selected supermarkets and Asian food shops.

2 tbs extra virgin olive oil, plus extra to drizzle
1 garlic clove, finely chopped
250g Swiss brown mushrooms, chopped
2 tbs dry Marsala (Italian fortified wine)
40 egg wonton wrappers
200g Taleggio cheese*, cut into 20 pieces
5 thin prosciutto slices, each cut into 4 small squares
Truffle oil*, small basil leaves and grated parmesan, to serve

Heat the oil in a frypan over medium heat. Add garlic and cook, stirring, for 30 seconds. Add mushrooms, season with salt and pepper, then cook, stirring, for 2-3 minutes until softened and any liquid has evaporated. Stir in the Marsala, then remove from the heat.

Lay a wonton wrapper on a work surface, then top with a piece of cheese, a teaspoonful of the mushroom mixture and a piece of prosciutto. Brush the edges of the wrapper with a little water, then top with another wrapper and press down to seal. Trim edges, then repeat with remaining wrappers and filling to make 20 ravioli.

Bring a large saucepan of salted water to the boil. Add the ravioli and cook for 3-4 minutes until they rise to the surface. Remove to a plate with a slotted spoon.

Divide the ravioli among 4 plates and drizzle with olive and truffle oils. Season with salt and pepper, then serve scattered with basil and parmesan.

* Taleggio (an Italian washed-rind cheese) and truffle oil are from delis and gourmet food shops.

greek-style pasta bake with lamb

Serves 3-4

This makes a perfect roast for two, with leftovers for the next day. I like to serve this dish with a salad of crumbled feta, kalamata olives and parsley, dressed with olive oil and a squeeze of lemon.

1 tbs olive oil
1 lamb mini roast or half leg (about 800g)
125g sliced pancetta, cut into strips
1 tbs chopped rosemary
150ml dry red wine
600ml tomato passata* (sugo)
600ml lamb* or chicken stock
1 tsp sugar
400g penne
280g jar marinated artichokes, drained, chopped
Lemon wedges, to serve

Preheat the oven to 180°C.

Heat the oil in a large frypan over medium heat. Season the lamb all over with salt and pepper, then add to the pan and cook, turning, for 5 minutes or until browned. Remove and set aside. Add the pancetta and rosemary to the pan and cook, stirring, for 4-5 minutes until the pancetta starts to crisp. Add the wine and bring to the boil, then add the passata, stock and sugar. Season to taste, then pour the tomato mixture into a roasting pan and stir in the penne.

Set a rack over the roasting pan, then place the lamb on the rack. Bake the lamb and pasta for 40 minutes or until the lamb juices run clear when pierced with a skewer and the pasta is al dente. Set the lamb aside in a warm place to rest for 10 minutes and stir the artichoke through the pasta.

Slice the lamb and serve with the pasta and lemon to squeeze.

* Passata (sieved tomatoes) is available in bottles from supermarkets. Lamb stock is available from butchers.

spicy squid spaghetti

Serves 4

1 tbs extra virgin olive oil
3 garlic cloves, finely chopped
1/3 cup (80ml) dry red wine
400g can chopped tomatoes
2 tbs harissa* (or to taste)
500g fresh baby squid, cleaned, hoods lightly scored
400g spaghetti or other long thin pasta
2 tbs chopped flat-leaf parsley leaves

Heat the oil in a frypan over medium heat. Add the garlic and cook, stirring, for 1-2 minutes until softened. Add the wine, tomato and harissa and cook, stirring occasionally, for 1-2 minutes. Add the squid and season to taste. Reduce heat to low and simmer for 30-40 minutes until squid is tender, adding a little water if the sauce becomes too thick.

Meanwhile, cook the spaghetti in a large saucepan of boiling salted water according to packet instructions. Drain the pasta and divide among bowls, then top with the squid mixture and garnish with parsley.

* Harissa is a North African chilli paste from delis and Middle Eastern food shops (see Glossary).

macaroni cheese with truffle oil

Serves 4

400g macaroni
2-3 tbs truffle oil* (to taste), plus extra to serve
1 tbs olive oil
2 eschalots, finely chopped
4 bacon rashers, finely chopped
2 garlic cloves, finely chopped
1 tsp fresh thyme leaves
1^1/$_2$ cups (375ml) thickened cream
3 cups (360g) grated good-quality cheddar
^{1}/$_3$ cup (25g) grated parmesan
Grilled bread and chopped parsley, to serve

Preheat oven to 180°C and grease a 1-litre (4-cup) baking dish.

Cook the pasta in a large pan of boiling salted water according to packet instructions. Drain, then return to the pan, toss with truffle oil to taste and season.

Meanwhile, heat the olive oil in a large, deep frypan over medium heat. Add the eschalot, bacon and garlic and cook, stirring, for 2-3 minutes until the eschalot softens. Add the thyme leaves and cream, then simmer for 3 minutes until thickened slightly. Add the pasta and three-quarters of the cheddar to the sauce, stirring to coat.

Pile the mixture into the prepared baking dish, then scatter with the parmesan and remaining cheddar. Bake for 30 minutes or until bubbling and golden. Sprinkle with parsley, drizzle with a little extra truffle oil if desired, then serve with grilled bread.
* Truffle oil is available from gourmet food shops and delis.

PASTA

japanese prawn, pickled vegetable & noodle salad

Serves 4

1 cup (250ml) brown-rice vinegar* or regular rice vinegar
1/4 firmly packed cup (50g) brown sugar
1 small carrot, cut into thin matchsticks
1 small cucumber, cut into thin matchsticks
250g soba or somen noodles*
2 spring onions, cut into thin matchsticks
1/4 cup each coriander and mint leaves
1 long red chilli, thinly sliced
1 cup snow pea sprouts, trimmed
20 cooked prawns, peeled, deveined
2 tsp toasted sesame seeds

Dressing
1 tbs honey
1/4 cup (60ml) tamari* or soy sauce
1/4 cup (60ml) brown-rice vinegar* or regular rice vinegar
1/4 cup (60ml) olive oil
2 tsp sesame oil

Place vinegar and sugar in a small pan and stir over low heat until sugar dissolves. Increase heat to medium-high and simmer for 10 minutes or until syrupy, then allow to cool. Add the carrot and cucumber and set aside to pickle for up to 1 hour – the longer you leave them, the better they are.

Cook the noodles according to packet instructions, then drain. Place in a large bowl with the drained pickled vegetables, spring onion, herbs, chilli, snow pea sprouts and prawns.

For the dressing, whisk all ingredients together in a bowl. Add to salad and toss to combine. Sprinkle with sesame, then serve.
* Available from Asian and health food shops.

sushi rice bowl

Serves 4

2 cups (440g) brown rice
Grated zest and juice of 1 orange and 1 lemon
2 tbs caster sugar
2 tbs Japanese shoyu* or regular soy sauce
2 tbs brown-rice vinegar* or regular rice vinegar
400g firm tofu, patted dry, cut into 2cm cubes
1 tbs sunflower oil
4 sheets nori seaweed*
4 spring onions, sliced on the diagonal
1 small Lebanese cucumber, sliced into long, thin strips
1 avocado, sliced into thin wedges
50g snow pea sprouts, ends trimmed
Black sesame seeds*, toasted white sesame seeds
    and pickled ginger (gari)*, to serve

Cook the rice in boiling salted water according to packet
instructions. Drain and allow to cool.

   Meanwhile, place the citrus zest and juice in a saucepan
with the sugar over medium-high heat. Stir to dissolve the sugar,
then boil for 1 minute. Remove from the heat and stir in the
shoyu and vinegar. Stir half the dressing into the cooled rice.

   Heat a chargrill pan or frypan over medium heat. Brush
the tofu with the oil and cook for about 1 minute, turning,
until golden on all sides.

   Line 4 serving bowls with the nori. Divide the rice among
serving bowls, then top with the spring onion, cucumber,
avocado and snow pea sprouts. Drizzle with the remaining
dressing then sprinkle with sesame seeds and ginger.
Serve with the chargrilled tofu.

* From Asian food shops and selected supermarkets.

chilli rice with barbecued duck

Serves 4

1 cup (200g) jasmine rice (or use 3 cups leftover cooked rice)
1 tbs sunflower oil
1 large red onion, thinly sliced
2 eggplants, cut into 2cm cubes
4 tbs chilli jam*
200g baby spinach leaves
1 Chinese barbecued duck*, meat removed, chopped
1/2 cup mint leaves
1/2 cup coriander leaves
Sliced long red chilli, to garnish

Cook the rice according to packet instructions. Cool.

Meanwhile, heat the oil in a wok over medium-high heat. Add the onion and stir-fry for 5 minutes or until starting to brown. Add the eggplant and cook, stirring, for 2-3 minutes until the eggplant starts to soften and turn golden.

Add the rice to the eggplant with the chilli jam, spinach leaves and duck meat and cook, stirring, for a further minute or until heated through. Remove from the heat, stir through the mint and coriander, then serve garnished with chilli.
* Chilli jam is available from selected supermarkets and delis. Duck is from Asian barbecue shops.

chicken paella

Serves 4-6

Olive oil
1 onion, finely chopped
2 chorizo sausages, peeled, sliced
3 streaky bacon rashers, rind removed, sliced into batons
2 cups (400g) calasparra* or arborio rice
1 tbs sundried tomato paste
280g jar chargrilled capsicum strips*, drained
3 tomatoes, seeds removed, chopped
3 garlic cloves, crushed
2 tsp smoked paprika* (pimenton)
1/4 tsp saffron threads
1.5L (6 cups) chicken stock
3/4 cup (185ml) dry white wine
1 barbecued chicken, cut into portions
1 tbs chopped flat-leaf parsley

Heat the olive oil in a large, deep frypan over medium heat. Add the onion, chorizo and bacon and cook, stirring, for 5-6 minutes until onion is soft and bacon is starting to crisp. Add the rice, stirring to coat in the mixture. Add the tomato paste, capsicum, tomato, garlic and paprika, then cook, stirring, for 2-3 minutes. Add saffron, chicken stock and wine, then bring to the boil. Simmer gently uncovered, stirring occasionally, for 15 minutes or until the liquid is evaporated and the rice is just cooked.

Meanwhile, cut the chicken meat into bite-sized chunks. Stir into the paella and cook for a further 2-3 minutes until heated through. Season to taste, then stir through parsley and serve.
* Chargrilled capsicum is available from supermarkets (see Glossary). Calasparra rice and smoked paprika are available from delis and gourmet food shops.

chicken & eggplant laksa

Serves 4

Chargrilled eggplant gives this laksa a wonderful smoky flavour.

4 slices chargrilled eggplant*, drained, cut into strips
250g thick rice-stick noodles
3-4 tbs laksa paste
400ml can coconut milk
600ml chicken stock
4 small chicken breast fillets, thinly sliced
1 lemongrass stem (pale part only), bruised
2 kaffir lime leaves*
150g sugar snap peas, halved lengthways or shredded
1 tsp brown sugar
Zest and juice of 1 lime
Thai basil* and coriander leaves, to serve

Pat the eggplant with paper towel to remove excess oil.

Soak noodles in boiling water according to packet instructions until soft. Drain, then rinse in cold water and set aside.

Heat a wok over medium heat and stir-fry the laksa paste for 1 minute or until fragrant. Stir in the coconut milk and stock, then bring to a simmer. Add the chicken, lemongrass and lime leaves and simmer for 6-8 minutes or until chicken is cooked through. Add the peas and eggplant and simmer for 2 minutes or until peas are just cooked. Stir in the sugar, zest and juice.

Divide the noodles among bowls and top with the laksa. Garnish with Thai basil and coriander, then serve.

* Chargrilled eggplant is from delis and supermarkets. Kaffir lime leaves and Thai basil are from greengrocers and Asian food shops.

chocolate torte

Serves 6-8

A version of this clever torte by Australian cook Di Holuigue appeared in *Vogue Entertaining + Travel* in the '80s and I've been making it ever since. I love the idea that you use the same mixture for the base and the filling – so simple yet sure to impress.

200g dark chocolate, chopped
200g unsalted butter, softened, chopped
½ cup (110g) caster sugar
6 eggs, separated
1 heaped tbs dry breadcrumbs
1 tbs unsweetened cocoa powder

Preheat the oven to 190°C. Line the base and sides of a 22cm springform cake pan.

Melt the chocolate in a heatproof bowl over a saucepan of simmering water (don't let the bowl touch the water). Stir until smooth, then set aside to cool.

Place the butter and sugar in the bowl of an electric mixer and beat until light and fluffy. Add the egg yolks, one at a time, beating after each addition, then stir in the melted chocolate.

In a separate clean bowl, beat the eggwhites until stiff peaks form. Fold one-third into the chocolate mixture to lighten, then gently fold in the remaining eggwhite. Place two-thirds of the mixture into a piping bag with a star nozzle and chill.

Add the breadcrumbs to the remaining mixture and spread in the prepared pan. Bake for 20-25 minutes until firm. Transfer to a rack to cool completely in the pan.

Turn out the cake and place on a serving platter. Bring the topping mixture to room temperature. Starting in the centre, pipe the topping over the cake in a spiral to completely cover. Dust with cocoa powder, then slice and serve.

no-bake chocolate tarts

Serves 6

200g shortbread or digestive biscuits
100g unsalted butter, chopped
1 tbs golden syrup
100g milk chocolate, chopped
100g dark chocolate, chopped, plus extra melted
  chocolate to drizzle and shaved chocolate to garnish
1 tsp vanilla extract
2 tbs pure icing sugar, sifted
200ml thickened cream, plus extra to serve
Unsweetened cocoa powder, to garnish
Strawberries, halved, to garnish

Place the biscuits in a food processor and pulse to form fine crumbs. Place the butter and golden syrup in a saucepan over low heat, stirring, until butter melts, then pour into processor and pulse to combine. Press the biscuit mixture into the base and sides of six 10cm loose-bottomed tart pans. Chill until required.

Melt the milk and dark chocolate together in a heatproof bowl over a saucepan of simmering water (don't let the bowl touch the water). Remove from heat, stir until smooth, then allow to cool for 5 minutes. Stir in the vanilla and fold in the icing sugar.

Whip cream until soft peaks form, then fold into the chocolate mixture. Pour into the tart pans and chill for at least 2 hours until the chocolate filling is set.

To serve, drizzle plates with melted chocolate, top tarts with extra whipped cream and sprinkle with shaved chocolate and cocoa powder. Serve with strawberries.

refrigerator cake

Serves 8-10

Serve this cake as a dessert or in thin slices with coffee.
Keep in the fridge for up to 1 week.

150g pitted prunes, roughly chopped
$1/3$ cup (80ml) Pedro Ximénez sherry*, plus extra to serve
250g digestive biscuits, roughly chopped
100g raw pecans, chopped
100g unsalted pistachios, chopped
15 (about 50g) glacé cherries
150g unsalted butter, chopped
5 tbs golden syrup
500g dark chocolate, chopped
Cocoa powder, to dust

Line a 25cm x 10cm loaf pan with plastic wrap, leaving some
overhanging the sides to cover.
   Place the prunes and sherry in a small bowl and leave to
soak for 2-3 hours.
   Combine the biscuits, nuts and cherries in a bowl. Place the
butter, golden syrup and chocolate into a heatproof bowl over
a saucepan of simmering water (don't let the bowl touch the
water), stirring gently, until the chocolate melts. Remove from
the heat. Add biscuit mixture, prunes and any soaking liquid,
stirring to combine. Press mixture down well into the loaf pan to
expel any air bubbles, cover with the overhanging plastic wrap
and chill for at least 4 hours, preferably overnight, until set.
   Invert onto a platter and dust with cocoa just before serving.
Cut into 2cm-thick slices and serve with small glasses of sherry.
* Pedro Ximénez is a sweet, sticky Spanish sherry, available
from selected bottle shops.

blender chocolate mousse

Serves 4

Who doesn't love chocolate mousse? In this version, you simply throw everything in the blender so it's quick and easy.

1 cup (100g) finely chopped dark chocolate,
   plus extra grated chocolate to serve
¼ cup (55g) caster sugar
1 tsp instant coffee granules
2 tbs brandy
3 eggwhites
¾ cup (185ml) thickened cream,
   plus extra whipped to serve (optional)

Place the finely chopped chocolate in a blender.

Place the sugar, coffee, brandy and ¾ cup (180ml) water in a saucepan over medium-low heat and bring to the boil, stirring to dissolve the sugar and coffee.

With the blender motor running, carefully pour the hot liquid through the feed tube, blending until the chocolate has melted. Add the eggwhites and cream and pulse the blender several times to just combine.

Pour the mousse into 4 serving glasses and chill for 4 hours or overnight. Serve topped with extra grated chocolate and whipped cream, if desired.

chocolate truffles

Makes 30

300ml thickened cream
1 tbs instant coffee granules
450g dark chocolate, chopped
¼ cup (60ml) Baileys Irish Cream or brandy
1 tsp vanilla extract
1 cup (100g) unsweetened cocoa powder

Combine the cream and coffee in a saucepan over medium heat, stirring, until coffee dissolves. Decrease heat to low and add the chocolate, stirring for 5-6 minutes until the chocolate melts. Set aside for 5 minutes to cool, then stir in the Baileys or brandy and vanilla. Pour into a shallow bowl, allow to cool, then chill for 4 hours until set to a fudge-like consistency.

Use a small ice-cream scoop to scoop balls from the chocolate mixture (or scoop out teaspoonfuls of the mixture and roll into balls wearing gloves) Place on a baking paper-lined tray in the fridge as you go – you should have enough mixture for 30 truffles.

Sift the cocoa onto a large sheet of baking paper. Roll the truffles in the cocoa to coat, then store the truffles in an airtight container or in the fridge for up to 5 days.

Bring to room temperature before serving, then dust with a little extra cocoa if needed.

rosewater cupcakes

Makes 12

These cakes are inspired by New York's famous Magnolia Bakery –
be generous with the icing, as that's what makes them so special.

180g unsalted butter, softened
350g caster sugar
4 eggs
1 cup (250ml) milk
1 tsp each vanilla extract and rosewater*
1^1/$_3$ cups (200g) self-raising flour
1 cup (150g) plain flour

Icing
500g unsalted butter, softened
350g pure icing sugar, sifted
Rose pink food colouring

Preheat the oven to 180ºC and line a 12-hole muffin pan
with paper cases.

Place the butter in the bowl of an electric mixer and beat for
5 minutes until very pale. Gradually add the sugar and continue
to beat for a further 5 minutes until very light and pale. Add the
eggs, one at a time, beating well after each addition.

Combine the milk, vanilla and rosewater in a bowl. Sift the
flours and gently fold into the egg mixture using a metal spoon,
alternating with the milk mixture, until combined. Spoon into
paper cases, filling to just over halfway. Bake for 20 minutes
or until a skewer inserted in the centre comes out clean and
the cakes are lightly golden. Stand in the pan for 5 minutes,
then turn out onto a wire rack to cool completely.

For the icing, beat the butter, sugar and a few drops of
colouring with electric beaters until light and fluffy. Use a
piping bag with a fluted nozzle to ice the cakes generously.
* From supermarkets and Middle Eastern food shops.

easy baklava

Serves 6

500g unsalted mixed nuts (such as
   walnuts, pistachios and almonds)
250g honey
250g caster sugar
Zest and juice of 2 oranges
2 cardamom pods, smashed
1 cinnamon quill
16 sheets filo pastry
80g unsalted butter, melted
Ice cream, to serve

Preheat the oven to 200°C. Spread nuts on a baking tray
and toast for 5 minutes. Cool slightly, then finely chop in
a food processor and set aside.

   Meanwhile, combine the honey, sugar, orange zest and juice,
cardamom, cinnamon and 300ml water in a pan over medium
heat. Boil for 5 minutes or until syrupy, then allow to cool.

   Lay 1 sheet of filo pastry on a bench and brush with butter.
Cover with another filo sheet and brush with more butter.
Sprinkle all over with a layer of nuts, leaving a 1cm border.
Fold in the 2 shorter ends and roll quite tightly into a log.
Place seam-side down on a greased baking tray, then repeat
with the remaining pastry, butter and nuts to make 6 rolls.
Bake for 5-6 minutes or until golden brown.

   Cool the rolls slightly, then cut into pieces. Place in a shallow
dish, pour over the cooled syrup, then stand for at least 1 hour.

   Serve with ice cream, drizzled with some of the syrup.

party lamingtons

Makes 18

I used to make huge platters of lamingtons for my two sons'
birthday parties. They're grown men now, but they still love them.

85g packet strawberry jelly crystals
85g packet orange jelly crystals
1 tbs unsalted butter
1 tbs cocoa powder
1/2 cup (80g) pure icing sugar, sifted
Twin-pack (350g) square vanilla sponge cake*
3 cups (270g) desiccated coconut

Boil 2 cups (500ml) water in the kettle. Place jelly crystals in
separate jugs. Pour 1 cup of boiling water over each and use
a fork to whisk until the crystals dissolve. Pour into separate
shallow dishes and chill for 1-1 1/2 hours until just starting to set.

Meanwhile, place the butter, cocoa powder, icing sugar
and 3 tablespoons boiling water into a shallow bowl. Stir
with a fork until coating consistency.

Cut each cake into 9 squares. Spread the coconut on
a large plate or a sheet of baking paper.

Dip 6 of the cake squares first in strawberry jelly, then
in coconut. Place on a rack to firm slightly. Repeat with
the remaining cake, dipping 6 in orange jelly and 6 in the
chocolate mixture, then coconut. (If the chocolate mixture
begins to set, stir in 1 tablespoon boiling water.)
* Available from supermarkets.

black forest cake

Serves 6

When I got married, it was the height of fashion to have a
Black Forest cake at your wedding. Times have changed,
but they're still a great cake for entertaining, especially
when you start with a ready-made chocolate cake.

680g jar pitted morello cherries, drained, juice reserved
2 tbs sugar
1/3 cup (80ml) kirsch* or brandy
2 tsp arrowroot
2 tbs pure icing sugar, sifted
300g mascarpone cheese
350g store-bought chocolate slab cake or chocolate brownies
2 tbs cherry jam
1 tbs finely grated dark chocolate, to garnish
Zest of 1 orange, to garnish

Place the cherry juice in a saucepan over low heat with the
sugar and half the kirsch or brandy. Mix the arrowroot with a
little cold water until smooth, then add to the pan. Heat gently,
stirring, for 2-3 minutes until thickened. Add the cherries to
the sauce, then remove from the heat and set aside to cool.
  Beat the icing sugar and mascarpone together in a bowl
with a wooden spoon until combined.
  Cut the cake into 6 pieces and place on a platter. Sprinkle
over remaining kirsch and spread with the jam. Pile the
mascarpone mixture on top of the cake pieces followed by
some cherries and sauce. Sprinkle with chocolate and zest,
then serve with remaining cherry sauce.
* Kirsch is a clear, unsweetened cherry brandy, from bottle shops.

chocolate mayonnaise cake

Serves 6-8

This is the perfect recipe for when you feel like baking a cake but discover you have no eggs! Who would've thought mayonnaise could turn into such a delicious dessert.

1²/₃ cups (250g) self-raising flour
60g cocoa powder
¹/₄ tsp baking powder
200g caster sugar
³/₄ cup (225g) whole-egg mayonnaise
3 tsp vanilla extract
100g unsalted butter, softened
100g cream cheese
1²/₃ cups (250g) pure icing sugar, sifted
1 shot (30ml) Kahlua (or other coffee liqueur)
Hazelnuts half-dipped in melted chocolate, to decorate

Preheat the oven to 180°C. Grease and line the base of a 23cm springform cake pan.

Place the flour, cocoa, baking powder, caster sugar, mayonnaise and 2 teaspoons of the vanilla in the bowl of an electric mixer with 200ml warm water and beat for 2-3 minutes until smooth. Spread into the prepared pan and bake for 40 minutes or until a skewer inserted in the centre comes out clean. Cool completely.

Meanwhile, make the icing. Process the butter, cream cheese, icing sugar, remaining 1 teaspoon of vanilla and Kahlua in a food processor until smooth. Spread over the cooled cake and decorate with nuts.

berries with white chocolate sauce & sweet pangrattato

Serves 4

Italians use pangrattato, crisp fried breadcrumbs mixed with garlic or herbs, as a topping for pasta and other savoury dishes. This sweet version is flavoured with cocoa and cinnamon, and is great sprinkled over berry desserts.

450g mixed fresh berries (we used raspberries, blueberries and chopped strawberries)
2 slices sourdough, crusts removed, torn into pieces
1/3 cup (40g) almond meal
1 tbs brown sugar
1 tbs cocoa powder
1 tsp ground cinnamon
20g unsalted butter
1/3 cup (80ml) pure (thin) cream
250g white chocolate, chopped

Preheat the oven to 180°C and line a baking tray with baking paper. Place the berries in the freezer to chill while you make the pangrattato and sauce.

Place the bread in a food processor with the almond meal, sugar, cocoa and cinnamon. Process the mixture to form fine crumbs, then add the butter and pulse to combine. Spread on the prepared tray and bake for 10 minutes or until crisp and dry. Remove from the oven and allow to cool.

Meanwhile, place the cream and chocolate in a heatproof bowl over a pan of simmering water (don't let the bowl touch the water) until chocolate melts, then stir gently to combine.

Divide the berries among plates, pour over the warm sauce, then serve sprinkled with the sweet pangrattato.

no-pastry pear tarts

Makes 6

If you don't have time to make your own poached pears, use fresh
pear or buy ready-made poached pears from gourmet food shops.

180g unsalted butter
50g plain flour
180g pure icing sugar
100g almond meal
2 tsp finely grated lemon zest
5 eggwhites
2 poached pears*, sliced (or 2 fresh pears, thinly sliced)
2 tbs flaked almonds
Icing sugar, to dust
Pure (thin) cream or ice cream, to serve

Preheat the oven to 200°C. Lightly grease six 7cm
loose-bottomed tart pans.
   Melt the butter in a small saucepan over medium heat for
1-2 minutes (watch closely and don't let it burn), until golden
brown. Allow to cool.
   Sift the flour and icing sugar into a bowl and stir in the
almond meal, lemon zest and melted butter.
   Use a fork to lightly froth the eggwhites in a separate bowl,
then fold into the dry ingredients. Divide among the tart pans
and place pear on top. Scatter with flaked almonds and bake
for 10 minutes. Reduce the heat to 170°C and bake for a further
5-6 minutes or until golden. Dust with icing sugar and serve
warm with cream or ice cream.
* Poached pears are from gourmet food shops (see Glossary).

little fig & rosewater pies

Makes 4

450g packet frozen sour cream shortcrust pastry*
  (or use a 375g block frozen puff pastry), thawed
4 fresh figs
4 sugar cubes
2 tsp rosewater*
1 egg, beaten
Icing sugar, to dust
Thin (pure) cream, to serve

Preheat the oven to 200ºC. Line a baking tray with paper.

Roll out the pastry on a lightly floured surface to 5mm thick. Cut four 10cm and four 12cm circles from the pastry.

Trim the stalk from each fig, then turn over. Cut a cross in the base, then squash down a little with your hand to flatten and open out slightly. Press a sugar cube into the cross of each fig and sprinkle with the rosewater.

Sit each fig right-way up in the centre of the larger pastry rounds and brush the border with beaten egg. Cover with the smaller pastry rounds, then fold in the edges of the larger pieces and pinch the edges to seal. Place on the lined tray. (You can keep the tarts chilled at this stage for 3-4 hours until ready to bake.)

Just before baking, brush the pies all over with beaten egg, then cook in the oven for 25 minutes or until the pastry is golden and the fig juices are starting to ooze.

Dust the warm pies with icing sugar and serve with cream.

* Sour cream pastry is available from delis and gourmet food shops (see Glossary). Rosewater is available from Middle Eastern and gourmet food shops.

apple galette

Serves 4-6

The secret to this wonderfully crisp galette is to bake it with another tray on top so the pastry doesn't have a chance to rise but remains crisp, thin and buttery.

6 Granny Smith apples
2 tbs lemon juice
375g block frozen puff pastry, thawed
100g unsalted butter, chopped
185g caster sugar
Cream or ice cream, to serve

Preheat the oven to 180°C. Line a baking tray or pizza tray with baking paper.

Peel and core the apples, then slice very thinly (a mandoline slicer is ideal). Gently toss with the lemon juice to prevent the slices from discolouring.

On a lightly floured surface, roll out the pastry to 5mm thick and trim into a neat 28cm-diameter circle. Place on the lined tray. Arrange the apple slices in overlapping circles – with each slice overlapping to ensure that they all fit on the base. Dot with the butter and sprinkle with half the sugar. Cover with another sheet of baking paper and second heavy baking tray. Bake for 35 minutes.

Gently remove the top tray and baking paper (being careful of the hot juices). Sprinkle with the remaining sugar, then return to the oven, uncovered, for a further 10-15 minutes until well caramelised. Slice the galette and serve warm with cream or ice cream.

simple summer pudding

Serves 6

When my husband, Phil, and I lived in England, working as a
butler and cook team, we made this pudding every weekend
for weddings and parties. Then we had the stress of unmoulding
them, but this simple version is made in a dish for easy serving.
For me, it's the quintessential English dessert.

600g frozen mixed berries
1/2 cup (110g) caster sugar
10 slices white bread, crusts removed,
    halved into triangles
Pure (thin) cream, to serve

Place the fruit in a saucepan with the sugar and 1/4 cup (60ml)
water and bring to the boil over medium heat. Reduce the heat
to low and simmer for 3-4 minutes until the sugar dissolves
and the fruit starts to give off some of its juice.

Layer one-third of the bread in a 1-litre (4-cup) serving
dish, cutting pieces to fit if necessary. Using a slotted spoon,
top the bread with half the berry mixture. Repeat with another
layer of bread and fruit, then finish with the final layer of
bread. Pour the liquid remaining in the pan over the bread,
pressing down well. Cover and chill for at least 30 minutes,
then serve drizzled with cream.

caramel pavlova bites

Makes 15 bites

When you make a pavlova, you always end up with leftover egg yolks, so I like to use them up in an easy caramel filling that's made in the microwave. With their crisp meringue shell, creamy caramel and tart raspberries, these little bites are quite addictive!

2 eggwhites
1 cup (220g) caster sugar
1 tsp white vinegar
1 tsp vanilla extract
1 heaped tbs cornflour
Thick cream, fresh raspberries and icing sugar, to serve

Microwave caramel
2 egg yolks
20g unsalted butter
1/2 cup (125ml) milk
1/2 firmly packed cup (100g) brown sugar
1 tbs plain flour
1 tsp vanilla extract

Preheat oven to 120°C. Line 2 baking sheets with baking paper.

Beat eggwhites using electric beaters until soft peaks form. Gradually add sugar, beating until stiff and glossy. Gently fold in vinegar, vanilla and cornflour. Using a piping bag fitted with a 1cm nozzle, pipe a 5cm circle onto the tray, then continue to pipe 3-4 rings on top of each other around the rim to form a nest. Repeat to make 15 meringues. Bake for 30 minutes, then leave meringues in switched-off oven to cool completely (at least 2 hours).

For the filling, whisk ingredients together in a microwave-safe bowl. Microwave on medium setting for 3 minutes, stirring every minute, until thickened. Beat well to remove any lumps, then cool.

Spoon caramel into the cooled pavlova nests, then top with cream and raspberries. Dust with icing sugar just before serving.

bread & butter pudding

Serves 4-6

Bread and butter pudding must be one of the easiest desserts to make, and a universal favourite. The secret to a creamy texture is to let it stand for at least 1 hour before baking.

1/3 cup (55g) sultanas
2 tbs brandy
10 slices white bread, crusts removed
50g unsalted butter, softened
5 eggs
300ml pure (thin) cream
300ml milk
1/4 cup (55g) caster sugar
1 tsp vanilla extract
Icing sugar, to dust
Thick cream or ice cream, to serve

Grease a 1-litre (4-cup) baking dish. Place the sultanas and brandy in a small pan and warm through over low heat for 3-4 minutes. Set aside.

Lightly butter the bread, then cut the bread into 2 triangles. Layer the bread in the baking dish, overlapping slightly, scattering with sultanas and any remaining brandy as you go.

Lightly whisk the eggs, cream, milk, sugar and vanilla until combined. Pour the mixture evenly over the bread and leave to soak for 1 hour.

Preheat the oven to 180°C.

Place the baking dish in a roasting pan and pour in enough boiling water to come halfway up the sides of the dish. Bake for 40 minutes or until the top is golden but the custard still has a slight wobble. Stand for 10 minutes, then dust with icing sugar and serve with cream or ice cream.

cheesecake in a glass

Serves 4

200g shortbread biscuits
1/3 cup (80ml) dessert wine or sweet sherry
2 gold-strength gelatine leaves*
Zest and juice of 1 lemon
250g cream cheese
500g thick Greek-style yoghurt
1/2 cup (110g) caster sugar
Berry compote or warmed berry jam, to serve

Place the shortbread in a food processor and pulse to form crumbs. Place crumbs and wine in a bowl, then stir to combine. Divide among four 1-cup (250ml) serving glasses. Set aside.

Soak the gelatine in cold water for 5 minutes to soften.

Meanwhile, heat the lemon juice in a microwave for 30 seconds. Squeeze excess water from the gelatine, then add the leaves to the hot lemon juice and stir to dissolve.

Place the cream cheese, yoghurt, sugar, lemon zest and gelatine mixture in a food processor and process until smooth. Pour over the biscuit mixture and chill for at least 2 hours or until set. Top with the berry compote and serve.

* Gelatine leaves are from gourmet food shops. Always check the packet for setting instructions.

limoncello soufflé

Makes 8

Melted butter, to brush
¼ cup (55g) caster sugar, plus extra to dust
6 eggwhites
Pinch of cream of tartar
325g jar good-quality lemon curd*
Grated zest of 1 lemon
2 tbs limoncello*, plus extra chilled to serve
Icing sugar, to dust

Preheat the oven to 200°C. Brush eight 150ml soufflé dishes
or ramekins with melted butter. Dust with a little extra caster
sugar, tapping to remove excess.

Use electric beaters to whisk the eggwhites and cream of
tartar until soft peaks form. Gradually add the sugar, beating
constantly, until the mixture is stiff and glossy.

Meanwhile, gently warm the curd and zest in a saucepan
over low heat. Stir in the limoncello, then transfer to a large
bowl. Use a large metal spoon to gently fold one-third of
the eggwhites into the lemon mixture. Continue to fold in
the remaining eggwhite until just combined, taking care not
to lose too much volume. Divide among ramekins and run
your finger around the inside edge of each ramekin. Bake for
12 minutes or until golden and risen. Dust with icing sugar,
then serve immediately with extra chilled limoncello.
* Good-quality lemon curd is from gourmet food shops and delis
(see Glossary). Limoncello is an Italian-style lemon liqueur,
available from bottle shops.

rosé wine jellies

Makes 6 individual or 1 large jelly

6 gold-strength gelatine leaves*
¾ cup (165g) caster sugar
2 cups (500ml) rosé wine
Pure (thin) cream and summer fruits (optional), to serve

Lightly grease six 150ml dariole moulds or one 900ml jelly
mould. Soak gelatine in cold water for 5 minutes to soften.

Place the sugar in a pan with 200ml water and stir over
low heat until the sugar is dissolved. Remove from the heat.

Squeeze excess water from gelatine and add the leaves
to the warm sugar mixture, stirring to dissolve. Stir in the
wine, then divide among moulds. Allow to cool, then chill
for at least 4 hours until set.

Turn the jellies out onto serving plates and pour over a
little cream. Serve with summer fruits such as raspberries
and peaches, if desired.

* Gelatine leaves are from gourmet food shops. Always check
the packet for setting instructions.

blanco y negro

Serves 6

Leche merengada is a lovely Spanish ice cream that's just so refreshing as it doesn't contain egg yolks. Topped with espresso, it becomes blanco y negro, the Spanish version of Italy's affogato.

2 cups (500ml) full-cream milk
150ml thickened cream
150g caster sugar
Grated zest of 1 lemon
2 cinnamon quills
1 tbs brandy
3 eggwhites
Hot espresso coffee, to serve
Almond praline (optional), to serve

Place the milk, cream and 100g of the sugar in a saucepan over medium heat with lemon zest and cinnamon quills. Bring to just below boiling point, then remove from the heat and stand for 40 minutes to infuse. Strain through a sieve into a large bowl, discarding solids, then stir in the brandy.

In a separate bowl, use electric beaters to whisk the eggwhites and remaining 50g sugar until stiff peaks form. Gently fold into the milk mixture.

Pour the mixture into a shallow container and freeze for 2-3 hours until frozen at the edges. Remove from freezer and beat with electric beaters, then refreeze. Repeat this process two or three times. (Alternatively, churn in an ice cream machine following manufacturer's directions.)

When ready to serve, place a large scoop of ice cream in four serving glasses. Pour a shot of espresso coffee over each one and serve with praline if desired.

pistachio & date kulfi

Serves 6

These make-ahead desserts are the ideal cooling finish to an Indian feast.

²/₃ cup (100g) unsalted pistachio kernels
395g can sweetened condensed milk
300ml thickened cream
125g fresh pitted dates, chopped
1 tbs orange blossom water*
3 oranges
¹/₂ cup (110g) caster sugar

Line six 150ml dariole moulds with plastic wrap, leaving some overhanging the sides.

Process pistachios and condensed milk in a food processor until nuts are finely chopped and you have a coarse paste.

Lightly whip the cream in a large bowl, then fold in the condensed milk mixture, dates and orange blossom water.

Divide the mixture among the dariole moulds, then cover with the overhanging plastic wrap and freeze for at least 6 hours or overnight until firm.

Zest the rind of 1 orange using a zester. Place in a saucepan with the juice of 2 oranges, the caster sugar and ¹/₂ cup (125ml) water. Stir over low heat to dissolve the sugar, then simmer for 5 minutes until the syrup has thickened. Set aside to cool.

When ready to serve, peel the remaining orange, then slice the flesh into rounds. Place on a serving plate and drizzle with some of the candied rind and syrup. Turn out the kulfi onto plates, then drizzle with the remaining rind and syrup and serve with the orange slices.

* Fresh dates are from greengrocers. Orange blossom water is available from supermarkets.

frozen ricotta & mascarpone puddings

Makes 6

These creamy little parcels are the perfect accompaniment to hot Christmas pudding or fruit mince pies.

1 cup (240g) fresh ricotta
1 cup (250g) mascarpone cheese
1 cup good-quality fruit mince*
1/3 cup (80ml) Grand Marnier or Cointreau
3 tbs thick cream
1 tbs icing sugar

Cut twelve 23cm squares of muslin. Lightly beat the ricotta, mascarpone, fruit mince and liqueur with electric beaters until combined. Stir in the cream and icing sugar.

Layer 2 muslin squares on top of each other and spoon about 1/2 cup of the mixture into the centre. Enclose in the fabric and shape into a ball, then tie with kitchen string. Repeat with remaining fabric and mixture. Freeze for 6 hours or overnight until firm. Serve with hot Christmas pudding or fruit mince pies.
* Good-quality fruit mince is from gourmet food shops.

profiteroles with ice cream and chocolate sauce

Serves 6

A yummy warm chocolate sauce and vanilla ice cream give the old-fashioned profiterole a new lease on life.

300ml good-quality vanilla ice cream
30 store-bought profiteroles*, split
250g good-quality dark chocolate, roughly chopped
1/2 cup (125ml) thickened cream
Splash of Cognac or brandy

Allow the ice cream to soften in the fridge for 30 minutes. Sandwich each profiterole with a scoop of softened ice cream, then return to the freezer on a tray as you go. This can be done up to a week in advance.

When almost ready to serve, place the chocolate, cream and alcohol in a saucepan over low heat until the chocolate has melted. Stir gently to combine, then serve the warm sauce drizzled over the profiteroles.

* From Italian grocers and selected supermarkets.

ice cream pie

Serves 6-8

400g chocolate cream biscuits (such as Oreos)
120g unsalted butter, melted
150ml dry white wine
2 tbs brandy
Finely grated zest and juice of 2 lemons
Finely grated zest of 1 orange
1 tsp vanilla extract
$1/3$ cup (70g) caster sugar
500ml thickened cream
2 mangoes

Line the base of a 22cm loose-bottomed tart pan with baking paper.

Pulse the biscuits to fine crumbs in a food processor. Add the melted butter and pulse briefly to combine. Press the crumb mixture well into the base and sides of the tart pan. Chill while you make the filling.

Clean the food processor, then add the wine, brandy, citrus zest and juice, vanilla and sugar. Process to combine and dissolve the sugar, then add the cream with the motor running and process for about 1 minute until the mixture is thick and well combined. Pour the mixture into the tart shell and freeze for at least 3 hours until firm. Transfer the tart to the fridge about 30 minutes before serving to soften slightly.

Meanwhile, clean the food processor again and blend the mango flesh to a smooth puree.

When ready to serve, remove the tart from the pan and place on a platter. Drizzle with some of the puree, then slice and serve with the remaining sauce on the side.

Apple and sage jelly (p 113)
Tracklements Apple & Sage Jelly from Simon Johnson,
1800 655 522, simonjohnson.com.au.

Bouquet garni (p 58)
Herbie's Spices, (02) 9555 6035, herbies.com.au.

Chargrilled capsicum (p 29, 139, 194)
Sacla Char-Grilled Capsicums from supermarkets.

Chermoula paste (p 144)
Greg Malouf, gregmalouf.com.au; or
Christine Manfield, christinemanfield.com.

Chilli chocolate (p 73)
Lindt Chilli Chocolate from supermarkets.

Frozen French-style crepes (p 12)
Creative Gourmet French Style Crêpes from
supermarkets.

Harissa (p 185)
Christine Manfield, christinemanfield.com.

Herbes de Provence (p 40)
Herbie's Spices, (02) 9555 6035, herbies.com.au.

Lemon curd (p 236)
Duchy Originals Organic Traditional Lemon Curd from
Simon Johnson, 1800 655 522, simonjohnson.com.au.

Peperonata (p 151)
Sacla Peperonata from supermarkets; or Woolworths
Select Peperonata from Woolworths supermarkets.

Peri peri spice mix (p 147)
Herbie's Spices, (02) 9555 6035, herbies.com.au.

Pikelet bites (p 32)
Golden Pikelet Bites from supermarkets.

Poached pears (p 223)
Simon Johnson Pears In Red Wine from Simon Johnson,
1800 655 522, simonjohnson.com.au.

Pomegranate molasses (p 78)
Mymouné Pomegranate Molasses from Simon Johnson,
1800 655 522, simonjohnson.com.au.

Porcini powder (p 77)
The Essential Ingredient, (02) 9557 2388,
essentialingredient.com.au.

Roasted cherry tomatoes in oil (p 51)
Sacla Sweet Cherry Tomatoes from supermarkets.

Sage and onion stuffing mix (p 119)
Tandaco Stuffing Mix Sage & Onion from supermarkets.

Sour cream shortcrust pastry (p 224)
Carême Sour Cream Shortcrust Pastry. For stockists,
visit caremepastry.com.

ACKNOWLEDGEMENTS

Firstly, a sincere thanks to the management team at News Magazines – particularly Sandra Hook and Wendy Miller for giving me this opportunity. Also to Brigitta Doyle and Liz White at ABC Books, for their invaluable input on this project.

To the editorial team on *delicious.*, I have to mention you all by name as I feel privileged to work with such a talented and dedicated group of people. Thank you to editor-in-chief Trudi Jenkins for all your encouragement and support over the past seven years. And to editor Kylie Walker, who joined us at a particularly crazy time but has thrown herself into the madness with such energy.

To deputy editor Danielle Oppermann (my rock), I couldn't have done this without your eye on the details and disciplined approach to making it all come together... just in time. To the subediting team of Sarah Macdonald, Molly Furzer, Selma Nadarajah and Amira Georgy, and editorial coordinator Alison Pickel – thanks for your all your efforts and your patience, particularly on those occasions when I was up to my elbows in food and couldn't come to the phone.

A thousand thanks to our senior designer Simon Martin, whose enthusiastic input into the book has helped to make it such a visual delight, and designer Liz Bucknell, again a new recruit, who has helped keep the magazine looking beautiful while we were somewhat distracted.

A special hug must go to my wonderful food team. To Olivia Andrews, my assistant food editor – although she was eating her way around China while we were shooting the book, she was no less involved – your support and hard work keep the magazine looking so great every month. And to Georgina Kaveney, who along with Youjin Kwon did such a great job in assisting on the book shoot and making it all run so smoothly.

Lastly, a heartfelt thanks to the amazing team on the book shoot. Photographer Brett Stevens, your talent has turned my basic vision into such beautiful images. Stylist David Morgan – I am such a fan, thank you for making every dish look so special. And last but not least, to our creative director Scott Cassidy, whose lack of cooking skill is certainly made up for by creative talent – thank you for going on this journey with me and taking the book to a level I could only have dreamed of.

THANKS TO THE FOLLOWING STOCKISTS

Design Mode International Mona Vale (02) 9998 8200; **Ici et Là** Surry Hills (02) 9699 4266, icietla.com.au; **Kris Coad** Stockists (03) 9690 6510, kriscoad.com; **Meïzai** stockists nationally 1800 674 455, meizai.com.au; **Mud Australia** Stockists nationally (02) 9519 2520, mudaustralia.com; **No Chintz** Willoughby (02) 9958 0257, Woollahra (02) 9386 4800, nochintz.com; **Parterre** Surry Hills (02) 9356 4747, Woollahra (02) 9363 5874, Fortitude Valley (07) 3666 0100, parterre.com.au; **The Bay Tree** Woollahra (02) 9328 1101, thebaytree.com.au.

254

The ABC 'Wave' device is a trademark of the Australian Broadcasting Corporation and is used under licence by HarperCollins*Publishers* Australia.

This edition first published in 2008 by ABC Books for the Australian Broadcasting Corporation.
Reprinted by HarperCollins*Publishers* Australia Pty Limited
ABN 36 009 913 517
www.harpercollins.com.au

Text copyright © 2008 ABC Books/News Magazines
Photography copyright © 2008 Brett Stevens & Ian Wallace

HarperCollins*Publishers*
25 Ryde Road, Pymble, Sydney, NSW 2073, Australia
31 View Road, Glenfield, Auckland 0627, New Zealand
1–A Hamilton House, Connaught Place, New Delhi – 110 001, India
77–85 Fulham Palace Road, London W6 8JB, United Kingdom
2 Bloor Street East, 20th floor, Toronto, Ontario M4W 1A8, Canada
10 East 53rd Street, New York NY 10022, USA

ISBN 978 0 7333 2427 7

Food Director: Valli Little
Photography: Brett Stevens (Ian Wallace p 151, 202, 212, 224)
Styling: David Morgan (Louise Pickford p 151, 202, 212, 224)
Creative Director: Scott Cassidy
Senior Designer: Simon Martin
Project Editors: Molly Furzer, Sarah Macdonald, Danielle Oppermann
Food preparation: Georgina Kaveney, Youjin Kwon

delicious. Editor-in-chief: Trudy Jenkins
delicious. Editor: Kylie Walker
International Business Director, News Magazines: Wendy Miller
Chief Executive Officer, News Magazines: Sandra Hook

Colour reproduction by PageSet, Victoria
Printed and bound in China by Everbest

8 7 6 5 4 3   09 10 11 12